IMAGES OF THE U.S. AROUND THE WORLD

SUNY series, Human Communication Processes
Donald P. Cushman and Ted J. Smith III, editors

IMAGES OF THE U.S.
AROUND THE WORLD

A Multicultural Perspective

Edited by
Yahya R. Kamalipour

Foreword by Majid Tehranian

STATE UNIVERSITY OF NEW YORK PRESS

Published by
State University of New York Press, Albany

For information, address State University of New York Press,
State University Plaza, Albany, N.Y., 12246

Production by Cathleen Collins
Marketing by Anne Valentine

Library of Congress Cataloging in Publication Data
Images of the U.S. around the world : a multicultural perspective /
    edited by Yahya R. Kamalipour : foreword by Majid Tehranian.
        p.   cm. — (SUNY series in human communication processes)
    Includes bibliographical references and index.
        ISBN 0-7914-3971-2 (alk. paper). — ISBN 0-7914-3972-0 (pbk. :
    alk. paper)
        1. United States—Foreign public opinion.   2. United States—
    Relations—Foreign countries.   3. Mass media—Political aspects—
    Foreign countries.   4. Mass media—Social aspects—Foreign
    countries.   I. Kamalipour, Yahya R.   II. Series.
    E840.2.I55   1998
    303.48′273—dc21   98-5278
                                                                   CIP

10 9 8 7 6 5 4 3 2 1

To my mother and in memory of my father
And for
Daria, Shirin, and Niki

Contents

Illustrations

Tables

Foreword

Ever since its inception in 1776, the United States has held an eternal fascination for the rest of the world. In 1776, any government in the world dedicated to life, liberty, and the pursuit of happiness would have been received with a combination of alarm from the ruling classes and delight from the ruled. For centuries, the normal practice of governments had been to dish out death, oppression, and taxation. From De Tocqueville to Lord Bryce, George Santayana, Alistair Cooke, and J. Baudrillard, distinguished European observers have looked at the American phenomenon with a mixture of disdain and admiration. Other parts of the world also have followed suit in their mixed emotions. Providence seems to have decreed that the world's First Nation, as Seymour Martin Lipset has characterized the American experience, should provoke such strong dual emotions—infatuation as well as revulsion, love as well as hatred, adulation as well denunciation. There are those who consider it the Leader of the Free World side by side with those who view it as the Great Satan. What is even more peculiar is that such contradictory images often emanate from the same countries and the same observers.

How can we explain the mystery of such a complex web of images? Images often tell more about the image holder than the image object. We construct an image of the other often in the idiom of our own cultural values and material interests. In such constructions, power and knowledge are inextricably intertwined. As Edward Said has argued in his *Orientalism*, the image of the Orient constructed by the Europeans during the colonial era projected all of their own repressed desires and deepest fears into an imaginary world of debauched harems and unbridled tyranny. The variety and complexity of Oriental societies was thus reduced into a homogeneous and simplified image of the other needing to be subdued and civilized. The rest of the world has similarly viewed the United States from the prism of its own contradictory material and cultural interests by portraying it either as a threatening colossus or as a benign champion of freedom and human rights. Neither image, clearly, comes close to reflecting the complexity and variety of United States history or society. Occidentalism is as guilty of oversimplifications as Orientalism.

However, as Montesquieu's satire of the eighteenth-century French society in his *Persian Letters* demonstrates, we can gain more insights by viewing ourselves as others see us. In this admirable volume of research papers, Yahya Kamalipour has gathered together a broadly conceived study of U.S. images in twenty countries around the world, as reviewed by thirty-three scholars. The book fills an important gap in several respects. First, it goes beyond the episodic media headlines to give us a historical depth of understanding with respect to the changing images of the United States in different parts of the world as U.S. interests evolve to collide or coincide with other nations. Second, it compares and contrasts the cultural perspectives with the media images as an important source of construction of reality. Third, it studies the extraordinary role of U.S. media exports as a critical factor in the global constructions of the U.S. image.

In all three respects, power relations appear as a critical factor in image formations. As a nascent nation rising against British colonialism, the United States provoked the deepest fears among the aristocrats while inspiring the fondest hopes among democrats and revolutionaries in Europe. In de Tocqueville's account, *Democracy in America*, we can clearly witness this ambivalence. As a European aristocrat, de Tocqueville was thus deeply suspicious of American democracy's uncouth manners and tyranny of the majority while convinced of its inevitability and robustness. In Latin America, however, where the United States dominated the continent through its Monroe Doctrine and gunboat diplomacy, it earned for itself a reputation as a bully. For the rest of the world, however, so long as the United States continued to be an isolationist power, it presented an image of a benign power to be befriended. Twice in this century, the United States appeared to save the world from the tyranny of newly emerging European imperialists. In the minds of the colonial peoples in particular, the United States came to stand as a symbol of anticolonial victory and national self-determination. At the conclusion of both world wars, the colonized expected the United States to come to their rescue against the European colonialists.

However, the postwar entry of the United States into the world arena in a relentless cold war against the Sino-Soviet camp led it to generally side with its Western European allies against the anticolonial national liberation struggles. The image of the United States thus gradually deteriorated from a friend to a foe. In the meantime, however, the flow of American soft power in the spread of its cultural influence around the world through its cultural exports (English language, books, films, music, radio and TV programs, blue jeans, Coca-Cola, Madonna, and Michael Jackson) has seduced the younger generation nearly everywhere into emulating the American ways. The repugnance against Americanization has led some critics of U.S. cultural influences to call it westoxification. Just like intoxication, the afflicted not only fall victim to its influence but revel in it. Others have employed the metaphor of Satanic to suggest how temptations of the flesh have corrupted the young and old into imitations of alien and ultimately destructive ways.

To paraphrase Lord Acton, power attracts and absolute power attracts absolutely. Just in the days of the Persian, Greek, or Roman empires, the American empire has similarly elicited both love and hate toward this dominant power in the world. It also has led to a construction of the other in stereotypes that need to be examined critically. In an increasingly interdependent, multipolar, and multicultural world, it is neither safe nor in one's own interest to engage in such stereotyping of others. Every act of dichotomizing, demonizing, and dramatizing the conflicts between self and other is an act of cultural violence nearly as damaging to the cause of peace as the exercise of manifest violence. However, to attract audiences or to propagate government policies, the mass media often engage in such acts of cultural violence, thus paving the way for physical violence in international and intercultural relations.

This volume unpacks such stereotypes, whether exercised through cultural or mass media practices. The editor and the authors should be therefore congratulated for their valuable contribution to international communication scholarship as well as to the cause of world peace.

Majid Tehranian
Professor of International Communication
University of Hawaii at Manoa
Director of the Toda Institute for Global Peace and Policy Research

Acknowledgments

I would like to offer my sincere gratitude to the contributing authors of this book, for without their genuine support and interest, this project could not have come to fruition. Also, many thanks to the contributing authors' institutions for providing them financial, administrative, and secretarial support during the course of this project.

A hearty note of appreciation goes to two special individuals, Michael R. Moore, dean of the School of Liberal Arts, and William L. Robinson, head of the Department of Communication and Creative Arts, at Purdue University Calumet, for their valuable support and encouragement throughout this project. Elizabeth Paschen, the department secretary, also deserve to be mentioned for her assistance. Furthermore, I would like to thank Linda Kostiba of Desktop Publishing at Purdue University Calumet for her support and Kaylie Gura-Luken for her creative design on the cover of this book.

I am grateful to Sandra Littleton-Uetz and Dennis H. Barbour of the English and Philosophy Department at Purdue University Calumet for their conscientious reviews and editorial assistance. Furthermore, Kuldip R. Rampal of Central Missouri State University deserves a special thanks for sharing his insightful comments relative to the overall structure of the book. I am also indebted to Clay Morgan, senior editor, State University of New York Press, for his patience and critical input throughout this project.

Finally, I would like to express my appreciation to my wife and children for their unconditional love, emotional support, and understanding.

Introduction

YAHYA R. KAMALIPOUR

> All free nations are vainglorious, but national pride is not
> displayed by all in the same manner. The Americans, in
> their intercourse with strangers, appear impatient of the
> small censure and insatiable of praise. The most slender
> eulogy is acceptable to them, the most exalted seldom con-
> tents them; they unceasingly harass you to extort praise, and
> if you resist their entreaties, they fall to praising themselves.
> It would seem as if, doubting their own merit, they wished
> to have it constantly exhibited before their eyes. Their
> vanity is not only greedy, but restless and jealous; it will
> grant nothing, while it demands everything, but is ready to
> beg and to quarrel at the same time.
> —Alexis de Tocqueville, *Democracy in America*

De Tocqueville's perception of early-1800s America was primarily based on
his personal observations and formed in a period when most contemporary
communications channels, particularly the electronic media, did not even exist. Today, even Americans form their perceptions of their fellow citizens, particularly ethnic minorities, through the mass media. In this electronic age,
when an array of carefully crafted television images spans the entire globe,
when mass media influence our perceptions of others, when multinational
corporations are at the helm, and when much of our cultural diversity is at
risk, I wonder, How would de Tocqueville rewrite his classic work, *Democracy
in America*?

The Impetus for This Book

This book is intended to provide a much needed balance to my earlier book,
The U.S. Media and the Middle East: Image and Perception (1995, 1997), in
which twenty-two scholars discuss and analyze the prevailing U.S. media

portrayals of the Middle East. In that book, most authors criticize the U.S. media for presenting a grossly distorted image of the Middle East and argue that the mass media contribute to the existing stereotypical images of Arabs, Muslims, Iranians, Turks, and so on. It was in the course of that project that I became intrigued with such questions as "How do other cultures perceive the U.S.?" and "How do the media of other nations portray the U.S.?" An extended library search yielded no published book aimed at answering those and other pertinent questions relative to the U.S. image abroad. Hence, I begun working on this project in mid-1995.

A World of Images

"An *image*," writes Hamid Mowlana (1997), "may be defined as a combinatorial construct whose subject is itself a collection of images in the individual memory of various aspects of reality. It is the totality of attributes that a person recognizes or imagines. Images are to varying degrees interdependent on one another. The structure of one is inferred or predicted from that of another; and change in one produces imbalance and, therefore, change in others" (3). Generally speaking, nations, much like individuals acquire—through their behavior relative to their own citizens and other states—a certain global image that becomes the basis for international relations. Obviously, a positive global image can greatly contribute to the success and prosperity of a given nation, while a negative image can hinder its domestic and international affairs. According to Michael Kunczik (1997), "Images of certain nations, however right or wrong they might be, seem to form, fundamentally, through a very complex communication process involving varied information sources. . . . But radio and TV transmissions of international programs, newspapers, books, news services, and so on are probably the strongest image shapers" (1).

Image Makers

Prompted by an array of new telecommunication technologies and a host of geopolitical and economic reasons, a new world is being forged before our very eyes. It is a world in which the mass media conglomerates such as General Electric, Time Warner/Turner, Disney/Capital Cities/ABC, and Westinghouse play a significant role in the way(s) that we perceive ourselves, our world, and our fellow human beings. It is a technologically driven, intensely competitive, and corporate-dominated world that was quite unimaginable to our predecessors merely a generation ago. Ours is a world of images, images of all kinds—images that are often consciously manipulated and manufactured to create an identity or status for selling mass-produced products or for promoting or demoting a political candidate, a company, a nation, or a religion by economically driven institutions or conglomerates whose major concerns are self-interest and in-creased monetary profits. Hence, a marketable image, to be used in advertising, can be accentuated by an already existing one, such as the prevailing stereotyp-ical images of ethnic groups, religions, nationalities, or geographical locations, or can be manufactured by the so-called media handlers, image makers, or pub-lic relations experts. These images are then fed through an array of sophisticated communication networks, particularly the mass media, by the very conglomer-ates that have penetrated practically every aspect of people's lives, whether they live in Chicago, New York, Beijing, Tehran, Cairo, New Delhi, Mexico City, Bogota, Moscow, Paris, Algiers, or Johannesburg. Products are glamorized, im-ages are commoditized, and are sold globally. In such a market-driven and me-dia-saturated environment, it is no wonder, then, to see teenagers in Ankara, Bangkok, Caracas, or other major cities of the world, wearing T-shirts with the imprints of universal or Western icons such as Michael Jackson, Madonna, Coca-Cola™, Snoopy, Adidas™, American Express™, Chicago Cubs, or a myriad of other Hollywood-TV-industry manufactured logos, icons, and celebrities. In short, when it comes to production of images, no nation holds more power than the United States in terms of reach and penetration into cul-tures of the world. Hence, many scholars contend that this phenomenon (the Americanization or "McDonaldization" of the global village), has resulted in the breakdown of traditional values or old ways of life in many countries. Conse-quently, argues Walter Truett Anderson (1990), ". . . a kind of unregulated mar-ketplace of realities in which all manner of belief systems are offered for public consumption" (6) has emerged in the so-called postmodern world. Hence, "Globalization provides a new arena (or theater) in which all belief systems look around and become aware of all other belief systems, and in which people every-where struggle in unprecedented ways to find out who and what they are" (6). In terms of politics, news, and information, the results might be confusion in the minds of, for instance, the citizens of Timbuktu as to "whom to believe?"—Voice of America (VOA), British Broadcasting Corporation (BBC) World Ser-vice, Radio Israel, Radio Canada International, or the Timbuktu media? In terms of beliefs, the results might be rejection of the old ways or modes of think-ing in favor of the media or corporate-generated and disseminated beliefs. In terms of values, the results might be alienation from indigenous values in favor of a new set of largely "corporate values" that has permeated practically every cultural group throughout the world, via the corporate-owned and American-dominated media.

Relative to a handful of media conglomerates manufacturing and dissem-inating the bulk of information and entertainment fare throughout the world, Ben Bagdikian (1996) argues that "Although the United States offers the prime model in the world of mass communications controlled by a few corporations, the same trend exists in western Europe and Japan. The large multinational corporations in those countries are already ensconced in their national economies—and expanding internationally" (10).

Americanization of the Global Village

Ironically, according to The Commission on Global Governance, the emerging global neighborhood is forging new bonds of friendship and interest, but it is also creating new tensions. Never before have so many people had so much in common, but never before have the things that divide them been so obvious (The report of . . . 1995). In such a milieu, comprehending the power and influence of global media is certainly a crucial step toward understanding the contemporary global society. Furthermore, working toward achieving a relative state of peace, mutual respect, and harmony in international relations requires knowledge of all the forces (war, hunger, economic inequalities, pollution, deforestation, diseases, overpopulation, etc.) that play a role in our lives, including those forces (mass media) that focus our thoughts on certain issues, distract us from other issues, or form our perceptions of other people and places.

The English-speaking nations, particularly the United States, dominate practically all aspects of communication and entertainment throughout the world. For instance, in the summer of 1994, I visited Iran for the first time in nearly eighteen years. Knowing that the governments of Iran and U.S. have been at odds with one another since the 1979 Iranian Revolution—largely because of the hostage crisis—it was quite fascinating for me to experience personally the prevalence of American symbols, media, and products practically everywhere. Even in remote villages, one could easily use the American dollar, in lieu of the Iranian currency (Rial), to purchase products. Satellite receiving dishes were prominent on the rooftops of millions of Iranian homes where families would gather around their Sony TV sets and view *Oprah, Donahue, America's Funniest Videos, Hard Copy,* or *Growing Pains.* Or one could turn to a variety of international channels such as "CNN," "BBC," "MTV," "STAR TV," "SKY TV," "Z-TV," where programs originating in Japan, China, India, Turkey, and so on were offered. Pepsi-Cola™ and Coca-Cola™ were the most popular soft drinks; Winston™ and Marlboro™ cigarettes were displayed by peddlers at practically every street corner; movies such as *Dances With Wolves* and *Silence of the Lambs* were circulating on videocassettes; *Pinocchio, Mickey Mouse,* and other Disney icons were visible in a variety of formats—from T-shirts, to books, to videos; American pop singers such as Michael Jackson, Madonna, and others (whom I had not even heard of!) were known to the youth; and although McDonald's™ wasn't selling hamburgers, McAli or others did! It seemed that at practically every intersection in the major cities, there were private institutes offering classes and certificates in learning the English language. Not only did the Iranians not seem to hate the Americans—as is commonly propagated by the U.S. media—on the contrary, they seemed to be fond of American goods and cultural products. Nonetheless, in terms of politics, Iranians have some legitimate grievances against the American government and its antagonistic and often counterproductive foreign policy toward Iran. In fact, the 1953 *coup d'état*, instigated by the Central Intelligence Agency (CIA), is often cited as an example of U.S. interference in the internal affairs of Iran. That coup resulted in the overthrow and detention of a popular nationalist leader, Dr. Mohammad Mossadeq, in favor of Mohammad Reza Shah Pahlavi, who had fled the country. Subsequently, the Shah was successfully returned to the Peacock throne to continue his autocratic rule, with the full support of the U.S., until the 1979 Revolution when Ayatollah Ruhollah Khomeini triumphantly returned from his lengthy exile in Iraq and a brief stay in France. The Ayatollah ended the Pahlavi dynasty and monarchy and established the Islamic Republic of Iran, headed by a president who is elected every four years.

Other major Iranian grievances relative to U.S. policy toward Iran include: the largely CIA-created Shah's secret police force, known as SAVAK, which systematically jailed, tortured, mutilated, and/or killed thousands of Iranians who opposed the Shah politically (Detmer 1997); the American support of Saddam Hussein of Iraq in his invasion of Iran, in 1980, and the subsequent eight-year Iran-Iraq war (Bill 1988); and the USS *Vincennes*'s downing, in 1988, of an Iranian civilian airliner over the Persian Gulf, which killed nearly 300 passengers. These and other incidents have largely contributed to the souring of American-Iranian relations in the past two decades.* Accordingly, the Iranian mass media have been highly critical and generally negative in their coverage of the American political establishment, and vice versa.

It is, then, no wonder that since the Revolution, "Cultural Imperialism," "Cultural Pollution," or "Cultural Invasion," by the West, particularly the U.S., has been passionately and fiercely debated in the Iranian Majlis

---

*Since the landslide victory of President Mohammad Khatami, in the 1997 Iranian elections, a window of opportunity has opened that may lead to renewed and productive relationships, at various levels between Iran and the United States. On January 7, 1998, in his address to the American people, via CNN, President Khatami spoke admiringly of American civilization and expressed his regrets for the hostage crisis. Likewise, on January 30, 1998, in his message, via Voice of America, President Clinton spoke admiringly of the rich cultural heritage of Iran, expressed his regrets for the soured Iranian-American relations, and hoped for renewed relations between the two countries. Furthermore, in February 1998, for the first time since the 1979 Iranian Revolution, an American wrestling team participated in the Takhti Wrestling Cup contest in Tehran—reportedly, the Iranians gave the American team a very enthusiastic and warm reception. Also, the Iranian and American soccer teams competed, quite admirably, in the 1998 World Cup in France.

(Parliament) and the media. In fact, during my visit, journalists repeatedly asked my views concerning this global phenomenon, which is also known as Westernization or Americanization, that is believed to displace traditional beliefs and cultural values of the Iranian people. Hence, to combat this threat, the Iranian government has not only banned the satellite receiving dishes, but has begun penalizing those who distribute, sell, consume, or manufacture products (e.g., clothing with Western icon imprints, recorded music, videos, publications, etc.) that are deemed to be harmful to Islamic values and the traditional way of life. By mid-1996, these restrictions were intensified when the United States inaugurated a one-hour TV program in Persian, transmitted to Iran daily, via satellite.

Furthermore, in the summer of 1996, I taught a course at Oxford, England. Once again, the cultural influence and presence of American products could visibly be experienced everywhere. For instance, not only a high percentage of programs on the Independent Television (ITV) network were American, but Oprah Winfrey's poster— advertising her talk show—was plastered on the shelter of nearly every bus stop throughout Oxford and other cities. Budweiser^{TM} seemed to be the most popular American beer; Ford^{TM} the favorite American automobile; while McDonald's^{TM}, Burger King^{TM}, Pizza Hut^{TM}, and other American food franchises were patronized by many— mostly youth.

In view of the above, it is extraordinary to think that "cultural imperialism" seems to have successfully conquered even England—one of the most powerful colonizers of an earlier period. In this vein, it then becomes convincing to argue that the "global village" is, indeed, becoming increasingly "Americanized." In fact, a popular notion among the developing countries, and even among the industrialized nations, including France and Canada, is that the U.S., through its media conglomerates and media contents exports, has attempted to dilute their traditional or indigenous cultures. Ironically, America, which was once colonized by the British, is now colonizing the United Kingdom through its media presence. Hence, "Cultural Pollution" or "Cultural Invasion" has become a major concern among most countries throughout the world, often sparking a heated debate. As noted in the Chapter, "As Others See the United States: A View from Canada," even ex-Prime Minister of Canada Pierre Trudeau once said that living next to the U.S. is akin to sleeping next to an elephant. You cannot help but be aware of its every movement.

Furthermore, the proliferation of satellite television networks (e.g., Cable News Network, Rupert Murdoch's Star TV and Star TV Plus satellite channels in Asia) in recent years has further fuelled these concerns and debates to the extent that countries such as Iran and Saudi Arabia have passed laws forbidding the ownership of satellite receiving dishes or viewing foreign satellite television networks. On the other hand, many other nations have imposed legal restrictions, or quotas, on the number of foreign programs, particularly American, that can be imported for domestic consumption.

In view of the above, Herbert Schiller (1996) argues that "The United States' global industrial pre-eminence may be slipping, but the domestic output and international sale of one of its manufactures is booming—packaged consciousness. Packaged consciousness—a one-dimensional, smooth-edged cultural product—is made by the ever-expanding goliaths of the message and image business." He goes on to say that "Gigantic entertainment-information complexes exercise a near-seamless and unified private corporate control over what we think, and think about" (*The Nation*, 16).

We now live in a world in which the physical boundaries between nations are becoming increasingly blurred. On the horizon lies a future that will be symbolically homogeneous, Westernized (read Americanized), corporatized, and culturally uniform.

America as the Only Superpower

After the collapse of Communism in the Soviet Union and the demise of a bipolar world order, the U.S. became the "only superpower" and hence acquired a unique position to influence and shape the future direction of our world, for better or worse, with the help of other nations, including those of Europe, Canada, Japan, Russia, and China.

Despite pronouncements such as the ushering in of a "New World Order," at the time that this book was being written, some forty major and minor wars and conflicts in Afghanistan, Albania, Chechnya, Bosnia, India, Israel, Liberia, Rwanda, Peru, Somalia, Zaire, and elsewhere around the world were taking place. The general global perception seems to be that, if willing, the U.S. and its allies, working through the United Nations, can indeed resolve most of these conflicts. At the same time, it is also perceived that the U.S. and its allies have often ignited (e.g., the Persian Gulf War, the Iran-Iraq War), or helped to ignite, some of the ongoing conflicts, either by meddling in the internal or regional affairs of other nations or simply by ignoring the conflicts, arguing that as long as U.S. interests, political or economic, are not jeopardized by domestic or regional conflicts, they may continue indefinitely, without U.S. intervention. A classic example for this argument would be the disastrous Balkan War which was largely ignored by the international community, including the European Community, for nearly four years. This war was finally halted after the U.S. and NATO intervened in early 1996, negotiated a settlement among the warring factions in Dayton, Ohio, and dispatched a peacekeeping force to Bosnia-Hercegovina. In the meantime, the United Nations began the process of finding and prosecuting the war criminals.

In my opinion, the global communication networks, coupled with a concerted effort by governmental and non-governmental organizations, can indeed help to pull the world's people closer together. In fact, it has been demonstrated that "Media images of human suffering have motivated people to express their concern and their solidarity with those in distant places by contributing to relief efforts and by demanding explanations and action from governments. The media's influence on the shaping of foreign policy is considerable in many countries" (The report . . . 1995, 31). However, some argue that the U.S. has turned inward and is often indifferent toward global conflicts, environmental problems, and human sufferings, while others point to its ineffective and inconsistent, or double-standard, foreign policy.

Purposes of This Book

A great deal of literature exists about the United States' cultural and political domination of the world through the exportation of news, information, and entertainment products, ranging from Walt Disney productions to Hollywood movies and television series. There is also a relatively sufficient amount of information about U.S. media portrayals of various ethnic groups, races, sexes, religions, and so on. However, to this date, no other book has focused primarily on what this volume, *Images of the U.S. around the World: A Multicultural Perspective*, is intended to accomplish:

1. to present a multifaceted analysis of the U.S. image in Africa, Asia, Australia, Europe, the Middle East, and South America;
2. to present examples of the U.S. image as portrayed by other nations' mass media (newspapers, magazines, radio, television, books, motion pictures, music); and
3. to discuss the influence of the exported media products (i.e., Hollywood movies, television serials, popular music, publications, etc.) on the U.S. image around the world.

As we approach the millennium and an increasingly global society, where information and communication more than ever before play a crucial role in enhancing international relations and mutual understanding, the book that you hold in your hands intends to provide a framework for describing and analyzing perceptions and misperceptions of the United States of America throughout the world. It goes without saying that in its brief history of just over 200 years, the U.S. not only has become the most advanced information society but also a culturally dominant force in global and regional affairs. And in view of the fact that, according to Walter Lippmann (1922), we generally act or react in accordance with "pictures in our heads," it would be worthwhile to learn how others "see" or "perceive" the United States of America—the master image maker and the leading producer and exporter of information and cultural products (i.e., TV programs and series, motion pictures, music) in the world.

It is important to note that the goal of this book is not to advance or propose any particular critical media perspective. Rather, *Images of the U.S. around the World: A Multicultural Perspective* attempts to present a comprehensive discussion and analysis of the U.S. image based on the work of thirty-four mass communication scholars and researchers throughout the world. Hence, one of the explicit goals of this volume is to take the reader beyond the pervasive "stereotypical" or "assumed" images of the United States.

Images of the U.S. around the World: A Multicultural Perspective is explicitly descriptive and implicitly prescriptive. It not only describes the role of modern communication technologies as the primary purveyors of news, information, and entertainment throughout the world, but also illustrates the influence of mass media on people's perceptions of "others" at the global level. It brings to the attention of the North American media conglomerates (Disney, Hollywood, broadcast networks, music industry, and publishers) a problem that continues to persist in the U.S. and elsewhere—an unrealistic portrayal of people, places, religions, races, and sexes by the mass media. In essence, this book is both reflective and self-reflective: reflective in that it illustrates the ways in which other cultures view the U.S.; self-reflective in that it illustrates the ways that the U.S.-produced and exported media products are interpreted and internalized by other cultures. Interestingly enough, as illustrated in this book, peoples' perception of the U.S. throughout the world is often based on the cultural products (i.e., television series, movies, music, etc.) that are produced in the U.S., exported, and consumed by other nations.

Who Should Read This Book?

This book should be extremely appealing to those individuals and organizations (e.g., college students, teachers, researchers, policy makers, journalists, travellers, international consultants, international businesses, etc.) that are keenly interested in learning not only "how the mass media in selected countries around the world cover the U.S." but also "how people of different nations perceive the U.S."

Furthermore, *Images of the U.S. around the World: A Multicultural Perspective* should be a valuable resource, either as a required or supplemental text, for college and university students enrolled in such courses as international communication, international relations, intercultural communication, international public relations, media effects, journalism, political science, sociology, and comparative studies.

Structure of This Book

The thirteenth-century Persian sufi teacher Mowlana Jelaluddin Balkhi (known in the West as Rumi) "told the tale of a group of blind men trying to describe an elephant by touch alone. One felt the trunk and described it as a rope; another felt the leg and described it as a tree while a third felt the ear and described it as a fan. The point of the story was to show how the unenlightened may miss the truth of the whole: the elephant as coherent reality" (Tomlinson 1991, 8).

From the outset of this project, it has been my desire to allow diverse voices, from diverse cultures, to express themselves freely, using any suitable methodology, writing style, and theoretical orientation, without imposing a prescribed framework for their studies. This freedom, however, has presented to me the challenging task of organizing twenty-four original essays, authored or co-authored by thirty-three scholars/researchers throughout the world, into a coherent and integrated whole. In any anthology of this nature and magnitude, where the contributing authors' primary language may not necessarily be English or in which some of them may not subscribe to the Anglo-European culture or perspective, obviously each essay ends up "reading" differently—in terms of writing style, language, or perspective—than any traditional work produced by a relatively homogeneous group of researchers/scholars in America would be. It goes without saying that ultimately what matters most is the quality and significance of the contribution that each author has made, from his/her own cultural perspective, to the study of the U.S. image abroad. Nonetheless, in an attempt to make the book more coherent and easier to read, I have organized the twenty-four essays, based on the overriding framework that is used by each author to explore the U.S. image, into the following sections:

1. *Introductory Perspectives*: This section begins with a broad study that gauges students' image of the U.S. in eleven countries throughout the world, followed by two global perspectives by McKenzie Wark of Australia and Herbert Schiller of the U.S. relative to the overall theme of this book.

2. *U.S. Image and the Political Factor*: This section contains studies that examine U.S. image in a largely political framework by illustrating the interconnection between media coverage of the U.S. in other nations relative to the quality of political relationships that those countries have with the U.S.

3. *U.S. Image and the Cultural Factor*: This section contains articles that examine U.S. image in a largely cultural framework by illustrating the influence of domestic values, belief, or traditions on other people's perception of the U.S.

4. *U.S. Image and the Entertainment Factor*: This section contains articles that examine the U.S. image in a largely entertainment- or media-related framework by illustrating the impact of cultural products such as TV series, movies, music on the perceived image of the U.S. in other nations.

In addition, a brief introductory perspective, at the beginning of each of the above sections, sets the stage for exploring the overarching image of the U.S. around the world.

References

Anderson, W.T. (1990). *Reality isn't what it used to be*. San Francisco: Harper & Row.

Bagdikian, B.H. (1996). Brave new world minus 400. In G. Gerbner, H. Mowlana, and H. I. Schiller (Eds.), *Invisible crises: What conglomerate control of media means for America and the world*. Boulder: Westview.

Bill, J.A. (1988). *The eagle and the lion: The tragedy of American-Iranian relations*. New Haven: Yale University Press.

Detmer, D. (1997). Covering up Iran: Why vital information is routinely excluded from U.S. mass media news accounts. In Y. R. Kamalipour (Ed.), *The U.S. media and the Middle East: Image and perception* [Paperback edition]. Westport: Praeger.

de Tocqueville, A. (1981). *Democracy in America*. New York: The Modern Library.

Kunczik, M. (1997). *Images of nations and international public relations*. Mahwah, N.J.: Lawrence Erlbaum.

Lippmann, W. (1922). *Public Opinion*. New York: The Free Press.

Mowlana, H. (1997). Images and the crisis of political legitimacy. In Y. R. Kamalipour (Ed.), *The U.S. media and the Middle East: Image and perception* [Paperback edition]. Westport: Praeger.

Schiller, H.I. (1996, June 3). On that chart. *The Nation* 262(22), pp.16–18.

The report of the Commission on Global Governance. (1995). *Our global neighborhood*. New York: Oxford University Press.

Tomlinson, J. (1991). *Cultural imperialism*. London: Printer Publishers.

Part I

Introductory Perspectives

This section provides an overall perspective for the study of the U.S. image abroad. Richard Harris and Joseph Krafa discuss college students' impressions of the U.S. in eleven countries, including Germany, France, Denmark, Switzerland, Austria, Morocco, Nigeria, Hong Kong, Argentina, Brazil, and Canada. Interestingly enough, they conclude that the major sources of students' impression of the U.S. were all media-based, primarily from television, film, and newspapers. Furthermore, they note that the identifications of these sources across the different nations were strikingly similar.

McKenzie Wark writes about America from a particular place, Australia, and at a particular moment in history, the post–Cold War period, relative to the tension between the U.S. and Japan. In his essay on cultural triangulation, he looks at particular expressions of anxiety about the troubled U.S.-Japan relationship in the news media. He also traces the mutual otherness of Japan's image of America, and of America's image of Japan, as seen from Australia. He argues that the rise of postmodern culture and intense global competition in manufacturing seems to coincide with the eclipse of American power.

Herbert Schiller's essay, although somewhat disconnected from the central theme of this book, offers a perspective that is quite challenging and useful to the study of international communication. He asserts that, in the late 1990s, not only does the U.S. not dominate the flow of international information and images, but cultural imperialism is "an anachronistic view." Schiller offers a view that is contrary to the prevailing universal assumptions about U.S. domination and to most of the assertions contained in this book. Nonetheless, I believe this contradiction encourages readers to question the implications of certain concepts and, at the same time, appreciate the diversity of voices, perspectives, and arguments contained in this book.

1

A Cultivation Theory Perspective of Worldwide National Impressions of the United States

RICHARD JACKSON HARRIS AND JOSEPH ANDREW KARAFA

Introduction

People form impressions of other nations and their people, often based on the most meager knowledge. What is the nature of these impressions and how might they be formed? We argue for the utility of using cultivation theory from communication literature to examine this problem (Gerbner, Gross, Morgan, and Signorielli 1994). This theory is especially useful in regard to the role of the media in the formation of national impressions.

Some past studies have extended social psychology research on interpersonal and intergroup attitude formation to the formation of impressions about different countries (e.g., Tims and Miller 1986; D'Adamo and Garcia-Beaudoux 1993, 1995). Other studies have used multidimensional scaling, cluster analysis, or factor analysis to identify the major factors involved in impressions of nations (Johnson, Oliveira, and Barnett 1989; Johnson and Tims 1985; Klineberg 1941; Robinson and Heffner 1967; Sherman 1973). A third approach to studying national impressions has compared impressions of one's own group (autostereotyping) with perceptions by other groups (heterostereotyping) (Marin and Salazar 1985; McAndrew 1990; Nichols and McAndrew 1984). Traditionally, autostereotypes have been more positive and uniform than heterostereotypes, but not always. The present study measured both auto- and hetero-stereotypes of people from the United States.

3

Sources of the Impressions

One important research problem in the study of national impressions concerns identifying the sources of these impressions. One variable that has been investigated is contact with people from other groups (McGrady and Mc-Grady 1976). Clearly, experience in a country, either through travel or residence, is a major factor, if such an experience exists. Contact with friends and other people from that country is another source. However, the effects of contact have not been consistent across the literature, no doubt due in part to the complexity of the construct of contact, the variety of the groups examined in the various studies, and the different methodologies used.

This inconsistency may also be due in part to a failure to consider other important variables. In particular, various forms of media compose another set of formative influences. One major component of this influence is news media, a major source of public information about other countries. Some studies have examined the impact of exposure to broadcast and print news on knowledge and attitudes about other countries (McNelly and Izcaray 1986; Perry 1987, 1990; Perry and McNelly 1988; Perry and Melson 1989). Persons who consume more media news have greater and more differentiated knowledge about other nations, and sometimes more positive and less xenophobic attitudes as well.

News is not the only media component, however. Entertainment programming on television, as well as movies, provides input to these national impressions, especially for countries that are frequent exporters of film and TV programming or are frequent settings for stories in such fiction. Although the effects of such fictional portrayals on national impressions have not been extensively studied, some research suggests that fictional portrayals of groups may actually have a greater effect on knowledge than do non-fictional portrayals, especially on those people with relatively less personal knowledge and experience with that particular group (Slater 1990; Tims and Miller 1986). This could be described by the availability heuristic, by which one makes decisions based on the ease to which examples can be generated (Tversky and Kahneman 1973).

Cultivation Theory

A useful way to conceptualize the role of the media in the formation of national impressions is through cultivation theory (see Gerbner et al. 1994 for a recent overview). This theory emphasizes the exposure to recurring patterns of stories, images, themes, and messages through media. It assumes an active role of the media consumer, whose interaction with the media comes to *cultivate* a world view or set of attitudes. In other words, what people see frequently on television is what they come to believe.

For example, people who watch more violent television believe the world is a more dangerous place than those who watch less TV (Gerbner and Gross 1976; Morgan 1983). Similarly, heavy viewers tend to have relatively more traditional gender-role conceptions (Morgan 1982, 1987) and hold more middle-of-the-road political views (Gerbner, Gross, Morgan, and Signorielli 1982, 1984). The latter finding from the U.S. was also obtained in Britain (Piepe, Charlton, and Morey 1990) and Argentina (Morgan and Shanahan 1991, 1995). These findings support the idea that the messages offered by TV affect a person's world view or sense of reality.

In terms of national impressions, cultivation theory is a promising theoretical framework from which to view the media contribution to the socialization of attitudes about other countries. Considering both news and entertainment programming, the United States would seem to be country about which many people worldwide would have an impression, due to its high profile in international news and the popularity of U.S.-made movies and television programs worldwide. Thus it seems that people's impressions about the U.S. might be especially likely to reflect media influences or cultivation effects. Surprisingly, although there have been several cultivation-theory studies within different countries (see Signorielli and Morgan 1990, for several papers of this type), few have looked at perceptions about other specific nations. In one exception, heavy exposure to U.S. television was associated with an enhanced Israeli perception of the U.S. standard of living (Weimann 1984). Therefore, one of the main goals of the present research was to investigate the role that media play in the formation of national impressions about the United States.

The Present Research

The present research assessed impressions of the United States, as viewed from inside and outside that country. The first study tested how lifelong U.S. residents viewed (a) people from their own nation (autostereotype), and (b) their perception of the "media image" of their nation.

The second study assessed the impressions about the U.S. in people living in several other nations around the world (international stereotype). These impressions of people who have never been to the U.S. were then compared to (a) the perceived media image, and (b) the autostereotype assessed by Study 1. It was predicted that the international stereotypes of people who have never been to the U.S. would more closely fit the media image profile than the autostereotype profile, thus suggesting a formative role of media in national stereotypes.

In order to retain some control of factors such as education, age, and socioeconomic class, only university students were tested. Presumably, university students would have at least as much access to influences other than television and movies as, and more possibly than most, other segments of many national populations. Because of a comparable educational level, as well as other commonalities of the university experience, one might also expect greater cross-cultural homogeneity worldwide than would be the case with a sample from the general population. Thus, if national differences occur across university students, such differences in more general samples should be highly likely and quite possibly much larger and even more media-influenced.

Study 1 Method: Autostereotype and Perceived Media Image

Participants were 348 introductory psychology students who participated for course credit. All had lived all or almost all their lives in the U.S. and were attending a diverse and comprehensive Midwestern U.S. university with open admissions.

Subjects received a two-part questionnaire entitled "Impressions of International Peoples," which read: "We are studying the impressions people have about the inhabitants of different countries. You are to evaluate some characteristics of people from the United States first in regard to the media image and next in regard to real people you have known."

Subjects then rated their perceived "images of the U.S. and its people presented in the movies and television produced in that country" on a 7-point Likert scale from 1 (strongly disagree) to 7 (strongly agree) for each of nineteen attributes. These attributes had been generated through intuitive reflection on media stereotyping and previous pilot testing. Subjects were also given the option of circling "Don't Know" if they "don't know or cannot determine" enough to make a rating. The complete text of each scale appears later in the chapter in Table 1.2. Finally, participants rated their "impressions of actual people from the United States" (i.e., autostereotypes) on each of the same nineteen attributes with the same 7-point scales.

Study 2 Method: International Samples

The second study gathered data on impressions of American people from samples of university students living in eleven different countries: France (Aix-en-Provence), Germany (Freiburg), Denmark (Aarhus), Switzerland (Basel, Neuchatel, and Zurich), Morocco (Fes), Argentina (Buenos Aires), Brazil (Sao Paulo), Canada (Calgary), Hong Kong, Austria (Klagenfurt), and Nigeria (Ile-Ife).

Thanks are expressed to colleagues Mark Helle, Brigitt Pitzinger, Abdelali Bentahila, Cheryl Frenck-Mestre, François Grosjean, Kirsten Nielsen, Orlando J. D'Adamo, Virginia Garcia Beaudoux, Gustav Habermann, Monica

Lasisi, Rumjahn Hoosain, Adail Victorino Castilho, Carlos Eduardo Amadori, and Michael Klassen for international data collection and to Mark Helle, Brigitt Pitzinger, Ana Braga-Henebry, Cheryl Frenck-Mestre, Elizabeth Nelson, Andrew Johnson, and Sonya Guerra for translations of the questionnaire.

Unlike in the first study, participants were given just one set of nineteen scales to rate "your opinion about people from the United States." No mention was made of the media image as distinct from "real people." At the end of the nineteen scales were listed ten possible sources of their impressions just given. Subjects were asked "From which sources below have you received information that you used to make the above evaluations?" They were asked to rank order the sources in importance, leaving blank those that "are of no importance in forming your impressions." The ten sources were television, movies, books, radio, magazines, newspapers, friends from the U.S., travelling in the U.S., living in the U.S., and the U.S. government. Finally, some general demographic information was collected, including where they had lived or travelled outside their home country. As appropriate, the questionnaire was translated into Spanish, German, Portuguese, or French by native speakers and checked by a second speaker.

Results

Demographics

Major demographic data from each of the foreign samples and from the pooled international sample appear in Table 1.1. Pooled data are presented with and without the Canadian sample. This sample was much larger than any of the other samples and, unlike any other national sample, more than ninety percent had visited the United States. A close examination of those few who had not been to the U.S. found many recent international migrants to Canada.

Overall, the pooled international sample was not quite two-thirds female, with a large majority in their early twenties. About two-thirds had travelled outside their home countries, but only about one-sixth of the non-Canadians had visited the U.S. This left an aggregate sample of 520 who had never been to the U.S.

Attribute Ratings

Table 1.2 presents the mean media image and autostereotype ratings for each of the nineteen attributes from the U.S. sample, along with the same mean ratings of the pooled foreign sample, minus the Canadians (International Stereotype). In addition, the percentages of the international sample responding "Don't know" to each attribute is shown.

Table 1.1. Demographic Characteristics of International Samples

Country	Total Number	Gender Male/Female	Mean Age	Living Abroad Yes/No	Living in U.S. Yes/No	Travel Abroad Yes/No	Travel in U.S. Yes/No
Argentina	61	9/48	23.6	9/50	0/58	35/24	9/49
Brazil	65	19/46	22.7	9/56	/64	34/31	13/52
Germany	58	32/26	24.7	28/30	6/52	58/0	16/42
Austria	10	4/6	24.3	8/2	2/8	10/0	4/6
Denmark	59	15/44	26.1	34/25	7/52	56/2	13/45
France	64	14/49	27.8	12/52	2/62	58/6	7/57
Switzerland	110	46/62	24.0	45/64	11/98	107/1	33/75
Hong Kong	63	15/48	19.4	3/63	1/62	39/24	4/59
Morocco	63	24/39	24.4	6/57	0/63	32/31	0/63
Nigeria	81	54/28	23.4	12/63	1/73	19/56	1/72
Canada	230	91/139	19.5	67/163	18/212	223/7	200/30
Total (excl. Canada)	634	247/442	23.9	166/459	31/592	448/175	100/520
Total	864	323/535	23.7	233/622	49/804	67/182	301/549

Nineteen one-way within-subjects analyses of variance were performed on the U.S. students' ratings of the media image and their autostereotypes of real U.S. people. Next, nineteen between-subjects analyses compared that media image with the pooled international stereotype. A final set of between-subjects analyses compared the autostereotype ratings with the pooled international stereotype. Pairs that differed significantly are so indicated in Table 1.2. The highly conservative alpha level of $p = .005$ was chosen due to the large number of univariate analyses and the resulting increased probability of alpha error.

Differences between the U.S. subjects' ratings of the media image and the autostereotype appeared on eight of the nineteen attributes. The media image of U.S. people was seen as more emotionally expressive, physically attractive, violent, sexually promiscuous, and having more free time than the autostereotype. On the other hand, the autostereotype, as compared to the media image, was seen as more prejudiced, more religious, and more prone to worrying about having enough money.

The media tified by the U.S. subjects did not differ significantly from the pooled international stereotype on five of the nineteen scales. Stereotypes were close to the rated media image in how fun-loving, selfish, and hard-working U.S. people are, and in the degree to which they worry about having enough money and in how well men treat women. Compared to the U.S.-

Table 1.2. Mean Attribute Ratings (1 = Disagree, 7 = Agree) U.S. and Pooled International Samples

	U.S. Ratings		International (Aggregate Number = 634)	
	Media Image Mean	Autostereotype Mean	Mean	% Don't Know
They are patriotic	5.47	5.35a	5.99b	5.5
They are fun-loving	5.55a	5.40a	5.49a	7.4
They are selfish	4.93ab	5.17b	4.79a	13.4
They are prejudiced	4.60a	5.07b	5.05b	10.7
They are emotionally expressive	5.53a	4.94b	4.69b	10.3
They are physically attractive	6.17a	4.80b	3.97c	6.3
They are friendly	5.26a	5.05ab	4.81b	6.6
They are politically conservative	4.31a	4.27a	5.03b	12.9
They like children a lot	5.05a	5.02a	4.28b	19.9
They worry about having enough money	5.39a	6.48b	5.33a	10.4
They are religious	3.85a	4.65b	4.50b	9.0
They have close families	4.63a	4.45a	3.44b	13.2
The men treat women well	4.32a	4.30a	4.21a	19.6
They are greedy and materialistic	5.29a	5.36a	4.94b	9.1
They have lots of free time	5.20a	3.41b	3.82c	15.9
They are intelligent	5.41a	5.07a	4.22b	10.9
They are violent	5.19a	4.49b	4.45b	9.1
They are hard-working	4.96ab	5.24b	4.77a	8.5
They are sexually promiscuous	5.94a	5.17b	4.50c	19.9

Note: Means with different letters differ from each other $p < 005$.

identified media image, international respondents rated U.S. people as being more patriotic, more prejudiced, more politically conservative, and more religious; they also rated them less friendly, less emotionally expressive, less greedy and materialistic, less intelligent, less violent, less sexually promiscuous, and much less physically attractive. In addition, the international stereotype found U.S. people as liking children less, having families that are less close, and having less free time than the media image.

Similarly, the U.S. autostereotype did not differ from the international stereotype on seven of the nineteen scales. In this sense the pooled international sample held similar impressions to the U.S. people on the scales of fun-loving, prejudiced, emotionally expressive, friendly, religious, violent, and in how well women are treated. However, the international stereotype saw U.S. people as being more patriotic, less selfish, less attractive, more politically conservative, less greedy and materialistic, less intelligent, less hardworking, and less sexually promiscuous than did the U.S. autostereotype. The international stereotype also found them to like children less, be less worried about having enough money, have less close families, and more free time.

The mean international stereotype ratings for the different national samples (with the exception of Austria, where $N = 10$) appear in Table 1.3. Although there was at least one pair of statistically significant differences in the means for each attribute, overall the similarity across national samples is more striking. Certain deviations are considered below in the discussion.

Finally, in order to examine dimensions underlying the nineteen attributes, a factor analysis extracted three reliable factors (via principal axis factoring with an eigen value cutoff of 1.0). The three factors had eigen values ranging from 2.06 to 1.08 and together accounted for 26.10 percent of the explained variance. Only items with factor loadings greater than .40 were included in the three factors. The first factor (antisocial) included violent, selfish, and greedy and materialistic. The second factor (extroverted/hedonistic) included emotionally expressive, fun-loving, and physically attractive. The third factor (prosocial) contained liking children, and whether men treat women well.

Formative Influences

Unless otherwise specified, all internationals who indicated they had ever been to the United States were eliminated from the analysis of the formative influences. The percentages rating each influence as important appear in Table 1.4, along with their mean rating of importance.

The primary perceived influence in the formation of stereotypes about the U.S. was television, both in terms of the highest percentage rating it "important" and in terms of the mean ranking of those who rated it important. In

Table 1.3. Mean Stereotypes for Different International Samples (1=Disagree, 7=Agree)

| | National Sample | | | | | | | | | | |
	France	Germany	Denmark	Switzerland	Morocco	Argentina	Brazil	Nigeria	Hong Kong	Canada	Mean*
Patriotic	6.02	6.21	6.52	6.30	5.46	6.34	6.44	4.75	5.14	6.43	5.99
Fun-Loving	5.36	4.95	5.26	5.16	4.96	5.82	5.88	5.54	6.07	4.55	5.49
Selfish	4.92	4.62	5.64	4.86	4.72	5.77	5.88	3.91	3.44	4.85	4.79
Prejudiced	5.75	4.56	5.30	5.35	4.00	5.41	6.38	4.30	4.14	4.97	5.05
Emotionally expressive	4.75	4.18	4.53	4.67	4.98	4.55	3.70	4.80	5.74	4.48	4.69
Physically attractive	3.54	3.05	3.50	3.53	4.63	4.11	4.02	4.96	4.39	4.12	3.97
Friendly	4.54	4.76	4.87	5.03	5.07	3.71	3.39	4.89	5.53	4.23	4.81
Politically conservative	5.75	5.54	6.11	5.58	3.70	5.84	5.81	4.43	2.92	3.58	5.03
Like children	4.85	4.18	3.92	4.70	3.82	4.10	4.15	4.10	4.04	3.47	4.28
Worry over money	6.00	4.75	5.86	5.15	5.19	6.77	6.12	4.49	3.42	5.63	5.33
Religious	5.63	4.89	5.40	4.81	3.13	4.09	4.44	3.66	4.29	3.46	4.50
Close families	3.81	4.12	3.77	3.84	2.66	2.62	3.34	3.27	3.21	3.31	3.45
Treat women well	3.89	3.93	3.47	4.18	5.12	3.50	3.51	4.72	4.37	3.56	4.21
Greedy	5.72	4.79	5.43	5.27	5.46	5.24	5.28	3.65	4.14	5.07	4.94
Have free time	3.95	4.14	3.55	4.30	2.28	3.26	4.00	3.78	5.13	3.36	3.82
Intelligent	3.88	3.52	3.66	3.78	5.15	4.76	3.79	5.11	3.96	3.95	4.22
Violent	4.34	4.33	4.36	4.51	3.95	5.22	5.14	4.25	4.48	4.85	4.45
Hard-working	4.36	4.39	4.95	4.59	5.56	5.36	5.22	5.17	3.10	4.26	4.77
Sexually promiscuous	3.63	4.32	4.00	3.96	5.25	4.93	4.06	5.27	4.93	4.06	4.50

*Includes all international samples except Canada.

Note: Underline indicates distance greater than +1 or −1 from overall mean.

Table 1.4. Percent Sample Never in U.S. Rating Influence Important

	Argentina	Morocco	Germany	Denmark	France	Switzerland	Hong Kong	Nigeria	Austria	Brazil	Mean All	Rating	Canada
Television	76	92	81	98	86	82	95	68	83	98	86	1.91	88
Film	69	81	64	89	79	82	93	60	50	98	79	2.47	65
Books	47	86	62	67	60	55	73	74	67	65	66	3.27	40
Radio	41	54	50	62	56	48	47	61	33	37	51	3.73	44
Magazines	43	76	69	53	68	48	81	64	50	85	65	3.19	63
Newspapers	63	68	74	78	70	78	86	68	0	79	73	2.74	70
U.S. friends	45	54	60	60	44	47	54	42	33	29	48	3.07	45
Travel in U.S.	6	3	12	4	16	8	8	18	0	0	9	3.70	75
Living in U.S.	2	20	2	0	9	5	7	17	0	0	5	4.75	9
U.S. government	33	27	24	20	33	34	36	17	0	46	30	3.90	36
N	49	63	42	45	57	75	59	72	6	52	520		230

Note: Canadian data include all participants, whether or not they had lived or visited the U.S.

all eleven samples, television was rated more important than any other influence, except for two countries where TV was tied for first. The second most important influence on both dependent measures was film, and the third was newspapers. Clearly, participants perceived that the media play a powerful role in forming their stereotypes of the U.S.

Discussion

National Images

Several conclusions may be drawn from these data. First of all, it is not the case that the international perceived image of people from the United States more closely fits either the media image or the autostereotype ratings in a general sense. The scale with the clearest suggestion of the media cultivating foreign impressions of the U.S. was the "worrying about having enough money" scale, where the autostereotype differed from both the media image and the foreign stereotype, which did not differ from each other. U.S. people saw themselves as worrying a lot more about having enough money than people elsewhere saw them or than they themselves perceived the media to portray. However, this was the only scale clearly to show this predicted pattern.

On the other hand, the most common pattern (six scales) occurred in which the international stereotype did not differ from the U.S. autostereotype, although both differed from the rated media image, on the scales of prejudice, emotional expressiveness, liking children, religion, greed, and violence. Influences other than the media must be the formative factors in these cases.

Another pattern (three scales) occurred in which the media image, autostereotype, and international stereotype all differed from each other (physical attractiveness, sexual promiscuity, and having lots of free time). Apparently, attributions on these factors are formed on the basis of factors not tapped in this study.

On the selfish and hard-working scales, only the U.S. autostereotype and the aggregate international stereotype differed from each other, with the U.S.-perceived media image intermediate and not significantly different from either. On the friendly scale, only the U.S.-perceived media image and the international stereotype differed.

A few extreme ratings are worthy of comment. The highest ratings on the perceived media image were physically attractive (6.17), sexually promiscuous (5.94), and fun-loving (5.55), whereas the lowest rating was religious (3.85); these clearly reflect the often-noted hedonistic characteristics of the media entertainment personality. On the other hand, the highest rating for the autostereotype was "worry about having enough money" (6.48) and the lowest was "have lots of free time" (3.41). This is a very different reality than what is reflected by the media image, although these two ratings may have been somewhat more extreme due to the fact that all participants were college students, who are traditionally very busy people on limited budgets.

Although the cross-national similarities in stereotypes presented in Table 1.3 are more striking than their differences, some of the latter are worth noting. For purposes of this discussion, only mean ratings that fell outside of the range of –1 to +1 around the pooled Likert-scale means are considered. These means are underlined in Table 1.3. First of all, it is noteworthy that only twenty-one out of 190 means (eleven percent) were outside this range, a small number considering the cultural differences in the samples. About half of these occurred in the samples from Hong Kong (six) and Morocco (four). In considering these deviations, we must keep in mind the overall Western European bias of the pooled international stereotype (four out of ten national samples). Four of the deviations (nineteen percent) appeared on the "politically conservative" scale and were probably due to the different meaning of that term in national political cultures.

Other deviations would appear to reflect at least the popular stereotypes held by their raters. For example, economically booming Hong Kong rated U.S. people far less hard-working than did any other sample; these respondents also thought U.S people had a lot of free time. Racially mixed and tolerant Brazil found U.S. people very prejudiced, while Islamic Arab Morocco found them much less so. Heavily Chinese Hong Kong found U.S. people more emotionally expressive than any other group did. Islamic Morocco found U.S. people the least religious of any of the samples.

Media Influences and Cultivation

Although the present study clearly did not test cause-and-effect relationships, the retrospective rankings of the various media sources, especially television and film, as highly important cannot be dismissed. All of the most important influences identified, as reported in Table 1.4, are media sources. As the examination of the attribute ratings suggests, it is likely that the actual media influence is considerably stronger in forming national impressions in regard to some attributes than others. Future research should work to identify attributes that are particularly vulnerable and those that are particularly resistant to media influence.

Conclusions and Future Research

The present research provides some suggestive evidence as to a formative role of media, especially television, in the cultivation of national impressions of people who have never visited a country. However, much remains to be done to determine which types of knowledge are disproportionately influenced by media. Samples from ten nations showed a striking degree of similarity in both their aggregate stereotype and their ratings of influencing factors. Because all samples were university students, there might, of course, be greater differences in representative samples of the various populations. On the other hand, university students have greater access than most people in many societies to influences other than media. It is entirely possible that national impressions may actually be more media-influenced in less-educated populations. Also, future research should include any additional formative influences not considered in this study. One potentially important factor suggested to the authors so far is school experience.

This study of course has the common cross-cultural research limitations of non-random samples and some degree of a Western European bias, although the non-European samples were more striking in their similarity than in their differences from the European samples. Also, it is of course a "cross-national" rather than truly a "cross-cultural" study, with some of the nations very culturally homogeneous (Denmark, France, Morocco), and others very heterogeneous (Brazil, Canada, Nigeria). Future research should assess more non-Western societies and examine impressions about other major communications-exporting nations (e.g., Mexico, Brazil, France, United Kingdom) as well as the U.S.

Finally, the limits of cross-national research using trait rating scales must be considered. Individualist societies, such as Western nations, where trait theories and other personality scales and theories were developed, generally see the self as an independent self-system, whereas collectivist societies use an interdependent self-system, defined in terms of one's relationships to others (Markus and Kitayama 1991). How such a difference might be reflected in ratings such as those gathered in the present study is not entirely clear, but the issue is worthy of considering.

References

D'Adamo, O.J., and V. Garcia-Beaudoux. (1993). La representacion social de los paises americanos: Un estudio en Argentina y Estados Unidos. [The social representation of countries in the Americas: A study in Argentina and the United States] *Interamerican Journal of Psychology* 28(1): pp. 93–104.

D'Adamo, O.J., and V. Garcia-Beaudoux. (1995). *El argentino feo.* [*The ugly Argentine*] Buenos Aires: Losada.

Gerbner, G., and L. Gross (1976). Living with television: The violence profile. *Journal of Communication* 26(2): pp. 173–199.

Gerbner, G., L. Gross, M. Morgan, and N. Signorielli. (1982). Charting the mainstream: Television's contribution to political orientations. *Journal of Communication* 32(2): pp. 100–127.

Gerbner, G., L. Gross, M. Morgan, and N. Signorielli. (1984). Political correlates of television viewing. *Political Opinions Quarterly* 48(1): pp. 283–300.

Gerbner, G., L. Gross, M. Morgan and N. Signorielli. (1994). Growing up with television: The cultivation perspective. In J. Bryant and D. Zillmann (Eds.), *Media effects: Advances in theory and research*, pp. 17–41. Hillsdale, N.J.: Lawrence Erlbaum.

Klineberg, F.L. (1941). Studies of the measurement of the relations among sovereign states. *Psychometrika* 6: pp. 335–352.

Johnson, J.D., O.S. Oliveira, and G.A. Barnett. (1989). Communication factors related to closer international ties: An extension of a model in Belize. *International Journal of Intercultural Relations* 13: pp. 1–18.

Johnson, J.D., and A.R. Tims. (1985). Communication factors related to closer international ties. *Human Communication Research* 12: pp. 259–273.

Marin, G., and J.M. Salazar. (1985). Determinants of hetero-and auto-stereotypes: Distance, level of contact, and socioeconomic development in seven nations. *Journal of Cross-cultural Psychology* 16: pp. 403–422.

Markus, H.R., and S. Kitayama. (1991). Culture and the self: Implications for cognition, emotion, and motivation. *Psychological Review* 98: pp. 224–253.

McAndrew, F.T. (1990). Auto- and heterostereotyping in Pakistani, French, and American college students. *Journal of Social Psychology* 130: pp. 341–351.

McGrady, R.E., and J.B. McGrady. (1976). Effect of direct exposure to foreign target groups on descriptive stereotypes held by American students. *Social Behavior and Personality* 4: pp. 233–239.

McNelly, J.T., and F. Izcaray. (1986). International news exposure and images of nations. *Journalism Quarterly* 63: pp. 546–553.

Morgan, M. (1982). Television and adolescents' sex-role stereotypes: A longitudinal study. *Journal of Personality and Social Psychology* 43(5): pp. 947–955.

Morgan, M. (1983). Symbolic victimization and real-world fear. *Human Communication Research* 9(2): pp. 146–157.

Morgan, M. (1987). Television, sex-role attitudes, and sex-role behavior. *Journal of Early Adolescence* 7(3): pp. 269–282.

Morgan, M., and J. Shanahan. (1991). Television and the cultivation of political attitudes in Argentina. *Journal of Communication* 41(1): pp. 88–103.

Morgan, M., and J. Shanahan. (1995). *Democracy tango*. Cresskill N.J.: Hampton Press.

Nichols, K.R., and F.T. McAndrew. (1984). Stereotyping and auto-stereotyping in Spanish, Malaysian, and American college students. *Journal of Social Psychology* 124: pp. 179–189.

Perry, D.K. (1987). The image gap: How international news affects perceptions of nations. *Journalism Quarterly* 64: pp. 416–421, 433.

Perry, D.K. (1990). News reading, knowledge about, and attitudes toward foreign countries. *Journalism Quarterly* 67: pp. 353–358.

Perry, D.K., and J.T. McNelly. (1988). News orientations and variability of attitudes toward developing countries. *Journal of Broadcasting and Electronic Media* 32: pp. 323–334.

Perry, D.K., and W.H. Melson. (1989). Cosmopolitan media use, knowledge, and attitudinal differentiation of countries. *International Communication Bulletin* 24(3/4): pp. 16–21.

Piepe, A., P. Charlton, and J. Morey. (1990). Politics and television viewing in England: Hegemony or pluralism? *Journal of Communication* 40(1): pp. 24–35.

Robinson, J.P., and R. Heffner. (1967). Multidimensional differences in public and academic perceptions of nations. *Journal of Personality and Social Psychology* 7: pp. 251–259.

Sherman, R.C. (1973). Dimensional salience in the perception of nations as a function of attitudes toward war and anticipated social interaction. *Journal of Personality and Social Psychology* 27: pp. 65–73.

Signorielli, N., and M. Morgan. (Eds.). (1990). *Cultivation analysis: New directions in media effects research.* Newbury Park Cal.: Sage.

Slater, M.D. (1990). Processing social information in messages: Social group familiarity, fiction versus nonfiction, and subsequent beliefs. *Communication Research* 17: pp. 327–343.

Tims, A.R., and M.M. Miller. (1986). Determinants of attitudes toward foreign countries. *International Journal of Intercultural Relations* 10: pp. 471–484.

Tversky, A., and D. Kahneman. (1973). Availability: A heuristic for judging frequency and probability. *Cognitive Psychology* 5: pp. 207–232.

Weimann, G. (1984). Images of life in America: The impact of American TV in Israel. *International Journal of Intercultural Relations* 8(2): pp. 185–197.

2

Latent Destiny

Perverse Readings of the Greater East Asian Co-Prosperity Sphere

MCKENZIE WARK

American Century

New York, Thursday, October 5th, 1989: In living rooms across the United States, Johnny Carson bows to the audience and says: "Good evening, fine people. Welcome to humble show. We were just bought by Sony." Sony Corporation had just paid $3.4 billion for American entertainment giant Columbia Pictures in Japan's biggest American takeover deal ever.

According to *Newsweek* (1989), "this time the Japanese hadn't just snapped up another building, they had bought a piece of America's soul." Then when Matsushita made an offer for MCA/Universal studios, it began to look as if Sony's move was the beginning of a trend.

Herbert Schiller (1990) points out this irony: "It [the Columbia Pictures acquisition] has caused the American news media, along with government foreign-policy makers, to recognize a problem whose existence they have steadfastly denied for the past 25 years—cultural domination by an external power." Schiller is quick to add that it is not the nationality of the buyer that ought to be cause for concern, but the "awesome concentration and control, domestically and globally, by private economic power, of the apparatus of human consciousness production." This is clearly an issue here, but not the only one. Capital has culture too, and the movements of capital affect the distribution of cultural power.

One can see this most distinctly in business culture itself, where the craze for Japanese "management wisdom" rose with the value of the Yen and eventually fell with the Nikkei index. Hence, in a *Newsweek* (1989) interview, the president of Sony America, Akio Morita, said: "After we acquired CBC records, I thought, 'Now we have become the largest maker of music software in the world. And Sony is the largest video hardware company. So why don't we have video software?' Ever since, my mind has been set on making an acquisition in video software." Speaking of U.S. economic decline, he said:

> Instead of seeking to buy key components from Japan, American industries should produce those components by themselves. The strength of my company is that we have a policy of producing all key components ourselves. Service industries, which make up more and more of the US economy do not add value. It's production that adds value.

It seemed that the American Century was to wind up a decade early, rather like a Hollywood spectacular that opened with a bang but ultimately failed at the box office. As Mike Davis recounts, the nightmare image of the "warfare state" purveyed in a movie like *Colors* is more than just an image. That mode of police thinking, which mobilizes the Panopticon with the helicopter and infrared night vision, actually exists in Los Angeles (Davis 1990).

In decline, the apparent unity of America, invested as a site of power, fell apart. Perhaps the unifying narrative of American hegemony is breaking down under fire from competing pressures from class factions, social forces, and regional demands. The empire seems to compensate for this unbecoming fragmentation at home by projecting its force abroad—as though by threatening its proliferating among others it could rally a sense of identity at home. The gulf war against Iraq, the drug war against Medellin, the trade war against Japan, and right-wing Presidential candidate Pat Buchanan's war against the foreign within seem to merge into a desperate effort to hold the center. Descriptive comments like the sale of "a piece of America's soul"—and one of its few successful, profitable export industries—appeared as a widening disintegrating gyre, threatening the center.

Replicant Culture

Is it a coincidence that the rise of postmodern culture seems to coincide with the eclipse of America? When I hear the word "culture," I reach for my revolver, but when I hear "postmodern culture," I reach for the remote control to flip channels before the show gets too boring. Perhaps, if we stay tuned long enough, there might be something worth watching in the dissonance between American and Japanese takes on this oh-so-contemporary notion of the meaning of the contemporary. Sony's big move from hardware to software failed. By the mid-'90s, the Japanese economy staggered to a halt, lurching from one political crisis to another, even its once sacrosanct civil service finally being called into question. If the postmodern was a moment lived in the United States, during the '80s in terms of heightened instability in the media sphere that met with even more transparent and ironic attempts to reanimate the vital center, then by the '90s it appeared as though Japanese popular media had caught the same virus.

In this speculative essay, I want to follow the way the simulacra of Japan in American media, and of America in Japanese media, appear as signs of disturbance within each other. These signs of disturbance, which both media spaces place as belonging to the "great other" across the Pacific, may actually say as much about the space in between. This is an essay, in other words, that muses on the logic of international representation in postmodern times. If the guiding assumption is that international codes of representation, and codes of representation of the international, have a particular kind of semantic instability stemming from the question mark that hangs over the once-unquestioned sign of American hegemony, then this essay is necessarily just as fragile.

We are all familiar with the notion of these being postmodern times. In the world of product design, that is taken to mean an end to the standardized, form-follows-function thinking and a proliferation of designer objects in which form-follows-whimsy. Objects are made not for mass consumption but for what Fujioka Wakao calls the micro-masses, subcultural niches who construct their in-group identity and their differences from other groups on the style map in terms of a semiotic glut of stylized objects (Fujioka 1986).

To this end, Japanese manufacturers are oriented toward producing differently finished products on the same assembly line, products that appear to owe their forms to the present information landscape rather than to the space of a modern, mechanical imaginary (Schodt 1988).

Looking at the huge variety of products pictured in Japanese magazines, we see what seem to be collections of hairdryers that do not know they are hairdryers, hi-fi speakers that think they are ceramic vases, motorbikes that think they are hovercars out of *Blade Runner*.

This interpretation is not entirely fanciful either, given that Sid Mead, a former "conceptual artist" for General Motors designed the hovercars and much else in the visual style of *Blade Runner*. He has since been employed in designing futuristic nightclub spaces in Tokyo. In all of these cases, cultural information and the technical artifact seem to merge. Indeed, it might be appropriate to think in terms of *technoculture*—a term that might cover a wide spectrum of interfaces and sites at which a miniaturized power operates between the flesh and the machine.

If there is an image which goes with this blurring of culture into technology, it is perhaps the Tyrell Corporation in Ridley Scott's *Blade Runner*, which takes technology to the nth degree with replicants who do not know they are inhuman. The punch line is that the replicant hunter Deckard is probably not human either, and the metaphor of the reproduction of the social relations of capital collapses back into the reproduction of the body. The crucial factor that pushes the replicant over the edge, from knowing it is a product of labor to believing it is "really" human, is information—the encoding of memory. This is the crucial point because the encoding of memory in postmodern culture is in the hands of ever-more-sophisticated cultural technologies. We no longer have roots, we have aerials!

George Lukacs spoke of a second nature, composed of the products of physical labor, over and against which living labor is formed and struggles. It would seem appropriate now to speak of a *third nature*, of an environment shot through with the products of intellectual labor, over and against which intellectual labor is formed and struggles (Wark 1994).

It is this third nature that replicates itself in us, and hence it is no small matter who owns this "little piece of America's soul." For we all grew up in America, in a place called Hollywood, a place where movie stars have been replaced in the image bank by teenage crackheads and serial killers.

Is it any accident that the margins of *Blade Runner* fill with Asian images? These images could be disturbing, or affirming, depending on one's point of view. The first phase of global third nature issued from America and replicated, as an image, elsewhere. In the second phase, the images return from elsewhere, weird hybrids recolonizing third nature, from the margins to the center (Mercer 1994). In *Blade Runner*, one can take this hybrid landscape as an optimistic sign of the collapse of the authority of a global third nature issuing from a hegemonic imperial source.

Things are a little more difficult in Ridley Scott's subsequent film *Black Rain*, which reinstates the centrality of the American sign at the center, challenged by the "bad other" of Japan. Interestingly, the threat comes from counterfeiting—from the production of illegitimate signs of value. But the irony of postmodern capital is that it is no longer an American prerogative to act as a center of value. There is no gold standard for the transaction of transnational cultural values.

Old Times

The passage from the modern to the postmodern is also the passage from Fordism to Sonyism, the passage of the locus of technocultural power from the manufacture of standardized, mass-produced goods to the manufacture of quality products designed to sit in a variety of specialized market niches.

That means the passage from standardized mass labor and mass consumption to a *split workforce*, some of whom perform complicated hi-tech functions, while the majority work in sweatshops and service industries for low pay. Fordism—under which almost everybody got a sliver of an ever-expanding pie through the culture of consumerism, may soon be a phenomenon of the past (Lipietz and Legbourne 1988; Kennedy 1988). Already, nostalgic postmodernism is looking longingly back at the '60s.

The expertise of the old Fordist system was always culturally encoded as a quintessentially American quality. The Ford motor company was so proud of its mass production system that whenever it set up a factory anywhere in the world, it made sure it was identical in layout to the ones back home—right down to the placement of the Coke machine. The irony is that that Japanese learned the lessons of Fordism and improved upon it, learning how to incorporate quality into serial production, learning how to make a plethora of design finishes on one production system.

A significant fact about American society in the postwar years is that the share of the world market for cars held by U.S. firms fell from 76.2 percent in 1950 to only 19.3 percent in 1982 (Halberstam 1987). Hence, the term Fordism is linked to an instance of the failure of American capitalism, which has more than symbolic importance for the thousands of workers it used to employ and the style of life they used to enjoy.

Here begins (or resumes) the agonizing business Paul Virilio calls "endo-colonization," wherein the modern state responds to the crisis by colonizing its own urban population (Virilio 1988; Wark 1988). In the *Robocop* films, this space of endo-colonization becomes the site for new Hollywood narratives. Not by accident, these films are set in Detroit, and the crucial site for the big shoot out is the old River Rouge plant—built in the '20s by Henry Ford.

If the postmodern has more than a flip significance then, it means a challenge to the mastery of American technoculture. The myth of the postmodern as an era when signs float free, when power is abolished, when a transpolitical miasma envelopes the surfaces of the globe is wishful thinking, deflecting attention from the partial transfer of power away from America and its cozy satellites toward new centers of power.

It is not insignificant that while postmodernism is associated in the United States with a loss of mastery, a dissolution of narrative trajectories, it is experienced in Japan in quite the opposite way. The triumphalism of liberal modernization theory gives way to a Japanese approach to postmodernism that stresses a leap from the premodern to the postmodern or a precocious overcoming of the modern as a singularly Japanese achievement. This is a discursive formation which is complex, dangerous, and interesting.

Infantile Capitalism

Asada Akira offers a fabulous parody of such teleologies of power in his essay on "Infantile Capitalism." He proposes a reverse trajectory which begins with elderly capitalism, passes through the stage of adult capitalism, and terminates in infantile capitalism. Asks Asada, "is this the goal of the global trajectory of capitalism that broke down territorial boundaries as it stretched from the Mediterranean Sea up north across Europe out to the ocean, crossed the Atlantic, crossed the United States, and finally traversed the Pacific? Is this the goal of capitalism's history as a parody of Hegelian world history?" (Akira 1989, 275).

Not exactly, but this parodic trajectory makes as much sense as the triumphalist ones being touted in Japan, and is intended as a line of attack on the ideological grandeur that appears as the almost inevitable correlate of economic power. Likewise, we might attempt a parodic extension of it to the United States. While American *manifest destiny* led it to project its power outward, perhaps its *latent destiny* is an unproductive, narcissistic self absorbtion—beautiful but dangerous.

Asada ends his hallucinatory text with a burst of properly Nietzschian laughter, but not before he has drawn attention to a certain irony in the position from which he is called to speak. In being invited to America for a conference on "Japan and Postmodernism," he is being offered a site from that to speak which confers on him some cultural authority, just as the American "modernization" experts packed off to Japan after its defeat by the Fordist war machine had an authority over the theory that supposedly underlay that success. So Asada assumes the mask and the mantle of the postmodern, offered him by his hosts, and the space on the agenda opened up by Japanese technoculture.

This situation emphasizes that theory is not a universal language. In principle, we all know that. In practice, we assume the problem away and discuss Foucault or Stuart Hall as if these were international commodities. Seen in this light, Asada's laughter indicates a decentering which theory has long advocated but not entirely practiced.

America Is Dead

"The Americans have colonized our subconscious," runs a famous line from a Wim Wenders film. When Sony bought CBS and Columbia, it was as if this quotation invoked the response. Matsushita's $6.6 million bid for MCA, parent company of Universal, and Japanese investments directly in Tri-Star and indirectly in a number of film production packages duly followed. If the Americans have the power to affect the world's psychic unconscious, there is no point in getting angry about it. Instead, one has to get even. So why not buy the economic infrastructure that made this psychic colonization possible? Johnny Carson's racist wisecracks quoted at the beginning of this essay point to the paranoia that lurks just below the surface of good old-fashioned American gung-ho, can-do confidence.

For a long time now, we have all been trying to understand the American culture that lurks in our own unconscious. To work in the culture industries in Sydney or Toronto or West Berlin has meant for several decades to work on psychoanalyzing our unconscious desire for America to work at resisting, or celebrating, or subverting, or playing out the American in all of us, the image of the master we all are still slave to. This is why Sony's buying Columbia is an event of paramount importance which has not quite had its full effects yet. America-heroic, phallic America—is dead!

Great God America had always proclaimed itself the paramount power, the vital cultural center, and all the other gods died laughing. Left alone in the cultural void, America became the lone target for resentment. So we killed America. Only we have not quite awakened to the fact that America *really* is dead. Our cultural life revolves around a void we have not quite realized is there.

A paranoid and reactionary response to the killing of America is to elevate some other cultural power into its place, which is exactly the move Johnny Carson is signalling. Japanese economic power and technoculture have not displaced America. While serious questions are emerging about the position of the United States in the Pacific region, the U.S. Navy retains an unparalleled ability to project force in the region. So why all the fuss? It is because America has colonized our subconscious in a way that Japan has not.

Symptomatic of the problem is Hollywood's answer to the psychic power of Japan—*Black Rain*. A flawed trans-Pacific Western, this veiled cowboy epic is transformed once again into a Pacific war film, only this time the war is a peaceful technocultural business.

The rodeo-ride image of American power always relied upon our knowledge that the power of Fordist technoculture stood behind it. Since the Vietnam war (when the "Indians," for a change, started winning) that power has been in crisis—and so has Hollywood. With the slow running down of the American economy, the engine that sustained and projected the power of both Hollywood and the war machine is no longer there to guarantee the power of either.

We think we understand America; we think we have neutralized its psychic power in our culture. We have created a "tremendous Canada of light" or some other institutional defense mechanism in the shadow of it (Powe 1993). We have spent several decades on the problem, and we think we have got it mastered, only America is dead, and our cultural life is an anachronism lagging far behind the dynamic power for change coming from the decline and fall of Fordism.

The paranoid model on which peripheral cultures worked, based on a tacit acknowledgment of America as a univocal, patrilocal center simply won't work any more. We need a new model for grasping the networks and flows of culture on a global scale without referring them back to the dominant center.

This is the tyranny of difference, lived acutely in my own country, Australia, where dependence on American cultural and military power has for decades been both inestimably large and deeply resented. Now, more than ever, we have to deal with forces and cultures we have no understanding or "arrangement" with.

Delicious Reading

In seeking to cope with the vacuum created and with our feelings concerning it, we look at ways of reading post modern phenomena. For example, Sigourney Weaver appears with the logo "delicious living." This is an advertisement for Parco, a major Japanese department store. The slogan is the invention of Shigesato Itoi, who is both an advertising copywriter and a media celebrity in his own right, credited with introducing a new style of advertising based on pleasure and difference. Nobody who has ever seen Sigourney Weaver in Ridley Scott's *Alien* would associate her with "delicious living," but here she is. How am I to read her image here?

Cultural studies still tend to assume some common ground between the person who interprets and the media product to be read. Such an interpretation isn't much help when confronted with Sigourney Weaver and "delicious living." Perhaps we need to add to Hall's modes of reading two new kinds: perverse and paradoxical reading (Hall 1980).

The perverse reading would be one that misinforms the reader. The reader ends with an interpretation that is not warranted within the range of interpretations available to the community from which the message comes. The reader has unwittingly read the text in terms of the conventions of the reader's own interpretive community.

Japanese appropriations of English often appear in such a way. English writing, words, and most importantly, sounds are often inscribed within the Japanese text as Japanese signs of another culture, a perverse reading that intentionally misuses English, making it Japanese (Saint-Jacques 1987).

Perverse rewritings are creative and adaptive uses of "foreign" signs for new uses. The "noise" of the foreign message is turned into a delicious addition by assigning it a range of meanings and incorporating it in the lexicon.

Paradoxical Reading

Besides perverse reading, there might also be a category of paradoxical reading, a category of reading that knowingly decontextualizes the message, which knowingly works on the lack of commensurability between the two cultures that intersect when a message strays or ricochets out of orbit.

Such a reading would work in what is increasingly becoming the double existence of any and every sign:

1. its meaning for a community, its "local" meaning where there is a strong degree of shared codes between the people who make the media product and the people who read it;

2. its second or "shadow" meaning, which would be its complete openness to reinterpretation in parts of the world where images are interpreted very differently.

Perhaps one might deliberately want to encourage a self-conscious, paradoxical reinscription effect, not as a substitute for properly contextualized rereadings, but as a playful counterpart. Asada's reading of triumphalist postmodernism in the context of Japanese-American exchanges might be an example of such a practice. Perhaps this strategy is more and more necessary as the information landscape grows more and more powerful and increasingly free of the constraints communities used to place on the movement and interpretation of information. The media vector is no longer constrained within the magnetic fields of the communal, the social, or the cultural.

This idea of deliberately paradoxical, knowingly decontextualized reading might have a purpose in a world in which we cannot always connect points of cultural difference together through the unifying medium of the vast overweening dominance of American culture. It might have a further use stemming from the fact that regardless of the balance of political and cultural power, the flow of information is increasingly a transnational affair, and when information strays from its culture of origin and ends up spreading over into other cultures, there will always be powerful effects stemming from the spillover.

So if confronted with an image like "delicious living," I might be less interested in having someone explain to me what that means to its Japanese audience than in reinscribing it in another series of meanings. I might prefer to make it an emblem of the passage from mass consumerism to the proliferation of consumer micro-masses, each interpreting delicious living through its own bizarre collage of images. Or I might read it as an index of the decline of American power: strategic, cultural, cinematic. It might be juxtaposed in an essay with Ridley Scott's films, the Johnny Carson Show, and cultural studies *à la* Stuart Hall.

An eclectic list to be sure—but then paradoxical reading requires a certain "bent" attitude mixed with a strong dose of the reality of power. Might that not be a reasonable way to respond to the planet of noise that exists now in the twilight of American global projections? Even if the reports of the death of America turn out to be greatly exaggerated, surely something is to be

wrested from this period of its eclipse in the name of the plurality and difference which is the as-yet-unrealized promise of the postmodern.

Post America

While the typology of dominant, resistant, and negotiated readings was a useful tool for the examples and contexts Hall and his "Birmingham School" colleagues were immediately concerned with, in the examples above we reach its
limit (Davies 1995). One obvious problem is the implicit assumption that the
cultural studies practitioner approaches the cultural artifact or practice differently than the audience being studied. The scholar's position as an insider in
relation to the hegemonic culture is still in place, and questioned from
"within" as it were.

Speaking on radio during his one visit to Australia, Hall said that the
problem with theories of ideology is that it always appeared to be something
suffered by someone else. Here we encounter the same factor: other people's
readings are resistant or negotiated, not the scholar's. The point of taking up
an example like "Delicious Living" is that the cultural studies scholar has no
particularly privileged relation to it. I, too, am obliged to find a particular way
of reading the artifact, or perhaps of misreading it. Hence the idea of paradoxical or perverse reading—both to account for the kinds of reading that increasingly occur in the globalized network of media vectors, and to allow for
a writing of such readings within cultural studies without dragging the latter
off in the direction of a universalizing discourse such as classical anthropology,
or a narrowly particularist one like professional "Japanology."

To open up a space for paradoxical reading is to open space for writing.
Some argue that there is too much emphasis on reading in cultural studies—
too much endless interpretation. A paradoxical reading is an act of cultural
production, a reading in a space as yet without rules, as opposed to a reading
within the institutional exchanges of criticism. At the antipodes of the new
vectors of media transit and the new distributions of the powers of technoculture, there is still an open space for (mis)reading and writing. This cultural
production has to negotiate the fragments left by the absent center of Hollywood and the "popular" it once produced.

Takahashi Gen'ichiro, one of the new breed of Japanese writers, offers a
fine example of the kind of paradoxical reading/writing which a similarly paradoxical, or even a tactfully perverse cultural studies might develop, wander-
ing amid the *papier-maché* ruins of Hollywood's epic Babylon. Writing from
Yokohama, site of one of the biggest American naval bases, Gen'ichiro proposes six ways to become Christopher Columbus and "discover America":
"The first way is to make a map for going to America, pack a lunch, and set

out one bright clear afternoon. Don't forget the compass and canteen. Wear sneakers. No special dress required" (Gen'ichiro 1991, 53).

Takahashi's method is not without its difficulties. Its first problem, of course, is the map. He provides quite a detailed map which commences in a coffeeshop and ends . . . in America. The only difficulty is which coffeeshop. A fellow traveller in search of America sends a New Year's card to Takahashi from China: "Please be very careful when you use that map. What I took for America landed me in China." Although he adds, "At least over here you can draw a salary to look for America. The Chinese call it 'modernization.' "

Of course, most of us in cultural studies have already found *that* America. What the West has in common with Japan now is a search for different Americas. Perhaps it's a question of deciding which coffeeshop to set out from—or perhaps there is an America waiting around the corner and down the lane from every coffeeshop? Or perhaps it isn't America anymore, but America-in-Yokohama, or maybe Yokohama-in-America? Who can tell? Perhaps the best thing to do in cultural studies, out on its edges, where the media vectors cross and collide like freeway pileups, is to make paradoxical maps and wander, writing and sending each other postcards from new worlds.

References

Akira, A. (1989). Infantile capitalism. In M. Miyoshi and H. D. Harootunian (Eds.), *Postmodernism and Japan*. Durham: Duke University Press.

Davies, I. (1995). *Cultural studies and beyond*. London: Routledge.

Davis, M. (1990). *City of quartz*. London: Verso.

Fujioka, W. (1986). The rise of the micro-masses. *Japan Echo* 13(1).

Gen'ichiro, T. (1991). Christopher Columbus discovers America. In A. Birnbaum (Ed.), *Monkey brain Sushi: New tastes in Japanese fiction*. Tokyo: Kodansha International, p. 53.

Halberstam, D. (1987). *The reckoning*. London: Bloomsbury.

Hall, S. (1980). Encoding/decoding. In S. Hall et al. (Eds.), *Culture, media, language*. London: Hutcheon, pp. 157–162.

Kennedy, M., and R. Florida. (1988, March). Beyond mass production: Production and the Labour process in Japan. *Politics and Society*, pp. 121–158.

Lipietz, A., and D. Legbourne. (1988). New technologies, new modes of regulation: Some spatial implications. *Society and Space* 6, pp. 263–280.

Mercer, K. (1994). *Welcome to the jungle*. New York: Routledge.

Newsweek. (1989, October 9). Japan goes Hollywood, pp. 10–23.

Powe, B.W. (1993). *A tremendous Canada of light*. Toronto: Coach House Press.

Saint-Jacques, B. (1987). Bilingualism in daily life: The Roman alphabet in the
    Japanese writing system. *Visible Language* 21(1), 88–105.
Schiller, H.I. (1990, December 31). Sayonara MCA. *The Nation*, pp. 828–829.
Schodt, F.L. (1988). *Inside the robot kingdom*. Tokyo: Kodansha International.
Virilio, P. (1988). Pure War, Semiotext(e) Foreign Agents Series. New York.
Wark, M. (1988). On technological time: Cruising Virilio's overexposed city.
    Arena 83.
Wark, M. (1994). *Virtual geography: Living with global media events*. Blooming-
    ton: Indiana University Press.

3

The Basis for Perception

HERBERT I. SCHILLER

Though this volume is focused on conceptions of America derived from U.S. cultural products on display around the world, prevailing doctrine has it that the idea, much less the reality, of United States domination of the global flow of messages and images in the late 1990s is outmoded. A variety of explanations are advanced by those who think cultural imperialism, if it ever existed, today is an anachronistic view. These outlooks can be categorized roughly as follows:

One disputes the assertion that domination ever existed. This represents mainly the official position, enunciated by governmental officialdom. This outlook eliminates the very possibility of domination by insisting that the "free flow of information" guarantees the ultimate, universal good however distorted that flow may be. If the global flow of information and culture is in one direction and issues from a tiny number of message producers, its U.S. proponents claim it still represents the essential condition for free expression which operates to everyone's benefit. This principle has been the bedrock of official U.S. information policy since the end of World War II and remains very much in place today.

A second view, which also has as its objective the denial of the influence of U.S. cultural product, is the now very fashionable, and widely expressed notion of the "active audience." This formulation, which cuts across literary as well as communication spheres, places great weight on the capability of audiences—viewing or listening—to make up their own meanings from the symbolic flow that we all encounter. In this interpretation, the character of the content makes practically no difference. The audience will rework it and produce its own meaning.

This theory, offered with scant empirical support, is especially popular in academic and intellectual circles. Its effect is to demonstrate the pointlessness of examining the structures and institutions of cultural and informational power.

A third perspective, more willing to at least take into account the material reality of the global cultural sphere, claims that the development of a transnational corporate world has replaced the once-powerful state system. In this scenario, cultural, as well as other power, shifts to the competing transnational corporate actors, and the cultural product flows come not from one clearly identified state center but from the corporate global system.

To an increasing extent this is happening. However, the global position of U.S.-based cultural-informational conglomerates remains preeminent, and foreign transnationals in this domain largely imitate the U.S. creations. In either case, people are the targets, not the autonomous selectors.

Somewhat related to the above is the contention that individual nation states have developed rapidly in the information-image-making sphere and are now in a position to challenge the U.S. position. Some examples offered are Brazil and Mexico, in the Latin American region, and India, in the Asian area. Undeniably, these and other nations have expanded their message and image-making capabilities, and some of their products reach audiences beyond their own national boundaries, but their influence on the world cultural-information scene remains slight.

Finally, the increasingly favorite argument of those who are intent on obscuring, if not eradicating, recognition of the role of concentrated corporate power and influence over consciousness, is the technological "solution." The spreading electronic circuitry is hailed as the answer to concentrated control over expression and creativity. With the Internet, for example, so the argument runs, cyberspace is seen as the solvent of hierarchy and one-way communication. Truly interactive and democratic exchanges, now already occurring, will become, it is averred, the dominant pattern for world communication. Again, the coffin lid comes down on cultural domination.

Taken separately or together, these arguments present a seemingly daunting refutation of the idea of concentrated corporate cultural control. Yet, ironically, there are other powerful interests in the United States that see no reason to apologize for seeking global domination. In fact, they wish to extend it.

One such perspective is set forth in *Foreign Affairs* (1996) the quarterly organ of the nation's foreign policy elite. Written by two highly placed members of the Establishment, Joseph S. Nye, Jr. the Assistant Secretary of Defense for International Affairs in the Clinton Administration, and William A. Owens, former Vice Chairman of the Joint Chiefs of Staff, also in the Clinton Administration, their message is directed to those who don't yet grasp what they see as the full possibilities of assuring U.S. global domination in the next century.

Titling their article, "America's Information Edge," they get right down to business—the business of running the world. Nye and Owens begin their piece with these words: "The one country that can best lead the information revolution will be more powerful than any other. For the foreseeable future, that country is the United States. America has apparent strength in military power and economic production. Yet its more subtle comparative advantage is its ability to collect, process, act upon, and disseminate information, an edge that will almost certainly grow over the next decade" (20). This capability they term "soft power."

Unlike those who deny the presence of existing U.S. cultural power around the world, Nye and Owens affirm it and press to employ the new information technologies to deepen and solidify it. The U.S. should take advantage of "its international business and telecommunications networks," they write, because American popular culture, already "dominates film, television, and electronic communications."

Also, unlike the cultural groups who see no evil, hear no evil, and speak no evil about the present global cultural condition, there is ready recognition by Nye and Owens that the instruments of global cultural control are multifaceted and are most effective when seen as an ensemble of inputs. So, for example, they include in their inventory of America's "soft power" the fact that "American higher education draws some 450,000 foreign students each year" (29).

Attention is paid also to [U.S.] governmental involvement in the global cultural arena. The Voice of America, for example, is regarded by Nye and Owens as an indispensable tool for reaching audiences that the American commercial media, for one reason or another, cannot corral.

Noted too, is a well-known activity, the International Military and Training program (IMET), which "has trained more than half a million high-level foreign officers in American military methods and democratic civil-military relations" [El Salvador and Guatemala?] (31).

Most intriguing, given the authors' aim to make the twenty-first century "the period of America's greatest preeminence" (35), is their statement of approval that "USIA [United States Information Agency] and the U.S. agency for International Development have worked to improve global access to the Internet" (34). How does this square with those who are touting the Internet as the means of overcoming disadvantage and dependence? Do these foreign policy heavyweights know something that the high-tech enthusiasts are either unaware of or do not want to acknowledge?

Hardly a week passes without the news of another entry of an American corporate cultural presence into some hitherto uninvaded realm. *Business Week* reports (1996), for example, that Hungarian media properties are "on the block." "Hungary represents a great business opportunity," says one American corporate executive. Such "opportunities" are present throughout what used to be called the Third World. Today, viewed as "emerging markets," scores of nations are being treated, with their leaders' acquiescence, as dumping grounds for U.S. cultural product.

Antonio Pasquali (1996), Venezuelan scholar and media theorist, recently wrote: "All macro-trend indicators show *less* democracy in communications for Latin America: Greater national concentration with fewer owners . . . growing advertising imbalance between omnivorous television and other media . . . a cascade of national telecommunications systems going to multinationals; abandonment of endogenous systems. . . . Increased presence of foreign services which do not give broadcast rights to the region . . . minimalisation of public services . . . more external interventionism against endogenous cultural industries . . ." (4).

These are the current realities of cultural domination, not limited to Latin America. Their acknowledgment would be a first step to changing them.

References

Business Week 199 (May 27), p. 58.
Nye, J.S., Jr., and W.A. Owens. (1996, March–April). America's information
    edge. *Foreign Affairs*, pp. 20–36.
Pasquali, A. (1996, Spring). Latin American protonorms. *Media Ethics* 7(2): p. 4.

Part II

U.S. Image and the Political Factor

In this section, authors reveal that the U.S. government's political relations with, and its foreign policy toward, other nations greatly influences the way(s) in which it is portrayed abroad. Perhaps more than any other factor, political relations determines what citizens of other nations see, read, or hear in their domestic media about the United States and vice versa. In other words, the quality of political relations between two countries is a critical factor in the image that they portray of each other in their mass media. Kuldip Rampal discusses the U.S. image in the elite Indian press in the context of United States foreign policy toward India. He notes that since India has been a founding member of the Non-Aligned Movement (NAM), India and the U.S. have often been at odds over geopolitical and international issues. There have also been significant differences between the two countries on issues such as the disputed territory of Kashmir, human rights, and nuclear non-proliferation. Jae-Kyoung Lee explores the U.S. role in South Korea's politics in the 1990s, and examines statements issued by democratic activists, historians, and literary writers to document the transformation of U.S. public image from the savior of the republic to a villain. Dina Iordanova illustrates the interconnection between domestic politics, international politics, and media portrayals of the U.S. She points out that the representation of America has been changing along with the changes in Bulgaria's post-Communist media. Ayseli Usluata examines the political cartoons published in the national newspapers in Turkey to see how the image of the U.S. has been reflected and/or constructed by the foremost political cartoonists of Turkey over a period of two decades. Laid Zaghlami traces the U.S.-Algerian political relationship, from the eighteenth century to the present, to illustrate the interconnection between politics, trade, and his country's media portrayal of the U.S.

Taken together, this section shows that the mass media do not function independently from the domestic, regional, or international politics. Rather, they often reflect the quality of the relationship that a given country enjoys, at a given time, with the U.S.

4

Image of the U.S. Foreign Policy toward India among Indian Media and Policy Makers

KULDIP R. RAMPAL

An influential Indian newsmagazine said in late 1995 that "[a]s Indo-US exchanges promised to turn high profile in the coming months, it is apparent that relations between the two countries have entered yet another phase of assessment and adjustment" (*India Today*, November 30, 1995, 61). The magazine's ambivalence regarding Indo-U.S. relations was characteristic of the image portrayed by India's elite English-language press for decades. The magazine said that even as India has been receiving special attention in recent years from the U.S. government, which has designated India as one of the ten most important emerging markets, Washington continues to arm its old ally, and India's archrival, Pakistan with sophisticated weapons.

The U.S.-Pakistan strategic relationship born out of alliance in the 1950s is seen by the elite Indian press as the reason for the ongoing foreign policy "tilt" in favor of Pakistan by the United States. The Indian press is also critical of the U.S. pressure on India to support nuclear non-proliferation and the proposed comprehensive nuclear test ban treaty without taking a full view of Indian security concerns. Perceptions of a "biased" nature of human rights concerns and "insensitivity" to foreign-sponsored terrorist activity on Indian soil are other areas raising doubts about U.S. foreign policy among Indian policy makers and opinion leaders.

Before we continue with a detailed analysis of the Indian perceptions of U.S. foreign policy, a brief explanation of India's ideological and foreign policy principles, and its security concerns about its large neighbors, is necessary to establish the framework influencing the perceptions.

India's Ideological/Foreign Policy Principles and Security Concerns

India, which received independence from British colonial rule on August 15, 1947, is a secular state with a parliamentary form of government based on universal adult franchise. The country's Constitution guarantees fundamental rights enforceable in courts of law by an independent judiciary. The architect of India's foreign policy was its first prime minister, Jawaharlal Nehru. In his very first policy statement after India attained freedom, Nehru declared

> The world, in spite of its rivalries and hatred and inner conflicts, moves inevitably towards closer cooperation and the building up of a world commonwealth. It is for this One World that free India will work, a world in which there is free cooperation of free peoples and no class or creed exploits another. (*India* 1990, 5)

In view of Nehru's One World vision, the central element of India's foreign policy became the quest for reduction in international tensions and the maintenance of peace. Peace to India did not merely mean the absence of war, but meaningful cooperation between nations. India's leaders, especially Mahatma Gandhi and Nehru, were convinced that the country could play a meaningful role in building an environment of peace and cooperation only by rejecting alignment with any power bloc. As Nehru declared: "We are in no camp and in no military alliance. The only camp we should like to be in is the camp of peace which should include as many countries as possible" (*India* 1990, 5).

The policy of non-alignment, formulated by Nehru as early as 1946, was launched in 1961 under the leadership of world figures like President Tito of Yugoslavia, President Nasser of Egypt, President Sukharno of Indonesia, and Nehru. The membership of the non-aligned movement swelled from twenty-six in 1961 to more than 100 countries by the 1980s. As a result of this policy, cooperation with other nations, irrespective of their ideological beliefs, has been an essential ingredient of India's foreign policy before, during, and since the Cold War. Pakistan, traditionally an important element in U.S. foreign policy toward the Indian subcontinent, became an ally of the United States through the Southeast Asia Treaty Organization (SEATO), a collective defense alliance established in 1954 by a group of eight nations to guarantee peace in Southeast Asia.

Apart from India's ideological and foreign policy principles, its security interests have also played a central role in its perceptions of U.S. foreign policy. India and Pakistan have fought three wars since independence in 1947, two over the disputed northern region of Kashmir and one over the secession of what used to be East Pakistan into an independent state of Bangladesh. India also fought a brief war with its neighbor to the northeast, China, in 1962 over China's territorial claims. Although no major border conflict has developed with Pakistan or China for many years, territorial disputes with both neighbors remain. Caught between what it perceives as two adversaries, India believes it has compelling national security interests to pursue.

We will analyze in the next section Indian perceptions of U.S. foreign policy within the framework of India's ideological, foreign policy, and national security considerations. Before we continue, however, a brief introduction to the Indian press is in order.

Article 19(1)(a) of the Constitution allows all citizens the right to freedom of speech and expression. While freedom of the press is not explicitly mentioned, it has been judicially determined that the freedom of speech and expression clause includes press freedom (Kurian 1982, 480).

The Indian press is diversified and independent, generating publications in Hindi and English, the official languages of India, and in fourteen other major languages across the country. The press has become increasingly aggressive since late 1977, when it regained its freedoms after an unprecedented twenty-two-month "State of Emergency" imposed by the government of the then-prime minister, Indira Gandhi. The investigative stories done by the *Indian Express*, among other publications, have been recognized by the U.S.-based *World Press Review* as exposing corruption and malfeasance in the highest councils of the government (Rampal 1984, 9). In its assessment of the Indian press, Hong Kong–based *Far Eastern Economic Review* noted in October 1995 that "the Indian press is getting more powerful and more independent" running "well-researched social exposes."

It is fully recognized by the Indian and overseas journalistic community that major newspapers—*The Times of India*, *The Hindu*, *The Hindustan Times*, *The Indian Express*, and the *Statesman*, among others—and magazines like *India Today* are important contributors to and arbiters of public opinion. The English-language press is singled out for analysis in this chapter because it is read by policy makers and opinion leaders in the country and, therefore, considered to be the most influential in India.

U.S. Foreign Policy Issues and Indian Press/Policy Makers' Perceptions

India's Planned Economy and Non-Alignment

Although the United States has long admired India's democracy, it has had little admiration for India's non-alignment policy and socialist economy. That is where the roots of ambivalence in Indo-U.S. relations lie. Until 1991, when the government of Prime Minister P.V. Narasimha Rao launched a policy of economic liberalization, India had a protected economy of public and private ownership, often resembling the planned economies of socialist countries. In view of the American aversion to any socialist pattern of state-owned economy, the U.S. governments have traditionally denied aid to India's public-sector industries, restricting aid to agriculture, and, to a lesser extent, to the military until the 1960s.

For example, having built a public-sector steel plant with Soviet aid, India turned to the United States in the late 1950s to seek aid for another such project, partly because heavy dependence on one country for machinery and technology was considered inadvisable, especially in the politically strategic area of steel. In several sessions, the U.S. Congress showed little enthusiasm to fund the proposed state-run steel project. The Indian government withdrew the request in 1963 after concluding it would be rejected by the Congress. The following year, the Soviet Union formally offered financial and technical assistance to India in building this steel plant. Interestingly, as writer Ved Mehta noted, even though India had received about $4 billion in aid from the United States by 1962, compared to only about $800 million from the Soviet Union, the Soviet aid, with its dramatic industrial projects, was making a greater impression in India (Mehta 1970, 304).

Although, as noted above, India would have preferred to have built this steel plant with American aid, it considered its acceptance of the Soviet offer fully consistent with its policy of cooperation based on non-alignment, irrespective of the ideological orientation of the country providing aid. As India pursued a policy of engagement and cooperation with both power blocs during the Cold War, the United States viewed India's non-alignment policy and friendly relations with the Soviet Union with skepticism. Ollapally and Ramanna (1995, 17) note that such a view by America was tied to the "paradoxical streak of universalism in America's philosophy of liberal individualism, which implies that 'those who are not with us are against us.' " John Foster Dulles, U.S. Secretary of State from 1953 to 1959, had called non-alignment opportunistic, and denounced India on moral grounds. Hari Kishore Singh, writing in the *Indian Express*, said that such a view by Dulles "naturally infuriated India. The power establishment in Delhi and public opinion in the country reacted sharply" (Singh, Dec. 8, 1995, 48). To India, non-alignment was born out of the bitter experiences of subjugation and exploitation of colonial rule, and it wanted to be left out of the Cold War power politics between the two superpowers.

As the superpowers began to expand their sphere of influence in the first decade of the Cold War through a chain of military alliances—such as NATO, SEATO, and the Warsaw Pact—and the Soviet-sponsored support of communist movements, the non-aligned countries were alarmed. Singh says that leaders like Nehru "resented the psychological pressure that emanated from this [movement] and became even more conscious of the designs of neo-imperialism." Nehru, along with other founding members of the non-aligned movement, were sharply critical of U.S. foreign policy under Dulles. "Indo-U.S. relations were thus a thorny issue right from the beginning," says Singh.

Disputed Territory of Kashmir

Perhaps no other U.S. foreign policy issue regarding South Asia receives as much attention in the Indian press as the U.S. statements on the territory of Kashmir, a disputed mountain region in the north of the Indian subcontinent. John Ward Anderson of the *Washington Post*, writing on November 7, 1993, explained that after India's independence in 1947 and Pakistan's breaking away, Kashmir's ruling prince agreed to become part of India in exchange for India's help in driving Pakistani forces from his state. Under the India Independence Act, 1947, as the sovereignty of the British Crown over the Indian states lapsed, the states contiguous to India or Pakistan could, if they so desired, accede to either of the two countries. At the time of Indian independence, the prince of the state of Jammu and Kashmir entered into what was called a "Standstill Agreement" with both India and Pakistan so that he could take the necessary time before reaching a decision on the issue of accession.

The prince of Kashmir, in a letter dated October 26, 1947, to Lord Mountbatten, the Governor-General of India, wrote, however, that Pakistan was not abiding by the Standstill Agreement. He said that Pakistani soldiers had crossed into the state and were advancing to capture the capital, Srinagar (Singh, October 26, 1947). The letter went on to say:

> With the conditions obtaining at present in my State and the great emergency of the situation as it exists, I have no option but to ask for help from the Indian Dominion. Naturally they cannot send the help asked for by me without my State acceding to the Dominion of India. I have accordingly decided to do so and I attach the Instrument of accession for acceptance by your Government.

After the Instrument of Accession was accepted and Indian troops were airlifted to Kashmir, the Pakistani government swiftly dispatched its own troops. British Field Marshal Auchinleck, however, flew to the Pakistani city of Lahore on the morning of October 28, 1947, and explained to the government of Pakistan that Kashmir was legally a part of India (Lekhi, November 15, 1993). Before the U.N. intervened in the conflict, Pakistan had taken control of approximately one-third of Kashmir, with the remaining two-thirds being under Indian control. A resolution passed by the U.N. on August 13, 1948, accepted the validity of the accession by recognizing India's right to station troops in the whole of Jammu and Kashmir, and insisted that Pakistan withdraw all its forces from Jammu and Kashmir (Dhar, February 24, 1994).

Dhar added that "this position was explicitly and unambiguously endorsed by the U.S.'s own permanent representative, Warren Austin." Another U.N. resolution called for holding a plebiscite to determine the future of Kashmir.

The territory of Kashmir remains divided under Indian and Pakistani control after two other wars between these countries, in 1965 and 1971. Following the 1971 war over the creation of Bangladesh, Indian and Pakistani leaders met in the northern Indian hill town of Simla and reached an agreement on July 2, 1972, on bilateral relations. The Simla Agreement said that the heads of both governments will meet in the future to settle, among other matters, the issue of Jammu and Kashmir (Simla Agreement, July 2, 1972). To India, the Simla Agreement supersedes the 1948 U.N. resolution which called for a plebiscite following vacating of the Kashmiri territory held by Pakistan. Under the Simla pact, the Kashmir issue is a bilateral matter to be resolved between India and Pakistan. Although India and Pakistan have held several foreign secretary-level meetings on the issue, Pakistan continues to see the issue falling under the purview of the 1948 U.N. resolution.

Pakistan claims that since a majority of the people in the Kashmir valley are Muslims, the territory should go to Islamic Pakistan. India says that accession legally makes Kashmir part of India, in addition to the fact that secular India has 131 million Muslims, more than the entire population of Pakistan. Indeed, the Hindu-majority India has the world's second-largest Muslim population, after Indonesia.

Indian perceptions of U.S. policy on the Kashmir issue have created a serious image problem for the United States among the Indian press and public opinion. A review of several editorials and news stories indicates that the U.S. stand on the issue is found to be inconsistent, biased in favor of Pakistan, or even opportunistic to suit America's own geopolitical interests. The strongest torrent of anti-American commentary was launched in the Indian press in 1993 following a statement by the newly-appointed Assistant Secretary of State for South Asian affairs, Robin Raphel. In a press conference with South Asian journalists on October 26, 1993, Raphel said the United States does not recognize the 1947 document ceding Kashmir to India "as meaning that Kashmir is forevermore an integral part of India" (Anderson, November 7, 1993). The Indian press interpreted the Raphel statement to mean that the Instrument of Accession was no longer final from the American standpoint, which never before had been perceived to be the American position.

The wording of Raphel's comments led many Indians to conclude that the United States questions the validity of India's independence and favors a second partitioning of the Indian subcontinent. Anderson cited headlines in Indian dailies that read, "America doubting the validity of India's independence," and, "To hell with the West." Arun Shourie, a leading newspaper columnist, complaining that the Indian government's reaction to the United

States had been too timid, wrote, "What in hell gives some pup of an American officer the right to question the boundaries of our country" (Anderson, November 7, 1993). The Indian government did lodge a strong protest with the United States, resulting in a clarification of the Raphel statement.

Dhar (February 24, 1994) saw hidden American motives behind the Raphel comment. He said that "questioning the validity of Kashmir's accession to India is not an aberration or a bit of impulsive thinking by a U.S. official. It is the product of careful homework by the State Department." He went on to note that "Some analysts have argued the U.S. began looking favorably on an independent Kashmir from 1949 onwards as part of [the] Pentagon's larger global strategy to contain the Soviet Union." Writing in the *Times of India*, Kirpekar (May 15, 1994) quoted a former minister in the Jammu and Kashmir government as saying that "Washington's objective is to create an independent Kashmir to enable it to gain a foothold in this part of Asia to keep an eye on China." The seriousness of Indian concerns about U.S. motives in Kashmir further emerged when a statement by Home Minister Shankarrao Chavan in late 1995 accusing Washington of having "evil designs" in Kashmir received a standing ovation in the parliament.

Such a perception of American goals is reinforced among Indian policy makers and the press when they consider that the U.S. formula for peace on the issue has evolved from "direct negotiations between India and Pakistan within the Simla accord" to taking into account the "will" of the Kashmiri people. The latter American position is seen as a radical change from earlier references to taking into account the "interests" and "wishes" of the people. To India, American references to taking into account the "will" of the people means that it is increasingly interested in a "third option" for Kashmir, its independence, so that America can use it to pursue its own geopolitical interests. K.K. Katyal, writing in the *Hindu*, said that the Clinton administration had made some significant departures on Kashmir from the Bush-era line by "losing its earlier zest" for the Simla agreement framework for Indo-Pakistan talks. "For example, the new U.S. ambassador, Mr. Frank Wisner, while pleading for direct negotiations, the other day favored a solution of the problem 'taking into account the will of the people of Kashmir.' In the past, statements from Washington spoke of the 'wishes of the people of Kashmir' " (Katyal, August 22, 1994).

Katyal went on to speak of a pro-Pakistan bias in America's Kashmir policy: "Whatever be its line on Kashmir, the U.S. is interested in saving [Pakistani Prime Minister] Ms. Bhutto and in warding off threats to her survival." Such a pro-Pakistan bias is widely perceived by the Indian press, although the U.S. denies having such a bias. Prem Shankar Jha, writing in the *Hindu* (Jha, July 9, 1994), said that although Pakistan is anxious to involve the U.S. in seeking a resolution of the Kashmir conflict, Americans are baffled over the lack of Indian enthusiasm for the same. The reason, he explained, was that there is a "deep distrust of the U.S. motives, and its ability to act impartially in this matter." *India Today* (November 15, 1993) noted that Indian concern over the exact U.S. policy on Kashmir was so high that one foreign ministry official complained that "America's policy on Kashmir should be made more transparent."

As a result of the uproar caused by what was perceived to be a change in America's Kashmir policy, Raphel returned to India in March 1994 to correct the "misperceptions." She said that America would support a negotiated end to the conflict in Kashmir within the framework of the Simla agreement. In September of the same year, however, U.S. Ambassador to India Frank Wisner, in an interview with the Press Trust of India news agency said that although the Simla accord provided a broad framework for India and Pakistan to resolve the dispute, the U.N. resolutions toward finding a solution in Kashmir "have their own standing and legitimacy" (*Asian Age*, September 12, 1994). Wisner also said, however, that he was not suggesting that a plebiscite was the only way of finding the will of the people, adding that early assembly elections in the state was one possibility. India noted that it had been holding such elections for more than four decades.

There was little indication from the Indian press comments that concerns about the U.S. Kashmir policy had been addressed. John Mallott, who was the first director of the South Asian bureau in the State Department before Raphel became its assistant secretary, was clearly concerned about the damage the American statements on Kashmir were causing in Indo-U.S. relations. In one of his last congressional testimonies, he said that the best thing for America was to "simply shut up on Kashmir" (Nayar, December 22, 1995).

Human Rights

The U.S. State Department's annual reports on human rights around the world have long acknowledged that India is a parliamentary democracy with a free press, a civilian-controlled military, an independent judiciary, and active political and civic associations. According to the Indian press, however, the U.S. seems to forget these attributes of Indian political life when commenting on human rights abuses in parts of the country ridden with separatist movements. In his address to the United Nations in 1993, President Bill Clinton referred to human rights abuses in Kashmir and Bosnia. To the Indian press, mentioning Kashmir and Bosnia in the same breath implied that India had a state-sponsored policy of human rights violations. Both the Indian government and the press have also felt that there has been an unwarranted censure of the government's human rights record by the U.S. government.

To put the matter in some perspective, India has faced violent separatist movements in the northern states of Punjab, Jammu, and Kashmir, and in parts of the northeast of the country. U.S. State Department reports have acknowledged that these militant insurgencies have resulted in the deaths of thousands of innocent civilians. More than 300,000 Hindu residents of Kashmir have been forced to flee their homes under the threat of death. India's census figures show that in 1941, Hindus formed 15 percent of the population in Kashmir, whereas in 1991 only 0.1 percent of the population in the valley was Hindu. India, claiming that Pakistan was fighting a proxy war in Kashmir and Punjab by training and arming the militants, deployed military and paramilitary forces in the two states. Pakistan has consistently denied that it is behind the militancy, but a U.S. House task force report (U.S. House Republican Task Force Report on Terrorism and Unconventional Warfare, August 24, 1994) noted that Pakistan's "insertion of terrorists into Indian Kashmir continued to escalate." A U.S. Senate resolution in 1993 (*The Hindu*, September 2, 1993) called on Pakistan to desist from "aiding and abetting the reign of terror" unleashed in Jammu and Kashmir by indigenous militants as well as by the terrorists infiltrating from Pakistan.

Against this backdrop, both the Indian government and the press have acknowledged that in the process of hunting for the militants, there have been instances of human rights violations by the police and paramilitary forces. But they attribute such violations to the problems associated with militant search operations rather than to any official policy, adding that rogue security men are routinely disciplined. *India Today* (November 15, 1993) said in an editorial that in the U.S. government circles, an image of India is being created of "cruelty as an instrument of state policy for cracking down ruthlessly on citizenry, in not only Kashmir but also Punjab and the Northeast." The editorial continued:

> There are a few things US Congressmen should consider. For one, repression is not a state policy. To be sure localised police brutality in India is rampant and accountability often negligible. But the key is that India possesses, as is the case with every working democracy, the institutions that check the state's excesses. It has a free press, parliamentarians and civil libertarians who wage a ceaseless campaign to exposes state high-handedness. . . .

The Free Press Journal (February 24, 1994) said in an editorial that a well-researched study by four European ambassadors in Kashmir had concluded that there had been human rights violations by the militants and the security forces, adding that "[t]he situation in the state would not have degenerated to the present level if there had been no material assistance from across the border [Pakistan]." The editorial went on to say: "This is the crux of the Kashmir problem, as in the case of Punjab problem, something which President Clinton and his pro-Pakistan Assistant Secretary of State for South Asian affairs Robin Raphel have been deliberately ignoring."

Kirpekar (*The Times of India*, May 15, 1994) wrote that "there is little doubt in the minds of people here [Kashmir] that the Clinton administration is backing Pakistan's sponsorship of terrorism in Jammu and Kashmir, which is responsible for the grave and massive violation of human rights of the victims of terrorist activity." He went on to say that people in the valley were wondering why Washington was ignoring "the mountain of evidence of the Pakistan government's involvement in terrorism and secessionism."

Kamath (*The Free Press Journal*, February 24, 1994) said that while receiving Pakistan's new ambassador to Washington, "President Clinton said he shared Pakistan's concerns about human rights abuses in Kashmir, again turning a blind eye to Pakistan's own role in sponsoring terrorism in Kashmir." And Jha (October 6, 1993), writing for the *Hindu*, said that "If the Indian government has an ounce of sense, it should declare that it is returning the $36.9 million of aid offered by the U.S. government rather than accept the censure on its human rights record."

Although the Indian government views the U.S. criticism of its human rights record as unwarranted, it appointed a Human Rights Commission in 1993 to induce greater accountability and transparency in the laws, procedures, and system of administration of justice. It also allowed to lapse in 1995 the Terrorist and Disruptive Activities (Prevention) Act of 1987, enacted at the height of militant insurgency in Punjab, which allowed detention of suspected terrorists for up to a year.

In a development that the Indian government and the press will no doubt see as a vindication of their position that human rights problems in Kashmir were linked to foreign-sponsored terrorist activity, the State Department's 1995 human rights report acknowledged that "Many of the terrorists are not Indian citizens" (India Human Rights Practices 1995, 11). The report noted that the "National Human Rights Commission continues to play a useful role in addressing patterns of abuse . . . as it seeks to create a 'human rights culture' through educational programs" (2). In its overall assessment of the situation, the report said that "During 1995, India made significant progress in resolving human rights problems" (2).

Nuclear Non-Proliferation and Test Ban Treaty

At the time of this writing in early 1996, another U.S. foreign policy issue receiving much attention among Indian policy makers and in the country's press was nuclear non-proliferation. This issue emerged high on the American agenda when the eighteen largest arms control and disarmament organizations in the United States joined together in December 1993 to form the Campaign for the Non-Proliferation Treaty (NPT). They worked for the indefinite extension of the NPT and for steps to strengthen the global nonproliferation regime, including the adoption of a Comprehensive Test Ban Treaty (CTBT).

Soon after assuming office in January 1993, President Clinton promised to spare no effort to get an indefinite extension of the twenty-five-year-old NPT, an objective he accomplished in May 1995 when 175 nations party to the treaty agreed to extend it indefinitely. Clinton announced on August 11, 1995, that his administration would also push for the adoption of the CTBT by June 1996, ending all nuclear weapons tests for all time.

India, among some other countries, refused to sign the NPT, saying it was discriminatory because it did not require the five acknowledged nuclear powers—U.S., Russia, China, Britain, and France—to dismantle their arsenals. India has followed a similar position on the proposed CTBT, which was being thrashed out at the Conference on Disarmament in Geneva in early 1996. Clinton wrote a letter to Indian Prime Minister Rao in September 1995 urging India's support for the CTBT, but no such commitment was forthcoming from India as of March 1996. India was insisting that the five nuclear powers agree to a time-bound program for the elimination of their nuclear weapons as a precondition to signing the CTBT (Evans, March 21, 1996).

At the summit of the non-aligned movement in Colombia in October 1995, India got member countries to back its stand for global disarmament. In an unusually tough speech, Rao asked: "If such a commitment is not forthcoming, what are we to make of a status in which a few hold on to their awesome arsenals, kept trim by sophisticated computer simulation techniques, while they want all others to watch on with empty hands (*India Today*, Dec. 31, 1995, 46–47). Reports in the Indian press had noted that signing CTBT would put an indirect cap on India's nuclear-weapon capability, which the U.S. and the other nuclear weapons states were seen to be wanting to do.

Ollapally and Ramanna (1995, 15) say the Indian position on NPT and related issues is rooted in its security concerns about its largest neighbor, China. They note that even though Sino-Indian relations are on the upswing, the memory of the 1962 war and the continuing border dispute between the two countries in the face of significant Chinese military superiority suggest that Indian concerns are not baseless. China, which conducted its first nuclear test in 1964, had carried out a total of forty-three such tests by the end of 1995 and had acquired a significant arsenal of nuclear weapons. India detonated a nuclear device in 1974, but has not attempted any similar experiments in the twenty-two years since. It also denies possessing any nuclear weapons.

Another matter of serious concern to India is the strategic link between China and Pakistan, especially the sale of M-11 missile components, which indicates that China views Pakistan as one instrument of its foreign policy toward the Indian subcontinent (Ollapally and Ramanna 1995, 15). In another development, the CIA concluded that in 1995, China provided Pakistan as many as 5,000 ring magnets for refining bomb grade uranium (AP, March 21, 1996). This policy resulted in the Clinton administration considering economic sanctions against both China and Pakistan (*The Wall Street Journal*, March 13, 1996, A20). The China-Pakistan nuclear cooperation was reportedly taking place even as a friendly American administration was lobbying for the Brown amendment, which in March 1996 released to Pakistan military ware worth $368 million held back on non-proliferation grounds (AP, March 21, 1996).

Indian policy makers say that the United States has a tendency to reduce their security concerns by continuing to focus on nuclear issues in South Asia as an Indo-Pakistani problem rather than viewing it in the context of the Chinese nuclear threat perceived by India. India also believes that the United States unfairly singles it out from Pakistan and Israel, two other key NPT nonsignatory states, in criticizing the Indian position on non-proliferation (Ollapally and Ramanna 1995, 13).

For example, M.R. Srinivasan, the former chairman of the Atomic Energy Commission and the Department of Atomic Energy in India (Srinivasan, December 22, 1995, 62), said that "there can be no clearer admission of the cynicism of the United States when it talks about its commitment to non-proliferation. No wonder Israel first and later Pakistan were helped in various ways by the United States to acquire nuclear capability." The Press Trust of India news agency quoted Gary Millhollin, director of the University of Wisconsin Project on Nuclear Arms Control, as saying, "It seems clear that Pakistan bought the magnets to make nuclear weapons. But has anyone complained? We have yet to hear a peep out of the Clinton administration" (Parasuram, March 24, 1996). *The Hindu* (February 14, 1996) noted in an editorial that India should continue to oppose the selective implementation of the U.S.-sponsored nuclear control regimes, adding that the U.S. uses one set of standards for nuclear states and friendly countries and another for independent, non-aligned countries such as India. Such selective implementation, continued the editorial, "must reinforce the determination of this country [India] to follow its policy of nuclear restraint while keeping the nuclear option and continuing to work for global disarmament."

Nayar, writing for the *Indian Express*, said that "India's reservations about the manner in which the United States and some of its Western allies are trying to hustle the 38 members of the Conference on Disarmament in Geneva into a comprehensive test ban arrangement stems from [Indian Prime Minister] Rao's belief that the Cold War is not entirely a thing of the past" (Nayar, December 29, 1995, 54).

Nayar said that at a number of brainstorming sessions within a close circle in 1995, Rao cited rising tensions between the United States and China, the prospect of a very powerful China, and the hitherto undefined roles of countries like India on the Asian scene as compelling reasons for the inevitability of another Cold War in the century that lies ahead. In such a context, said Nayar, time-bound and complete nuclear disarmament naturally becomes a priority for countries like India.

Nayar also noted that it was ironic that during Rao's official visit to the U.S. in 1994, he had received strong support from Clinton for the elimination of nuclear weapons. Simultaneously, they spoke of "cooperative efforts" to achieve a CTBT. "But today, there is no mention of the elimination of nuclear weapons as Clinton looks upon the CTBT merely as one of the instruments for his second term in the White House," Nayar said.

A widespread impression held by the Indian press in early 1996 was that the United States was trying to twist India's arm to get it to support the CTBT. This impression resulted from a news report in the *New York Times* on December 15, 1995, which said India might be preparing for its first atomic weapons test in more than two decades. The Indian government called the report highly speculative and later denied that it was planning such a test. In spite of India's denial, the story persisted in the *Times* and other newspapers, including the *Wall Street Journal* and the *Washington Post*. This story was followed by visits to India by the Clinton administration officials, who were reported to have registered their concerns over India's stand on the CTBT (*India Today*, December 31, 1995, 47).

Indian opposition parties from the right-wing BJP to the communists lashed out at the *Times* report, claiming it reflected the views of U.S. officials who want India to sign a global test ban treaty. "If the story was planted with a view to pressuring India, then I find it laughable. We do not subscribe to a world in which racial apartheid is replaced by nuclear apartheid," Jaswant Singh, a leader of the BJP, said. "We must recognize that the treaty hurts India's national interest more than it does that of the others. The challenge is to balance vital national interests with valid international concerns about proliferation," Singh said (*India Today*, December 31, 1995, 47). *The Hindu* reflected the sentiments of several other Indian newspapers in saying that the U.S. administration's aim was to "step up pressure on India to give up its insistence on nuclear disarmament" (Reuters, December 16, 1995).

The findings of an opinion poll further underscored a strong national consensus in favor of resisting international efforts, led by the U.S., to curb India's nuclear weapons capability. "This is a question of national security on which there must not be any compromise," Janata Dal leader Sharad Yadav said. "The government should fight such pressure from the U.S."

The poll, commissioned by a private polling organization, showed sixty-two percent of the respondents would approve if India exploded an atomic bomb to develop its nuclear weapons capability. Thirty-five percent would oppose. Among those who would approve of a test, fifty-four percent said they would favor developing nuclear weapons, even if it meant that countries such as the United States and Japan would impose sanctions which could affect India's economic growth. The main reason cited for retaining India's nuclear capability was to protect against nuclear threats from China and Pakistan (*India Today*, December 31, 1995, 48–49).

Outlook

As the United States and India continue to reassess their relationship in the wake of the demise of the Soviet Union, Indian policy makers and press recognize that the American perception during the Cold War of India essentially being in the Soviet camp was largely responsible for putting a strain on Indo-U.S. relations. Indian leaders and the media, however, had always maintained that India's friendship with the Soviet Union was wrongly interpreted as an alliance with America's former adversary. The Indian position over the years was that if the friendship with the Soviet Union was getting too close, it was because of India's security concerns over China and the well-publicized American foreign policy "tilt" in favor of Pakistan during the 1971 Indo-Pakistani war over the creation of Bangladesh. The Indian position that it was not in the Soviet camp was supported by an American expert on South Asian affairs in 1982. Professor Leo Rose of the University of California at Berkeley wrote: "India is not a client state of the USSR; it is also not so heavily dependent upon the Soviets economically, politically or militarily that it is in danger of becoming one. Although there are extensive ties between the two powers that are vital to India, New Delhi has other options that it can, and does, use freely at its own discretion and at times in the face of quiet objections from Moscow" (Rose 1982, 51).

In any case, the Indian political establishment and the press have been hoping that with the dropping of the political baggage that went with the Cold War, Indo-U.S. relations would enter a new phase based on "mutual respect and understanding." The Indian press welcomed a flurry of visits to India by cabinet-level American officials in the early 1990s and the talk of strategic cooperation between the two countries. The U.S. statements on Kashmir and human rights, mentioned earlier, continue to give the Indian press and political establishment a sense of uncertainty over the future of ties between the two countries. The successful American pressure on Russia in 1993 to cancel a contract to transfer cryogenic engine technology to India for its civilian space program, and Indo-U.S. differences over the route to nuclear non-proliferation and CTBT, have also contibuted to the Indian uncertainty regarding relations with the United States.

In addition to these differences is the strong Indian perception that the United States does not take India seriously. John Ward Anderson of the *Washington Post* wrote in late 1993 that "It is widely contended in India that the United States does not treat this country with the respect that should be afforded the world's largest democracy" (Anderson, Nov. 7, 1993). Former Secretary of State Henry Kissinger appeared to identify with this Indian concern when he told a journalist in November 1995 that "My position was always that India was a major country which should be treated respectfully" (*India Today*, November 30, 1995, 69).

There were clear indications from the Indian press and political discourse in 1996 that one nemesis to good relations with the United States, the economy, may very well turn out to be their most significant building block as India's socialist economy continued to open up following its liberalization, which began in 1991. The United States had become the largest foreign investor in India, and American officials and corporate chiefs were projecting a multi-fold jump in investments, following the Indian general election in May 1996. The trade between the two countries, put at $10 billion for 1995, was projected to grow very substantially. As Kissinger told *India Today*: "I would think that over the next 10 years, the economic relationship between the United States and India will develop explosively" (*India Today*, November 30, 1995, 69). Visiting American entrepreneurs spoke of the "strong fundamentals" in India—its democracy, independent judiciary, free press, a large pool of technically skilled workers, and use of the English language. To the Indian press and political establishment, this was a long-overdue beginning toward an understanding and appreciation that they believed India deserved from the United States.

The high level of economic engagement between India and the United States is beginning to pave the way for better political ties between the two countries. U.S. Ambassador Frank Wisner said in July 1995 that as a result of a continued upswing in trade and investment ties, the two countries had increased cooperation in areas such as the environment, defense, and bilateral political dialogue. In January 1996, Rao told the visiting U.S. Agriculture Secretary, Dan Glickman, that the U.S. and India had to understand each other's roles and perspectives in the world (Graves, January 29, 1996). On January 6, 1997, the New York-based Council on Foreign Relations, the most prestigious think tank in the United States, published a study that recommended that the U.S. take a new approach in dealing with issues of contention and forge a close strategic partnership with India. Titled "A New U.S. Policy Toward India and Pakistan," the study recommended that South Asia should become a foreign policy priority. It also noted that "India has the potential to become a full-fledged major power. It is a democracy whose economic ties with the United States show great promise and whose strength can help promote stability across Asia. We should explore the formation of a real strategic partnership" (Haass and Rose, January 5, 1997, C02). Echoing the response to the study by India's elite press, the *Economic Times* of Bombay said that "This study is the most sober and balanced analysis on Indo-U.S. relations to come out of the United States" (*The Economic Times*, January 8, 1997).

References

Anderson, J.W. (November 7, 1993). U.S. official's remarks irk India. *The Washington Post*. Retrieved from the Internet.

Associated Press. (March 21, 1996). U.S. to deliver arms and spare parts to Pakistan, but not the F-16s. Retrieved from the Internet.

Asian Age. (September 12, 1994). Plebiscite is not the only solution in Kashmir: Wisner. Retrieved from the Internet.

Dhar, O.N. (February 24, 1994). Uncle Sam's sovereign remedy. *The Telegraph*. Retrieved from the Internet.

The Economic Times. (January 8, 1997). Sober Notes from U.S.

Evans, R. (March 21, 1996). India insists on disarmament link in test ban pact. Reuters news story retrieved from the Internet.

The Free Press Journal. (February 24, 1994). Editorial: Let Clinton read it. Retrieved from the Internet.

Graves, N. (January 29, 1996). India and U.S. say relations are excellent. Reuters news story retrieved from the Internet.

Haass, R.N., & R. Gideon. (January 5, 1997). Facing the nuclear facts in India and Pakistan: It's time to refine a simple-minded U.S. policy. *The Washington Post*.

The Hindu. (September 2, 1993). Editorial: A Diplomatic offensive against Pakistan? Retrieved from the Internet.

The Hindu. (February 14, 1996). Editorial: A policy under test. Retrieved from the Internet.

India: A Democracy on the Move. (1990). Washington, D.C.: Embassy of India.

India Human Rights Practices. (1995). Washington, D.C.: U.S. Department of State.

India Today. (November 15, 1993). Straining credibility, p. 18 (21).

India Today. (November 30, 1995). Indo-U.S. relations: Changing equations, p. 20 (22).

India Today. (December 31, 1995). India's nuclear policy: Testing times, p. 20 (24).

Jha, P.S. (October 6, 1993). India must be firm on Kashmir. *The Hindu*. Retrieved from the Internet.

Jha, P. S. (July 9, 1994). Can the U.S. help in Kashmir? *The Hindu.* Retrieved from the Internet.

Katyal, K.K. (August 22, 1994). The Kashmir agenda. *The Hindu.* Retrieved from the Internet.

Kirpekar, S. (May 15, 1994). Valley refugees feel U.S. is backing Pakistan. *The Times of India.* Retrieved from the Internet.

Kurian, G. (1982). India. *World Press Encyclopedia.* New York: Facts on File.

Lekhi, A. (November 15, 1993). The logic and validity of accession. *The Indian Express.* Retrieved from the Internet.

Mehta, V. (1970). *Portrait of India.* New York: Farrar, Straus & Giroux.

Nayar, K.P. (December 22, 1995). Beware of even-handedness. Reprinted in *News-India Times* by arrangement with the *Indian Express.*

Nayar, K.P. (December 29, 1995). U.S. seeks to perpetuate nuclear apartheid. Reprinted in *News-India Times* by arrangement with the *Indian Express.*

Ollapally, D., and R. Ramanna. (January/February, 1995). U.S.-India tensions: Misperceptions on nuclear proliferation. *Foreign Affairs.*

Parasuram, T.V. (March 24, 1996). Pressler condemns Clinton on Pakistan policy. Press Trust of India news story retrieved from the Internet.

Rampal, K. (1984). Adversary vs. developmental journalism: Indian mass media at the crossroads. *Gazette,* p. 34 (1).

Reuters. (December 16, 1995). Indian nuclear test report sends out shock waves. Retrieved from the Internet.

Rose, L.E. (1982). U.S. Policy in Asia: The India Factor. In R.H. Myers (Ed.), *A U.S. Foreign Policy for Asia.* Stanford: Hoover Institution Press.

Simla Agreement. (July 2, 1972). New Delhi: Government of India Publication.

Singh, H.K. (December 8, 1995). Unfriendly from the Start. Reprinted in *News-India Times* by arrangement with the *The Indian Express.*

Singh, H. (October 26, 1947). Text of letter from the Maharaja of Jammu and Kashmir to Lord Mountbatten, the Governor-General of India. New Delhi: Government of India Publication.

Srinivasan, M.R. (December 22, 1995). Self reliance is the key. Reprinted in *News-Times India* by arrangement with *The Hindu.*

The Wall Street Journal. (March 13, 1996). Editorial: Asia's other danger zone.

U.S. House Republican Task Force on Terrorism and Unconventional Warfare. (August 24, 1994). House Republican Research Committee. Washington, D.C.: Superintendent of Documents.

5

From Savior to Villain

Redefining America in South Korea

JAE-KYOUNG LEE

Introduction

The United States underwent a radical image shift in South Korea in the 1980s. Once the universally accepted protector of the republic, suddenly, over a period of only several years, it turned into an irrefutable symbol of malicious exploitation. This chapter attempts to explain what has brought about this fundamental image change. Most political scientists assume that the presence of American troops and the alleged intermittent U.S. intervention into Korean domestic affairs were the primary causes of the negative turn of public perception. This chapter radically departs from this line of reasoning. Instead, it considers communication processes as more central to the problem. Communication processes here refer to the conscious efforts made in order to influence various channels of public discourse, such as the mass media, grassroots publications, and other forms of public persuasion.

Owing to the difficulty in dealing with all the elements of communication processes, this chapter focuses on just one aspect of the phenomenon, namely, the cultural and symbolic struggles against the United States by various movement groups. Its main argument is that the rapidly erupted anti-American sentiments in Korea were largely a product of concerted articulative efforts of the anti-military, democratic forces to redefine the United States as one of the main enemies of the South Korean people.

Historical Context

In 1945, the United States ended Japanese colonial rule over the Korean peninsula. Then it helped the South Koreans fight against the aggression of North Korea during the Korean War in the early 1950s. Ever since, the U.S. has remained a special friend to the South Korean people. Because of these two major experiences, Koreans held a predominantly positive view of the U.S. up to the beginning of the 1980s. The traditional tendency of the general perception of Koreans about the U.S. is clear in expressions such as the "midwife" of the republic, the "ultimate guarantor" of the nation's security, and a "generous provider of economic aid" (Kim 1988).

This view underwent drastic changes in the 1980s. Beginning abruptly in 1980, anti-Americanism became an everyday phenomenon. Street demonstrations, whether staged by students, farmers, or laborers, featured anti-Americanism as a main theme. The number of intellectual and literary publications criticizing the U.S. increased dramatically. The phenomenon did not stop at mere verbal attacks or symbolic acts such as burning the American flag, but became most problematic with violent attacks against diplomatic and military installations. Following the first arson attempt at an American Cultural Center in 1980, various groups of activists launched twenty-nine attacks against American installations during the decade (*Joongang Ilbo*, May 10, 1989, 11).

What is widely considered to be the single most important event associated with the turn of the Korean attitude is the Kwangju incident and the perceived role of the U.S. in it. The city of Kwangju is in the southern region of Korea, with a population of about one million. The Kwangju incident refers to an armed clash between civilian protesters and soldiers in the city in May 1980, which resulted in the loss of almost two hundred civilian lives. Because of the pivotal significance of this incident in the contemporary history of Korea, the civic groups' anti-American struggle also started in this city. As a consequence of the incident, South Korea saw the rise of the second military regime led by General Chun Doo-hwan. The military rule lasted till February 1988, when a democratically elected government took office.

The democratic regime change apparently resulted from a series of massive civic protests against the authoritarian military government. The success of the anti-dictatorship civic movements depended largely upon strenuously staged symbolic and cultural struggles which helped mobilize popular support for democratic forces. Anti-Americanism was the central element of these struggles. This essay shows how the anti-American theme has grown to be a major objective of South Korea's democratic movement. It also explains how, in the minds of the Korean people, the U.S. has become the archvillain responsible for most of the ills in the country.

Social Persuasion and Anti-Americanism

Studies on social persuasion (Bailyn 1967; Kessler 1984; Stewart et al. 1989, among others) suggest that a major change in the collective perception of reality involves complicated communication processes. Most of all, the agent that breaks the existing conception of the world must emerge as a new cultural force. Its role is "to persuade the people to perceive history and society in the way organizers of the movement see them" (Stewart et al. 1989, 122). In other words, a key to the success of a movement lies in upsetting what Eco (1979) calls the "dominant code" of interpretation and presenting a viable alternative. Gramsci's notion of hegemonic struggle as well as Hall's (1982) idea of "the politics of signification" speak to the same point.

In his documentation of the history of pamphleteering by the colonists before the American revolution, Bailyn (1967) offers a good example of social persuasion. According to him, the Revolutionary War was a result of the long-waged revolution in people's minds, which started in 1760, in all colonies, in the pages of newspapers, broadsides, almanacs, and pamphlets (1). The emergence of anti-Americanism in South Korea was similar. Literature on anti-American movements (Chang 1988; Kim 1990; Shorrock 1986, among others) testifies that various civic organizations were continuously involved in the vehement anti-American struggles. Ambassador Gleysteen's (1986) comment on "the intentional articulations by some malicious elements" in South Korea is a good instance of U.S. recognition concerning the problem (96).

The Dissident Press

In the 1980s, South Korea saw a remarkable proliferation of what is called *minjung* (or grassroots) cultural activities. Citizens' voluntary publications, such as leaflets, pamphlets, booklets, cartoons, and posters, as well as underground newspapers and magazines, were essential vehicles in this cultural protest. It was more so because *minjung* groups' access to the mainstream media was almost completely denied, and the establishment media were consistently manipulated to marginalize the oppositional activities. Consequently, most of the energy of the oppositional activities concentrated on what Gramsci (1971) calls the "war of position" or on engaging the minds of the people, and on changing the popular perception of reality.

These oppositional activities were harshly suppressed by the military. Many people suffered severe punishment for producing and distributing the cultural products, and sometimes even for merely possessing a publication. However, the increased availability of information technologies, such as copy machines, personal computers, tape recorders, and even VCRs, made it easier to produce and disseminate materials for cultural protest. The anti-American ideas were also first articulated, debated, and disseminated in these publications.

The grassroots publications came in four major forms: leaflets, pamphlets, posters, and underground newspapers. Among these, leaflets were the most readily available and widely used. A leaflet is a typed—sometimes handwritten—single-page printout distributed to the public and to the press at sites of street or campus demonstrations. The pamphlet refers to a longer and theoretically more developed form of what may be called an internal document distributed, primarily, to members of movement organizations. The wallpaper refers to a traditional Asian method of public announcements. It is a handwritten text, on a large sheet of white paper, posted on walls and bulletin boards. The underground newspapers and magazines are illicit periodicals. Following the format of mainstream newspapers, they include editorials, opinion columns, straight news, and analysis. Underground newspapers are usually weeklies. Magazines adopt largely a monthly or quarterly production schedule (Hwang 1986, 38).

However, the lack of a systematic study of this press makes it difficult to obtain a reliable estimate of how many underground periodicals were published nationwide. Even so, by the mid-1980s, several underground newspapers were published at each university by different student groups. By 1986, many non-student civic organizations also began to produce similar publications intended for much larger general audiences. To build villainous images of the military regime and the U.S., movement organizations also used other media such as cartoons, films, and various other types of visual representation. These media largely served to reinforce the themes already articulated in texts.

On many occasions, the expression of anti-Americanism took the form of action, such as collective demonstrations, violence, and even terrorism. As Melucci (1988) maintains, social movements or collective actions in contemporary society no longer operate as the situation-specific "characters," but as "signs" with broader contextual implications (249). He argues that their primary function is not to fix any immediately felt grievances, but rather "to challenge and upset the dominant codes upon which social relations are founded" (248). In this case, the dominant code is the decades-old positive popular perception of the United States.

The Rise of Anti-American Writings

Several natural breaks mark the evolution of anti-American articulation in South Korea. This essay identifies three stages. The first stage covers the period from June 1980 to May 1985. This is the time during which some civic organizations, for the first time, began to raise questions about the role of the

U.S. in South Korea. The scene changed fundamentally into a full-blown U.S. bashing during the second stage, from mid-1985 to the end of 1986. This period was represented by the emergence of the U.S. imperialism thesis. The third stage refers to the period of the popularization of anti-American sentiments. The beginning of this period coincided with the toppling of the military regime in June 1987 by the coalition of civic forces and continued through the early 1990s.

Early Anti-American Writings (June 1980–May 1985)

The military regime's violent suppression of the popular protest in Kwangju in May 1980 ended the brief period of liberalization. The machineries of the police state were immediately restored to full capacity. Most opposition organizations were disbanded and their leaders arrested. In the face of an apparent defeat and the reemergence of another military regime, democratic forces—student leaders, labor activists, religious leaders, and progressive intellectuals—had to abandon the idea of open confrontation. They went underground and embarked on a painful process of regrouping and revitalization. The immediate task of the opposition intellectuals was to analyze the causes of the failure, and to articulate objectives and strategies for future action.

Gradually, criticisms about the U.S. emerged. The first group that seriously questioned the role of the U.S. was the civic leadership in Kwangju. In a pamphlet published in June 1980, movement leaders in Kwangju expressed their deeply felt sense of betrayal. The pamphlet said, "Finally we need to change our view of the U.S." It further stated that the U.S. must now be rejected in South Korea as it was in South America, as well as in Iran (Chonnam Institute for Social Problems 1988, 207).

These remarks represented the frustration felt by the Kwangju citizens, who had repeatedly asked for U.S. intervention during their confrontation with the military. In fact, in the eyes of the Kwangju people, the U.S. alone possessed the ability to stop the military repressions. Instead of taking action, the U.S., it appeared, fully supported the forceful suppression. This image of American collaboration with the Korean military was partly a misunderstanding that had resulted from the massive distortion of U.S. reactions by the government-controlled media (Lee 1994). What matters, however, is that this was how most people in Kwangju understood U.S. reactions.

In the same month, a leaflet, issued in the name of the "Voice of National Democratic Youths and Students," reiterated the previous pamphlet's call. Its tone was highly emotional, condemning the U.S. for allowing Chun's regime to use military forces. The leaflet warned that "if the U.S. should continue its present Korea policy, protection of American lives and properties in South Korea is no longer guaranteed" (*Hankyoreh Shinmun*, May 21, 1988, 4).

Its warning was transformed into action six months later. On December 9, 1980, a group of Kwangju youths attempted what is called the "arson struggle" by setting fire to the roof of the American Cultural Center, located in downtown Kwangju. In the arsonists' court testimony, this group attacked the cultural center because U.S. support of the military during the Kwangju uprising was a "clear betrayal" of South Korean people's expectations (Kim 1990, 86–87). Perhaps more significant was the mode of attack—the act of targeting the U.S. installation as an object of violence. Although it was inherently a simple act of violence, the political implication was enormous. As it turned out, the act of attacking the U.S. Cultural Center became a statement in itself, a special cultural text or a sign, in Melucci's (1988) terms, that conveys the message far more effectively than any written statements.

The second attack on an American installation came on March 18, 1982. This time, it was in Pusan, the second-largest city in South Korea. Four university students threw inflammatory materials into the entrance of the American Cultural Center, resulting in substantial property damages and the loss of a library visitor's life. The leaflet distributed shortly afterward stated that "the U.S. should no longer treat South Korea as a subject state, and immediately leave this land" (*Shindong-a*, January 1990, supplement, 116). This was a shocking statement at the time, strongly challenging the deeply engrained pro-American sentiments of most South Korean people. More astonishing was that this was exactly the same rhetoric North Korea used.

The idea of U.S. imperialism, first expressed in the Pusan leaflet, was conceptually enriched in the following year. A booklet published in January 1983 maintained that the "fascist military regime" in South Korea was only the "vicarious ruling force" that ultimately served the imperialistic interests of the U.S. (Kim 1990, 95). This document was a precursor of the consequent development of the U.S. imperialism thesis. However, few mainstream South Koreans were ready to accept such a radical statement yet.

Perhaps this was why the focus of anti-American articulations returned to the question of U.S. involvement in the Kwangju incident in the spring of 1985. For instance, a pamphlet published by the Korean Christian Students Federation concluded that U.S. actions during the Kwangju incident indicated "wholehearted" support of the military regime, and clearly signalled that the U.S. was undeniably a "patron" of the regime (Chonnam Institute for Social Problems 1988, 278). It went on to say that the U.S. considered South Korea merely as a part of its global market, on the one hand, and as a forward military base for containing the Soviet expansion, on the other. The pamphlet cited President Carter's remarks as indisputable evidence to support this argument. According to its account, President Carter said, in his interview with CNN on June 1, 1980, that the U.S. could not turn South Korea over to the Soviet Union merely for human rights reasons (278). It is important to remember here that factual information used in this pamphlet, such as President Carter's remarks, largely came from local news reports, which were mostly objects of egregious distortion by the military censors.

By far the most attention-grabbing event in 1985 was the seizure of the Seoul U.S. Information Service (USIS) building. Seventy-three students from the National Students Federation occupied the second-floor library in the heart of the capital city. They represented a newly formed umbrella organization recognized by most student associations across the nation. The stunning seizure lasted four days, from May 23 through May 26, when students voluntarily walked off the U.S. premises in time for a historic meeting between South and North Korean officials in Seoul.

Again, the primary motivation behind this move by the student group was perceived grievances over the U.S. role in the Kwangju incident. In a leaflet titled, "Why We Had to Enter the USIS," students stated that "now we want to ask the U.S. to bear its responsibility for supporting the military's suppression of the Kwangju uprising" (*Shindong-a* 1990, supplement, 125–126). Students then demanded that "the U.S. should disclose detailed facts of the incident to clarify the deepening skepticism of the Korean people," and that the U.S. should "openly apologize to the Korean people for supporting the military leaders during the Kwangju massacre" (126).

Radicalization of the Rhetoric (1985–1986)

The language of the anti-American discourse took a decisive leftward turn in the fall of 1985. Statements issued by student and other movement organizations began to show a dominant tendency of incorporating the imperialistic interpretation of the U.S. and its policy. According to Lee, (1988) "The crystallization of anti-Americanism" took place during the 1985/86 winter (p. 18). He observed that "it was then that radical students agreed that America was the cause of all the problems that Koreans were facing" (18).

Now the U.S. was no longer criticized as merely a foreign supporter of the dictatorial military regime; neither was the anti-American articulation by the democratic forces limited to exposing the U.S. role in the suppression of the Kwangju incident. For instance, a pamphlet published in the fall of 1985 defined, in highly agitating language, the U.S. as the main, not the secondary, target of struggle. It asserted that "political soldiers, conservative bureaucrats and monopoly capitalists in South Korea are only servants of the U.S." (*Shindong-a*, January 1990, supplement, 128–129).

The pamphlet tried painstakingly to convince the reader that "the principal contradiction" of South Korean society did not lie in the domestic labor-capital relationship. It was rather the contradictory relationship between the Korean people and U.S. imperialism that constituted the origin of all social and historical problems in South Korea. Therefore, the apparent logical conclusion was that Koreans should rise up to break the "exploitative structure of domination" built by U.S. imperialists (129).

An important event, closely intertwined with this trend, was the takeover of the national student movement leadership by the group advocating "national liberation," in the spring of 1986. This meant that from then on most efforts of student movement would concentrate on the struggle against the U.S. (Lee 1988). The fiery anti-American inaugural statement by the Jamintu (or the Committee for the Struggle towards National Autonomy and Democratization) was charged with an appeal to patriotic nationalism. The beginning lines read: "Patriotic fellow students! We are burning with a desire for vengeance against U.S. imperialists and their puppet, Chun Doo-hwan's military regime. We can no longer merely stand as spectators of the shameful reactionary history" (*Shindong-a*, January 1990, supplement, 135–136). It is interesting that students now use blatant expressions, such as "imperial invasion," "U.S. imperialists conspiracy," "malicious plot," and "U.S. fascist repression" in characterizing U.S. actions in South Korea (Kim 1990, 92–93).

The shift of emphasis of the student movements to the struggle against "U.S. imperialism" also explains the intensified anti-American publicity campaigns by various student groups from 1986. Particularly, the number of violent attacks multiplied and objects of attacks expanded virtually to the whole range of U.S.-related offices, including the embassy, the ambassador's residence, four regional American Cultural Centers, as well as the U.S. Chamber of Commerce in Seoul, and even to some military facilities.

Popularization of Anti-American Rhetoric (Beyond 1987)

South Korean society reached a major turning point in 1987. The coalition for democratization finally prevailed over the military regime in June 1987. As a matter of fact, the declaration on June 29, 1987, by Roh Tae-woo, the head of the ruling party, was widely interpreted as a surrender of the authoritarian regime to the irreversibly mounting popular pressure to obtain democracy. The rapid and unavoidably chaotic process of democratization, or perhaps more appropriately, the process of de-authoritarianization, naturally accompanied a swift expansion of the freed space for public debate.

The popularization of anti-Americanism progressed at a remarkable speed as well, by and large, due to these almost revolutionary cultural circumstances. During this period, many mainstream Koreans also jumped on the bandwagon of the radical movements. Three main elements conspicuously contributed to the penetration of the radical anti-American rhetoric into the mainstream society. They include: (1) the widespread reproduction of previously students-centered anti-American ideas by virtually all grassroots publications; (2) the advancement of revisionism in history that diametrically contradicted the traditional interpretation of U.S. roles in South Korea; and (3) the active incorporation of anti-American themes into popular literary works.

The Grassroots Press. Reproduction of anti-American themes appeared in almost every grassroots publication across the country. Some of the leading and relatively more influential periodicals that actively engaged in anti-American articulation include: *Mahl* (or Speech), the *Voice of the Minjung* (or the people's voice), the *Minjung Shinmun* (or the people's newspaper), the *Workers' Voice*, the *Nation and Education*, the *Christian Workers' Shinmun*, and the *Minjung Munhwa* (or the people's culture). These publications used various modes of writing, such as news, editorials, opinion columns, or background analysis, to characterize the U.S., without exception, either as a villainous manipulator of the South Korean political scene, or as the self-centered exploiter of the fragile Korean economy.

Unquestionably, *Mahl* was the prominent leader in setting the tone of U.S. bashing and in elaborating on concrete issues suitable for public condemnation of the U.S. Founded by a group of purged journalists with proven moral integrity under the military regime, the magazine was widely appreciated and respected by intellectuals inside and outside the movement. The anti-American tendency of the magazine was apparent from the time of its inception. *Mahl* explicitly stated, on the cover of every issue, its editorial philosophy of supporting the cause of what is called *Minjok Haebang*, or national liberation.

Accordingly, it carried countless articles of an anti-American nature. For instance, there was a series of articles on the joint military structure under which an American general exercised full operational authority over most of South Korea's armed forces. In its March 1987 issue, citing an American general's comment, the magazine described the standing military arrangement as a "remarkable alienation of sovereignty" rarely found in other parts of the world (*Mahl*, March 20, 1987, 46). In subsequent issues, it gave a considerable amount of coverage to U.S. nuclear weapons in South Korea. Some major ideas proposed by the magazine included: (1) nuclear weapons were unilaterally brought into South Korea by the U.S. neither with the consent nor with the knowledge of the South Korean people; (2) nuclear weapons were serving only U.S. global strategies in its Cold War confrontation with the Soviet Union; (3) it was time for grassroots organizations to start an anti-nuclear campaign as a part of the anti-American struggle to reduce the possibility of a nuclear war on the Korean peninsula.

The Kwangju incident and the alleged U.S. support of the military regime were other main issues intensely covered by the magazine. For example, an article in the March 1987 issue characterized the U.S. as a "counter-democratic element," because it had singlemindedly pursued only its own national interests (*Mahl*, March 20, 1987, 29–30). The same perspective persisted even after Roh's June 29th declaration. An editorial, analyzing the June 29th concession statement by the ruling party, concluded that the ruling party's decision was, more than anything else, a result of a "behind-the-curtain political maneuver" by the U.S. The main motivation, needless to say, was "to maintain its imperial interests by reforming the South Korean political system under its supervision" (*Mahl*, December 10, 1987, 17–22).

The *Minjung Shinmun's* expressions were far stronger in their character-ization of the U.S. For instance, in one article, analyzing the general political situation, the U.S. was described as a "plunderer who took away the blood and sweat of the South Korean people by remote-controlling the killers' regime" (*Minjung Shinmun*, February 14, 1987, 14). In other stories, the U.S. was de-picted either as the "instigator of the Kwangju massacre" (*Minjung Shinmun*, May 13, 1987, 1), or as the "main obstacle" for the Korean reunification (*Min-jung Shinmun*, February 28, 1987, 2).

Reflecting the same trend, the *Workers' Road* described South Korea as "a U.S. forward military base," "a launching pad of U.S. nuclear arms," "a market for U.S. commodities," "and a low-wage labor warehouse for U.S. businesses." The article went on to say that "in order to secure its permanent control of this precious commodity, the United States keeps 40,000 troops as well as 1,000 nu-clear warheads in this land" (*Workers' Road*, December 5, 1987, 3).

Revisionist History. Independently, and yet closely associated with the democratic organizations, the revisionist historians also played a significant role in the popularization of anti-Americanism. Their most notable contribution was to provide an academic justification for the action-oriented, anti-American struggles in the streets. The list of publications produced by the revisionist historians includes: *A Re-Interpretation of South Korea–U.S. Relations,* volume 1 (1990) and 2 (1991); *A History of South Korea–U.S. Relations* (1990); *Rewriting Contemporary South Korean History,* volume 1 (1988) and 2 (1989); *A History of U.S. Imperial Invasion* (1989); "The South Korean Politics and the United States: The Structure and Historical Process of Intervention" (1988); "The Kwangju Minjung Uprising and the Role of the U.S." (1989). As the titles of these books and articles clearly suggest, revisionist historians devoted themselves to "unmasking the U.S." so that the image of the U.S.engraved in the minds of South Koreans as "liberator," "blood-ally," and "protector of democracy" could be correctly understood as an outcome of extensive ideological manipulation (Park et al. 1990, 3).

This is why these authors concentrated their efforts on "exposing how and through what structural mechanisms the U.S. has maintained its domi-nation over South Korea" (Ryu 1990, 326). A good illustration is *A Re-Inter-pretation of the South Korea–U.S. Relations* (Duri 1990). Featuring eleven essays by different authors, it deals with issues ranging from the nature of the U.S.

military government during 1945–1948, CIA operations in South Korea, and U.S. support of successive military regimes, to the structure of economic exploitation and the influence of the U.S. on every level of education in South Korea. The preface explicitly states its objective to appropriately "position" the overly glorified U.S. in South Korea's history, and to provide "scientific verification" for such a re-positioning (3).

Guided by this basic objective, each essay attempts to demystify various aspects of the U.S. presence in South Korea. For instance, the first chapter raises a question of whether the U.S. Army should be interpreted as the "army of liberation" from the Japanese colonial rule, as has been maintained, or as the "army of yet another occupation" (13). The author concludes that the U.S. Army came to South Korea as a conqueror, not as a liberator, and established a hostile and repressive regime toward the people of South Korea (36). The next essay turns to the mechanisms of U.S. "neo-colonial" control. An apparent alteration of strategy, according to the essay, was the change from direct rule by the U.S. military government to a subtler, "low-intensity" strategy of establishing a "manageable" South Korean regime (62). An essay about CIA operations describes the CIA station chief as the "real director of South Korean politics, controlling the life-line of the dictatorial regime through an invisible hand" (165). Examining the "structural educational dependence" on the U.S., an article on education notes that "Korea's higher education is dominated by U.S.-trained Ph.D.s who tend to worship almost everything American" (314).

Anti-American Poetry. Dissident poets played an equally significant role in the spread of anti-American sentiments. This is, by and large, due to the legacy of the Confucian tradition, in which critical intellectuals would use poetic forms to express their political dissent. Nicholas Kristof, a *New York Times* correspondent, commented on the poetic activism, writing that dissident writers "hurled verses instead of bricks" in their fight against the military regime. He wrote that "the brick-throwers may lose their battles for control of the streets, but the poets have mostly won the battle for Korea's soul" (*New York Times*, July 31, 1987, A2). The philosophy behind this type of poetry is succinctly summarized by Ko Un, one of South Korea's best-known dissident poets. According to him, "The role of a poet in Korea is not just to write about sentiments, but also to write about movements in history. Poetry is the song of history" (*New York Times*, July 31, 1987, A2).

The overall scope of what may be called anti-American poetry was well represented by an anthology, published in 1988, with the title, *America: the Ocean of Shit* (Im and Lee 1988). It featured altogether 112 poems, most of them written in the 1980s, by ninety-three different poets from across the nation.

For instance, a work by Ki-hyung Lee entitled, "Good-bye U.S. America," has the following passage: "Mr. President/ Simply switch your position with ours./ Suppose your great nation is divided into the North and the South along the 40th parallel,/ and the Korean army has stationed in the South for/ the past forty years./ Then, imagine that somewhere in the South,/ say in Dallas,/ something comparable to the Kwangju incident took place,/ and that under the Korean military's operational control./ Under these circumstances,/ think carefully at least once/ about how your students and youths,/ the proud descendants of their fathers/ who early proved their valor in conquering the West,/ would react to it." (Im et al. 1988, 24–25).

Another poet, Ha Kyong, in a poem titled "Oh America," wrote that in the name of liberal democracy, America "still offers prison instead of freedom," and "dictatorship instead of democracy" (30–31). There were poems that were more specific in their thematic focus. For instance, Park Mong-ku dealt with the perceived U.S. role in the Kwangju incident: In the streets,/ under the authority sanctioned by them,/ a number of brothers and sisters were hunted down./ They,/ our friends,/ let it happen with their eyes closed" (30). A poem by Kim Jung-hwan entitled, "Our Love, Struggle, Production and Labor," gave the same image of the United States: When we rose up,/ there were the military regime,/ guns and swords,/ and behind all these/ were your blood-tainted hands" (37).

Aside from these, there were numerous other poems that dealt with various negative aspects of the U.S. presence in South Korea, ranging from U.S. economic and cultural domination to the plight of the so called "base-towns," where "American princesses"—Korean prostitutes serving U.S. soldiers—provided a pertinent poetic symbol of the one-sided bilateral relationship. A poem, "The Dollar 3," by Kim Nam-ju, represented a group of works depicting U.S. domination of South Korea's economy. "Where the dollar is headed/ and the gunman from the Wall street goes,/ There is no liberty./ Liberty/ is immediately cut off by the neck,/ the moment it comes into being" (82).

Paik Nak-chung, a notable South Korean literary critic, observed that poetry was important for the success of the democratic movement, by spreading protest and inspiring dissent (*New York Times*, July 31, 1987, A2). Indeed, as Kristof noted, in a country, "where anthologies of verse sell the way the spy novels do in the United States" (*New York Times*, July 31, 1987, A2), the power of poetry could hardly be ignored.

Conclusion

An American teacher in Seoul, who wrote about South Korean popular sentiments toward the domestically reported U.S. reactions to the Kwangju incident, observed that "shock is an insufficient word to describe the reaction when people read these words in black and white in the newspaper." He also commented that "the sense of betrayal was so great that 'anti-Americanism' is a simplistic label for the popular emotions" (Shorrock 1986, 1202). This shock and the sense of betrayal took almost a decade to transform into a national movement. Nine years later, the *Christian Science Monitor* noted a fundamental change in the people's attitudes, suggesting that South Koreans were "openly questioning the U.S. presence" in their country. "More and more, Koreans of all political persuasions resent the military's presence as a painful reminder of a dependency on the U.S. that they want to put behind them" (*Christian Science Monitor*, January 3, 1989, 4). The newspaper described this phenomenon as an expression of "raw" nationalistic feelings.

The 1980s marked a decade of movements as well as an era of anti-Americanism in South Korea. This essay has portrayed how the anti-American articulation has grown; how extensive the persuasive efforts have been; and how many organizations and individuals have participated in this macro-scale communicative processes. The major objective of the essay was to reject the widely accepted view that the growth of anti-Americanism is a mere reflection of changed structural conditions, such as the rise of postwar generations and the arrival of the affluent society. Instead, what it suggests is that for an adequate understanding of the rise of anti-Americanism, one must take account of the highly concerted cultural and symbolic struggles for the creation of a new interpretive framework, a new sense of history and society.

References

Bailyn, B. (1967). *Ideological origins of the American Revolution*. Cambridge: Harvard University Press.

Citizens of Kwangju. (1988). Truth of the Kwangju civil uprising. In Chonnam Institute for Social Problems (Ed.), *The May 18 Kwangju minjung uprising: Collected documents*, pp. 193–208. Kwangju: Chonnam Institute for Social Problems.

Chang, D. (1988). Anti-American movements and the Korean politics. In *A re-illumination of the Korean-American relations*, pp. 123–143. Seoul: Kyungnam University Press.

Criminal acts of the United States and Chun's military regime. (1987, February 14). *Minjung Shinmun*, p. 2.

Eco, U. (1979). *A theory of semiotics*. Bloomington: Indiana University Press.

Eight years since the Kwangju incident. (1988, May 21). *Hankyorch Shinmun*, p. 4.

Gleysteen, W. (1986). Korea: A special target of American concern. In D.D. Newsom (Ed.), *The diplomacy of human rights*, pp. 85–99. Lanham, Md.: University Press of America.

Gramsci, A. (1971). *Selections from prison notebooks*. Q. Hoare and G.N. Smith (Eds.). New York: International Publishers.

Hall, S. (1982). The rediscovery of ideology: Return of the repressed in media studies. In M. Gurevitch, T. Bennett, J. Curran, and J. Woolacott (Eds.), *Culture, society and media*, pp. 56–90. Beverly Hills: Sage.

Hwang, U. (1986). *Student movement in the 1980s*. Seoul: Yeochogak.

In, H., and Y. Lee. (Eds.). (1988). *America: The ocean of shit*. Seoul: Indong Publishing.

The June 29 declaration and the United States. (1987, August 1). *Mahl*, pp. 115–120.

Kim, H. (1988). The 1987 political crisis and its implications for U.S.-Korean relations. In I. Kim and Y. Kihl (Eds.), *Political change in South Korea*, pp. 221–241. New York: Korean PWPA.

Kim, S. (1990). A history of anti-Americanism in the 1980s. In *A reinterpretation of the Korean-American relations*, pp. 85–120. Seoul: Duri.

The Korean Christian Students Association. (1998, April). Oh Kwangju, the holy cross of the nation and the minjung. In Chonnam Institute for Social Problems (Ed.), *The May 18 Kwangju minjung uprising: Collected documents*, pp. 259–264. Kwangju: Chonnam Institute for Social Problems.

Lee, J. (1994). Manufacturing American patronage: Korean military regime's management of U.S.-related news in the 1980s. Paper presented to International Communications Section at the 1994 IAMCR convention in Seoul (July 3–8).

Lee, M. (1988). Anti-Americanism and South Korea's changing perception of America. In M. Lee, R.D. McLaurin, and C. Moon (Eds.), *Alliance under tension: The evolution of South Korean–U.S. relations*, pp. 7–27. Boulder: Westview Press.

Let us unmask the United States. (1987, March 13). *Minjung Shinmun*, p. 1.

Melucci, A. (1988). Social movements and the democratization of everyday life. In J. Keane (Ed.), *Civil society and the state*, pp. 245–260. London: Verso.

The National Democratic Students Federation. (1985, May). Reinterpretation of the Kwangju minjung uprising. In Chonnam Institute for Social Problems (Ed.), *The May 18 Kwangju minjung uprising: Collected documents*, pp. 269–289. Kwangju: Chonnam Institute for Social Problems.

Park, Y., and K. Kim. (1990). Introduction. In Y. H. Park & K.S. Kim (Eds.), *The South Korea–U.S. relations*, p. 3. Seoul: Shilchon Munhak.

Ryu. S. (1990). Controversial points and perspectives in the study of South Korea–U.S. relations. In *A re-interpretation of the South Korea–U.S. relations*, vol. 1, pp. 325–339. Seoul: Duri.

Shorrock, T. (1986). The struggle for democracy in South Korea in the 1980s and the rise of anti-Americanism. *Third World Quarterly* 8(4): pp. 1195–1218.

Solidification of division. (1987, February 28). *Minjung Shinmun*, p. 2.

South Korean democratization and the United States. (1980, March 20). *Mahl*, pp. 29–30.

South Koreans redefine ties to U.S. (1989, January 3). *The Christian Science Monitor*, p. 4.

Statements of national democratic movements in the 1980s. (1990, January). *Shindong-a* special supplement, pp. 116, 125–140, 150–152.

Stewart, C.J., C.A. Smith, and R. Denton Jr. (1989). *Persuasion and social movement*, 2nd ed. Prospect Heights, Ill: Waveland Press.

The United Minjung Movement for Democracy and Unification and the Youth Federation for Democratization Movement. (1986). *The uprising never stops.*

The United States—an accomplice of the Kwangju massacre. (1987, May 13). *Minjung Shinmun*, p. 2.

The United States Information Service in South Korea. (1989, May 10). *Joongang Ilbo*, p. 11.

The United States should stop interfering with South Korean affairs and leave. (1987, December 5). *Worker's Road*, p.3.

U.S. nuclear strategy in the Pacific. (1988, March 1). *Mahl*, pp. 89–92.

Voice of dissent in South Korea speaks in verse. (1987, July 31). *The New York Times*, p. A2.

6

Political Resentment versus Cultural Submission

The Duality of U.S. Representations in Bulgarian Media

DINA IORDANOVA

Introduction

The post-communist transformation of the media in Bulgaria unravelled generally along the lines outlined in numerous studies of the changing media landscape throughout Eastern Europe. Little has been published in the West on Bulgarian media specifically, however (Engelbrekt 1992; Ognianova 1993; Iordanova 1995b; Deltcheva 1996).

The new features of the East European media economy, media legislation, journalism, and other print and broadcast media, along with many surviving characteristics of the rigid communist-type media organizations, have been studied by scholars involved in observing various national media systems in Eastern Europe, such as Tomasz Goban-Klas (1994) and Karol Jakubowicz (1995) on Poland, Slavko Splichal on Slovenia (1994), and Peter Gross on Romania (1996). Their conclusions hold true for Bulgaria as well, and the specifics of the Bulgarian situation do not blur the general picture offered in their studies. The same validity can be claimed for the general trends in restructuring of journalism and journalistic education outlined at many international conferences by Owen Johnson, Ray Hiebert, and Lisa Schillinger, and for the theoretical considerations offered by John Downing (1996).

The issue of cross-national images has not been the focal point of either one of these studies, however. There is, indeed, a relatively recent study devoted to the exploration of mutual images of the U.S. and the USSR (Dennis,

Gerbner, and Zassoursky 1991), but it is thoroughly marked by the congratu-latory, elevated spirit of *perestroika* and the end of Cold War times. In spite of the fact that it presents some interesting observations, this volume can hardly be cited as offering many insights or a deep theoretical context. Thus, in my in-vestigation of the U.S. image in Bulgarian media, I have been mostly on my own. On the one hand, this freedom gave me the opportunity to speculate, but on the other it made me perceive the project as a very demanding one, as I have been fully aware of the responsibilities that setting a precedent carries. In the study that follows, I am continuing the work of a previous study, which dealt with the image of Bulgaria in the West and its use in domestic media (Iordanova 1995a).

The representation of America has been changing along with the changes in Bulgaria's post-communist media. The Cold War attitude toward the U.S. as an instigator of war is no more, and political cartoons of Uncle Sam carry-ing a smoking missile are no longer seen in newspapers. The cartoons have been gradually replaced, however, with images of the U.S. as a global police force, often incompetent and guilty of partiality. In an environment saturated overnight with tried and true American exports—lifestyle products, fast food, popular music, and more—Bulgarians hear frequent media attacks on the United States' international bias and political hypocrisy. Today, the enthusi-asm about all things American that accompanied the "velvet revolution" is considerably diminished. Most pro-American leanings are now forgotten, re-placed by bitterness and disenchantment after the previous great expectations.

The American Way: Takeover in Culture and the Media

The signs of globalization are everywhere in Bulgaria, but most often in the form of American cultural icons, even if the actual products originated in the Middle East or Turkey. The old claim of media and development scholars that "the poorer a country is, the more dependent it is on foreign imports for en-tertainment" (Nam 1983) proves true in Bulgaria. As the socialist system col-lapsed at the end of the 1980s, many East bloc countries came to look like the Third World, Bulgaria included, and today that new look is very evident in Bulgarian media.

In 1996, after six years of transition, the Bulgarian media are volatile and serve clashing political interests. The end of state ownership and control of the media has been marked by a mushrooming of new publications. Many go bankrupt in a fortnight, but new ones continue to appear on the market. The subscription and distribution system that served the state-controlled media is ruined, and most of the new publications are sold from street stalls in the cities. A few make it to the villages. The several dailies that have a larger read-ership, and the several weeklies that enjoy a relatively good reputation are mostly affiliated with a political party or other interest group. The rest are tabloids featuring gossip (usually about Western celebrities), sex (illustrated mostly with reprinted Western photographs), and untrustworthy astrological and money management advice. Good reputation in the Bulgarian print media, however, is based not so much on the objectivity of the information offered, but on the opinionated stance that the journalists of a given publication take.

In broadcasting, two nationwide TV channels are owned by the state and managed by the socialist government. So owned too is the national radio network, which came to prominence at the end of 1995 with controversies involving censorship allegations and firings of disobedient journalists. Some private TV enterprises are licensed locally, and there are a number of small commercial radio stations. The signals of cross-border operations such as Radio Free Europe, Deutsche Welle, and the BBC are no longer jammed. They continue broadcasts in Bulgarian, and some even have offices in Sofia.

All opinions have a relevant media outlet. Journalism is not only free, but free-and-easy, with even respected publications showing a footloose and irresponsible attitude. Journalists think of themselves as shapers of public opinion, and it is a commonly shared belief that to be a good journalist means to be as highly opinionated as possible. Disinformation in small doses is considered to be an indispensable tool of the trade. Excesses in biased news coverage spark controversies between publications belonging to rival interest groups (Like the one that developed in 1995 between Media Holding, which publishes *Trud*, and the press group 168 Hours, which puts out *24 Chasa* and *168 Chasa*). The media are constantly accusing each other of distorting reality. Such cases, however, become events in themselves, and attract even wider readership. It seems that the audiences do not care too much about accuracy in reporting; instead, they find the controversies and recriminations in media most entertaining. The absence of a demarcation line between the information and entertainment functions of the media is one of the main features of post-communist media. Often a publication can be correctly described as a reliable source of information and a tabloid at the same time (a feature analyzed in detail in Peter Gross's analysis on media in neighboring Romania, 101–121).

In this environment, American cultural imports remain prevalent. The flair of "forbidden fruit" that made American products so attractive in the past is no longer a factor, but their popularity has not diminished. There is an abundance of cheaply got-up paperbacks featuring translations of American romance, self-help, true crime, mystery, and horror publications. Hollywood blockbusters play in the theaters. Video outlets offer pirated versions of trashy action and horror films. There are public eateries called "Americana" and "B-B-Q," and the cafeterias use umbrellas with Coca-Cola™ and Marlboro™ logos. One can barely find a T-shirt without *Power Rangers*, or *Pocahontas*.

With the end of state funding for domestic production of TV and radio programs, the electronic media were flooded by American TV shows and popular music. CNN International can be watched even without cable, and *The Funniest Home Videos* is being broadcast on prime-time TV. It is interesting to note, however, that not only mass culture, but American independent films and numerous other alternative American cultural products also make it to Eastern Europe.

Domestic programs, when they are made, often imitate the American model. Adenoidal radio voices announce the latest rock and roll hits, and domestic television productions pattern themselves after well-known American shows. *Nevada* and *Top-Family* borrow from *The Price is Right*, *Wheel of Fortune*, and *Jeopardy*. A TV talk show with comedian Todor Kolev (the Bulgarian David Letterman) is entitled *How to Catch Up* (with the Americans), and in spite of its technical awkwardness, it enjoys wide popularity, mostly due to its witty title. Even *Nablyudatel* (Observer), still considered an example of serious political journalism, is respected mostly because the two hosts are known as experts on all things American.

Print media also "borrow" a lot from the American models—in layout, advertising, and in newly emerged genres, notably gossip columns. The Westernization of press language, which John Murray wrote about in respect to Russia, can be observed in Bulgaria as well:

> Following the collapse of the Soviet power structures and the liberation of the press from the party stranglehold, Russian journalists turned to the Western press to find a replacement ideology for the discredited Leninist creed. This has taken the form of genre-borrowing, a process that is proving much more influential than word-borrowing in shaping the emerging Russian press. The appearance of non-Soviet genres in the press has facilitated the introduction into the public discourse of words which previously did not appear in the pages of the press. Most of these words, while new for the press, are not new to Russian, though in the Soviet era they received sparse if any coverage in less public genres. Obvious examples would be words to do with sex and capitalist economies. (196)

In Bulgaria the media have adopted many words and expressions that have an existing equivalent in the Bulgarian language but sound more fashionable in their English version: "body," "top model," "top banker." In addition, new words are introduced when an English word is used with a Bulgarian ending as in *fanove* for "fans." Many Bulgarians do not have a good command of the English language, as is seen everywhere on signs and posters. A major feature of the new semantic environment is the fact that more and more messages in the information environment contain a verbal component that is incomprehensible to the audience. Noting this same situation in Russia, Condee and Padunov distinguish it as a new type of communication environment in which the visual takes over and displaces the verbal. For them:

> This collapse of verbal into visual messages points to the genuine (counter-) revolutionary development in Russo-Soviet society: "cultural literacy" has been displaced by capitalism's drive for "brand-name" or "consumer literacy," even if those names have not yet appeared on the local market. (78)

Ironically, in this environment saturated with references to American consumer culture, reporting on news in the U.S. is not a priority of the Bulgarian media. Of course, there are many reports about American politics and economics, but this attention is only due to the dominant presence of the U.S. in international politics. Regular reporting on the U.S. is detached and disinterested, and whenever an attitude is taken, it is usually critical. Not much is left of the Bulgarian-American dream of the first post-communist years. The mid-1990s are marked by a shift in attitudes, and now it is mostly disappointment that is revealed in Bulgarian media coverage of the U.S. One laments the loss of a rapprochement that could have taken place, but did not.

American Interests: Political Disillusionment

Students of mutual images have noticed that because the images of a country are "largely a result of the media and other products of popular culture" (Mickiewicz 1991, 21) there is a significant "asymmetry" in what Americans and East Europeans know about each other (Dennis, Gerbner, and Zassoursky 1991). Thus, for most ordinary Bulgarians the U.S. is still the out-of-reach country of sex, drugs, guns, and rock and roll, or else a land of endless opportunity and affluence. The elimination of restrictions on international information, however, has led to a situation in which educated Bulgarians gradually have lost their initial unquestioning enthusiasm for all things American. While they remain generally respectful of American democracy and its accomplishments, a sobering process has begun for them. They saw inconsistencies in the U.S. policy toward Bosnia; they became suspicious about the American commitment to Turkey; they heard profuse rhetoric followed by little practical help; they realized the frightening extent of American consumerism; they encountered exploitative American businessmen who treated Bulgaria like a "banana republic"; and they witnessed gaffes on the part of U.S. diplomacy. (In 1995, a donation of medical supplies from a former base in Germany made by the spouse of the U.S. ambassador to Bulgaria to a provincial hospital turned out to contain medications aged past their expiration date. It was an embarrassing incident that gave journalists an opportunity for many bitter remarks.) All this has caused many "critically thinking"

Bulgarians to react to the ongoing Americanization of the cultural landscape by articulating strong anti-American sentiments.

Two major anti-American arguments are in circulation now. The first one is based on the realization that, contrary to expectations, the U.S. did not get involved with implementing political and economic change in Bulgaria, or at least it did not provide the expected support needed for the changes to take hold. The other argument is nationalist in tone, and its point is to make explicit the U.S. commitment to promoting (hostile) Turkish interests at Bulgaria's expense.

I will explore these two arguments separately.

"They Do not Care about Us, Why Then Should We Care about Them?"

Bulgaria has a satellite syndrome—a consciousness that it must inevitably play satellite to one bigger power or another. The question has always been, to which one?

The period of post-communist transition in Bulgaria has been marked by reflection on the topic of which big power would be interested in having the country as a satellite in these new times. Before 1989 Bulgaria was called "a sixteenth Soviet republic." Cultural and historical involvement with Russia was strong, and Bulgaria's economy and politics were closely tied to their Soviet counterparts. The dominant portion of Bulgarian exports went to guaranteed Soviet markets. Soviet bookstores operated throughout the country, a variety of Soviet print periodicals were imported, and Soviet television began broadcasting to Bulgaria in 1986.

By the end of 1989, however, it was clear that the countries of the East bloc could consider taking a separate road from Russia. Most of Eastern Europe had experienced dependency on the Soviets as an obstacle to their own development. Certainly this was the case in Czechoslovakia, East Germany, Hungary, and Poland. Communist countries in the Balkans, such as Albania, Romania, and Yugoslavia, had been less dependent on Russia and diminishing Russian interference did not substantially affect their politics. Bulgaria was the only country that needed to decide if it would remain in position as satellite to Russia or change its orbit.

The country tried to go the way of the East-Central European countries—to take a course that would emancipate it from the Soviets. It severed many of the old Soviet ties and turned to new foreign partners in the West. Or rather, it tried to. Initially, Bulgaria believed that the reorientation of the East bloc to the West would be a package deal: since the East European countries had been assigned to the Soviet sphere of influence *en bloc*, one expected that they would also be taken in by the West *en bloc*. Very soon, however, it became clear that the West was not looking at the situation this way, thinking instead in terms of individual countries and favoring only some of the East-Central European ones. Inequalities appeared and grew deeper. By 1994, no one from the West had expressed much interest in Bulgaria. No entrepreneurs were rushing to invest in the economy, and no new markets were opening up. The country felt abandoned. It had quit its traditional orbit, but it had not found a new one, and was now hovering in the dark.

In 1989/90, it was expected that the United States would get involved in Bulgaria, would try to wrest the country from the Soviets and facilitate its turning to the West. In spite of the fact that these events did not happen, for a while the media (and the politicians) were doing their best at pretending that America was really interested in Bulgaria. Any minuscule exchange between Bulgaria and the U.S. would be blown out of proportion and covered as if it was a turning point in relations between the two countries, a triumphant opening up of Bulgaria to America. A few hours stopover in Bulgaria by then Vice President Dan Quayle in 1992 was covered as if it was an extended presidential visit.

The radical "democratic forces" that emerged after 1989 and introduced the trend toward Westernization managed to hold power for a short time only. They were gradually replaced in 1992 by a moderate government, and then in 1994, the reformed communists came to power. Quite naturally, the change of governments led to changes in the foreign political and economic orientation of the country, and the idea of patching up relations with Russia started to dominate discourse in politics and the media. Now there is a serious effort to show that reorientation toward Russia is the only natural approach. Media reports on Russia, which in 1989–1994 had been dominated by explorations of its past practices, have lately been replaced by reports depicting it as an abandoned, wounded, and good-natured giant that is now exposed to all sorts of unscrupulous international ransacking. The book of the Russian director-turned-politician Stanislav Govorukhin, *The Great Criminal Revolution*, which powerfully enhances this image, was one of the best-sellers on the 1995 Bulgarian book market. That year was also the one in which a Bulgarian-Russian digest of the Russian press was successfully launched.

Public opinion has shifted in favor of reviving economic, cultural, and political linkages to Russia. In a policy document called "The White Book" put out by the socialist government in 1995, the reform governments that immediately preceded the socialists were accused "of leaving Bulgaria without security guarantees, of causing a deteriorating relationship with the West, and of 'exchanging one Big Brother for another'—the Soviet Union for the United States" (Krause 1995, 32). The 1995/96 discussion in the pages of the Socialist party daily *Duma* about the prospect of joining NATO run along the same lines.

An interesting example of anti-American inclinations is the coverage that *Duma* gave to the visit of Zbigniew Brzezinski when he attended a conference in Bulgaria in April 1995. Just a few years earlier, his visit would have been celebrated uncritically. In 1995, however, several articles recalled that as an anticommunist advisor to the American government in the 1970s, Brzezinski used to recommend maintaining ethnic tensions in the region as a way to counteract the successes of socialist construction. Thus, in 1995 he did not have the right to blame Balkan nationalism on the communists-turned-nationalists. In an editorial ("What did the oracle Zbigniew Brzezinski guess and what did he not," 1995), *Duma* wrote:

> But are not these [the nationalist inclinations] fruits of the system-atic American anti-communist foreign policy strategy after W.W.II? Brzezinski was one of the brightest ideologues of this strategy. In his works back in the 1960s he was developing the thesis that igniting nationalist tendencies was one of the most important methods of the so-called internal erosion of socialism. These tendencies, he was claiming, were a major weapon of anti-socialism. (5)

Currently, most Bulgarian print media refer negatively toward the U.S. Bulgarian journalists rarely miss the chance to remind the public of the lack of real U.S. involvement in Bulgaria and often allege hypocrisy in American for-eign commitments.

It would be hard to claim, however, that the prevailing negative media image of the U.S. was masterminded by the powers that be in a massive gov-ernment-directed media campaign. Rather, it has been carried out by emerg-ing business formations disappointed with lagging U.S. involvement. The negative image of the U.S. in the Bulgarian media would probably be there no matter who was in power. Because its appearance coincided with the reorien-tation in foreign policy conducted by the socialist government, the media vil-ification of the U.S. has simply had more outlets and greater play.

U.S. Promotion of Islamic Fundamentalism

Media reports that express disillusionment with American involvement in the Balkans claim that the U.S. actually promotes Islamic fundamentalism. One of the fundamental tropes of national feeling for all Slavic peoples in the Balkans is their pride in having served historically as a barrier to Islamic penetration of the West, making the project of the European Enlightenment possible through their sacrifice. Five centuries under the Ottoman empire held back their own development, but they prevented Islam from entering Europe and spreading further. The Slavs from the Balkans, no matter if they are Serbs, Macedonians, or Bulgarians, believe that the West should be eternally thankful. To them the Islamic threat is Issue Number One in politics.

Bulgaria has tried to maintain a neutral attitude toward the Bosnian con-flict, but most ordinary Bulgarians subscribe to the view that it is unacceptable to see a Muslim state taking hold in the region. This might explain why the Bulgarian media have been relatively silent about Serb atrocities against the Muslims, while diligently reporting every occasion when the Muslims were responsible for war crimes. In this context, U.S. concern for the Bosnian Muslims has been interpreted as promoting Islamic interests against the Orthodox Slavs.

But this is only part of the concern. There is also concern about the political and economic involvement of the U.S. with Turkey. To the U.S., Turkey may be the most progressive force in the Middle East, but to Bulgarians it is the embodiment of an imminent Islamic threat. Even though Bulgarians trade with much more fundamentalist countries such as Iraq and Iran, paradoxically, only when dealing with Turkey is the Islamic fundamentalism issue taken into consideration. Still, the Black Sea economic zone proposed by Turkey was well accepted by Bulgarians, and they participate in a number of joint ventures. Yet, the geographical proximity of this potential source of Islamic influence makes Bulgarians think of Turkey as a potential political threat, with alleged intentions to claim parts of Bulgarian territory, based on the fact that they are populated mostly by ethnic Turks. The media call this threat "the Cyprus scenario." The facts that Turkey is a member of NATO and that it is favored by American politicians make Bulgarians look upon the U.S. as a promoter of hostile interests.

Nationalistic newspapers such as *Zora* and *Bulgarski Pisatel* have published numerous pieces suggesting that Americans are unable to understand the history and importance of the Balkan cultural tradition, and thus their interference in any Balkan conflict is unjustified. In *Bulgarski Pisatel*, for example, Kliment Konstantinov (1995) claimed that since the U.S. has yet to build a proper national culture, it just does not know how to pay proper respect to the importance of the national idea. In spite of the fact that the American society and economy are very developed, he claimed, American culture is not. This is why Americans oppose national cultural values and even strive to destroy them. Konstantinov used the argument of cultural differences as an argument against American involvement in solving the problems of Balkan nationalism:

> In other words, the U.S. are only a state that pretends to be a nation. This is true, as it is true that Americans do not have ethnos, but are "citizens of the world." Americans want to impose their model on the entire world. They oppose things such as national education, national history, and national intelligentsia. The attempt of the Americans to encourage Western Europe to develop an administrative structure similar to the U.S. model was resisted by Europeans. . . . The penetration of Americanism in Bulgaria has reached such a high

level due to the lack of criticism toward this phenomenon. Some of us are misguided, others are irresponsible, third ones are sell-outs, who, supported by the offsprings of the old elites and by a significant part of the riff-raff populace, are leading a struggle to build an American type society in our country, believing that this is the only way to get rid of the past, which they designate with the cursed label of "communism." In fact, however, their politics could be described as "manipulative Bulgarophobia" where the concept of democracy has been assigned an entirely mechanical function and does not comply with the historical legacy of the nation and its cultural specifics. (16)

Other print media have explored various conspiracy theories: in *Duma*, Paunka Gocheva (1995), for example, developed the thesis that the Turkish interests have powerful promoters among top U.S. politicians. In her article, she listed numerous Turkish lobbying organizations that she believes play a major networking role and often convince American politicians to take an anti-Bulgarian stance. The journalists of *168 Chasa* have written extensively, insisting that the American ambassador to Bulgaria was involved in a wider conspiracy aimed not only at increasing the Muslim presence in the Balkans, but also at escalating the Bosnian war to include the neighboring Slavic countries. Some suggestive titles in 1995 were: "Montgomery Killed Our Hopes" (May 29–June 4, 1995); "Clinton's Administration Dreams of a Balkan War" (June 5–11, 1995); "The U.S. Promised to Arm the Muslims As Soon As the Peace Accord is Signed" (November 27–December 3, 1995).

The Open Society Foundation Conspiracy

Often, media reports link alleged U.S. conspiracies with the activities of the Open Society Foundation, established and run by financier and philanthropist George Soros. A common belief is that Soros actually represents not just himself and his financial empire, but the American government. He is being portrayed as an evil force, systematically working behind the scenes toward destroying Bulgaria's national integrity. Using various media formats, many Bulgarian intellectuals have been lamenting the situation in which they are reduced to beggary. They also have been claiming that a few coins are being tossed to them any time Soros has given new money to some project in the arts.

The media criticism of Soros seems to be part of an international trend. Initially welcomed across Eastern Europe, in 1995 the activities of the Open Society Foundation have been banned in countries such as Slovakia and Serbia, and are scrutinized with suspicion by politicians and the media in Croatia,

Macedonia, and Bulgaria. Western publications critical of Soros are being reprinted, and reports on the troubles of the foundation in other countries are featured. Soros is depicted as someone who is trying to dictate to governments, and his meetings with Bulgarian government officials in May 1995 while on a visit to Sofia did not prove very productive.

The conspiracy theories and allegations about Soros appear mostly in newspapers such as *24 Chasa* and *168 Chasa*, but also in *Trud* and *Duma*. Some of the titles of articles that appeared in *168 Chasa* were: "Soros Is Buying Off Bulgaria's National Security" (May 8–14, 1995); "Is Soros Using Open Society as a Mafia Structure?" (May 15–21, 1995); "Open Society Discarded Our National Heroes from the History Textbooks" (June 5–11, 1995). *Bulgarski Pisatel* also published numerous articles speculating on Soros's conspiracy. Many of these articles can be attributed to journalist Milena Boycheva, whose pieces have aimed at proving the subversiveness of all projects supported by Soros.

One of the specifically Bulgarian accusations is that funding is allocated mostly to projects promoting what Americans would call ethnic diversity, but what Bulgarians call Islamic influence. A populist stance taken by some journalists suggests that ethnic Bulgarians have their own troubles, and more attention should be paid to them and not to the minorities, especially not to minorities confessing Islam. The Open Society foundation is "exposed" for its support of projects such as a Gypsy textbook (Gypsies are stereotyped in the media as voluntarily illiterate and uninterested in education) and the film *Burn, Burn, Little Flame*, which deals with the violent human rights abuses committed against the ethnic Turks of Bulgaria in the mid-1980s. There are also masterpieces of "investigative" journalism alleging that Open Society provides funding for projects that would give the foundation access to classified information, such as a computerized information pool for police forces, or an on-line cataloguing project for the National Library. For example, in *Soros Is Buying Off Bulgaria's National Security* (1995), one claims:

> Soros has provided computerized networks and books to all possible university and departmental libraries. Which means that he is already granted access to the literary treasures of our state. But his efforts to make a full inventory of our museums run upon the rocks for now. In the white countries similar information is considered part of the national security and is not to be bought with a bunch of computers, what the American tycoon is trying to do in our country. (11)*

Ironically, it is not the Bulgarian government but Soros who systematically provides funds for original East European projects and who is giving local

---

*"White countries" here denotes the developed capitalist societies of the West.

artists the opportunity to survive in an environment that has been ruthlessly taken over by the imports of American mass culture. Thus, the only American effort that supports higher culture is branded as conspiracy.

Duma's *Coverage of the United States*

In order to illustrate and support the claims made above, I would like to offer a short overview discussing the content analysis of *Duma*'s coverage of United States-related issues between April and June 1995.

The Bulgarian dailies with the widest circulation are *24 Chasa* and *Trud*. They are overtly anti-American and often not very trustworthy. Other popular dailies are *Kontinent*, *Pari*, and *Standard*. *Demokratsia*, the newspaper of the oppositional Union of Democratic Forces, founded in 1990, has never established a viable audience, and its circulation is steadily declining. I chose *Duma* for two reasons. First, it is published by the ruling Bulgarian Socialist Party and is thus regarded as an official government newspaper. Second, it offers relatively balanced and trustworthy international coverage, and although it can also be considered anti-American, its anti-Americanism is not excessive.

Duma is the former *Rabotnichesko Delo*, which used to be published by the Communist party. The newspaper changed its name in 1990, approximately at the time when the Bulgarian Communist Party itself changed its name to the Bulgarian Socialist Party. Its editor in chief since 1989 has been Stefan Prodev.

The period analyzed runs from April 1, 1995, to June 17, 1995. Sixty-six issues of the newspaper came out during that period, usually in twelve-page editions. *Duma* was published daily except Sundays and national holidays (such as May 1 and May 24). It carried relatively little advertising, publishing mainly journalistic reports.

Amount of Coverage. During the period in consideration, *Duma* run 295 stories dealing with the U.S. (the sports page was not included in the count). On the average, 4.46 U.S.-related stories were featured in each issue.

Dateline. About half of the stories were reported from the U.S., with the other half originating from various locations around the world.

Length. Fifty percent of the reports were short features (20–30 lines), 15 percent were tiny ones (5–7 lines). Long features accounted for only 7.5 percent of the total (22 stories).

Location. Fifty-six percent of the reports about the U.S. and its international relations appeared on pages four and five, which are traditionally reserved for foreign news. Authored or editorial articles were published on the editorial pages (traditionally p. seven, eight, or nine) and totalled forty-six. Of the fifty-two reports that were run on page one, only four were long and detailed reports, whereas fifteen were tiny ones, filling the space in the margins. Stories about the U. S. rarely appeared on the business pages.

Source. Most reports were from the Big Four wire services (mostly Reuters and the Associated Press) or other bigger international agencies, such as ITAR-TASS. In fifty-four cases (18 percent) the reports were from *Duma Press* which means its own correspondents were not identified by name. There were forty signed reports (14 percent).

Type. The majority of the stories were reports on current news (171, or 57 percent). Sixteen percent featured soft news, mostly dealing with culture, celebrities, and curiosities. Seventeen editorials discussed issues touching on various aspects of the international actions of the U.S., and there were thirty authored comment articles (10 percent).

Regions Covered. Only 23 percent of the reports dealt with issues relating only to the U.S. The majority of stories (240, or 81 percent) featured information regarding the international activities of the U.S. Of these, 30 percent dealt with U.S.-Russian and U.S.-Balkan issues.

Forty articles (17 percent) dealt with the relations between Bulgaria and the U.S. (or organizations such as NATO, which are considered to be dominated by the United States). Of these, most commented on the imminent expansion of NATO, followed by reports on joint ventures or cultural exchanges. Other topics of discussion were the ousting of a deputy from the Bulgarian Parliament over a controversy involving his alleged U.S. citizenship, issues of the Bulgarian diaspora in the U.S., and the coverage that Bulgaria receives in the American media.

Attitude. Most reports (72 percent) did not take any particular attitude toward the U.S.. Explicitly positive attitude was expressed in 5 percent, and a negative one in 23 percent (total of sixty-three). The majority of the articles that took negative attitudes were authored pieces or editorials, while the positive ones were reports by *Duma Press* correspondents.

Of the sixty-eight stories that expressed negative attitude, seventeen (or 25 percent) dealt with the potential expansion of NATO, fifteen criticized U.S. policies in the Balkans, seven attacked Soros's Open Society Foundation, five were criticisms published during the visit of Zbigniew Brzezinski, and the rest commented on various human rights abuses—on racism and mistreatment of immigrants in the U.S. About ten stories contained allegations of unacceptable interference by the U.S. military or the CIA in the domestic affairs of other countries.

A positive attitude was taken mostly in reports on Bulgarian-U.S. joint ventures and cultural exchanges. Of the seventeen stories that expressed an explicitly positive attitude toward the U.S., thirteen featured business or cultural interaction.

Topics. Mostly, issues of international politics and international conflict (particularly the Balkan one) received coverage, followed by coverage of issues of terrorism (especially at the time of Oklahoma City bombing). These were followed by soft news in the fields of education and health, and some sensationalist reporting. Only occasionally was there coverage of U.S. domestic policy issues.

It is interesting to note that the most attention was paid to the Oklahoma City bombing during the first days after the explosion when it was still believed that Islamic fundamentalist terrorists were accountable for the incident. During these days, *Duma* published a number of materials by their own U.S. correspondent, and ran several authored pieces commenting on issues of international fundamentalist terrorism. Eventually, when the investigation pointed in another direction, interest in the topic declined.

During the same time period (April 1–June 17, 1995) a Lexis/Nexis search indicated that Bulgaria was mentioned in thirty stories published by *The New York Times*. Of these mentions, the most numerous were in the field of sports (ten articles), followed by history (three stories), Russian and Balkan issues (three stories each), international business (three stories), and once each in stories of international terrorism, illegal migration, drug smuggling, Turkey, culture, and fortune telling. During the same period, the word "Bulgaria" appeared in *The New York Times* headlines on three occasions altogether.

Conclusion

A more active involvement of the U.S. with Bulgaria in the early 1990s would have been beneficial for Bulgaria. Since it did not happen, however, Bulgaria seems to be taking a new path in its foreign orientation, one that will bring it closer to Russia again and emphasize its difference from the West.(This trend has been noted by U.S. journalists and commented upon in the American press. See for example the articles of Kinzer and Perlez in *The New York Times*.)

Media have taken an important part in setting the stage for this reorientation. The portrayal of the U.S. that dominates Bulgarian media is one of incompetence and fishy political and economic interests. More and more reports can be seen that depict failures in American foreign policies and investment strategies. This media picture might have been quite different had the U.S. shown more interest in Bulgaria. For now, however, only American mass culture has a firm presence in Bulgaria. It is the only American manifestation that is there to stay.

References

Boycheva, M. (1995, March 6–13). A flame in the haystack. [Trans. from Bulgarian by Dina Iordanova] *Bulgarski Pisatel*, p. 1.

Clinton's administration dreams of a Balkan war. (1995, June 5–11). [Trans. from Bulgarian by Dina Iordanova] *168 Chasa*, p. 1.

Condee, N., and V. Padunov. (1994). Pair-a-dice lost: The socialist gamble, market determinism, and compulsory postmodernism. *New Formations*, p. 70.

Deltcheva, R. (1996). New tendencies in post-totalitarian Bulgaria: mass culture and the media. *Europe-Asia Studies* 48(2).

Dennis, E., G. Gerbner, and Y. Zassoursky, (Eds.). (1991). *Beyond the cold war: Soviet and American media images*. Newbury Park, Cal.: Sage.

Engelbrekt, K. (1992). Bulgaria. (assessment of the mass media). *RFE-RL Research Report* 1(39), p.30.

Goban-Klas, T. (1994). *The orchestration of the media: The politics of mass communication in Communist Poland and the aftermath*. Boulder: Westview.

Gocheva, P. (1995, March 17). The Turkish lobby in the U.S. is pretty influential. [Trans. from Bulgarian by Dina Iordanova] *Duma*, p. 7.

Gross, P. (1996). *Mass media in revolution and national development: The Romanian laboratory*. Ames: Iowa State University Press.

Iordanova, D. (1995a). The image of Bulgaria abroad and its domestic use. In *Communications in Eastern Europe*. Mahwah: Lawrence Earlbaum.

Iordanova, D. (1995b). Provisional rules and directorial changes: Restructuring of national TV. Ljubljana: Javnost/*The Public*. Vol. 2/ 3.

Is Soros using Open Society as a mafia structure? (1995, May 15–21). [Trans. from Bulgarian by Dina Iordanova] *168 Chasa*, p. 27.

Kinzer, S. (1995, April 28). Bulgaria: Not sure whether it should turn East or West. *The New York Times*, p. A11.

Konstantinov, K. (1995, March 6–13). Eradication. [Trans. From Bulgarian by Dina Iordanova] *Bulgarski Pisatel*, p. 16.

Krause, S. (1995, June 23). The white book: Pointing the finger. *Transition*, p. 32.

Martin, J. L., and A. G. Chaudhary, (Eds.). (1983). *Comparative mass media systems*. New York: Longman.

Mickiewicz, E. (1991). Images of America. In E. Dennis, G. Gerbner, and Y. Zassoursky (Eds.), *Beyond the cold war: Soviet and American media images*, p. 21. Newbury Park, Cal.: Sage.

Montgomery killed our hopes. (1995, May 29–June 4). [Trans. From Bulgarian by Dina Iordanova] *168 Chasa*, p. 27.

Murray, J. D. (1994). *The Russian press from Brezhnev to Yeltzin*. Hants: Edward Elgar.

Nam, S. (1983). Media entertainment in the third world. In J. Martin and A. G. Chaudhary (Eds.), *Comparative mass media systems*, p. 209. New York: Longman.

Ognianova, E. (1993). On forgiving Bulgarian journalists/spies. *Journal of Mass Media Ethics* 8(3): p. 156.

Open Society discarded our national heroes from the history textbooks. (1995, June 5–11). [Trans. from Bulgarian by Dina Iordanova] *168 Chasa*, p. 34.

Paletz, D., K. Jakubowicz, and P. Novosel, (Eds.). (1995). *Glasnost and after: media and change in Central and Eastern Europe*. Cresskill, N.J.: Hampton.

Perlez, J. (1995, May 21). In Bulgaria, Russia eyes a renewal of old ties. *The New York Times*, pp. 1, 13.

Soros is buying off Bulgaria's national security. (1995, May 8–14). [Trans. from Bulgarian by Dina Iordanova] *168 Chasa*, p. 1.

Splichal, Sl. (1994). *Media beyond Socialism: Theory and practice in east-central Europe*. Boulder: Westview.

The U.S. promised to arm the Muslims as soon as the peace accord is signed (1995, November 27–December 3). [Trans. from Bulgarian by Dina Iordanova] *168 Chasa*, p. 34.

What did the oracle Zbigniew Brzezinski guess and what did he not. (1995, April 1). [Trans. from Bulgarian by Dina Iordanova] *Duma*, p. 5.

7

U.S. Image Reflected through Cartoons in Turkish Newspapers

AYSELI USLUATA

Introduction

Editorial or political cartoons in the national daily newspapers in Turkey, as "graphic expressions" (T. Selçuk, 1995) or as "pictorial satire" of current events, while contributing to political images also provide pictorial documents for the in-depth study of political and social trends. Inseparable from the pictorial renderings of political events is their imagery which, as Watson and Hill (1990) in their dictionary point out, "reflects opinion since the image does not merely reproduce, it interprets." Thus, what cannot be expressed verbally can be displayed in drawing. According to Reeves (1991, xi), "What can rarely be found in learned and footnoted analyses of foreign affairs is at the core of political cartooning" (cited in King 1991, xi).

Studies have demonstrated that political cartoons are powerful weapons of the daily papers in showing immediate reactions to both national and international events, in interpreting and/or criticizing political and social affairs humorously or maliciously in pictorial form, and in choosing an image that conveys its message independent of any restriction (George 1959; Dennis 1974; Reeves 1990 in King; Palmer 1995). Political cartoonists with artistic inclinations, who are "fierce in their independence" from conflicts of interest, "feel themselves less restricted" (Parker, 144; Al-Hajji and Nelson, 224) from portraying what others cannot dare to put into words; that is why their cartoons are defined as radical, oppositionist, and disruptive (George 1959; Dennis 1974).

For the foremost humor writer of Turkey, Aziz Nesin (1973, 15–41), humor replaces protest; he argues that under oppression people, feeling powerless and unable to deal with the oppressors, use humor as a weapon and at the same time a tool to relax through laughter. As "artists of protest," political cartoonists during times of crisis can afford drawing to "ridicule" or "satire" since what they are doing is what Hewison (1997, cited in Watson and Hill, 29) calls "drawn humor" and treating politics as "a struggle between right and wrong and truth and falsehood" and as "weapons of controversy" (George, 13). As Watson and Hill (28) note, "the serious nature of caricature and its particular significance in expressionism, which sets people protesting rather than laughing" was emphasized by Gombrich in 1958. In Turkey, nearly all editorial and/or political cartoonists who are conscious of being artists in a developing country have been practicing their art as leftist-radicals and have undertaken the mission of enlightening the public by reflecting paradoxes and exposing exploitation or corruption (T. Selçuk 1992, in interview by Çeviker 1995, 51; I. Selçuk 1995). Their cartoons display the contradiction between acceptance and resistance and the conflicts between what Gordon (1989, xiii) identifies as "acculturation and rejection," "dependence and independence," and "alienation and identification."

Nations are connected by images through their inherited imagery and pressure of events, and while images of the "Other" nations in the West are distorted and stereotyped, and this often applies to well-informed people as well (Becker and Ganzel 1978, in Wahlström, 3; Galtung 1992; Gumpert and Cathart 1983; Parker 1995), the developed nations can afford to transmit positive images of themselves abroad. As Gordon (27) points out, "the technological and scientific revolution of the West has produced a cosmopolitan culture fashioned according to Western values," and an imbalance in communication. The flow of news, films, TV programs, and commercial products from those countries with power and technological means to the developing world, and of "news and entertainment coming primarily from the U.S." (Schiller 1976), "lead to dependence on one side and domination on the other" (McBride 1980, 149). The predominant position of the U.S. in economic and political life is reflected in the images of the U.S. among university students from Denmark, Finland, Sweden, and the USSR as positive, according to research conducted in the early 1990s. Surprisingly, "Soviet respondents made a more positive assessment of the United States than did the students from all the other countries and had more positive associations to the U.S. than to their own country" (Bjersted et al. 1993, 16). Also, in Egypt the young generation has a positive image of the U.S., as a "like-to-live-in country" (Tayie 1988, 539). The American image in Turkey has been shaped by U.S.-made products: movies, TV programs/series, news, and commercial products. Multinational corporations, international organizations, and travel have all contributed to the formation of the image of the U.S. in Turkey, as in other developing nations.

Over the last thirty years, the United States of America has played and continues to play a crucial role in the politics, economy, and social life of Turkey. Although a lot of books and articles have been written to evaluate and/or analyze this role and the relationship between Turkey and the U.S. (Barkey 1992; Bozer 1990; Mango 1975; McGhee 1990), the manner in which the U.S. has been perceived and reflected in Turkish editorial cartoons has not been investigated. Only one section of a collection of Turkish cartoons, "Of the U.S.," shows "that there is a bit of America in every land" (Eren 1959). However, relations between the two countries can be traced through negative or positive images conveyed in the editorial and political cartoons of the daily newspapers.

"Turkey and the U.S. have always been allies in spite of a few crises in their relationship," writes Abramovitz (1995, 179), a former U.S. ambassador to Turkey, who depicts NATO, bases, and military aid as "three imperatives" that have directed Turkish-U.S. relations. In fact, these are the "imperatives" that Turkish cartoonists have protested and criticized most bitterly in their political cartoons as obstacles to national independence. Their resentment of the "image of omnipotence" (Schiller 1976) has been fed by what Gordon calls "Western self-congratulation" (1989, 14).

Purpose of the Study

This chapter will examine the messages of political cartoons in the national Turkish newspapers in terms of the images of the United States of America during the last thirty years. The purpose is to study the use of cartoons as political and social statements, analyze the images of the U.S. created by cartoons in the daily newspapers by the foremost editorial cartoonists of Turkey, and trace the changes in those images over the period covered by this study.

Hypothesis

Editorial or political cartoonists with artistic power can survive with their own ideology intact, can afford to be independent and bold even in conflict with the interests of the newspapers they work for, and can counterbalance the dominant policy of those in power or influence by pointing to "facts" versus "beliefs" (Chomsky and Herman 1979). Thus, political cartoons can bring insight to what is not put into words, because, as one of the foremost Turkish political cartoonists, T. Selçuk, has said, "lines start when words end."

Method

The cartoons—the symbols and themes—have been analyzed in three steps: the translation, the explanation, and the relation to the subject (Holsti 1963, 124). Editorial and political caricatures in the national newspapers, and collections of the works of political cartoonists, have been surveyed to identify the symbols used for the U.S. by different cartoonists and by the same cartoonists over time. Change in perceptions and images has been registered qualitatively in terms of the empathy or antipathy the images evoke. Personal interviews with the cartoonists were conducted. The majority of the political cartoonists (A. Ulvi, T. Selçuk, S. Balcioğlu, F. Doğan, T. Oral, B. Koraman, H. Soyöz, R. Yakali, S. Memecan) who have been considered in this study, especially those who are classified as the third generation (T. Selçuk, F. Doğan, A. Ulvi, S. Balcioğlu, T. Oral), are left-wing radicals; however, their cartoons can still be presented in papers whose policy does not necessarily agree with theirs because of their circulation value and because they cannot be replaced. Best known of all Turkish national daily newspapers carrying more than one editorial and/or political cartoon are *Cumhuriyet*, a leftist newspaper, and *Milliyet*, a liberal newspaper, and editorial or political cartoonists have been working for them for more than twenty years. Other foremost political cartoonists of Turkey have been working for other national newspapers.

While dealing with historical events concerning crucial issues in Turkish-U.S. relations, the citations used are mostly drawn from foreign sources—academicians and/or politicians—in order to provide a more objective view and a comparison between foreign and Turkish interpretations.

Cartoons covering three periods corresponding to periods of strain or conflict in Turkish-U.S. relations have been investigated in three groups: the *first period* included the years between the late 1960s and 1970s that were years of internal conflict, and public hostility toward the U.S. was reflected in the cartoons; in the *second period*, that is, in the 1980s, U.S. relations were perceived in the international arena; and the *third period* covered the early- and mid-1990s, years of close relations between the leaders of the two countries when the U.S. was perceived as a country of refuge and investment.

Humor and political cartoons in Turkey

Turkish caricature has its roots in the West; however, humor, especially oral humor, has a long tradition. Aziz Nesin, in his work on Turkish Humor, declares that humor depends on the society one is born into, and that economic and social conditions, cultural level, history, traditions, cultural national differences are reflected in humor.

For Turkish people, anecdotes have a special importance, especially during times of crisis. When people cannot deal with those in power, they start
ridiculing them, creating legendary characters such as Nasreddin Hodja to
take responsibility for the anecdotes, because they are afraid of the oppressors
(Nesin 1973, 15–41).

Visual humor or caricature is, in the political cartoonist Selçuk's words,
"drawing with an element of humor" (Selçuk, 8). According to the *Encyclopae-
dia Meydan Larousse*, "Ridicule, satire and criticism have united to form Turkish pictorial satire." Four generations of Turkish cartoonists have demonstrated
to the masses the power of an art that has surpassed the written word. The
third generation of political cartoonists "has broken away from pictorial art and
the art through lines (graphic art) have predominated in the cartoons" (F.
Doǎan, T. Selçuk, A. Ulvi, B. Koraman), and the "graphical expression" has
been defined as a form of art (Y. Kemal 1974, in *Güldiken*). The political cartoonists of the 1950s have reflected the struggle of men with a changing world.
With the political cartoonists of the 1960s social and political problems have
gained considerable importance in Turkish newspapers. In 1995, political cartoons in animated form were included in the main evening news program of a
private TV channel owned by the newspaper on which the creator of the cartoons, Salih Memecan, works as an editorial cartoonist.

A few lines with or without words can reflect what is actually happening
and display social contradictions, paradoxes, and absurdities that may not be
pleasing to everyone, but that may address the feelings of the majority of the
people. The political cartoon as a form of art in daily contact with its viewers
has been an influential medium in Turkey, and the possible threat posed by
their cartoons to the established order has caused those in power or influence
to react against their creators, the cartoonists. Thus, some of the Turkish political cartoonists who probed into the depths of social problems and criticized
social injustices and/or contradictions in the country were arrested in 1970s.
It seems that one of the most respected cartoonists, T. Selçuk, was released because of public opinion (*Pardon*, Germany, Jan. 1972 No. 7, in *Güldiken* 1995,
125), which illustrates the power wielded by a political cartoonist (Parker
1995) and proves a direct relationship between political cartoons and public
opinion (Palmer 1995, in Kamalipour, 140).

That editorial cartoons can be more "offensive" than pages of writing
and that they can stimulate newspaper readers or just "newspaper viewers" to
think has repeatedly been voiced both by authorities on the subject and by
the man in the street. Turkish editorial cartoonists are supporters of the view
that newspapers are indispensable factors in the transition to democracy and
that political cartoons are indispensable features of newspapers. The foremost Turkish cartoonists support a democratic Turkey. Their cartoons reflect
respect for human rights and loyalty to secularism and oppose absolute

dependence upon the industrial powers; for them, as for Gordon (159), the terms could be reversed—the core is also dependent on the periphery, creditors upon debtors. Thus, they defend mutual dependence or interdependence rather than dependence on the superpower (T. Selçuk 1994, in *Güldiken* 1995).

While dealing with the Turks' perception of the U.S., Turkish political cartoons reflect what Chomsky and Herman (ix) call "dual focus." While in one cartoon the American soldier is greeted by a "Welcome" sign written in English (F. Doǒan, 1967) between the two minarets of a mosque (S. Balcioǧlu 1967), in another, birds of peace chase an American soldier with a "Yankee Go Home" sign (T. Selçuk, *Cumhuriyet*, July 31, 1977). These two cartoons summarize the social contradiction of simultaneous acceptance and protest. The discrepancy is between the perception that the United States is "dedicated to furthering the cause of democracy and human rights throughout the world," which Chomsky and Herman call "beliefs" (ix), and the perception that "the United States has organized a system of client states ruled mainly by terror and serving the interests of a small local and foreign business and military elite," which Chomsky and Herman call "facts" (ix). These two perceptions have prevailed in the minds of people interchangeably for the last thirty years, and while those in power or influence have almost always been the believers of the "beliefs," most of the political cartoonists have been trying to illustrate in their cartoons that "beliefs" are not "facts." While drawing to protest, Turkish political cartoonists try to portray the political life with new insights, using "the slang of graphic art" (Geipel 1972, in Watson and Hill 1990) or the "ungentlemanly" art (Hess and Kaplan 1968).

Findings: Images of the U.S.

When Turkish satire established itself, Turkish cartoonists inherited an international or Western symbolic language to form common images—Turkish newspaper readers or viewers could understand that Uncle Sam symbolized the U.S. and a white dove with a branch of olive tree symbolized peace. The U.S. image in the political cartoons of the national newspapers in Turkey display both the artistic and satiric talents of the foremost Turkish editorial cartoonists. In times of crisis in Turkish-U.S. relations, the number of cartoons has increased and their messages have been overloaded with exaggerations in accordance with the word *caricature* (which has its origin in an Italian verb meaning "to overload with exaggeration").

The main cartoon stereotype of the U.S. in Turkish political cartoons is Uncle Sam—the famous universal symbol, a tall thin figure with high head, chin whiskers, starry coat, and starry pantaloons—sometimes just a starry and striped sleeve if the body is not shown. He is mostly portrayed as cunning.

Then come the images of a cowboy with a wide hat and boots, with dollars pouring out of his pockets and a gun in his belt; the American flag; the Statue of Liberty; a dollar or a dollar sign; military bases; IMF; Coca-Cola™; a sheriff; and an old pleasant cowboy city. These symbols reflect either positive or negative images according to the message they aim to convey. Offensive images have been portrayed in case the cartoonists feel they have "the right to be offensive" (Platt 1995).

Historical Developments

"Westernization" and "modernization" have been synonymous terms in Turkey; for a long time to be modern has been assumed to be European in manner and lifestyle. Later on, with the coming of "democracy," the U.S. became a new model for Turkey. "Americanization" was voiced after the 1969 elections; Prime Minister Demirel, when the Justice Party (AP) increased its majority, promised to make Turkey a "small America," something that is still being satirized by famous political cartoonists. In a recent cartoon, Turhan Selçuk portrays Demirel in front of the 6th Fleet holding a Turkish flag in one hand and an American flag in the other and shouting happily, "Hooray! We are becoming small America!" and asks "What has happened to the GREAT TURKEY that was established after the independence war by Gazi Mustafa Kemal [in other words, Atatük]?" (*Milliyet*, November 1995). A cartoon by Ferruh Doğan (1969, 92) satirizing the change in the national economic policy of Turkey exposes the new goal of the country as dependence upon the U.S. In three cartoons, he displays the closure of the "village educational institutions" that trained teachers and the establishment of "USA bases" in their place.

The 1960s and 1970s were years of unrest in Turkey. In the 1965 elections, the Democrats or the new Justice Party (Demirel) won a majority, and according to Mango (1975) many Republicans attributed their defeat to "intrigues by the American Embassy in Ankara" and portrayed the Justice Party as the "representative of a collaborationist bourgeoisie intent on sharing imperialist robbery in Turkey." Ferruh Doğan, in his social satire, criticizes the "collaborationist bourgeoisie," portraying the same people who are always on the scene (popular), who have no ideology, who only think of their own interests, and who are always on the side of those in power. In his cartoon with a caption, "Political Economy, Long live the monarch! Long live the Republic! Long live democracy! and long live America! "cries the same rich, fat man changing appearance in accordance with the ideology in power (Doğan 1969, 85).

Student radicalism in Turkish universities in 1968 created tensions in Turkish-U.S. relations. The imperialist "ugly American" image was used to express suspicion toward the U.S. for its manipulation of Turkey as the gendarme of the Middle East, thus impeding its development. The 1969 agreement (Co-operation Agreement Concerning Joint Defense) took into account "Turkish sensitivity in matters of sovereignty in governing the use of facilities in Turkey by Americans." In 1970, the American presence in Turkey was reduced, and Turkish control over joint installations strengthened. Violence spread beyond the campuses in 1970. The armed forces intervened on March 12, 1971, martial law was declared, and political cartoonists were among those who were arrested. Turkey's orientation in foreign relations continued to be toward the West; the government's commitment to NATO and "to the primacy of the connection with the U.S. within the alliance" was confirmed. In 1970–71, relations with the U.S. were dominated by concern over the drug trade, with the U.S. demanding that Turkey eliminate opium poppy production. The cultivation of opium was thus banned in 1972. President Nixon announced that the U.S. would initiate new forms of technical and financial aid to assist Turkish agriculture in compensation for losses due to the ban on the cultivation of opium. Banning symbolized the desire of those in power and influence to do business with the United States (Mango 1975, 57–68; McGhee 1990, 68–169).

T. Selçuk (*Ortam* 1971) criticizes the involvement of the U.S. in the internal politics of the country. A fat cowboy with a dollar sign on his hat watches the voting for the new Constitutional Law from the balcony of the Grand National Assembly, and when everyone says "yes" to the Law, his hand points down—showing that he does not approve. The cartoonist is protesting such an interference. A cartoon by F. Doğan reflects a "mission impossible" in Turkey: the cartoon shows Turkey as an island that needs help, and an Uncle Sam coming to the capital, Ankara, and opening an "Information Center" (1969, 86). A great number of political cartoons express suspicion of the aid the government receives from the U.S. T. Selçuk, in a cartoon in *Milliyet* (April 27, 1968), depicts the U.S. as a monster, called Imperialism, that crawls into the country and gives dollars as aid. F. Doğan satirizes development through debt; in one cartoon with a caption, "development," a politician or a businessman looks up happily to get the dollar handed down to him (112), and in a strip cartoon, in the first panel a man looks at a dollar in the sky happily; in the second, the dollar changes shape; in the third, it becomes a bomb descending onto him; and in the fourth, the man is running away (F. Doğan 1969, 128).

Under the Demirel government of October 1965–March 1971 and under the military-backed administrations of March 1971–October 1973, relations with the United States improved, largely because the anti-Americanism of the local radicals, which had been tolerated by the opponents of Demirel, was suppressed. Other types of U.S. economic and military aid, including an agreement to sell some F-4 Phantom aircraft to Turkey, continued in 1973. After the 1973 elections, the Republicans (B. Ecevit) formed a coalition with the National Salvation Party in 1974 supporting an anti-capitalist program, and in 1976 the oil crisis threw the economy into a deep recession (Mango 1975; McGhee 1990, 68–169).

In Mid-1970s, with the Cyprus crisis, Turkey faced some "facts" in foreign policy and had to turn away from total reliance on the West. Following the 1974 Cyprus operation, the decision of the U.S. Congress to impose an embargo on arms shipments to Turkey in 1975 was a shock to Turkey. Until then, all Turkish politicians to the right of the Radicals had relied on the U.S. and valued the American connection, but until then disagreements between the two countries had centered on economic problems, and when it came to political needs, the situation changed. After the Cyprus operation, Turkey realized that her interests were not protected by NATO and had to consider two alternatives—relations with the Soviet Union and relations with the Third World (Mango 1975; McGhee 1990). One cartoon in particular shows deep trust in Turkish-U.S. bonds and may offer an explanation of the shock the decision created in Turkey: Uncle Sam says "Embargo!"—which was perceived as a bluff by the Turks (Rasit Yakah, *Dünya*, June 20, 1975).

In March 1975, a right-wing coalition government was formed. The Turkish response to the U.S. by the Demirel coalition government was given in the following statement: "Over the 30 years Turkey and United States have maintained friendly ties, have helped each other on matters of mutual security. From the point of view of American interests, this decision is inappropriate." On July 25, 1975, following the refusal of the U.S. House of Representatives to lift the arms embargo, the Turkish government began to take over American military facilities—for internal political reasons. "Certainly the ties of interest that bind Turkey with the West in general and the Atlantic Alliance in particular are strong" (Mango 1975). An editorial cartoon in *Dünya* reflects the manipulation of Uncle Sam by the Greeks by depicting him with his chin whiskers in the hands of the Greek government (Rasit Yakah, *Dünya*, July 29, 1975). A cartoon by T. Selçuk in *Cumhuriyet* contains a warning against full reliance on the U.S. by depicting in one the Statue of Liberty in New York sinking with the rising water (October 1, 1977).

In the 1980s, the perception of the U.S. by the Turks was based on the international situation. In the early 1980s, Turkey entered a new area of export-led economic growth, and the 1980 military intervention brought about attempts to restructure the economy (Çeçen 1994, 37–56). The Cyprus-related arms embargo against Turkey was lifted by President Carter in April 1978, and Turkish-U.S. relations have improved since then. The U.S.-Turkish Defense and Economic Cooperation Agreement was signed in 1980 and renewed in 1986. In 1988, a new base agreement was signed. The

Reagan administration recognized the importance of Turkey in Western defense and "attempted to provide generous military support" (McGhee, 168).

At the beginning of the 1980s, when the Reagan administration took office, a Turkish politician protesting the restrictive attitude by industrialized countries toward exports of textiles from developing countries demanded a freer international trade system and wrote: "attachement to the ideals of peace, freedom and democracy provides a strong basis for Turkish-American relations. The United States is completed by its superpower status to pursue a multidimensional foreign policy. It is natural that the responsibilities, burdens and benefits should be mutually and equitably shared. We will need assistance from the allies and such assistance is for mutual benefit" (Kahveci, 226–230, in Schmergel 1991).

The U.S. sale of arms abroad mostly to underdeveloped countries has been criticized by various cartoonists. In an cartoon by Tan Oral in *Cumhuriyet*, Mrs. Reagan says to President Reagan, who is in bed with his cowboy hat and rifle, "Dear, let's invest our money in gold and land" (2 October 1981). When the U.S. planes keeping a watch on Libya took off from bases in Greece, Ali Ulvi criticized the U.S. policy of selling arms for peace in three cartoons (*Cumhuriyet*, November 4, 1981). He tries to expose in the three cartoons to what end arms are sold: in the first one, a salesman with a cowboy hat is selling arms on his tray to people from different nationalities— Arabs as well; in the second picture, those who buy the arms start firing at each other; and in the third picture, the salesman with his cowboy boots gets in between them with an olive branch and tries to be a mediator. On May 1, 1984, a cartoon by A. Ulvi in *Cumhuriyet* shows a flag of peace on a rocket. Another cartoon portrays an American cowboy, as a superpower, sitting on top of the world with his guns and boots as if riding a horse (T. Oral 1981).

Hypocrisy in the relations of the two superpowers is displayed in a cartoon by A. Ulvi. In spite of the cold war between the two superpowers, they are bound by secret commercial ties. In his depiction, the two men, one with an American flag on his arm and the other with the Soviet flag, sitting at opposite sides of a table, quarrel while the U.S. sells a package of wheat to the USSR, who hands him money underneath the table (Ali Ulvi, *Cumhuriyet*, February 10, 1982). Another example of hypocrisy is a cartoon by Ali Ulvi taking as its subject the Labor Union leader's visit to the United States. His getting advice from the U.S. and the close relationship with the employer/owner is criticized. Another cartoon depicts an employer/capitalist at a tennis court. A man calls, "Sir, you have a telephone call from the U.S. The labor union leader will talk to you on the rights of the workers" (A. Ulvi, *Cumhuriyet*, August 8, 1984).

In the 1990s, the U.S. "still maintains rights in six military bases in Turkey which are valuable assets for U.S. defense, as well as for the defense of

Turkey and NATO" (McGhee, 173). Besides two crises in world politics, the Gulf war and the war in Bosnia, which have determined the agenda of the editorials, the close relations between the leaders of the two countries have been the most criticized topics. During the Gulf crisis in August 1990, Özal had allowed American use of Turkish air bases despite İnönü's declaration that the Turkish people did not want war. "After Gulf War, Özal sought to institutionalize ties with the United States. He believed that a strong American connection would enhance Turkish economic growth, political stability, and prospects for entrance into the EC and Western European Union. He envisioned 'strategic cooperation': an expansion of U.S.-Turkish relations and political cooperation in troubled areas" (Abramovitz, 178).

According to Abramowitz (1978–79), today Turkish and American leaders are closer together, and Turkey is less dependent on the United States. The "imperatives" that once directed U.S.-Turkish relations—NATO, bases, and military assistance—are quickly disappearing. The American military presence in Turkey has been cut in half, trouble spots like Iraq demand closer U.S.-Turkish consultations, and "senior Turkish officials repeatedly emphasize the importance of Turkey's American connection." The United States also serves as a tremendous source of investment, technology, and education and is Turkey's second largest trading partner, still providing Turkey with foreign aid after the disintegration of the Soviet Union in 1993.

The symbol of the U.S. in the 1990s is as the home of the leaders of Turkey and the rich in Turkey and refuge for those Turks who are trying to transfer their money in the U.S. and evade the laws of their country. The money is the ruler of the world. The first woman prime minister of Turkey, Prof. Çiller, was educated in the States and owned property there. Thus, she is seen by the political cartoonists as the product of the U.S. T. Selçuk's "Barbie Doll" is made in the USA; for S. Balcioğlu she has been doped in the USA (21), she is a wind from the USA (29), she wears two flags, Turkish and American, on her neck (22) with the eagle emblem of the U.S. behind her Prime Minister's table (28) and stands as a "Statue of Liberty" holding a sign reading "YES" (78). In T. Selçuk's cartoon Çiller is a Barbie Doll that can speak English and knows the Koran, packed in the U.S. and sent to Turkey (in *Milliyet*, September 3, 1993). In another cartoon, a hand of a man with stars and stripes writes her fate on Çiller's forehead (Kurtcebe, *Cumhuriyet*, September 17, 1995).

The U.S. as powerful protector: A strip by T. Selçuk in *Milliyet* (April 21, 1995) shows the handsome young president of the U.S. who summons the prime minister with his finger (body language unfamiliar to Turkish culture and regarded as impolite). When they kiss, everybody claps, "Here is Turkish-American friendship; this is our history's greatest victory." A cartoon by Haslet Soyöz shows Çiller with a grin on her face pushing everybody away in order to have her picture taken next to Clinton (*Milliyet*, November 8, 1995). The prime minister asks the U.S. government to help her, warning them, "If I go, the religious fundamentalists will come" (*Vakit*, April 22, 1994).

An American-educated artist working as editorial cartoonist on *Sabah*, the pro-government newspaper, has started to depict the daily political life of Turkey as if it were taking place in an old American western city, with the title "BizimCity"(Our City) written half in English and half in Turkish. The sheriff is the prime minister. Thus, on the first page of a popular national newspaper, the biting image of the U.S. has been converted into a milder one with the image of an "Americanized" Turkey. The Americanized names stress the extent the U.S. has penetrated the Turkish media. T. Selçuk, in his cartoon called "cultural imperialism," satirizes the use of English in daily life and by the media. A villager says "by, bye"; a small child shows surprise by exclaiming "wau!"—all unfamiliar to Turkish vocabulary (*Milliyet*, June 12, 1995).

According to Abramovitz (180), "increasingly the United States is seen as the sole superpower and the only country capable of mobilizing world action." A cartoon by Selçuk in *Milliyet* (1995) and a cartoon by T. Oral in *Cumhuriyet* both show the U.S. as a superpower embracing the world in his arms. T. Selçuk's cartoon strip, "Space War," in the national daily *Milliyet* represents the U.S. as the superpower where Truman II says, "We have an umbrella over the sky. From now on we will treat Japan as we did the underdeveloped countries. We are the most powerful country on the earth and in the space. I will conquer the earth and space" (October 14, 1995).

Conclusion

The newspapers are able to display real democracy in reflecting images of the U.S. contrary to those preferred by persons of power or influence due to the independence of the political cartoonists as artists and to their popularity with the readers. Different and contradictory views, such as that the U.S. tries to exploit Turkey for its interests on the international level and that Turkey benefits from this alliance, are all reflected. In other words, the paradox between what Chomsky and Herman (1979, ix) call "facts" and "beliefs" in the perception of the United States are displayed.

Since it is mostly crises in political, economic, and social relations with the U.S. that evoke cartoons, through the images their effects on Turkey can be traced. The American interest in Turkey has been depicted by Abramovitz (181), the former American ambassador to Turkey, "as maintaining a democratic Muslim country in an area of turbulence, poverty, and religious radicalism." How this interest has been perceived by the Turks can best be traced in the political cartoons. The so-called "third generation"—the leftist radical—political cartoonists have a mission on behalf of a democratic, independent, and secular country and a mission to counterbalance "cultural imperialism" and display the "facts." Thus, cartoons have dealt with the relationships in terms of:

1. *internal affairs*: the involvement of U.S. officials in internal Turkish affairs is resented by the cartoonists. They defend the "independence of the country"—rejecting aid and military aid, arguing that interdependence requires both countries to be independent, questioning Turkey's independence, and warning not to rely on superpowers;

2. *international peace in the world*: they criticize hypocrisy and the sale of weapons; and

3. *"cultural imperialism"*; they are against the use of English as an outlet of superpower domination.

For the some of the "new generation" cartoonists, since the U.S. is a nation, both countries need to protect their interests—each working to exploit the other for its own interests.

In conclusion, in the 1960s and 1970s, the response of the political cartoonists to the U.S. was the creation of the "ugly American" image, which reflected internal turmoil and the dependence on a developed country through debt. The Cyprus problem in the mid-1970s led to criticism of the U.S. in the international arena. In the 1980s and 1990s, the U.S. policy in the Gulf War, the war in Bosnia, and, on the economic level, the protectionist barriers that prevent Third World countries from exploiting their advantages have been criticized. In the "new world order," "Uncle Sam" is depicted as a giant holding the world in his arms or as a "cowboy" sitting on top of the world. In the 1990s, the U.S. has also been depicted as sending Turkey leaders, or giving shelter to those who can pay for it. One editorial cartoonist, however, has turned the biting image of the "ugly American" into a milder one by using English words and by depicting the image of an "Americanized" Turkey.

References

Abramowitz, M.I. (1993, Summer). Dateline Ankara: Turkey After Özal. *Foreign Policy*, 91: pp.164–181.

Al-Hajji, M.N., and J. Nelson. (1995). American students' perception of Arabs in political cartoons. In Y.R. Kamalipour. (Ed.), *The U.S. media and the Middle East: Image and perception*. Westport: Greenwood.

Balcioğlu, S. (1994). *Galeri Çiller*. Istanbul: Kaynak.

Barkey, H. (1992, September). Turkish American relations in the post-war era: An alliance of convenience. *Orient* 33, pp. 447–464.

Bjersted, A.; J:P. Jensen; S. Keldorf; O. Melnikova; R. Wahlström. (1991). *Enemy images among university students in four countries*. (Report published as a handbook) Denmark.

Bozer, A. (1990). Turkish foreign policy in the changing world. *Mediterranean Quarterly*: pp.15–25.

Çeçrn, A.S. Dooꞌruel, and F. Dooꞌruel. (1994). Economic growth and structural change in Turkey (1960–88). *International Journal of Middle East Studies*: pp. 37–56.

Çeviker, T. (1995). Interview with Turhan Selçuk in *Güldiken*.

Chomsky, N., and E.S. Herman (1979). *The Washington connection and Third World Fascism*. Boston: South End Press.

Chomsky, N. (1969). *American Power and the New Mandarins*. New York: Pantheon Books.

Dennis, E.E. (1974). The regeneration of political cartooning. *Journalism Quarterly*, pp. 51, 66.

Dooꞌan, F. (1969). *Çizgili Dunya: Karikatürler*. Istanbul: Ant.

Eberhard, D. (1993, January). Propaganda and caricature in the first world war. *Journal of Contemporary History*, 28: pp. 163–193.

Eren, N. (1959). *Of the world*. Istanbul.

Fast, J. (1991). *Turkish American relations*. Washington, D.C.: Wilson Publishing.

Galtung, J. (1992). Supra-nationalism. Paper presented at London University.

George, D.M. (1959). *English Political Caricature* Vols. 1–2: London: Oxford University Press.

Gumpert, G., and R. Cathcart. (1988). Media stereotyping: Images of the foreigner. Paper presented at the Conference of the IAMCR, Barcelona, Spain, pp. 500–520.

Güldiken Journal of Humorous culture: The World of Turhan Selçuk. (1995). Istanbul.

Gordon, C.D. (1989). *Images of the West*. New York: Rowman & Littlefield Publishers.

Kahveci, A. (1991). American foreign policy: A Turkish view. In G. Schmergel (Ed.), *US Foreign Policy in the 1990s*. London: Macmillan.

Kamalipour, Y.R. (Ed.). (1995). *The U.S. media and the Middle East: Image and perception*. Westport: Greenwood.

King, N. (1991). *A Cartoon History of United States Foreign Policy*. New York: Pharos Books.

Koraman, B. (1995). Interview in *Elit*. 1(2).

Hess, S., and Kaplan, M. (1968, 1975). *The history of American political cartoons: The ungentlemanly art*. New York: MacMillan.

MacArthur, B. (1990, July 22). When political cartoons are no laughing matter. *Times Newspaper Limited* [electronic search].

Mango, A. (1975). *TURKEY: A delicately poised ally*. London: Sage.

McBride, S. (Ed.). (1980). *Many voices, one world: Communication and society today and tomorrow*. London: unipub/Unesco.

McGhee, G. (1990). *The US-Turkish-NATO Middle East connection*. New York: St. Martin's Press.

Memecan, S. (1995). *BizimCity*. Istanbul: Mart.

Nesin, A. (1973). *Cumhuriyet Döneminde Türk Mizahi*. Istanbul: Yelken.

Oral, T. (1993). Karikatür. *Güldiken*, No. 1: pp. 46–53.

Palmer, A. (1995). The Arab image in newspaper political cartoons. In Y.R. Kamalipour. (Ed.) *The U.S. media and the Middle East: Image and perception*. Westport: Greenwood.

Platt, S. (1994, March 18). The right to be offensive: Political cartoonists and political correctness. *New Statesman & Society* 7: p. 294.

Schiller, H.I. (1976). *Communication and cultural domination*. White Plains: International Arts and Sciences Press.

Schiller, H.I. (1992). *Mass communication and American empire*, 2nd ed. Bolder: Westview Press.

Selçuk, T. (1995). *InsanHaklari/Human Rights*. Ankara: Turkish Ministry of Culture.

Selçuk, I. (1995). Enlightenment of caricature. *InsanHaklari/Human Rights*. Ankara: Turkish Ministry of Culture.

Tayie, S. (1988). Influence of mass media in forming foreign images of young Egyptians of foreigners and foreign countries. Paper presented at IAMCR Conference, Barcelona, Spain.

Ulvi, A. (1995, October 16). Interview in *Cumnuriyet*, p. 14.

Wahlström, R. (1989). *Enemy Images and Peace Education*. Malmö, Sweden: School of Education, No. 660.

8

Mass Media and the U.S. Image

An Algerian Perspective

LAID ZAGHLAMI

Introduction

The U.S. image and its perception in the Algerian media should be considered in light of the historical, economic, political, and cultural dimensions of relations between Algeria and the United States. This chapter briefly highlights several major national, regional, and international events as the basis for assessing their impact on the Algerian mass media and on people's perception of the U.S. Clearly, the media as a vehicle for education, information, and entertainment exert a great deal of influence on the general public. Before the Algerian parliament's adoption of the Information Act in 1990, the media were an intrinsic part of the political system. Thus, the media were heavily dependent on the authorities' instructions and rules, which were ultimately reflected in the U.S. portrayal—always in tune with the nature and evolution of the bilateral relations, which were defined by Algerian officials, the presidency, and the foreign ministry.

As U.S.-Algerian relations went through periods of friendship, denunciation, sometimes condemnation, to sympathy and fascination, the media were poised to adapt political messages and discourses accordingly. In the eighteenth century, Algeria developed a cordial relationship with the U.S., partly because of Algeria's geo-strategic position and notably because of its strong maritime fleet. In modern times, as international politics and priorities have shifted from the Cold War era to a New World Order, relations between the two countries have been generally turbulent.

Since the Algerian independence in 1962, many events in the world have prompted the U.S. and Algeria to pursue different policies and strategies. Further, some turning points in their mutual relations have strategically forced each side to adopt opposing and often contradictory principles and guidelines in their foreign policy. Consequently, these shifts have contributed to the ways in which the Algerian media have covered the U.S. in different periods.

Four main periods have characterized the Algerian media's evolution and editorial policy: (1) The 1960s, during the Algerian revolution, leading to independence from France, and its positive echo worldwide; (2) The 1970s, when Algeria opted for socialism and distanced itself, on political grounds, from the U.S. by joining the international socialist movement; (3) The 1980s, when Algeria began to implement a democratization process which ignited a new era in its political structure and led to the liberalization of its economy; and (4) The 1990s, when the democratization process was constituted and a free market economy was realized.

The 1960s: The American Friendship

The 1962 independence brought with it sympathy and support from the U.S. and elsewhere. Even before that, the U.S. had wholeheartedly supported the Algerian cause. In fact, President John F. Kennedy openly supported the Algerian people's struggle for gaining self-determination. He demonstrated his expressed admiration for independence by providing economic support through consistent humanitarian aid and political backing in United Nations debates. Along the same line, Redha Malek (1995) stated that few people would deny the international impact of the Algerian revolution throughout the world. Obviously, Algerian media appreciated the U.S. position and attitudes toward events in Algeria. Hence, many reports emphasized the Americans' role during the revolutionary period. Following the independence, Ahmed Benbella, who was elected President, paid a visit to the U.S. He was cheerfully greeted as the first head of the newly independent Algeria. He even received a red carpet welcome in Washington, D.C. Diplomats and journalists who accompanied him would not forget that memorable visit and the warmest greetings that they received from President Kennedy and his staff. Accordingly, media reports in Algeria were highly positive and enthusiastic about the atmosphere that had prevailed during the visit. They even praised the close relationship that Algeria was forging with the U.S.

However, on his return trip from U.S. to Algeria, Ahmed Benbella unexpectedly stopped in Cuba and met with Fidel Castro. This presented a problem in that Castro had forged an alliance with the Soviet Union and, furthermore, Havana was in a state of hostility with Washington, exemplified by the missile crisis and the Bay of Pigs invasion. That stopover in Cuba was, of course, seen by the White House as slap in the face and a clear indication of Algerian support for the Cuban side in the conflict with Washington.

Undoubtedly, the Algerian president revealed his true political intentions to the While House when he embraced socialist values and ideology. His frequent subsequent visits and meetings with leaders and politicians from socialist regimes confirmed his intentions as well as the United States' apprehensions. President Benbella infuriated U.S. officials, as they could hardly understand the logic of that "undiplomatic gesture"!

Ultimately, the brief honeymoon spirit between the two countries faded away. The U.S.-Algerian relation was headed for turbulence, as was later confirmed when President Houari Boumediene came to power in 1965. The country opted for socialism, and consequently political relations assumed a low profile. However, economic trade, especially the flow of petroleum, with the U.S. continued.

The 1970s: U.S. Imperialism

World events in the mid-1960s and 1970s brought to both countries a great deal of misunderstanding and further tension. Two conflicts took place in the Middle East that heightened tensions between the U.S. and Algeria: the Arab-Israeli war in 1967, and the Arab-Israeli war in 1973. Hence, the U.S. and Algeria adopted strong opposition by favoring one or the other side of the warring factions: Washington supported Israel as its ally in the region. Algeria, as part of the Arab world, naturally supported the Palestinians and the other Arab countries, both militarily and otherwise, during both wars. At the same time, the U.S. established an arms agreement with Israel and armed it to the teeth (Saadi 1974).

Furthermore, Algiers hosted the 1973 non-aligned movement summit, where more than seventy-five heads of state and government attended. Washington perceived the summit as a hostile gathering and opposed its world policy (Malley 1973). At the economic level, the 1973 world oil crisis again put both countries at cross purposes. In 1974, mutual mistrust between the two nations reached its peak level when President Boumediene gave a speech at the United Nations calling for a new economic world order, based on mutual respect and cooperation between developing and developed countries. Once more, Washington disagreed with the Algerian president's demands.

The 1970s is also remembered for the Vietnam war and the heavy involvement of the U.S. in the bombing and killing of many Vietnamese. That war was a prominent issue in the Algerian media. The media reported that the inhabitants of Belghimouze, a village built during the heyday of socialism, "condemn(ed) with virulence the U.S. imperialism and call(ed) for the withdrawal of its forces." Slogans such as "Yankee Go Home," "Imperialist Uncle

Sam," and so on were expressed in the national media rhetoric as well as in political discourse. Sit ins and demonstrations were held to denounce the imperialistic policy of the U.S. and its involvement in Vietnam.

The 1980s: Rapprochement Policy

In 1981, Algeria played a crucial role in the release of American hostages in Iran. The Algerian Minister of Foreign Affairs and the Ambassador to the United Nations were at the heart of the negotiation process. Algerian diplomacy finally succeeded in releasing the U.S. hostages. Subsequently, in many American cities, there were scenes of jubilation, congratulations, and acknowledgments of the Algerian deed.

Nevertheless, successive events once again prevented the U.S. and Algeria from promoting friendly relations. In 1980, Iraq invaded Iran, sparking an eight-year war. Two years later, Israel invaded Lebanon. In both cases, the U.S. and Algeria opted for different and often opposing policies. Relations worsened when President Ronald Reagan ordered the bombing of Libya in 1986.

In 1986, the first attempts were made to revise some of the socialist principles, in the National Constitution, which were approved massively in 1976. Such attempts gradually led to political and social reforms and paved the way for the liberalization of the economy. Once again, Algeria experienced a complete turnaround in national politics and in its culture of public service ownership.

After the liberalization movement, history repeated itself, and President Chadli Bendjedid, who came into power in 1978, traveled to the U.S. and met with President Reagan, twenty-five years after the first visit by Benbella. Later, Vice President George Bush paid an official visit to Algeria. Criticism emerged in a few media about the visit, as he was the former director of the "cynical" Central Intelligence Agency (Djabri 1986). Coverage of Chadli's visit to the U.S. likewise brought anger and outcry from ordinary people who were apparently inspired by some critical articles in the Algerian media. Strikes and riots occurred in the historic patrimony of the Casbah. Slogans such as "Chadli in USA while people live in the caves" were cried out by the socialist old guard and leftists who were utterly opposed to any kind of rapprochement with Washington.

Externally, intensive contacts with the U.S. after Chadli's visit irritated Paris. French officials were uneasy about the prospect of Algeria falling into the "Hands of the American Imperialist Ghost" (Laurent 1995). They considered these contacts as threats to their presence in the Maghrib region and particularly in Algeria. The French have always viewed the Maghrib area as their sphere of influence. One French official from the Ministry of Culture on a visit to Algeria offered free French programs to Algerian TV, in an attempt to counter the British and American cultural influence (Ministry of Culture 1982).

The 1990s: Pragmatism and Realism

Generally speaking, the 1990s prompted more sympathetic and amicable attitudes toward the U.S. Many books were imported by American authors such as William Faulkner and Ernest Hemingway, as well as more modern writers. Books on the U.S. political system, society, trade unions, and culture became available at competitive prices. Literature on liberalization and free market economy gained popularity in Algeria. The national media that had fiercely opposed "American imperialism" gradually changed their tune, parallel to the government's policies, by using moderate, even friendly terms in their coverage of the U.S. The new rhetoric includes such phrases as "American dream," "American way of life," and "the land of opportunity"!

Official contacts are encouraged by both countries. In fact, the U.S. Information Office provides facilities and services in Algeria for teaching English, promoting exchange programs, and organizing visits by U.S. diplomats, scholars, and parliamentarians to lecture on a wide range of topics, through WorldNet facilities. On the other hand, many Algerian journalists, artists, scholars, managers, and diplomats attend or participate in conferences, video conferences, and the celebration of U.S. independence that take place in the U.S. or Algeria.

U.S. Image at Owners' and Editors' Mercy

With regard to media coverage and the Algerian perception of the U.S., it is important to mention that the 1989 Constitution paved the way for a multiparty system. Although the print media (newspapers and magazines) are both publicly and privately owned, the electronic media (radio and television) remain in the hands of the Algerian government. Hence, despite heavy pressures, including assassination threats and financial constraints, the print media have managed to sustain a great deal of impartiality and freedom. Radio and TV, on the other hand, are often criticized by various factions for their lack of democratic access and impartiality in their news reports and debates (Zaghlami 1993).

Consequently, the political orientation, interest, editorial policy, and ownership of mass media in Algeria influence the way(s) in which they portray America. This was apparent during the Gulf war when the print media could generally cover the war from different perspectives, whereas, the TV awaited authorities' instructions before airing its newscasts. The radio, on the other hand, seemed to be more impartial and less constrained in its coverage of the war.

Public pressure, nonetheless, forced television to report the events more accurately despite some opposition from the government, who had called for the use of "moderate and impartial terms" in covering the Gulf war. In reality, some journalists from the public media found it hard to report the events on a professional basis. This was partially because they were not allowed to report freely and partially because they were accustomed to following governmental instructions.

Sequels Die Hard

It is quite clear that previous experiences and precedents established during the socialist era still exert some influence on the way(s) in which the Algerian media cover national and international events. For instance, in the 1970s and 1980s, the Algerian media were in perfect harmony with the socialist rhetoric. This meant that they had to portray the U.S. in a negative and sometimes sarcastic manner. A great amount of demagoguery, manipulation, and misinformation were used in concert with political discourses. Hence, to some extent, the sequel continues, in terms of media coverage of the U.S.

In the meantime, despite negative media rhetoric, economic trade, student exchange programs, and cultural exchanges between Algeria and the U.S. have increased tremendously in recent years. Many U.S. teachers have joined several high schools and universities to teach English and American literature and civilization. In fact, the Institute of English at the University of Algiers has set up a permanent cooperative program with American scholars and universities. In view of these developments, it is not a coincidence that Bencherif Benosmane, a former professor of American culture and civilization at Algiers University, was appointed Algerian Ambassador to Washington, in 1995.

Politically at Crossroads

As illustrated earlier, political events in the Middle East, Africa, South America, and elsewhere have at times positioned the U.S. and Algeria at a turning point. The Algerian media have accordingly reflected the prevailing political mood of the country relative to the political relations between the U.S. and Algeria. In other words, the media appear to be in tune with the prevailing views of those in power.

U.S. Movies

In the 1970s, many Algerian movies were produced, and the majority of them dealt with the Algerian revolution and its bloody fight with the French. Hence, it was politically inappropriate to import or air U.S. media products that would contradict the spirit of that period. Algerian TV, however, often showed films from India, socialist countries, and Arab nations as they were in concert with the prevailing values and political ideology of the socialist regime.

In the 1980s and 1990s, as a new democratic era emerged in Algeria, many Hollywood films were imported and shown in movie theaters or on television. For instance, in 1987, 262 movies were imported from Franc, of which about 80 percent were produced by U.S. companies based in Paris. In 1993, more than 25 percent of Algerian television programs were of Western origin, particularly American, including films, soap operas, serials, documentaries, and special reports. For instance, of the 1,048 hours of film shown on television, 750 hours were U.S. films. By 1994, more than 28 percent of the programs aired on Algerian TV were produced by Western countries (Djezairi 1995). In October 1995, Algerian TV broadcast seventy-six hours of U.S.-produced movies, twenty-five hours of films produced in Arab countries, and only three hours of films produced in Algeria. It broadcast nearly thirty-five hours of soap operas produced in Arab countries, twenty-two hours of soaps produced in Western countries, including the U.S., and only 4.5 hours produced in Algeria. Music features broadcast consisted of twenty-three hours Western, twenty-two hours Arabic, and fifty-four hours Algerian (Algerian National TV Enterprise 1995). Overall, in October 1995, Western motion picture productions, aired on Algerian TV, comprised about 22 percent, while entertainment (e.g., features, soaps, music, quiz shows) counted for about 39 percent of the total programming schedule.

The Impact of American Soap Operas

The impact and contribution of the U.S.-produced media products are quite visible in Algeria. Algerian TV broadcasts many popular American series, including *Dallas*, *Miami Vice*, *The Cosby Show*, *Golden Girls*, *L. A. Law*, *M*A*S*H*, and *Mission Impossible*, *Starsky and Hutch*, and *Invaders*. Many of these series have been repeatedly shown on Algerian TV. Likewise, the Algerian movie theaters schedule many Hollywood pictures on a regular basis.

Consequently, Hollywood celebrities such as Michael Douglas, Michael Jackson, Madonna, Clint Eastwood, Arnold Schawarzeneger, Lee Marvin, John Wayne, Elizabeth Taylor, Silvester Stallone, and other American movie and music stars have acquired many admirers in Algeria, particularly among the younger generation. It is also believed that American soaps and films have influenced Algerian viewers' way of life. Many youths have adopted Western styles of clothing, haircuts, and behavior. These influences are quite visible in the streets of the major cities in Algeria. Furthermore, the impact of American soaps has been such that some Algerian cities have been nicknamed

Dallas and Miami, in direct connection with the two television series, *Dallas* and *Miami Vice*.

It should, however, be noted that formal "media research and broadcast ratings services on public opinion and audience analysis have not yet been launched. Hence, the Algerian television, radio, and print media lack substantial information concerning public opinion and public attitudes" (Zaghlami 1995).

American-Algerian Relations

As explained earlier, since the 1980s, the U.S. image in the Algerian media has gradually shifted from a "hostile imperialistic power" to a more friendly country. The success of Algerian diplomacy in securing the release of American hostages, and, later, the visit of President Chadli to Washington, paved the road to improved U.S.-Algerian relations. In parallel with the establishment of political and economic ties, U.S. portrayal in Algerian mass media has also gradually become more positive.

The U.S. embassy in Algiers has played an active role in bringing relations between the two countries to the acceptable level of friendship and cooperation. For instance, U.S. ambassador Christopher Ross was successful in establishing personal ties with many Algerian officials and diplomats who were interested in Anglo-Saxon culture. His successor, Anne Mary Casey, who speaks Arabic fluently, continued that policy and succeeded, in concert with Algerian officials, in revising the negative and aggressive tone of the press relative to the U.S. to a more friendly and amicable one.

Of course, many political changes in the 1990s, including the collapse of the Soviet Union, the end of the Cold War, the fall of the Berlin Wall, and the revised geopolitical world map have had direct effects on the political, economic, and cultural aspects of Algerian society and the development of a mutually productive relationship with the U.S.

In addition to establishing of a host of educational, cultural, and scientific links between the U.S. and Algeria, the WorldNet facilities in the U.S. embassy are available to Algerian journalists for producing a variety of TV programs or partaking in worldwide video conferences with American media experts, politicians, and scholars.

In the meantime, economic and political reforms were introduced by Algerian Prime Minister Abdelhamid Brahimi, who was educated at American universities. He put in motion, despite fierce opposition from trade unions and the old guard within the government and the National Liberation Front party, a reconstruction process to revive the ailing national economy. While in power, he was successful in revising many socialistic and dogmatic principles, reducing the omnipotence of the trade unions, and lowering public spending. In fact, these changes were made with the support and approval of some editors in the media who advocated a new discourse. A weekly newspaper *Alg,Àrie Actualit,Às*, in 1986, supported the political reforms, by depicting the errors, damages, and hardships that socialism had brought to the country, and by praising liberal and pragmatic views. Furthermore, during 1986 and 1988, scenes of violence and riots in many Algerian cities were routinely shown on national television, affirming that political and economic reforms were needed. Eventually, the internal pressures and global shifts compelled the Algerian government to discard socialism in favor of capitalism and a multiparty system.

Not only are Western values depicted in the media, but people are encouraged to form new consumption habits, which are thought to have relaxed some of the economic barriers related to foreign trade and state monopoly. In this new political climate, Algerian media portray the U.S. as the strongest driving force in world affairs.

UPI, AP, VOA, and the *Herald Tribune*

The presence of U.S. media correspondents in Algeria from United Press International (UPI), and the Associated Press (AP) has also helped to improve the image of the U.S. The international daily, *Herald Tribune*, is also available and has published many reports about Algeria. The Voice of America (VOA), with its powerful transmitters in Dakar (Senegal), which is heard clearly in Algeria and the entire Maghrib region, further contributes to the prevailing perception of the U.S. in Algeria. Many Algerians listen to VOA, particularly the Arabic program, consisting of features about the region, special reports, news, music, and interviews with Algerian officials and members of the opposition. On the other hand, the United States Information Service in Algeria provides journalists and scholars with adequate literature, books, magazines, audio and video tapes about the U.S. It also distributes many scientific and cultural programs to Algerian Radio and TV for broadcasting. Hence, these media services and products along with the domestic media form the basis for the image and portrayal of the U.S. in Algeria.

Conclusion

At both domestic and global levels, mass media exert a great deal of influence in forming people's perceptions of themselves and of other cultures. As illustrated in this essay, media in developing countries such as Algeria tend to reflect the political and cultural forces that are operative in certain time periods. Hence, several elements including political ideology, domestic conditions, economics, and external relations with other countries contribute to what people read, see, or hear via their domestic communication media. In recent years, despite domestic unrest and censorship, Algerian print media have secured for themselves a great deal of liberty and autonomy relative to earlier periods when the prevailing political ideology was socialism. They provide a forum for the expression of opinions, thereby not only contributing to the society as a whole but fostering a more free atmosphere. In some cases, they have managed to disclose and report cases of corruption, wrongdoing, and mismanagement.

In terms of U.S. portrayal, the print media in Algeria have succeeded in presenting different perspectives relative to U.S. foreign policy and its global strategy. The diversity of these reports allows Algerians to gain a better understanding of the U.S. and form a more accurate perception of it. Clearly, any perception or misperception of the U.S. largely depends on the nature of the media coverage, including commentaries, visual presentations, editorials, and factual information. For instance, during recent domestic unrest in Algeria, some newspapers were critical of the U.S. policy *vis-à-vis* offering political asylum to the Islamic Salvation Front's (FIS) representatives. Other newspapers praised the U.S. policy relative to cutting its support to the Algerian authorities. In general, there continued to be many both positive and negative reports about the U.S. and its policies toward Algeria. Ultimately, Algerians' perception of the U.S. will continue to fluctuate as it has in the past decades and will not be necessarily uniform at any given time. In addition to the mass media, culture, education, religion, language, age, sex, social position, and conditions influence public perception or misperception of the United States.

References

Algerian National TV Enterprise. (1995, October). Statistic and Analysis Department. Algiers.

Djabri, A. (1986, November 24). Le President Chadli Benjedid a Washington. *Revolution et Travail* 786: pp. 28–30.

Djezairi, R. (1995, December 17). Programmes TV, Statistiques et Analyses. *The Horizons*: pp. 6–8.

Djezairi, R. (1995, May 12). La Politique de l'Information. *The Horizons*: pp. 3–14.

Laurent, E. (1995, May). La Politique US au Maghreb. *Esprit Libre* 25: pp. 12–22.

Malek, R. (1995, December). Debates in Geneva on his book *l'Alg, Àrie . . . À Evian*. Algiers.

Malley, S. (1973, September 12). l'Imperialisme US dans le Monde. *Afrique Asie* 1245: pp. 23–28.

Ministry of Culture. (1982, September). Talks between Algerian and French officials on bilateral cultural policy. Algiers.

Saadi, M. (1974, May 23). Les Mesaventures de l'Oncle Sam. *Revolution Africaine* 1384: pp. 24–26.

Zaghlami, L. (1993, October 13). Pouvoir et Contre-Pouvoir des des Medias. *The El Watan*: pp. 12–15.

Zaghlami, L. (1995, December 18). Redha Malek: Aux Origines de la Revolution. *The El Watan*: pp. 7–8.

Part III

U.S. Image and the Cultural Factor

Cultural factors play a crucial role in practically every aspect of our daily lives; hence, any analysis of communication processes, or image studies, must take these factors into consideration. In addition to political factors, values, beliefs, traditions, and an assortment of cultural artifacts can also influence people's perception of other nations. In this section, authors focus on the cultural factors that impact U.S. image abroad. Robert M. McKenzie presents a study analyzing perceptions of a group of American students who took a three-week college class in France, and a group of French students' perception of America. Allen W. Palmer and Tom Hafen explore the ways in which German adolescents use American television programs as a social resource in their lives and reconstruct the meanings of these programs in the context of their own culture. Jane Stokes examines the U.S. image and representation of American culture in British television advertisements, and explains how images of America are used to construct an "Americanicity" that is unique to British imagination. Sherry Devereaux Ferguson, Hilary Horan, and Alexander Ferguson explore Canadian impressions of the U.S. within the ongoing debate over the "Americanization" of Canada. Drawing on value studies by social psychologists, the authors focus on American values, Canadian values, and the consistency between American and Canadian self-perception. Alex Fernando Teixeira Primo explores Brazilian's perception of the U.S., based on a public opinion survey, and explains the ways in which the Brazilian mass media portray the U.S. Peggy Bieber-Roberts and Pauline Abela focus on Malta's mass media and their impact on the Maltese perception of the U.S. Udita Das examines the influence of American cultural products on the Indian youth on the basis of a selected sample of advertisements, films, and video programs. Finally, Ersu Ding examines portrayals of the U.S. on Chinese prime-time television.

115

9

Images of the U.S. as Perceived by U.S. Students in France

ROBERT M. MCKENZIE

Introduction

Have you ever travelled to another country for your Spring Break? Or have you ever taken a vacation with your family or friends to another country? If you have, by the end of your trip, after watching TV or reading a newspaper in that country, did you end up learning—perhaps not intentionally—a lot of things about your own country?

This chapter explores the idea that media in another country can teach you about your own country. Furthermore, this chapter offers a twist to the study of *Images of the U.S. around the World*, the focus of this book. The chapter is a study not only of U.S. images as perceived by U.S. students, but of students using media in a "foreign" environment in France. Data for this chapter came from the students' own words describing their exposure to media in France during a three-week college course called Comparative Media, which I taught in July 1995 at the University of Nancy in Nancy, France. The city of Nancy has a population of approximately 350,000 people, and is located approximately three hours due east of Paris by bus.

Unfortunately, media research projects of an international nature have, on the whole, neglected France as a primary site of investigation, even though France has high visibility in international relations, and a uniquely blended mix of government-funded and commercially-sponsored media. Instead, the literature on international media studies tends to polarize and juxtapose the media studied as capitalist versus communist (or totalitarian) media. I have argued elsewhere that we need to heighten our awareness of the ways in which media, both domestic and foreign, shape our perceptions of all the countries of the world—and especially of those countries we have never visited (McKenzie 1994; see also Ball-Rokeach and DeFleur 1976). No doubt, we are living in a world where ignorance about other nations is being eradicated through society's increasing exposure to other countries and cultures of the world, primarily through the lens of cable and satellite TV programs. Random examples just of U.S. television shows furnishing us with images of foreigners and foreign lands include MTV's *The Real World* (the one set in London), CNN's *Worldview* news, and many of the programs on the Arts and Entertainment (A&E) cable channel. In examining how foreign media convey a country's images, we gain the advantage of looking at domestic culture from the outside in.

This chapter tracks the perceptions of a group of U.S. students in France as those perceptions evolved over the course of their stay in France. At the outset of the study, I posed the question, "How are the U.S. students' perceptions of U.S. imagery reinforced, challenged, enlightened by their exposure to media in France?" In addressing this question, the chapter should disclose some of the texture in social and political relations between France and the United States, and provide an insight into what it is like to break out of home-country perceptions shaped exclusively by home-media coverage.

I have divided the rest of this chapter into four sections. In the first section, I select literature from the field of *Cultural Studies* to put together a theoretical framework and methodology for guiding the study. In the second section, I present *Situational Information* about the study to help contextualize the interpretations I present immediately thereafter. In the third section, I analyze *Perceptions of Images* offered by the students in response to questions I asked them about images of the U.S. that they perceived as coming through the media they used in France. And finally, in the last section I return to *Cultural Studies* to speculate upon larger *Implications* for society and the involvement of media in the formation of our world perceptions.

Cultural Studies

To the academic community, the phrase Cultural Studies means a wide variety of subject matters and methodologies related to the study of meaning arising from the mundane practices of everyday life (Nelson, Treichler, and Grossberg 1992). In this study, however, Cultural Studies is used to refer to that body of literature concerned with unfurling insights into the images of a "culture's way of life" (see Thompson, Ellis, and Wildavsky 1990). Moreover, the Cultural Studies literature I draw from is used to generate concepts related to media use, which in turn are applied to yield insight into the role of media in the formation of images of the U.S. (see also James 1995).

Thus, my use of Cultural Studies in this chapter represents only a basic application in a particular situation. As such, the chapter does not adequately present the finer fissures in the debates that surround this increasingly popular but uneven mode of academic inquiry. To describe the essence of the debate, the literature called Cultural Studies is split into two somewhat disparate schools of thought, each of which emphasizes a different underlying cultural structure that serves to configure meaning for the nation, the culture, the community, or the individual. One school of thought, that of political economy, focuses on inegalitarian economic symbolic structures that create a class system as the dominating influence on lifestyle and beliefs (Garnham 1995). The other school of thought, that of social identity, focuses on identity (race and gender, for example) as the dominating influence on lifestyle and beliefs (Grossberg 1995). Despite their disparate emphases on dominating influences, both the political economy approach and the social identity approach seek to critique and repudiate existing power structures that control the making of meaning. Moreover, cultural studies normally include a substantial component of analysis on mass media because of the media's pivotal role in hosting and directing the making of meaning in the public sphere (Murdock 1995).

In order to investigate this divide in Cultural Studies further, I refer the reader to an issue of *Critical Studies in Mass Communication* (1995, Volume 12, Number 1), which presents a colloquy of fiery debating articles between leading scholars about the accomplishments and shortfalls of Cultural Studies thus far and how they should proceed in the future. Also, I refer readers to a book titled *Cultural Studies* (edited by Grossberg, Nelson, and Treichler 1992), which offers a large collection of articles from prominent scholars applying, critiquing, and theorizing about cultural studies in a variety of contexts. Beyond these two sources, their bibliographies should lead to other works that have been published over the last thirty years or so in the expansive field of Cultural Studies.

The use of a cultural studies framework in this study is derived from a political economy approach designed to point the analysis to economic symbolism woven throughout the students' reactions to U.S. imagery presented by the media they used in France. For the analysis, the framework makes use of three central terms of cultural studies theory: *false consciousness, articulation*, and *change*. *False consciousness*, originally a term of cultural critique in Marxist theory, has been transformed to mean the assumptions we hold about life without knowing that we hold them—moreover, assumptions that lead us to form ideology about whatever aspects of life we are considering (Hall 1985). Ideology is a particular way of seeing the world, and an ultimate evaluation about whether a social practice is good or bad.

Garnham maintains that false consciousness is the way in which "our relations to social reality are mediated" (1995, 68). The idea that our relations are mediated at all offers the curious proposition that experience can precede observation. Moreover, it raises the question of why we should accept an ironic phrase initiated by the word *false*, a term that in most other circumstances would sound rather insulting. This is a question that Garnham addresses:

> Once one accepts the idea that on the one hand, our relations to social reality are mediated via systems of symbolic representation and, on the other hand, that we live within structures of domination—the mechanisms and effects of which are not immediately available to experience—then a concept like false consciousness becomes necessary. (1995, 68)

Put simply, when mass media come between us and the actual events we learn about, we are vulnerable to hidden assumptions we have no way of identifying. Moreover, assumptions related to imagery of foreign countries are especially stealthy because we typically are not able in our daily routines to compare those media messages with TV and radio programs of another country's media. Therefore, in this study, an analysis of false consciousness is used to disclose and explain the students' assumptions that lie behind the perceptions that they themselves describe.

The disclosure of false consciousness in Cultural Studies is arrived at through the process of *articulation*, our second theoretical term of analysis. Articulation is capturing in words the relationship between a dominant social structure and an individual's lifestyle and beliefs (Grossberg 1995); it is the piecing together of parts of a highly textured collage of government, economy, media use, and social identity into an analysis of "meaning making."

The practice of articulation involves a quirky concession that any social structure "constrains and oppresses the people, but at the same time offers them resources to fight against the constraints" (Fiske 1992, 157). In this study, I articulate how the students' perceptions are related mainly to the students' social structures of their national identity, their normal patterns of media use, and their French language capabilities. My articulation of these components is meant to reveal how the U.S.-dominant social structures "back home" for the students ended up clashing with images of the U.S. abroad invoked by experiences of media in a French social structure. In the analysis I invoke a concept of "cultural myopia" to explain some of the perceptions of U.S. imagery. I believe the concept of cultural myopia demonstrates how a way of life in a particular culture can be tethered to not-so-obvious assumptions about the self-evident virtues of certain cultural practices, some of them more complex (foreign policy toward another country, for example), some of them less complex (barbecuing on the 4th of July, the U.S. Independence Day, for example). Cultural practices include how we as a culture watch TV and use other media, and how our media use contributes to our formations of self-identity associated with the national (home) culture. Therefore, to articulate perceptions of U.S. imagery arising from the students' use of media in France, as well as the assumptions that those perceptions reveal, is to chart a strategy for resisting hasty conclusions unchecked against foreign experiences and media use, conclusions about merits of the way of life in our national culture.

This articulation strategy revolves around the concept of *change*, the third and final term of cultural studies theory used in the analysis in this chapter. Specifically, change in opinion about U.S. imagery is how the concept will be operationalized for this study. Change in opinion results from the "cumulative impact of successive anomalies or surprises" (Thompson, Ellis, and Wildavsky 1990, 69). In this study, when the analysis of data showed that the students were surprised, those reactions were treated as potential changes in awareness, opinion, and ultimately, assumption.

To assess the cumulative impact of surprises on the students, as well as the changes in their thoughts about U.S. images, I designed a methodology that involved the students in four data-gathering exercises spread out over the duration of the course. First, on the airplane trip to Paris, I had the students fill out a *questionnaire* asking them about their usual media habits in the U.S., their previous travel experience, and what images of the U.S. they guessed might be present in France. Then after a week in France, I assigned the students an *essay* in which they were required to react to French TV news and French newspapers. Then after two weeks in France, I conducted a *private interview* with each student according to a six-question protocol, which I recorded on cassette tape, transcribed on computer, and then printed out for analysis. Lastly, after three weeks in France, I collected *journals* from the students in which they were asked to record on a daily basis their reactions to U.S. images mainly on television shows, billboards, magazine covers, newspaper headlines, and radio songs, all of which they experienced not only in Nancy but other places around France as well. These four exercises were handled incrementally over the duration of the course in order to render the evolution of the students' changes toward their understandings of their national culture's imagery. In the analysis of each exercise, my overriding goal was to let the students tell in their own words their perceptions of U.S. images in media in France, while using our three terms as theoretical guideposts for analyzing the students' thoughts.

Situational Information

An important feature of Cultural Studies is the provision that the researcher may involve him or herself in the collection of data as a participant-observer: one who both collects the data, and who participates with the subjects supplying the data in their way of life (Clifford 1992; Fiske 1992). The particular advantage of conducting a study as a participant-observer is that the situations being analyzed can be contextualized with subtleties not accessible through more detached-researcher roles. One can argue that conducting a cultural study as a participant-observer is paramount to detailing the inner workings of human relations. However, only if the researcher reveals his or her potentially relevant biases, and only if the closeness of the researcher to the subjects of study is presented accurately, will the overall analysis be meaningful (James 1995). Accordingly, I offer the following situational information about my ethnographic observation with the students in this study.

Starting with myself: I was born in the U.S. to British (Scottish and English) immigrant parents. I was raised and educated in the U.S. In terms of travel related to this study, I have visited numerous countries of western Europe—including all those surrounding France—in various contexts: backpacking, vacationing, working, presenting academic papers, visiting family and friends.

I turn now to the connection of that part of my life in relation to the themes of this chapter. Through my European travel experiences and my acquaintances with Americans in Europe, I have come to believe that enlightenment is in store for most Americans travelling abroad for the first time. Why? Because prior to travelling abroad, many American citizens seem to lack basic knowledge about the ways of life in a variety of foreign countries (see also Perry 1987). This statement may sound harsh, but consider the obstacles that U.S. residents face: for one, the United States' geographical isolation is not conducive to U.S. citizens being substantially exposed to a wide variety of non-tourist foreigners. Additionally, most U.S. citizens normally do not travel to other parts of the world to "live" in a foreign culture (either temporarily or permanently), while many Europeans do. For me, discovering this situation has led to a bias I enact in some of my teachings, including courses such as Comparative Media. In such teachings, I make it a point to expose American students to foreign media because I want them to realize that there are often substantially different conventions to foreign news, sitcoms, films, and other media content than the conventions present in the U.S. media. A final obstacle I wish to mention is that most U.S. television viewing is ethnocentric—that is to say the available selection of TV shows offers programming mostly about American people in U.S. locations (Merrill 1991). Ironically, however, France is another country where TV viewers select from mostly national channels. In fact, France is a country where American media programming is restricted to help obviate an influx of American traditions at the expense of French traditions (Merrill, 1991). At any rate, the low exposure of Americans to foreign cultures makes for fertile exploration of foreign imagery in the university classroom.

The course generating the data for this chapter was Communication Studies 410: Comparative Media; I taught this course as part of the Study Abroad program administered through Indiana University of Pennsylvania.

The students, from several regions of Pennsylvania, registered for the course through my employer, East Stroudsburg University. The three-week class consisted in the morning of three-hour classes, and in the afternoon of a variety of excursions to towns, cathedrals, a vineyard, a French TV station, a French newspaper, and other sites and attractions. Enrolled in the class were nine students, four of whom were asked in advance of the course to participate in the study because of their similar age range (18–22), and because of their limited overseas travel experience (the three female students had never been abroad, while the one male student had previously been to England for eight days). Eight of the nine students, as well as myself, were not fluent in French, but all of us knew some basic French vocabulary and could understand French sentences better than we could speak them. The ninth student in the course was fluent in both French and U.S. English, and voluntarily served as a translator of French for the class and the study.

In the course, we discussed subjects like global media philosophies, the world's media systems, international media controversies, and the flow of world news, while reading from the textbook *Global Journalism* (1991), by John C. Merrill. To buttress our discussions with actual foreign media use, we incorporated the following categories of media experiences into the classwork. For television, every day we watched French national news to start the class, and sometimes, afterward, we channel surfed to gain some general impressions of other kinds of French television. The news we watched was an even mixture of two commercial (private) TV news channels and two public (government-funded) TV news channels. On two occasions after watching French news, we watched BBC news, and on two occasions we watched CNN news; we also spent several days comparing headlines and the gist of stories in a variety of French and British newspapers. French newspapers we read included the nationals *Le Figaro* (known to be conservative), *Le Monde* (known to be moderate), and *L'Humanité* (known to be communist), and also the regional *L'Est Republican*. British newspapers we looked at included *The Sun*, *The Daily Telegraph*, *The Guardian*, and *The London Times*. For magazines, we spent a class looking at French versions of the internationals *Elle* and *Cosmopolitan*, as well as several local/regional French magazines. For radio, we spent one class spinning the radio dial, which meant that we often did not know which French radio station we were hearing.

Outside of the class, all of us lived in the same dormitory, which was a ten-minute walk from our classroom. These living arrangements sometimes had me involved in non-academic activities with the American and the other students, like doing laundry, having a beer, figuring out a train schedule, etc. Similarly, the living arrangements also had me conversing with the students outside of the classroom about concepts we had discussed earlier inside the classroom.

Perceptions of Images

Before we begin the analysis, let me define "image" as a basic and mostly visual impression of a subject (i.e., the U.S.) created and reinforced over time by a collage of media messages. This definition of image lends itself well to this study because we are not trying to tie a student's reaction directly to a particular French media message; instead, we are trying to gauge the broad and memorable impressions that came to mind when the students were asked about their reactions to their use of media in France. Because of the nature of their consent and involvement in the study, the students will hereafter be referred to as "participants."

Beginning Images Identified by the Questionnaire

From the questionnaire administered to the participants before they arrived in France emerges a variety of responses showing a slight bias to the question, "What do you think America is known for in other countries?" Participant 1 answered, "fast food, a nation on the go, violence." Participant 2 answered, "freedom, opportunity, wealth." Participant 3 answered, "money, power, military, ingenuity." And participant 4—the only student who had travelled abroad previously (to England)—answered: "In general, I think Europeans do not like us, yet they envy us. We seem to have it so good."

One collective inference we might draw from these answers is the image of being "well off," which was alluded to by three of the students. "Well off" as an image in the minds of the participants at this stage most likely had come from their interactions with people in the U.S. and their experience of media in the U.S. But it does indicate a perception of the U.S. image abroad as that of one of the wealthier countries, perhaps in a different class than other nations, at least in terms of material goods. A reaction to this image was highlighted by the participant who had been to England, when he commented that the image of wealth creates an "envy" of the U.S., from which other nations ostensibly would like to have the "goods" that the U.S. has.

Answers to a second question reveal further repercussions from this image. When asked, "What stereotypes of Americans do you think people in other countries may have?" the answers were not very positive. Participant 1 answered, "we're stupid," while participant 2 answered, "spoiled." Taking these basic images further, participant 2 answered, "bold, aggressive, selfish, motivated, successful, bad mannered, uncultured." And participant 4 answered, "we're pushy; we are the founders of McDonald's. What more needs to be said?"

The cynicism evident in these answers may be attributable in large part from the connotation that a question about stereotypes necessarily means "bad stereotypes." But still there is an indication that the participants sensed an image of America as a spoiled materialistic bully, forcing its way with business brashness in its relations with other countries. Where these images came from is difficult to tell, but the participants at this stage of the study obviously perceived some problems with America's image abroad.

Images in French TV News Identified by the Essay

The essay asked the participants to compare French TV news to their past experiences of viewing U.S. TV news. At the time of this question, the participants had seen French news for nine days. The idea behind this question was to bring forth a comparison between the two countries' news presentations in the hopes of revealing images of U.S. TV news itself—not necessarily what it covers.

The participants' answers to this question disclose a consensual perception of the image of French news as longer and more detailed than American news. Participant 1 wrote:

> The story length in French news is a lot longer than that of the U.S. They spent much more time focusing on an event. In France, the average length seems almost twice as long as the U.S.

Similarly, participant 2 wrote:

> For one thing, the stories on the French news are much longer. In American reporting, there is a big emphasis on cutting to the chase, making things urgent.

Again, participant 3 wrote:

> The [French] stories are longer if the subject/topic demands it.

And once again, participant 4 wrote:

> The time spent on a single story could probably fill two or three story spots on American television. American news tends to give you the updates without spending the same amount of time as when the story first "broke."

From these answers we see an image of American news as brief and fast-paced, perhaps even shallow, with the emphasis on providing just the basic facts.

Perhaps adding further explanation for the image of brevity in U.S. news is another theme that emerged from two participants' writings in the essay:

the idea that U.S. news is more concerned with the dramatic and the visual than French news.

Participant 2 wrote: "French news is far less glamorous and visually appealing than American news." And participant 4 wrote: "American news tends to pick stories that are of shock value. The more that they shock you, the more outrage you feel. Americans seem to like disaster and chaos on the screen. We have a bias towards it."

The "bias" referred to in participant 4's notations can be taken as an inherent interest on the part of American TV news producers in the visually sensational. It is not clear whether this participant believes that such a bias has been cultivated solely by U.S. media producers, but it is clear the participant believes the interest in shock, as evidenced by "chaos" on TV news, is ingrained in the U.S. way of life. Since this was the only participant who had travelled abroad, perhaps he had developed this realization by comparing U.S. TV news to TV news in both England and France.

The final comparative aspect of French news that was brought out by the essays involved the concept of ethnocentric coverage. Many of the writings from the course textbook as well as our classroom discussions alluded to American news coverage as being parochial, but surprisingly, the participants directed this same criticism toward the French news they saw.

Participant 1 wrote: "In France, they only seem to cover what is news in their country and the countries they have negotiations with." Similarly, participant 2 wrote: "What we have seen of French news thus far is very nationally focused." Again, participant 3 wrote: "the coverage of international topics is limited, and only things dealing with France." And again, participant 4 wrote: "All the news covered in France will be in relation to France." The combination of these comments indicates an ethnocentric selection of media in France.

Since our viewing of French TV news was limited, it is difficult to know if what we saw was truly representative. Although we did see some stories on the U.S.—mostly stories about U.S. efforts to end the war in Bosnia—the following news stories and time lengths that we noted for one newscast appeared to be typical of our experience: Weather (2:08), Tour de France (2:10), a Serbian Offensive (1:56), French Troop Movements in Bosnia (1:35), Renault Workers On Strike (1:45), French Agricultural Output (:29), The French Legislature's Budget Discussions (1:00), and Life for a Frenchman After His Release From Prison (2:17).

Thus, from our sampling, little imagery of the U.S. came through the forum of French TV news. Therefore, possibly in the absence of regular French news coverage of the U.S., images of the U.S. abroad are gleaned more from alternative sources such as Hollywood TV and rock and roll music. Not surprisingly, both of these sources showed up in the participants' journal entries.

Images of the U.S. around France Identified by the Daily Journal

For this exercise, the participants were asked to make an observation of one U.S. image per day contained in a media message that they had come across during their wanderings outside of the classroom. As part of their observation, the participants were required to react in any way they wanted to what they saw.

For all of the participants, the medium they overwhelmingly made observations upon was music—American music. They commented that sometimes the music had lyrics in American English, and sometimes the lyrics were dubbed in French. Participant 1 made six journal entries on American music. This entry shows her perception of the French avidly listening to U.S. music as hypocrisy:

> We were on the way to Toul on the bus and someone turned on the radio. Once again, it was American songs. I have two reactions to what I'm hearing. The first is refreshing because it feels good to hear English and something I am familiar with. The second is annoyance. The French think we're stupid and pains in the asses, yet they do everything we do. I don't get it.

The surprise at the French partaking of American culture through music and other cultural forms ("they do everything we do") was interpreted by participant 2 not as jealousy, but as sheer surprise at the playing of American music in the context of celebrating a sacred French national holiday. One of participant 2's four journal entries on American music in France noted:

> Here we are in Cannes waiting for the fireworks to start in celebration of Bastille Day. It's amazing. But, here's the funny thing. All the music I hear is Tina Turner, Aretha Franklin and Michael Jackson. It's kind of weird that on their national holiday, they're playing American music. On the 4th of July in America, you would never hear anything but American music.

This theme of realization and surprise at American ethnocentricism was expressed also by participants 3 and 4. Here is one of participant 4's four journal entries on American music in France:

> Yesterday I noticed that American music seems to be very popular. The music I heard was at a social ice-breaker, a dance. French people may not be too fond of Americans, but they do seem to like our music.

From these collective entries, we can tell that our participants have two general but strong reactions to their experiences of American music around

France. One is their surprise at the popularity of American music across a variety of contexts (even national holidays) in France. And second is the placing of this surprise within the evolving assumption on their part that the French partake in American music in spite of not being "fond" of Americans.

Lasting Images of the U.S. as Identified by Personal Interview

For this section of analysis, I interviewed each student privately about his/her lasting thoughts of U.S. imagery since they were at the end of their stay in France. When asked, "What have you learned about the U.S. in terms of the world's perception of the U.S. that you did not know before?" all the participants responded with what I took to be a "realization" about America's role in world affairs. Participant 1 answered:

> I think they see us as a pretty powerful nation. I really didn't think that before I came here.

Participant 2 echoed the earlier theme of the pampered American:

> I think there's kind of this image that we're spoiled. I really see that kind of image as people are like "oh, here comes the Americans again."

Participant 3 alluded to a similar theme, but explained it as a function of capitalism as a U.S. social structure.

> We are still looked at as more capitalistic than any place in the world, and it really is a lot stronger than I thought it was.

Participant 4 alluded again to the theme of being spoiled, but blamed it squarely on the U.S. TV shows that French watch:

> It's amazing how many representations we get just because of the TV shows we export. I mean for countries three thousand some miles away to watch *Baywatch* or *Dallas* or some of these shows where everyone seems to be rich and beautiful—I don't think they can possibly get an understanding that it's not like that.

Implications

In this final section of the chapter, I would like to speculate on the implications of the students' various perceptions of U.S. imagery as experienced through the media they used in France. Accordingly, I return now to our three theoretical terms of cultural studies—false consciousness, articulation, and change. Obviously it would be a mistake to surmise that the students' thoughts were informed exclusively by French media when other media (mainly American and English) were also experienced in the context of their three-week French way of life. Moreover, certainly the students' interactions in France with Americans, other visiting foreigners, and the native French added much to their interpretations of American imagery. Therefore, the students' thoughts in this study are conglomerate images in which their media use added a significant piece to the larger puzzle of interpreting American imagery in France.

False Consciousness

One implication is that the use of media in France by the U.S. students appeared to cause an enlightenment on their part that the image of Americans as spoiled may be promoted and sustained in large part by the U.S.'s own media exports. American rock songs and Hollywood TV programs appear to be the main ambassadors carrying this meaning. Hence, we have exposed a false consciousness or imagery—namely, that Americans who have not travelled abroad may sense that when some of the French and other foreigners think of the U.S., they think of a people who have it easy in comparison to their situation. And in the absence of travelling to the country in question, it is easy for Americans to be puzzled by and resentful of this perceived attitude. But human nature leads to a drive for explanations to such mysteries, so it may be assumed before travelling abroad that the French media are to blame for the stereotype of the spoiled American, or alternatively that the French people are snobby or even jealous. However, exposure to the environment of media use in another country like France reveals that this consciousness is significantly false because it ignores that much of this imagery is created by the U.S.'s own media.

Articulation of Cultural Myopia

Another implication for this study is that all of the students experienced a globalization of experience. The fact that they were exposed to U.S. images in the context of another country's social structure helped them overcome what I call "cultural myopia," or the shortsightedness of evaluating a foreign culture according to the assumptions of one's own culture. One manifestation of cultural myopia, for example, is that the accumulation of material goods can be equated to being well off. And in the U.S., lots of material goods are available. One only needs to look on any single day at the deluge of TV advertisements presenting a swirling assortment of material goods to be had, like beauty products, fast foods, appliances, and cars.

In contrast, a lack of material goods can be equated with not being well off. At the beginning of our trip, for example, I heard the students complaining on many occasions that some of their normal material goods were missing from French life: showers in France are not always hot, soft drinks in France rarely come with ice, and ketchup costs extra at fast food restaurants in France. Such thoughts—initially devoid of a recurrent experiencing of French culture—may be related to the students' thoughts expressed in their answers on the opening questionnaire, in which they predicted that there would be negative stereotypes of Americans principally in the area of wealth or being spoiled. But after witnessing firsthand in France the imagery of Hollywood-style dramas and sitcoms and the prevalence of American music, and after adapting to the French way of life without some of these material goods, the students appeared to overcome the myopia of seeing the image of a materialistic U.S. as totally unjustified. Thus, the students all commented in the interviews that once they got used to their French way of life, they really enjoyed it.

Another breaking out of cultural myopia occurred in the students' collective realization that U.S. news is generally more flashy, more sensational, and more prone to a directive of grabbing the audience's attention than to explaining in depth the nature of the news event. To know the impact of a capitalist society on its own media, involves directly experiencing a society's media selection that is not so capitalist. Indeed, we can recall that one of the students noted that she did not realize how capitalistic the U.S. was until she witnessed media in France. Moreover, I argue that only in viewing American images of material wealth (through news, sitcoms, advertisements, etc.) in the context of another society's culture can one realize the pervasiveness of the U.S. profit motive in most human endeavors, the inadvertent consequence of which is sometimes to cheapen or trivialize serious and pressing issues like theft, destruction, and murder.

A final form of cultural myopia that was overcome by the students was their realization that French TV news, perhaps like U.S. TV news, is first and foremost nationally self-serving. For French news, this service means covering stories in a way that makes the issues predominantly about French people or about countries with cultural or economic connections to France. Therefore, the students' unified realization that the preoccupation of French news with relating issues back to the nation's interests perhaps reinforced the idea that the U.S. is no different from France or other countries in the tendency to select and then frame the news mainly on the basis of stories that relate to the home country.

Change

We can now speculate on three main changes in the students' perceptions of U.S. images in French media during their stay in France. First, it is clear that the omnipresence of American music throughout France puzzled the students at first. But it is clear also that later the students realized that to consume the culture of another country in the context of a domestic culture's sacred holiday is not unpatriotic. Rather, it can simply be a celebration of a similar sentiment that the other culture has to offer. American music on the French independence (Bastille) day?—Why not? After all, America went through an independence period too, at basically the same time in history.

Second, it is clear that the students' beginning image of the U.S. as a spoiled nation was somewhat reinforced by their stay in France. However, this recognition evolved into an understanding that Americans face a natural language barrier that leads to this image. Because Americans get little chance to practice French or other high school languages due to the geographical isolation of the U.S. mentioned earlier, there often is a reluctance on the part of Americans to try speaking a foreign language in another country when given the chance. This reluctance, in turn, can be misinterpreted by foreigners to mean that Americans are spoiled because they refuse to speak the country's language. As one participant put it in the interview:

> The biggest stereotype I had to overcome was that I was rich and spoiled. And everyone thought I wasn't speaking French because I didn't want to speak French. And then I felt like every time I talked to another student from another country, I had to say to them, "Well, yeah, I had four years of French but I haven't spoken it for three years. But look at where I live."

Therefore, perhaps the lasting change for the students from their experiences of media in France and their French way of life is their greater understanding that images of America are promoted largely by American media. Moreover, this understanding should extend to an understanding of the awkwardness many Americans have with communicating in foreign tongues. Such images may be difficult to overcome, but they are worth overcoming if one's experience of a way of life in another culture is to rise above making assumptions about a culture's envy and jealousy toward one's home country, to a higher and more worthwhile feeling that a country can celebrate through media the imagery of another country purely for enjoyment or kindredship.

Third, we can see how national identities (American, French) can give way to boundaries of social identity defined by media use, or identity with media programming—(Garnham 1993). In a world carrying these boundaries to the extreme, no longer would we perceive of ourselves primarily as American or French or whatever nationality from the country where we have been raised. Instead, we would identify ourselves primarily with the imagery of media programming. This world might consist of organizing identities (like "Generation Xers," "Classic Rockers," "News Hounds)" we take on based on the media habits we have. Such identities would grow out of our aggregate media use over time.

Where the imagery becomes all-encompassing, however, is at the international level. For here, human beings must find commonality, based on the single principle of being human. In the course of this process, we must overcome our cultural myopia through travel to another country and the use of media within that country. Studying U.S. imagery around the world is a useful exercise, not only for those who live in the U.S., but also for those who see or hear U.S. programming in much of their own domestic media selection. And since that audience encompasses many cultures of the world, a study of this nature is ambitious, but perhaps necessary.

References

Ball-Rokeach, S.J., and M.L. DeFleur. (1976). A dependency model of mass media effects. *Communication Research* 3: pp. 3–21.

Clifford, J. (1992). Travelling cultures. In L. Grossberg, C. Nelson, and P. Treichler (Eds.), *Cultural Studies*, pp. 96–116. New York: Routledge.

Fiske, J. (1992). Cultural studies and the culture of everyday life. In L. Grossberg, C. Nelson, and P. Treichler (Eds.), *Cultural Studies*, pp. 154–173. New York: Routledge.

Garnham, N. (1993). The mass media, cultural identity, and the public sphere in the modern world. *Public Culture* 5: pp. 251–265.

Garnham, N. (1995). Political economy and cultural studies: Reconciliation or divorce. *Critical Studies in Mass Communication* 12(1): pp. 62–71.

Grossberg, L. (1995). Cultural studies vs. political economy: Is anybody else bored with this debate? *Critical Studies in Mass Communication* 12(1): pp. 72–81.

Grossberg, L., C. Nelson, and P. Treichler, (Eds.). (1992). *Cultural Studies*. New York: Routledge.

Hall, S. (1985). Signification, representation, ideology: Althusser and the post-structuralist debates. *Critical Studies in Mass Communication* 2(2): pp. 91–114.

James, B. (1995). Learning to consume: An ethnographic study of cultural change in Hungary. *Critical Studies in Mass Communication* 12(3): pp. 287–305.

Jensen, K.B. (1987, Winter). News as ideology: Economic statistics and political ritual in television network news. *Journal of Communication*: pp. 8–27.

McKenzie, R. (1994). Uniting disparate cultures with like-minded journalism: A case study of *U.S.A. Today* and *The European. History of European Ideas* 20(1–3): pp. 591–597.

Merrill, J.C. (1991). *Global Journalism*. New York: Longman.

Murdock, G.M. (1995). Across the great divide: Cultural analysis and the condition of democracy. *Critical Studies in Mass Communication* 12(1): pp. 89–94.

Nelson, C., P.A. Treichler, and L. Grossberg. (1992). Cultural studies: An introduction. In L. Grossberg, C. Nelson, and P. Treichler (Eds.), *Cultural Studies*, pp. 1–22. New York: Routledge.

Perry, D.K. (1987). The mass media and audience generalization about groups of foreign countries. *World Communication* 16(2): pp. 101–120.

Thompson, M., R. Ellis, and A. Wildavsky. (1990). *Cultural Theory*. San Francisco: WesTView Press.

10

American TV through the Eyes of German Teenagers

ALLEN W. PALMER AND THOMAS HAFEN

Introduction

Recognizing the interpretive, or active audience paradigm, this study seeks to clarify how German adolescents assimilate, resist, or reinvent the meanings of American television programs within the contemporary understandings of German culture. David Morley's (1985, 1989) framework of audience studies postulates that youth subcultures develop methods to interpret media from the perspective of the preferred reading as well as in oppositional modes, suggesting media texts are both polysemic and open and the interpretation process is complex (Fiske 1989). This study focuses on defining how German youth view popular American television programs in light of a half-century of U.S. influence in Western Europe in general, and Germany in particular.

One central assumption of this study is that it is possible to consume and even enjoy a cultural artifact without accepting any of its assumed ideology. As Liebes and Katz (1989) observed, "Dumb genres do not necessarily imply dumb viewers" (223). The extent to which American popular culture affects adolescents will almost certainly fall somewhere along a spectrum between complete adoption or complete rejection of American cultural values.

Method

To determine the level to which German adolescents might either criticize or deconstruct, or both, the American programs the German youths watch on television, forty-two adolescents were invited from two German communities,

Iserlohn and Hagen, to view selections from four American television programs. The German youth then participated in focus group discussions about their responses to the programs. The programs selected for the study contained a variety of social dilemmas and problems from *Beverly Hills 90210*, *The Cosby Show*, *Married with Children*, and *Melrose Place*.

Demographic information about the German television audience collected by (RTL) television in Cologne indicates *Beverly Hills 90210* was seen by two to four million German viewers every week, and reached a height of 5.2 million viewers during 1993. Most of the viewers were women, 62 percent, a slight majority of viewers are older than age thirty. Apparently, more women watch who are age fifty and older than those who are age fourteen to nineteen.

To chart the "oppositional readings" of the programs, an adaptation of a scheme around four increasingly sophisticated types of audience opposition to determine the level at which an audience is able to resist the concepts they see in the mass media was used (Hacker, Coste, Kamm, and Bybee 1991). Use of the four categories of audience response—criticism, resistance, challenge, and deconstruction—empowers television viewers in the producer and consumer power continuum and opens a discussion to how the viewers accept or reject the influence of the popular culture surrounding them. By adapting these findings, we constructed four broad categories of critical viewing:

1. *Naive acceptance.* The viewer does not distinguish between text and reality and adopts positions shown as fact. Discussion of characters or events in a television episode does not acknowledge any difference between the viewer's actual life and that presented in the show.
2. *Sophisticated acceptance.* The viewer agrees with the show's position on its own terms, but is conscious of alternate arguments drawn from viewer's own life or extrapolated from the show itself. Discussion of characters or events may make direct or implied comparison with the viewer's life.
3. *Sophisticated Rejection.* The viewer disagrees with the show on its own terms by arguing from the viewer's own experience or extrapolated from the show itself. Discussion of characters or events may make direct or implied comparison with the viewer's life.
4. *Deconstruction.* The viewer is conscious of the show as a manufactured product. The viewer bases arguments on the fact that the show is created by the producers and writers with their own agendas.

The ability to grasp the multidimensional aspects of television varies with the accumulated experience of audience members (Faber, Brown, and

McLeod 1986). Because the participants in this study were from various up-per-middle, lower-middle, and working class families, it was expected that age and experience had more to do with deconstructive ability than socioeco-nomic background. As media and cultural scholars, we had no reason to pre-sume that deconstructive ability had any bearing on whether youth audiences attributed their interest to entertainment values.

Results

Naive Acceptance

A large percentage of the comments in this initial non-critical category relate in some way to characters portrayed in the television shows—either their ap-pearance, strengths, or flaws. Most of the comments referred to characters as if they were the viewer's neighbors or members of their family. Participants of-ten used first names to describe characters in this way, suggesting a personal familiarity—almost a friendship with them. For example, when describing why she thought the girls in *Beverly Hills 90210* were interesting, one girl said: "Donna and Brenda and Kelly and Andrea all have such beautiful hair . . . and they are all so nice." The admiration for the television characters went beyond physical admiration; interpersonal qualities like being "nice" were also impor-tant. It was as though the viewer's relationship with the characters was not at risk because the figures on the show were simply too "nice" to reject anyone they might encounter.

Other comments about interpersonal relationships revealed an emphasis on social qualities. A sixteen-year-old said he admired the relationship be-tween characters on *The Cosby Show*, Theo and his girlfriend Sheila: "I liked how they talked. Also, how they dealt with each other, those two, Theo and Sheila. I like their relationship . . . how they hang out together." Another young woman emphasized the fact that on *Beverly Hills 90210* Brandon wrote an article opposing racism because he "really liked" one of his African-Amer-ican friends. More than just a part of the story, the friendship among the char-acters seems to reassure these viewers that all is fine in their homes and also in Beverly Hills.

The many viewers who discussed how characters in the shows helped each other reinforced the belief that the viewers in this category lived in a so-cially-constructed community with the television characters. Volunteers from all four different groups commented on how friends on the show helped each other in times of need. The viewers were conscious of how the characters sup-ported one another in an interpersonal network, a network in which the view-ers seemed involved. The network was supportive against personal weakness. A thirteen-year-old boy found in a particular episode how "Brandon helped

Dillan to stop drinking. I thought that was good because it showed friendship." He later said, "I wish that Dillan hadn't gotten drunk," a comment suggesting that he saw himself in the same role as Dillan's other saviors on the show. The characters' friendships were often regarded to be proactive; that is, the characters not only helped each other in times of need, but they also sought to prevent each other from harming themselves.

The viewers did not always depict those whom they were describing favorably. Two participants described Al Bundy on *Married with Children* as addicted to money and sex. One young man characterized Bundy's son as "dumb." Several other participants described their reaction to *Beverly Hills 90210* similarly. Although the viewing youth did not necessarily like everything about the characters they watched, that did not prevent them from exhibiting a closeness to the television characters.

Similarly, other major groupings of comments in this category dealt with close familial relationships. When discussing the *Cosby* family, several viewers commented that they liked the Huxtables' willingness to help each other. One young man stated: "I like how the family sticks together. When someone does something bad they get together and life goes on." A *Beverly Hills 90210* fan sprang to the defense of Dillan's absentee mother, saying that she really did want to have a close relationship with Dillan; it's just that no one understood her background. He continued: "I thought it was good that the mother came back after so many years, even though the other people didn't like it. The father gave her money to leave him [the son] alone and she came anyway." The same themes surfaced in "category one" when the participants discussed family as when they discussed friends: reliability, loyalty, and amicability.

As evidenced by the heavy emphasis on the characters' social abilities, those who did not distinguish between their life and television found aspects of television experience that provided ersatz fulfillment of some basic needs. The fact that Germans can develop relationships with U.S. television characters suggests that they do not see cultural barriers stopping them from importing media figures from another country into their lives.

Beyond discussing relationships, comments in this category often displayed a thin awareness of the difference between television, America, and Germany. For example, one ten-year-old said that she did not learn anything about America from *Beverly Hills 90210* because "America is just like Germany, except that they speak another language there." Restating her comment, the moderator asked: "So you don't see a difference between what is on the television and life here in Germany?" Her reply was "No, not at all." The view that America on television is the same as real America, which is the same as the Germany around them, does not distinguish between different sorts of artificial and real cultures, which sets the stage for possible trans-cultural vision of relationships.

Other viewers in this age group were also accepting of America as they saw it on television. One young man said that, by watching *Beverly Hills 90210*, he learned that there were really pretty cities in America. Another said that there must be very beautiful women there, based on those represented on television. Although these participants did not accept the show to the same degree as those mentioned above, they also showed that some young Germans do accept U.S. television as an artificial reality.

Sophisticated Acceptance

The preponderance of comments in this category described the reasons why the volunteers viewed their favorite programs. The ways in which the participants recounted why they "watch" a particular program distinguished these comments from category one because of the implied distance between the viewer and the program.

Some strong similarities existed, however, particularly among the people in groups who said they watched television to see the relationships between certain characters. One sixteen-year-old viewer said: "I watch because I am interested in what happens to the people. For example, I am interested in what schools they will attend or who they will start dating." Another expressed similar reasons for watching the show: "I watch out of curiosity. I am really curious to see what is new. Dillan was together with Kelly! That is so dumb."

A closer look at those who were involved in the show's relationships and those who were distanced from them revealed a gender gap, suggested women's speech as more cooperative and less hierarchical than men's, the primary concern being connection with others. A strong indication that certain women participants have relationships with television characters is in their comments about how watching television helps them from becoming lonely. One woman said: "I like how they sit around during a break and talk. There are always people together there." Another said: "When I am alone and watching TV, I like to watch people who are together like that. There is always something going on there."

In stark contrast to the women who demonstrated heavy involvement with TV characters were the men who watched without strong connections to those in the show. A young man said that he liked *Married with Children* because "the daughter is hot and has a good figure." Noting that "nothing preoccupies young people like sex," another participant said that he looked forward to the graduation episode of *90210* because of sexually oriented themes.

Other volunteers made overt comments on characters' looks such as "I like to watch it for the girls" and "I just like the cute girls." Those who watched television because of the characters' appearances seemed more intent on visual and pseudo-physical stimulation than fulfilling social or emotional needs. They appeared to want a one-sided relationship in which they could take what the characters offered rather than a two-way relationship in which emotional giving and taking occurred.

Demonstrating similar distance from the show, a sixteen-year-old said he watched *The Cosby Show* "just to laugh." Another said that he "watched [*The Cosby Show*] to while away my time. . . . People watch what they think is funny. When I am at home, I watch things that are fun—things I just have to laugh about. Nothing sad."

Noting that he found the relationships on *Married with Children* unrealistic, a fifteen-year-old said that the show was "funny just because it is so stupid." Oriented toward exterior aspects of the show, these comments revealed little legitimate concern about the interior world of the characters or their relationships.

Comments about the social relationships of TV viewers with fictional characters indicated that viewers did not see the American origins of these shows as cultural barriers keeping them from involvement in the characters' lives. One could speculate that a foreign exoticism of American relationships drew them even further into the show, except for the fact that the men did not seem more inclined to become involved in an American show than in domestic television. The gender gap already noted between female (relationship oriented) viewing and male (externally oriented) viewing seems consistent even when Germans are watching American television.

Other comments in this category revealed traces of a debate among German youth regarding the definition and merits of realism in U.S. television. This debate is important because it casts doubt on a simple characterization of youth as accepting as real what they see on TV. The discussion of realism is important in terms of relationships with media figures because most of the comments revolved around realism in how friendship and familial relationships are portrayed.

Along with the relationships with TV characters discussed earlier, the high number of participants who embraced something produced outside their country as "real" shows, apparently, that they do not see cultural distance separating them from the "reality" of the show. Although they may be aware at some level that the families they watch are American, their descriptions of "real" seem more universal than particular to the U.S.

Three participants in one discussion group said that the realism of Bill Cosby made it their favorite program. "That it is like it really is," remarked one student. Another said: "Bill Cosby has money and he is a doctor. All of their kids go to college. It is more realistic." A young woman thought that Bill Cosby was realistic because "the parents do something for the family. The kids go to school. They discuss realistic problems." The viewers tied characters on *The Cosby Show* to "reality" although the characters seemed in many ways to lead an "ideal" existence.

On the other hand, many characters and situations on *Married with Children* were considered part of an unrealistic world. One participant observed: "No family would really talk to each other like that." Another believed that "no father would actually talk to his wife that way." Beyond character attributes, certain actions in the show, such as writing on the neighbor's fish in the refrigerator or spending the afternoon wrapped in a towel, were cited as being unrealistic. Yet, for most of these viewers, the lack of reality provided an entertainment value of the show. As one young man stated: "What I liked about it is that it was pretty senseless—I mean it was moronic. So it was really funny because there is no sense in any of it. I could just laugh myself silly."

Comments from other groups confirmed this attitude. A participant observed: "There are just impossible things there." By finding the show amusing because it lacked realism, the participants were free to enjoy behavior they apparently would not approve of if it were "real."

The overt purpose of the viewers' comments in this section was not directed at defining programs in terms of fantasy or reality, but to explain why they were enjoyed. Their perception of the reality within the show seemed to have direct bearing on their enjoyment of it. Shows like *Married with Children*, which they considered "stupid," "superficial," and "exaggerated," could be dismissed as fantasy even though ideal family situations like *The Cosby Show* were typified as real.

Sophisticated Rejection

Most of the participants saw the dichotomy between realism and lack of realism in terms of how it benefited them as viewers. Non-realistic shows existed for entertainment, and realistic shows could be instructive. However, a significant minority, comprised mostly of older youth, sensed a lack of realism in U.S. television that interfered with their ability to enjoy the programs. Similar to the other two sections, many comments in this third level of viewing revolved around the viewers' satisfaction with familial and friendship relationships as they were portrayed on the show.

One probable reason why the portrayal of unrealistic relationships would be bothersome to German adolescent viewers is that some of them are not able to enjoy unlikely friendships or improbable resolutions of conflict. This may stem from the fact that relationships as portrayed on TV are at odds with a viewer's own experience. As one young woman said about the easy resolution of a conflict among friends, "I can't imagine that America is like that. I think that the people in Germany are pretty much like those in America."

A participant said that he didn't like American shows because "there is always 'good vs. evil' . . . always the hero and the villain which you don't have in real life." Similarly, some viewers had difficulty accepting relationships which had been dramatized into conflicting roles and then segmented to fit within a fixed time period. In their own experience, real life did not develop according to artificial boundaries. It was difficult for them to accept important developments of a person's life artificially accelerated to fit between a game show and the evening TV news.

Although it was obvious that many of the viewers did not like unrealistic relationships as portrayed on TV, it was not readily apparent why they did not like them. If a primary reason for watching a show was to become involved socially with the characters, it was likely that viewers would become frustrated by shows that were not realistic enough to involve them. Several participants expressed outright disgust at the way difficult problems were portrayed alongside easy answers.

The concern for realism in interpersonal relationships as shown on TV may have reflected the frustrated desire either to have a relationship with the characters on the show or to use the program as a social resource. These wishes became problematic if the relationships on television were not dealt with realistically enough to be adopted into a viewer's life. Alternatively, there might have been a concern that someone with whom the viewer had a relationship would use the show as a flawed source of social relations. A few responses seemed to bear out these fears, such as that of one young woman who observed that "[e]verything is solved. . . . Then you think that the problems are not so hard."

Doubting whether a situation in Germany could turn out as well as in America presupposed that the same situation could come up in both places. Questioning the authenticity of a social situation where everything should turn out all right suggested both that the viewer was reluctant to rely on the show as a personal social resource and that he was afraid for others who might internalize aspects of relationships that he suspected were not consistent with real life.

Participants discussed the lack of realism in familial relationships with emotions similar to those with which they discussed friendships. Some became visibly upset as they discussed the way some television shows did not portray family roles and relations as they would have liked them to be presented.

These viewers separated ideal situations, which they called normal or "real," from non-ideal circumstances that they saw as not normal. Their ideal expectations were located in what the viewers, as children, saw in a "normal" family: food, trust, communication, and caring. Because the Bundys did not provide those things for their children, the Bundys were rejected by these viewers; the viewers did not care to enter a relationship with parents who gave their children dog food when they asked for food.

Deconstruction

Although comments of this type were not frequent, participants from eight of the ten focus groups in the research study that revealed an awareness of the shows as artificial productions created by those who sought something from the viewers. The groups that showed no inclination toward deconstruction were much younger than the others. The proportion of Germany's youth who accept U.S. television as reality declines as the young people progress toward adulthood. By the time a German youth approaches adulthood, around age eighteen, he or she is probably much more conscious of television as an artificial production than when he or she was age ten or twelve.

Participants seemed particularly oriented to the question of image vs. reality. One young man admitted that he liked to watch *Beverly Hills 90210* to see the girls. But he continued to say that his other friends wanted to see the women as well because

> Aaron Spelling (the director) didn't want to get old, normal people in the show. He wanted young, good looking actors. I believe that is pretty clear. If I were Aaron Spelling and I wanted to film a show like *Beverly Hills* I wouldn't want to have normal people in it who don't look so good. Look at Jason Priestly and how the girls swarm around him. Let's look at Luke Perry and Jennifer Gass. If they had normal people in the show, maybe it wouldn't have been so successful. I mean, who doesn't like to look at good-looking people?

Many comments suggested that the viewers saw TV producers as using attractive images to induce people to watch their shows. Participants realized how these images translated into profits for the producer. One volunteer observed,

> I know the sister of a friend . . . addicted to *Beverly Hills*. It began with buying cookbooks from *Beverly Hills*, then it went to cocktail books, books on how to make pizza, collecting things from the press, and so on. That was a typical example of how to sell a show perfectly and how to market it toward a particular age group.

Viewers' consciousness that the shows were made for profit did not seem to inspire anger toward the producers. Some volunteers even expressed a grudging admiration:

> Look at how many girls like the guys [in the shows] and how many guys like the girls. That is why they buy all the posters and magazines in Germany. The sales are huge. Why? Because these young people are hooked. It is easy to see. Whoever thought of this was pretty clever.

Although participants from most of the groups noted unrealistic images in the shows, very few saw them as harmful to the viewers. Deconstructionists saw the images more as an American delusion, perpetuated to show those at home and abroad that America is more wealthy and less racist.

Most of those who ascribed motives to the producers of the show considered it unfortunate that the producers of popular culture did not portray life more accurately, but they also recognized that market forces dictated the content of popular programming. Discussing why problems seemed so easily resolved on American television, one woman said, "If they weren't solved so easily, then I don't think very many people would watch them." Others acknowledged that producers showed the version of America that people expected to see. A participant commented, "I know a lot of people who watch [*Melrose Place*] because they are huge fans of America, and they watch it because they see how people live there, and they really believe that is how it is."

The extent to which the viewers were conscious of a show as a constructed artifact, made by people with their own agendas, did not keep them from enjoying the shows. For some, a show was enjoyable precisely because it was an absurd creation; the artificiality of the productions only contributed toward their main purpose: entertainment. A volunteer described why she was not disturbed that the producers did not show poverty and other "real" social issues:

> Poverty isn't shown. But you sit in front of the TV in order to relax. You want to see love, you want to see riches, you want to see problems that can be solved. You don't want to see what is really out there. Only that which is nice. Television is simply the self-contained world we all wish for somewhere. A world that will probably never exist.

Those who noticed the artificiality of TV did not seem to enjoy it any less. On the contrary, producers who are able to command a wide audience are earning a good living by "selling the American dream." Even though several of the viewers doubted the authenticity of the programs, they were the same participants who said they could suspend their disbelief and watch the shows, relax, and laugh.

We assumed that most German youth who saw television as an artificial production would ascribe harm to the manipulative effects of the producers' ideology. Instead we found that those who deconstructed television often expressed a modest level of appreciation for the producers' ability to create a well-received product. The distortions of reality that come with popular culture were viewed more as necessary evils than harmful manipulation.

Discussion

The responses of the participants in this study indicate that German youth have both egalitarian values and a vision of a global society. Although they are conscious of American stereotypes, they also discuss interpersonal relationships as if familial, friendship, class, and racial relations should be equitable. Of course, these ideals may or may not carry over into their everyday lives, but the evidence suggests that these values are strongly present whether the viewers are discussing the TV shows as fact, comparing them to their own lives, or deconstructing them.

German adolescents' vision of a global society is evidenced in the social aspects of their interaction with American TV. The participants were conscious of the programs coming from the U.S. when they discussed particular aspects of American life on the programs, but that did not happen as often as we expected. Indeed, when the research groups discussed relationships, national origins were rarely discussed; the participants seemed to be least conscious of the source of the programs when discussing the topics that were the most important to them. The closeness of the relationships with some TV characters and the fact that so many volunteers used the programs as a personal social resource suggests that the "Americaness" of the television programs is not a barrier between the viewers and the text.

For many German adolescents, not only do the shows reflect their own egalitarian values, but they become a source for them as well. The desire for equality between Al Bundy and his wife, the approbation of the Huxtables' familial relationships, and the appreciation of the helpful Beverly Hills crowd testify that these qualities are consonant with the viewers' ideals. The way in which the discussion of friendships evolved into a conversation on personal values suggests that American television used as a social resource necessarily evolves into an ideological resource as well. One group of TV viewers could not discuss Brandon's relationship with a black friend without applying the message to their relationship with foreigners in Germany, although there was resistance to mapping the intimate details of the American experience onto the German immigration controversy.

Although many of these subjects displayed at least some deconstructive ability, that was not the major response to the TV programs they viewed here. Most participants said they watched U.S. TV because they were entertained by it. Whether they accept the shows as reality or deconstruct the programs, the German youth will watch the shows as long as they enjoy them. The youths negotiate this enjoyment with the text on social, ideological, and personal levels which both reflects and determines the character of those who watch.

References

Faber, R.J., J.D. Brown, and J.M. McLeod. (1986). Coming of age in the global village: Television and adolescents. *Intermedia: Interpersonal communications in a media world*, 3rd ed., pp. 550–572. New York: Oxford University Press.

Fiske, J. (1989). Moments of television: Neither the text nor the audience. In E. Seiter, H. Borchers, G. Kreutzner, and E. Warth (Eds.), *Remote control: Television, Audiences, and US cultural power*. New York: Routledge.

Hacker, K., T.G. Coste, D.F. Kamm, and C.R. Bybee, C. R. Oppositional readings of network television news: Viewer deconstruction. *Discourse and Society* 2(2): pp. 183–202.

Liebes, T., and E. Katz. (1988). Primordiality and seriality in popular culture. In J.W. Carey (Ed.), *Media, myths, and narratives: Television and the press*, Vol. 15, pp. 113–125. New York: Sage.

Liebes, T., and E. Katz. (1989). On the critical abilities of television viewers. In E. Seiter, H. Borchers, G. Kreutzner, and E. Warth (Eds.), *Remote control: Television, audiences, and cultural power*. New York: Routledge.

Morley, D. (1989). Changing paradigms in audience studies. In E. Seiter, H. Borchers, G. Kreutzner, and E. Warth (Eds.), *Remote control: Television, audiences, and cultural power*. New York: Routledge.

Morely, D. (1985). Cultural transformations: The politics of resistance. In M. Gurevitch and M. Levy (Eds.), *Mass Communication Yearbook*. Newbury Park: Sage.

11

Anglo-American Attitudes

Affirmations and Refutations of "Americanicity" in British Television Advertising

JANE STOKES

Introduction

In his vision of television, Marshall McLuhan postulated that visual broadcasting would lead to the creation of a "global village" in which everyone would communicate with each other across the entire globe, as equal participants in a new, transnational society (McLuhan 1964). The expansion of television has continued apace since McLuhan did his most famous work in the 1960s, but the neophiliac excitement for the new medium has waned. Today, television, and especially American television, is more likely to be seen as an agent, less of community spirit than of "cultural imperialism" (see, for example, Dowmunt 1993).

The expansion of television across the globe is just one element of the phenomenon recently identified as "globalization" (Featherstone 1990; Featherstone and Lash 1995; King 1991; Robertson 1992; Waters 1995). The term is used to apply to multiple processes across many fields of life, including economics, culture, politics, and religion. Globalization describes the process by which people are believed to be acting, thinking, behaving, and comprehending events and situations on an increasingly global scale. Roland Robertson asserts that globalization is "a concept [which] refers both to the compression of the world and the intensification of consciousness of the world as a whole" (Robertson 1992, 8).

A central characteristic of globalization is the expansion of the consumerist ethic to include more of the world's peoples, accompanied by an increasingly popular acknowledgment of, and suspicion of, consumerism. A key industry in the globalization of consumerism is advertising, an international industry that grew up with the twentieth century itself (Sinclair 1987; Mattelart 1991). Entwined with the expansion of advertising has been the growth of television services around the world.

Great Britain has a mixed economy in television, with public and commercial services existing together as approximate equals in a duopoly that has evolved only very slowly over the past forty years. From 1936, when the British Broadcasting Corporation (BBC) first began to broadcast television, until 1955 when Independent Television (ITV) was launched, British television was exclusively public. When television advertising was first introduced, there was concerted and aggressive resistance to it from a number of sectors (Briggs 1995). The antipathy was largely based on the perception that advertising was an intrinsically American phenomenon, television advertising even more so, and that to permit such a thing in Britain would be one more slide on the inevitable decline toward "Americanization."

A fear of America as a base, commercial culture has a long history in British (especially English) thinking (Bigsby 1975; Webster 1988; Hebdige 1988). America is an Other of huge proportions for most Europeans (Baudrillard 1988), probably equal in significance to the Orient (Said 1978). But the image of America has another connotation in British culture, more in keeping with America's own preferred national identity: America is a symbol of freedom, opportunity, and wealth to many Britons, especially those who feel that their liberties and opportunities are constrained. Thus, the idea of America has at least two different manifestations in the British imagination: it is feared by current potentates lest it diminish their control; but for the British disenfranchised, America holds the promise of an alternative way of life.

Given the British popular enchantment with all things American, it is hardly surprising that the iconography of American popular culture references have been employed to sell a whole range of products to the British public, from Goodfellas™ pizza to Pirelli™ tires. Are these images contributing to the process of Americanization? Is Britain culturally subjugated to America by the preponderance of images culled from American culture? Can cultural artifacts, especially blatantly commercial ones like advertisements, contribute to the erasure of British national identity?

Advertisements and National Identity

Roland Barthes's famous analysis of an advertisement for the Italian produce and pasta company, Panzani, has become one of the foundational works of semiotics (1984 {1964}). Barthes claims that advertisements are especially ripe for semiotic analysis:

> Because in advertising the signification of the image is undoubtedly intentional; the signifieds of the advertising message are formed *a priori* by certain attributes of the product and these signifieds have to be transmitted as clearly as possible . . . the advertising image is *frank*, or at least emphatic. (Barthes 1984, 33)

In "The Rhetoric of the Image," Barthes attempts to separate the denotative (literal) message from the connotative (or implied) message in a French advertisement for Panzani. Barthes's objective is to answer the fundamental question of visual semiotics: "how does meaning get into the image?" At its simplest, the image means what it depicts; in this case, groceries and produce arranged in, and around, a string shopping basket. Yet Barthes shows that there is more to an image than its denotational content; meaning also rests in what the picture implies or connotes. The Panzani advertisement carries connotations of freshness; the full shopping bag with groceries tumbling out implying a recent return from the market. Further, the colors employed, red, yellow and green, echo the colors of the Italian flag and enhance the connotation of "Italianicity" which adheres to pasta products generally.

In order to appreciate the connotation of national identity one must be aware of the relevant codes by which Italianicity (or any other "icity") is signalled. The cultural knowledge called upon requires one to be conversant not with Italy the country, but with the identity of Italy for French people.

> It is a specifically French knowledge (an Italian would barely perceive the connotations of the name, no more probably than he would the Italianicity of tomato and pepper), based on a familiarity with certain tourist stereotypes. (34)

The advertisers have added meaning to the image of the groceries and value to Panzani products by foregrounding connotations of Italianicity.

Advertisers are in the business of promoting products and services through creating positive images and identities for them. As Robert Goldman says, "advertising constitutes an apparatus for *reframing meanings* in order to add value to products" (Goldman 1992, 5). Nationally constituted meanings of other countries are ripe for such reframing. There is no more omnipresent national identity than the United States of America. To extend Barthes's term, Americanicity is a powerful signifier in many cultural codes used to attach a valuable image to the "commodity-sign," or "the image that attaches to a product" (Goldman 1992). How do British television advertisements employ the value of Americanicity to enhance the meaning of their commodities?

Americanicity in British television advertisements

An evening watching British television advertisements will reveal that advertisers employ the codes of Americanicity quite freely, whether their products are American or not. Many advertisements for American products make the country of origin a feature of their commodity-sign, e.g., Levi's™ jeans. In the following analysis, I categorize these as displaying signs of Authentic Americanicity. However, many advertisements for products that are not American in origin, such as those for Peugeot™ cars or Heineken™ beer, also feature American iconography. I will refer to these as exhibiting Borrowed Americanicity. A third category of advertisement describes those that are promoting products popularly known to be American, but which eschew all signs of Americanicity and even promote a self-consciously British image for their product. McDonald's™ current campaign is a paradigm case of the way Americanicity is denied; I refer to these as carrying the signs of Un-Americanicity.

Authentic Americanicity

Many television advertisements for American products play freely on an established iconography of America as a place of high glamor. Promotions for Max Factor™ cosmetics, for example, rely on the already established identity of the products as American. The current television advertisement is letter-boxed, enhancing the connotations of Hollywood glamor through this formal reference to the difference between the aspect ratio of the cinema and television. The advertisement shows Allen Weisinger, identified as "make up artist for *Age of Innocence*," endorsing Max Factor's™ products. "Believe me, it's not easy looking natural on film," says Weisinger, while applying cosmetics to a young woman. He advises us of the advantages of Max Factor™ cosmetics in giving one "a beautiful look, naturally!" The opportunity to cash in on the company's link with its famous founder is not lost: the closing shot is of flower petals blowing across Max Factor's star on Hollywood Boulevard. Unabashed "Hollywood glamor" is the value of the sign being added to the product here, albeit tempered to British taste by the final voice-over, which is identifiably an English woman's, informing us that Max Factor™ is: "The Make-Up of Make-Up Artists." Americanicity is unequivocally affixed to the meaning of the product.

The television advertisement for Budweiser™ beer shows a middle-aged-to-elderly black man tap dancing in a large loft with images of the Budweiser™ logo and of pouring, bubbling beer superimposed. No words are spoken, and the only linguistic messages are those to be found on Budweiser™ bottle tops and labels, except the closing slogan: "the genuine article." Here, the idea of black Americans as the ultimate source of modern popular music and thus "the genuine article" is linked with the beer. Budweiser™ is promoted as "genuine" America by cashing in on America's (black) popular culture heritage. Both Max Factor™ and Budweiser™ advertisements exploit a romantic image of America and use the iconography of popular culture to enhance the commodity-sign of their product.

Borrowed Americanicity

The American cinema, often referred to as "the popular cinema of the world," provides a regular source of references and ready-packaged meanings which can be articulated to sell products of any national origin. An advertisement for the chain of home improvement stores, B & Q, begins with an overhead view of twelve men sitting round a large table. Overhead is a ceiling fan, behind the men is an American flag, and a large water bottle sits in the corner; none of which would be noticed by an American audience, but all of which connote Americanicity to Britons as surely as the elements of the Panzani advertisement signal Italianicity to the French. Crumpled papers are scattered on the table, and a man at the head of the table is reading from slips of paper: "Guilty . . . guilty . . . guilty." The advertisement is a clear homage to *Twelve Angry Men* (*dir*. Sidney Lumet, 1957), but it is a playful one since it is self-evidently not the movie. Trained by experience to expect humor in such a circumstance, we wait for the punch line. The chairman reads from a fourth piece of paper with mounting surprise: "Yale cordless burglar alarm only 149.99 pounds at B & Q?" The camera cuts to a smiling man before we are shown the burglar alarm in question, and an English accent delivers the suturing punch line: "B & Q. Prices so low you just have to tell somebody."

The American West provides the most recurrent iconography to sell many European products. An advertisement for Heineken™ beer begins with a classic Western scene of a cowboy at a campfire at night, the scene cuts to the cowboy riding a horse through various landscapes. A title identifies the locale: "Montana 1899." The soft American-accented voice-over adds to the setting:

> In 1899 Montana was still an unspoiled wilderness. A place where a man could put aside the cares of civilization and find himself in the sanctity of nature.

The image cuts to the interior of a barroom, and there is an abrupt change in register of the voice to expostulate: "But then again, there's only so much of *that* you can take." The cowboy is served a bottle of Heineken™ beer which, we are told, was "introduced to America in 1894," while the text at the end reads: "Heineken Export™. The world's favourite import." An idyll of the

American West is created only to be undermined by the image of the superior satisfaction offered by more urban, European, and civilized pleasure of beer drinking. Americanicity is used as the foil for European culture, which is sociable and fun-loving in contrast to the isolated and challenging life of the cowboy.

The French compact automobile, the Peugeot 106™, is advertised by borrowing the Americanicity of popular images of Hollywood. However, this advertisement shows English people at first seeing through the hype of Hollywood, then succumbing to its charms before finally, literally, smashing through the facade. Two young English women are driving their Peugeot™ through Los Angeles, the locale being signalled compactly by the famous Hollywood sign. "Trouble with this town," they say, "is that everyone wants to be in the movies!" Halted at a stoplight, a cigar-smoking man wearing a baseball cap in an adjacent car invites them to be in a movie, and they jump at the opportunity. In a blaze of lights and sirens, they find themselves being filmed in the middle of the desert. After the filming stops, the director calls "cut" and orders the "real actresses" to take the place of the English women, who look at one another in shocked amazement. The car faces a huge cliff, reminiscent of the final scene of *Thelma and Louise* (*dir.* Ridley Scott, 1991); the women exclaim: "Give *them* the 106? I'd rather die!" And they drive toward the precipice at speed. The twist in the tale is that they drive, not over a cliff, but through a movie flat and out onto a road on the other side. As they drive off into the Western landscape, they enjoy a final laugh at the expense of the flabbergasted American film crew.

The image of America as "fake" has been reinforced. They have shown how British people are superior to Americans (or at least Angelinos). The English women have penetrated the false appearances of Americans, and Britons are affirmed as superior to the narcissistic, vulgar Americans.

Un-Americanicity

While the two categories of advertisement discussed above use Americanicity to add value to their products, the advertisements I will discuss now eschew Americanicity in order, I presume, not to add negative value to their commodity-sign.

That giant symbol of American consumerism, McDonald's™, is clearly sloughing its American identity in its advertisements. The current campaign shows a young girl, about six years old, asking her father to explain "How do you get babies?" Filmed in tight close up to create an impression of a familiar relationship between the two characters, the father's embarrassment grows as his daughter pesters him with requests for further explanation. Finally, the father suggests that they go to McDonald's™, hoping this will distract his daughter. She accedes to his suggestion, adding by way of a punch line: "*then you can tell me all about it.*" McDonald's™ is thus associated with a very informal, intimate family situation within an identifiably English middle-class home, and all hint of Americanicity is erased.

KFC™, the food chain formerly known as Kentucky Fried Chicken, have a British campaign which also eradicates all traces of Americanicity from their product identity. A young man plays his video games in an obviously British living room while his girlfriend is trying to get his attention. "Kev," the English girl asks, "we've been going out for two years now; can you tell me what you really want?" Balloon images above her head indicate that she is thinking of marriage. He answers her in a Scottish accent: "Well, a KFC™ chicken fillet burger." This is evidently the wrong answer, but he describes the burger in great detail, and we are shown supporting illustrations of the sandwich. During the course of his description he hardly takes his eye from the television screen, but when he turns around she has left the house. "Perhaps she's gone to get me one?" he proffers, hopefully. Appealing to young teens, this ad shows no trace of Americanicity, and yet is for a product which had classically been promoted on the basis of its American origin.

Some advertisements, such as those for Levi's™ and Burger King™, seem to be adopting a futuristic setting in order to eschew any global location. The extraterrestrial location of the current Levi's™ advertisement is a case in point. Levi's™ jeans have long been advertised exploiting the connotation of the American West, which the product and the company represent for most people. The wide open spaces of the American West figured strongly in a recent campaign which captured the scope and grain of a John Ford western perfectly as it showed a settler family crossing the plains in beautiful, crisp monochrome. The current advertisement has no earthly locale, being set in what appears to be an alien planet colonized by humans at some future time. "Space Man" is the musical soundtrack accompanying images of the few human inhabitants of the planet performing such terrestrial acts as spraying the lawn, riding skateboards, and borrowing Father's vehicle. The human activities are all reminiscent of American suburbia. Although not located in the American West, it continues with the theme of expansionism, except instead of expanding to the West, space is now "the final frontier." The colonists are not cowboys or astronauts, but American suburbanites. The connotation is that Levi's™ will still be worn in the next incarnation of the American frontier.

While we can observe that British products are often sold on their putative, or borrowed, Americanicity, many products that are strongly identified as American in the public imagination, e.g., McDonald's™ or Coca-Cola™, seem to be denying all traces of Americanicity and adopting a self-consciously British identity through which to promote their products. Others still aim for a location removed from current space and time. An interesting hybrid has also emerged that blends American and British iconography, most evident in Miller's recent campaign, Miller Time.

Miller is an American beer sold, like many other American beers, on its Americanicity in the British market, but clearly in need of some differentiating edge. In the run-up to the busy Christmas 1995 advertising season, a series of poster and magazine advertisements appeared promoting the forthcoming Miller Time on Channel 4 at 11:25 on Friday nights. In a very aggressive move, Miller's agency purchased an entire three minute advertising slot for four successive weeks leading up to Christmas. The slot was scheduled between the animation series *Crapstone Villas* and *Eurotrash*, both late-night programs aimed at a youth audience. Miller Time features a late-night talk show host, Johnny Miller, a cross between Jay Leno and David Letterman who is introduced in the manner of Johnny Carson on *The Tonight Show* with the slogan, "Heeeeere's Johnny!" All the iconography of the late-night talk show is present, including a live audience, an onstage band, a window with an (American) city view, etc. Recurring characters are featured, as in the talk shows it refers to, such as Benny, the band leader, and Elastic Message Man—who enters from stage left in each episode harnessed to a piece of elastic which always pulls him back off the stage. Each advertisement is unique, again, challenging the idea of what an advertisement is. Through its placement, promotion, and format the advertisement announces *"this is not an ad"* (Goldman 1992, 168).

Americanicity of a very particular kind is being articulated in this campaign, which is carefully niche-marketed to reach a hip young audience. A strong degree of reflexivity is displayed through the series of advertisements and in the trailers for the advertisements. In one such trailer, James Belushi appears with "Johnny" and tells us: "we'll be humiliating some guy who's been masquerading as a talk show host." As Goldman says:

> Reflexivity in such ads exposes the meta-discourse that constitutes the code so that sophisticated consumers can then consume their own savvy-ness. (Goldman 1992, 168–169)

When we look closely, it is evident that the advertisement is not simply selling the beer through these images of Americanicity, however knowing they may be. There are many English elements of Miller Time that remind us that this is an English advertisement masquerading as an American talk show. The first advertisement shows Johnny in drag—hardly popular on American television, but common enough in England where camp is generally more prevalent. In the final Christmas advertisement, the British iconography jars most creakily with the American. Here Elastic Message Man appears in drag, as a fairy of the kind that features in British pantomime or on the top of British Christmas trees. Center stage is a giant Christmas cracker—an indispensable feature of the iconography of English Christmases, but largely unknown in America. One of the items revolves around Terry the Turkey—turkey being the typical English Christmas meal, whereas in the United States, the bird is more usually served at Thanksgiving. This is Americanicity for the English. According to John Kelley, writing in the advertising business magazine, *Campaign*, Miller Time is:

> A clever balance between product sell and program style. It's good TV advertising. And good TV. Leno and Letterman look out. (Kelley 1995, 30)

To use an Americanism, I don't think so. Americanicity is blatantly exploited here, but it is never beyond the comprehension of British audiences. Moreover, the advertisements are peppered with an iconography that is clearly not American.

Conclusions

A key anxiety of the twentieth century is that globalization and its concomitant homogenization is an inevitable process that will result in creating a monolithic culture of monolingual people. Americanization has served Europeans as the epitome and harbinger of this uniformity. American culture may well be the popular culture of the world, but this does not necessarily imply that the world is being hegemonized and homogenized by Americanicity. "Cultural analysis is intrinsically incomplete," says Clifford Geertz (1973, 29), and my conclusions are necessarily provisional. Nonetheless, close analysis of the advertising images on British television reveals that Americanicity is a product of the British mentality. The images of America mesh with British concepts and images of America and have little to do with America per se.

    Whether the products advertised are American or not, it is evident that British audiences are familiar with the classics of American cinema and the iconography of American popular culture. I cannot agree with Stuart Hall when he says that "global mass culture" is a "homogenizing form of cultural representation" (Hall 1991, 28), nor that "the new kind of globalization is not English, it is American" (Hall 1991, 27). Rather, I support Antonio Gramsci's assertion that "In Paris Americanism can appear like a form of make-up, a superficial foreign fashion" (Gramsci 1971, 318). Americanicity is a mask, a pretty facade to borrow at will; it is a construct of the British imagination, used to sell products of all kinds to a British public.

References

Barthes, R. (1984). Rhetoric of the image. *Image, music, text.* Translated by Stephen Heath. London: Fontana paperbacks.

Baudrillard, J. (1988). *America*. Translated by Chris Turner. London: Verso.

Bigsby, C.W.E., (Ed.). (1975). *Superculture. American popular culture in Europe.* London: Paul Elek.

Briggs, A. (1995). *The history of broadcasting in the United Kingdom. Volume V: Competition.* Oxford: Oxford University Press.

Dowmunt, T., (Ed.). (1993). *Channels of resistance: Global television and local empowerment.* London: British Film Institute.

Featherstone, M., (Ed.). (1990). *Global culture.* London: Sage.

Featherstone, M., and S. Lash. (1995). Globalization, modernity and the spatialization of social theory. In M. Featherstone, S. Lash, and R. Robertson (Eds.), *Global modernities.* London: Sage.

Geertz, C. (1973). *The interpretation of cultures.* New York: Basic Books.

Goldman, R. (1992). *Reading ads socially.* London: Routledge.

Gramsci, A. (1971). Americanism and Fordism. *Selections from prison notebooks.* Q. Hoare and G.N. Smith (Eds. and Trans.). London: Lawrence and Wishart.

Hall, S. (1991). The local and the global: Globalization and ethnicity. In A. King (Ed.), *Culture, globalization and the world system.* London: Macmillan.

Hebdige, D. (1988). Towards a cartography of taste, 1935–1962. *Hiding in the light.* London: Routledge.

Kelley, J. (1995, November 24). Private view. *Campaign.*

King, A.D., (Ed.). (1991). *Culture, globalization and the world system.* London: Macmillan.

Mattelart, A. (1991). *Advertising international: The privatization of public space* (M. Chanan, Trans.). London: Routledge.

McLuhan, M. (1964). *Understanding media: The extensions of man.* New York: McGraw-Hill.

Robertson, R. (1992). *Globalization: Social theory and global culture.* London: Sage.

Said, E.W. (1978). *Orientalism.* New York: Random House.

Sinclair, J. (1987). *Images incorporated: Advertising as industry and ideology.* London: Croom Helm.

Waters, M. (1995). *Globalization.* London: Routledge.

Webster, D. (1988). *Looka yonder! the imaginary America of populist culture.* London: Routledge.

12

As Others See the United States

A View from Canada

SHERRY DEVEREAUX FERGUSON, HILARY HORAN,
AND ALEXANDRA FERGUSON

Introduction

Canadians are seasoned observers of American culture. Almost three-quarters of Canadians live within 100 miles of the U.S. border. Movement of people and goods between the two countries is comparatively free. Canadians make twenty-five million visits to the United States each year, and Americans make thirteen million visits to Canada (Statistics Canada 1992). Canada and the U.S. have long been partners in commerce, political alliances, military undertakings, and cultural enterprises. The economies of the two countries are interdependent, to the extent that Canada has tied its dollar to the American dollar. Canada is America's biggest trading partner. Anglophone Canadians and Americans share a common language, compatible cultural histories, and similar political traditions. One historian called Canada and the United States "the Siamese twins . . . who cannot separate and live" (cited in Innis 1972, 1). In describing the impact of the U.S. presence on Canada, ex-Prime Minister of Canada Pierre Trudeau said that living next to the U.S. is akin to sleeping next to an elephant. You cannot help but be aware of its every movement.

Canadians participate actively in American culture, in the sense that television and radio signals do not recognize national boundaries. Seventy percent of Canadian households have cable television, which includes the American networks. Canadians watch such American artifacts as *Mad about You*, *Current Affair*, and *Bay Watch*. They follow *Days of Our Lives*, NFL football, NBA basketball, and the O.J. Simpson saga. They agonize with Americans when

157

bombings occur in Oklahoma City, earthquakes in San Francisco, or riots in Los Angeles. The yearly migration of Canadian seniors to Florida has resulted in their being dubbed "the snowbirds." In other words, Canadians think they know and understand American culture.

Despite this long history of trust and shared concerns, Canadians are frequently adamant in asserting that they differ from their American cousins in respect to social values and ideologies. Canadians engage in a near-national pastime of searching for self-definition—which usually translates into defining themselves in terms of what they are not rather than what they are; and, to the average Canadian, what they are not is American. As one author observed: "So conscious are we of the presence and power of our big neighbour that the nationalism of Canadian people often seems anti-American rather than pro-Canadian" (Innis 1972, 1).

Thus, in their ongoing search for Canadian identity, Canadians engage in much discussion of American values. Whatever the validity of these views, they permeate the academic literature, the print and electronic media, and the conversation of ordinary Canadians. These references to American values most often appear in the context of discussing their impact on Canadian culture (e.g., increasing violence in society as a result of American TV programs), policies (e.g., health care), and the economy (e.g., the impact of lowered trade barriers on small business).*

This chapter is divided into four parts. Part one establishes a framework for the study by reviewing the results of Americans' efforts to define their own values. Part two identifies the values selected for study in this research project. Part three presents the results of a survey of Canadian university students, in which the students report their impressions of American behavioral characteristics on a semantic differential. Part four describes the results of a content analysis of Canadian newspaper articles in which American values are discussed. The authors examine Canadian perceptions of American values, as evidenced in the ongoing debate over the "Americanization" of Canada. The conclusion of the chapter explores the degree of consistency between how Americans see themselves and how Canadians view Americans.

Defining the American Value System

The first part of this chapter addresses the question: How do Americans define their own values? A number of attempts have been made to define the American value system. Interest in measuring values has been growing steadily

---

*For additional information on Canadian views of the U.S., see Cairns, 1975; Doran & Sewell, 1988; Hawes, 1989; Innis, 1972; Lamorie, 1976; Moffett, 1972; Ogmundson, 1980; Orchard, 1993; Smith, 1988.

over the past half-century (Miller 1991, 470). The trend is reflected in the inclusion of this topic in many recent texts on intercultural and interpersonal communication (e.g., Adler and Rodman 1994; Althen 1988; Berman 1990, 112–113; Samovar and Porter 1995; Stewart and Bennett 1991; Trenholm and Jensen 1992, 156–158).

Early interest in measuring values surfaced in the 1940s (e.g., Crissman 1942). The largest body of research concerned with the definition of American values dates to the 1950s, with Allport et al. (1950) publishing their classic *Study of Values*. Between 1951 and 1970, Williams (1970, 452–502) arrived at fifteen major themes, or value orientations, based on an extensive study of historical, economic, political, and sociological data. Carter (1956) and Scott (1959) also sought to identify the critical values underpinning American society, and Thurstone published his major work *The Measurement of Values* in 1959. Maslow's (1954) delineation of a hierarchy of needs was a seminal influence on much of the early—and later—values research.

Other benchmark studies, such as the work of Kluckhohn and Strodtbeck (1960) and Cantril (1965), appeared in the 1960s. The Rokeach Value Survey, first published in 1968, became the foundation for almost every values study that followed (Crosby, Bitner, and Gill 1990). In subsequent years, some researchers undertook to identify the underlying factors in Rokeach's list of thirty-six values (e.g., Crosby, Bitner, and Gill 1990; Munson, McIntyre, and McQuarrie 1988; Prakash and Munson 1985; Vinson et al. 1977). Others such as Steele and Redding (1962) also made important contributions in the 1960s to the growing body of research on American values.

Rokeach (1973) defined values as "enduring beliefs that specific modes of conduct (instrumental values) or end-states of existence (terminal values) are personally or socially preferable to opposite or converse modes of conduct or end-states of existence" (5). He said that values may be inferred from what a person says or does. According to Rokeach (1979, 124), every individual holds hundreds of thousands of beliefs, thousands of attitudes, but only dozens of values. Rokeach (1968, 1973) identified eighteen instrumental values (ideal states of behavior: e.g., being generous or ambitious) and eighteen terminal values (ideal states of existence: e.g., a comfortable life or a sense of accomplishment) that appear to be among the most important values held by people.

The 1980s and 1990s produced a number of marketing studies that focused on values research. Mitchell (1983) published the results of his Values and Lifestyle Typology (VALS), which divided people into nine categories, ranging from poor struggling "survivors" to affluent, spiritually-motivated "integrateds." Kahle et al. (1986) and Beatty et al. (1988) confirmed the validity of Mitchell's typology. Kahle (1983, 1986) contributed the LOV typology, which differentiates between external values (e.g., being well-respected and warm relations with others) and internal values (self-respect and sense of fulfillment). Other marketing studies centered on values related to materialism and consumption behavior (Antil and Bennett 1979; Antil 1984; Beatty et al. 1985; Beatty, Homer, and Kahle 1988; Belk 1984, 1985; Leonard-Barton 1981; Lichtenstein, Netemeyer, and Burton 1990; Moschis and Churchill 1978; Inglehart 1981; Richins 1987; Richins and Dawson 1990; Richins and Dawson 1992, cited in Bearden 1993; Scott and Lundstrom 1990; Tashchian, Slama, and Tashchian 1984; Yamauchi and Templer 1982) and pursuit of leisure activities (Unger and Kernan 1983).

Many values studies have a cross-cultural component. For example, Hofstede (1980) administered surveys to 116,000 employees of a multinational organization, based in forty countries, over a six-year period. These surveys elicited work-related values. The results enabled Hofstede to identify four value dimensions (power distance, uncertainty avoidance, individualism vs. collectivism, and masculinity vs. femininity) that could be used to describe and differentiate the cultures of the forty countries.

The majority of social psychologists and anthropologists agree that a finite number of values guide human action. Introductory comment in *Understanding Human Values* (Rokeach 1979) noted: "In every full-fledged society, every one of Rokeach's 36 values will appear—as will each of the values or themes listed by C. Kluckhohn, F. Kluckhohn, R. F. Bales and Couch, C. Morris, M. Opler and R. Williams" (17). The majority also concur that value sets are relatively enduring and unchanging.* Shifts in values are much less likely than shifts in beliefs and attitudes. Confirming this point, Lipset (1967, 119) observed that no completely new value orientations had appeared in American society during the twentieth century. Williams (1970) concluded that American values had showed little change between 1950 and 1970. Using the Rokeach Value Survey, the National Research Center sampled a national population of Americans in 1968, then again in 1971. The study found that values remained stable over the three-year period (Rokeach 1979). A study by Kahle, Poulos, and Sukdial (1988) showed stability over a decade in how Americans evaluated the importance of many social values.

Williams (1970) and Rokeach (1979) concluded that changes in values are more likely to manifest themselves in the ordering of the values than in the matter of their presence or absence in the value set. For example, Williams (1970) and Yankelovich (1981) found that the importance of achievement as a value declined in the same period that success increased. Other studies found that American commitment to equality showed significant erosion in the 1970s (e.g., Ball-Rokeach, Rokeach, and Grube 1984). Since the 1960s, an increasingly large number of Americans have recognized the importance of environmental values

---

*See, for example, Lipset, 1967; Williams, 1970, p. 455; Rokeach, 1979, pp. 17, 129, 143; Allport, 1954, p. 231; Lasswell, 1967, p. 17; Bem, 1970, p. 17; and Williams, 1979, p. 18.

(Kempton, Boster, and Hartley 1995, 3–4). Research into political values demonstrates the increasing influence of the Christian Right (Persinos 1994) and fundamentalist religions (Badaracco 1992, 32). The number of Americans valuing honesty and integrity in political candidates has grown dramatically in the post-Watergate decades (Roelofs 1992, 123). Two recent surveys of American youth (reported in Easterlin and Crimmins 1991) have confirmed a "modest turning away from the public interest," a "sharp decline in emphasis on personal self-fulfillment," and a "sharp shift toward private materialism." The youths reported a greater tendency to support capitalist institutions and to believe that corporations are doing a good job. A large number call themselves conservative; at the same time, relatively few are politically active.

Other common value shifts may occur in terms of the consistency with which the population at large adheres to the values (i.e., the number of people at any point in time who believe in the value) or the extent to which the society tolerates conflicts in the values (i.e., the extent to which people can reconcile apparent contradictions in two strongly held values, such as an achieving vs. a caring society). Kalish and Collier (1981, 3) discuss a process called values clarification that forces individuals to confront situations where they hold inconsistent or unclear values. (See Raths, Harmann, and Simon 1966, and Simon, Howe, and Kirschenbaum 1972, for the derivation of the values clarification concept.)

In conclusion, researchers vary in how they choose to label certain values. They sometimes dispute the results of others' attempts to narrow the list of values through factor analysis techniques. Finally, they often point to the fact that—at different points in time and in different cultural contexts—people rank-order values in a different way, are more or less tolerant of conflicts in values, and adhere in smaller or larger numbers to certain values. However, whatever their differences, most researchers agree on a core set of relatively unchanging values held by most Americans. Bearden, Netemeyer, and Mobley (1993) have compiled one of the best contemporary surveys of the results of these value studies.

Values Selected for Study

The values selected for inclusion in this study have been identified by numerous researchers in the 1950 to 1990 period. A debate is often waged over whether it is appropriate to separate value listings into instrumental and terminal categories (Crosby, Bitner, and Gill 1990). Those who oppose the distinction argue that such differentiation can be confusing. We have chosen to frame the values in this study in instrumental terms because Canadians cannot know the terminal values of Americans—for example, whether Americans value an exciting life over a comfortable life. Canadians can only infer the values of Americans, based on behaviors that they witness; and behaviors reflect instrumental values, as defined by Rokeach (1968, 1973). The following list indicates (1) our label for the value, framed in instrumental terms; and (2) labels applied by other researchers to the same or related value constructs (sometimes framed as an instrumental value and sometimes as a terminal value). The first adjective in each adjective pair represents the American value examined in this study.

Achievement-oriented/Non-achievement-oriented: Ambitious (Rokeach 1968, 1973), Achievement and success (Williams 1970), Successful and self-made (Steele and Redding 1962), Ambitious, successful, and self-made, achievers (Mitchell 1983), Ambitious (McQuarrie and Langmeyer 1985).

Active/Passive: Exciting life, or stimulating active life (Rokeach 1968, 1973), Activity and work (Williams 1970), Activity (Kluckhohn and Strodtbeck 1961), Hard-working (Mitchell 1983), Adventure, vitality, and stimulation (Yankelovich 1981).

Competent/Incompetent: Capable (Rokeach 1968, 1973), Competent (Vinson et al. 1977), Capable (McQuarrie and Langmeyer 1985).

Caring/Uncaring: Helpful (Rokeach 1968, 1973), Compassion (Vinson et al. 1977), Generosity and consideration of others (Steele and Redding 1962), Humanitarianism (Williams 1970), Concern for others (Mitchell 1983), Caring relationships and commitment (Yankelovich 1981).

Competitive/Noncompetitive: Competitive (Steele and Redding 1962; Mitchell 1983).

Conformist/Nonconformist: Conformity (Crosby et al. 1990), External conformity (Steele and Redding 1962; Williams 1970), Obedient (Rokeach 1968, 1973), Obeys (Alwin and Krosnick 1985).

Cultured/Uncultured: World of beauty (Rokeach 1968, 1973), Aesthetics (Prakash and Munson 1985).

Democratic/Authoritarian: Democracy (Williams 1970), Authoritarian (Adorno).

Dominant/Submissive: Power (Hofstede 1980), Powerlessness (Neil and Seeman 1964).

Efficient/Inefficient: Efficiency and practicality (Williams 1970), Puritan morality, including efficiency ethic (Steele and Redding 1962).

Egalitarian/Nonegalitarian: Equality (Rokeach 1968, 1973; Williams 1970; McQuarrie and Langmeyer 1985), Power distance (Hofstede 1980), Equalitarianism (Lipset 1963, 1964, 1986).

Free/Restrained: Freedom (Rokeach 1968, 1973; Williams 1970; Mc-Quarrie and Langmeyer 1985; Yankelovich 1981).

Imaginative/Unimaginative: Imaginative (Rokeach 1968, 1973; Mc-Quarrie and Langmeyer 1985), Creativity (Yankelovich 1981).

Independent/Dependent: Independent (Rokeach 1968, 1973; McQuarrie and Langmeyer 1985); Self-Direction (Crosby et al. 1990), Self-reliant (Mitchell 1983), Autonomy and connectedness (Yankelovich 1981).

Individualistic/Collectivistic: Value of the individual (Steele and Redding 1962), Individual personality (Williams 1970), Individualism vs. Collectivism (Hofstede 1980), Group-oriented vs. individualistic (Kluckhohn and Strodtbeck 1961), Individualistic (Mitchell 1983), Concern with community (Yankelovich 1981), Individualism (Lipset 1963, 1964, 1986).

Intelligent/Unintelligent: Intellectual (Rokeach 1968; McQuarrie and Langmeyer 1985).

Logical/Intuitive: Logical (Rokeach 1968, 1973), Science and secular rationality (Williams 1970), Masculinity vs. femininity (Hofstede 1980).

Materialistic/Spiritualistic: A comfortable life, inner harmony (Rokeach 1968, 1973), Material (Williams 1970), Material comfort associated with happiness, size equated with goodness, quantity over quality (Steele and Redding 1962), Hedonism (Crosby et al. 1990), Materialism, outward-directed versus inner-directed (Mitchell 1983), Inner harmony (McQuarrie and Langmeyer 1985), Materialism (Belk 1985; Wallendorf and Arnould 1988; Ger and Belk 1990).

Moral/Immoral: Virtuousness (Crosby et al. 1990), Integrity (Vinson et al. 1977), Honesty (Rokeach 1968, 1973), Moral orientation (Williams 1970), Puritan morality (Steele and Redding 1962), Good vs. evil in human nature (Kluckhohn and Strodtbeck 1960), Honest (Mitchell 1983), Moralistic (Lipset 1990).

Optimistic/Pessimistic: "Best is yet to be" (Steele and Redding 1962).

Patriotic/Unpatriotic: Patriotism (Steele and Redding 1962; Mitchell 1983), Nationalism and patriotism (Williams 1970).

Peaceful/Warlike: A world of peace, Inner harmony (Rokeach 1968, 1973).

Progressive/Retrogressive: Necessity of progress and change (Steele and Redding 1962), Progress (Williams 1970).

Idealistic/Realistic: Idealism (Crosby et al. 1990).

Responsible/Irresponsible: Responsible (Rokeach 1968, 1973), Personal responsibility (Steele and Redding 1962).

Social/Antisocial: Sociality (Steele and Redding 1962), Cheerful (Rokeach 1968, 1973), Polite (Rokeach 1968, 1973), Warm relations with others (Kahle 1983).

Family-oriented vs. Non-Family-oriented: Family security (Rokeach 1968, 1973; McQuarrie and Langmeyer 1985), Security (Crosby et al. 1990; Vinson et al. 1977), Importance of family (Mitchell 1983).

Survey of Canadian Perceptions of American Values

Method

The survey instrument consisted of the above twenty-seven paired adjectives, placed at polar ends of a seven-point semantic differential scale. The polarity of a number of the adjectives was reversed in order to ensure against response set. Canadian respondents were asked to evaluate the "typical American," using these semantic differential scales. The second part of the survey requested information on the demographics of respondents and their experience with Americans.

The study sampled ninety-eight students; of that number, fifteen failed to meet the criterion of being a Canadian citizen or landed immigrant. Thus, the final sample consisted of eighty-three undergraduate students enrolled in four different communication courses at the University of Ottawa, taught by English-speaking professors. The students, in fact, represented a cross-section of most of the undergraduate faculties of the University. They also represented all four undergraduate years, with the majority in second and third year Arts and Social Sciences. Seventy-two percent of the sample was female. While ages ranged from below twenty years to over fifty, most respondents (83 percent) were in their twenties. Almost all respondents had visited the United States; their impressions of Americans derived, at least in part, from that experience. A number had visited the United States "hundreds of times," but the average number was "once a year." A large percentage of students also drew their impressions from media depictions of Americans: television (81 percent), newspapers (62 percent), magazines (58 percent), and radio (18.5 percent).

Results

Canadians saw Americans as highly patriotic (a semantic score of 6.7), materialistic (6.5), competitive (6.4). They also saw Americans as dominant (6.1). Achievement-oriented received a rating of 5.8.

Respondents appeared to be ambivalent on how they saw Americans on a number of the value dimensions. Value ratings that fell into the middle range included active (a semantic score of 5.2), independent (5.1), free (5.1), conformist (4.9), optimistic (4.9), family-oriented (4.9), realistic (4.8), progressive (4.7), social (4.7), individualistic (4.7), democratic (4.7), efficient (4.6), competent (4.4), intelligent (4.4), imaginative (4.3), and logical (4.3).

The instrumental values receiving the lowest overall ratings by Canadians were peaceful (a semantic score of 2.0), cultured (3.5), moral (3.6), responsible (3.8), egalitarian (3.9), and caring (3.9).

Respondents showed a high level of consistency (standard deviations of .5 to 1.3) in how they rated Americans on materialism, patriotism, levels of aggressiveness (warlike vs. peaceful), and family orientation. On the other hand, significant variations (standard deviations of 1.6 to 2.2) occurred in how respondents scored the instrumental values related to conformity, culture, imagination, individualism, and sociality. For example, the average score on conformity was 4.9; however, further analysis reveals that 46 percent of the responses were in the 6.0 to 7.0 range. The average score on culture was 3.5; however, the average was skewed by 29 percent of the respondents rating Americans in the 2.0 range. Imagination generated an average of 4.3; however, the distribution of responses was bimodal, with 33 percent of the responses in the 6.0 to 7.0 range and 21 percent in the 1.0 to 2.0 range. The responses to the value of individualism were heavily skewed by 47 percent of the respondents rating Americans in the 6.0 to 7.0 range and 25 percent in the 1.0 to 2.0 range. Thus, the 4.7 mean on individualism failed to show the strength of opinion on that attribute. The average on sociality was 4.7; however, 40 percent of respondents placed Americans in the 6.0 to 7.0 range.

Cross-tabulations were conducted to uncover any gender differences in responses. The only significant findings ($p < .05$) involved the instrumental values individualistic, intelligent, and logical. Males tended to see Americans as more individualistic, less intelligent, and less logical than did females.

Content Analysis of Newspapers

Method

The content analysis covered the July 1994 to July 1995 period. The researchers conducted data base searches, using the key words "American values" and "Americanization." The search generated 220 articles from eleven large circulation anglophone newspapers, representing all major population regions in Canada (the Atlantic, Quebec, Ontario, the Prairies, and British Columbia). The newspapers included the *Ottawa Citizen*, the *Financial Post*, the *Spectator* (Hamilton), the *Toronto Sun*, the *Toronto Star*, the *Gazette* (Montreal), the *Daily News* (Halifax), the *Vancouver Sun*, the *Calgary Herald*, the *Edmonton Journal*, and the *Province* (Vancouver). The researchers discarded all articles that originated in other countries; for example, wire stories from the

U.S. They also included only one copy of each article in the analysis, eliminating duplicates that appeared in more than one newspaper. The final article count, considered in this study, was ninety-eight.

Referring to the list of twenty-seven American values, the coders noted each time one of the twenty-seven values (or its polar opposite) appeared in each of the ninety-eight articles. The unit of analysis was the article; that is, no matter how many references to a trait appeared within a single article, the coders only noted the value once for each article. After reading all the articles, the coders computed the total number of times that values (or their polar opposites) appeared.

Results

Table 12.1 gives the results of the frequency count, with high frequency values appearing early in the list. References to values previously identified as part of the American value system appear in the second column (e.g., competent, individualistic, caring, etc.). References to traits that suggest the opposite of expressed American values appear in the third column (e.g., incompetent, collectivistic, or uncaring).

Discussion

Newspaper references to American values tended to be more frequently negative than positive. The most common theme to appear in the coverage related to the domination of Canada by the United States. Americans were perceived as strong, aggressive actors on the international scene. For example, Canadian journalists said that American culture is "swallowing up the whole planet" (Ruttan 1994). The trait that received the largest number of references was dominant—which relates to the values of power, activity, competition, and independence.

Many Canadian journalists commented on the American threat to Canadian culture—especially the Canadian film industry, television, and radio (Lapierre 1994). The *Province* urged Canadians to take a stance against "American cultural imperialism" (Hauka 1995). Some spoke of the "severe consequences" (Kainz 1994) of Americanizing Canada's broadcasting system. Others warned of hazards to the performing arts and clothing industries (Dunn 1995) and the book publishing trade (McLeod 1995). The *Ottawa Citizen* encouraged Canada's film, television, and video game industries to "work with foreign producers in an effort to ward off further Americanization of Canadian culture" ("Film, TV industry," 1994). Values at the heart of these concerns included competitiveness, independence, activity, and culture.

Table 12.1. Canadian Perception of American Values

American Value	Number of References to American Value	Number of References to Polar Opposite
Dominant	40	
Caring	1	26
Individualistic	25	
Materialistic	25	
Competitive	18	
Egalitarian	5	16
Peaceful		16
Achievement-oriented	8	
Competent	8	1
Independent	6	
Progressive	5	1
Efficient	4	2
Moral	4	
Patriotic	2	
Imaginative	2	
Family-oriented	2	
Social	1	1
Conformist	1	1
Imaginative		2

Note: Values with fewer than 2 out of a possible 98 references do not appear.

Canadians also expressed fears that their sports were being Americanized, particularly hockey and the Canadian Football League. Many believe that Canadian sports are becoming more aggressive and competitive—traits that they believe to reflect American values. One Canadian journalist wrote: "Americans haven't just embraced the game of hockey; they've taken control" (Starkman 1995). Referring to the Toronto area, another observed cynically: "The secret's out; basketball comes to America's 51st capital" (O'Leary 1994). Others spoke of American competition "killing off" Canada's "venerable league" (O'Leary, 1994). Values at stake in these discussions related to competition and independence. Canadians also saw Americans as active to the point of being aggressive.

Other Canadian journalists addressed the Americanization of Canada's welfare system ("Campaign Blasts," 1994) and other social systems: The "failing status quo will eventually lead to the Americanization of our safety net" ("How Not to Run," 1994). Another warned: "We're losing our patience. Our capacity for compassion is weakening. We're becoming more and more like the Americans" (Kennedy 1994). Many see the American health care system as less caring; they contrasted Canada's "fair and caring public health care system" with the American Medicare system (Mardiros 1995). They saw the American health care system as more individualistic, materialistic, and non-egalitarian.

Canadians were also concerned that their companies were being taken over and controlled by Americans; e.g., Scott Paper (Hamilton 1995) and the Loewen Group (Schreiner 1995). Historically, many have feared that Canada would be "swallowed up by the American empire," as multinational corporations consolidated their "control of the country's resource and manufacturing sectors" (Laxer 1994). The values referenced in these discussions related to competition, materialism, independence, and a deficit of egalitarianism.

Some journalists saw American society as "violent": "Every day we witness the American dream in action. Forgotten homeless people living in filthy squalor on filthy American streets. Children gunning each other down in broad daylight." (Regan 1995). In a fashion typical of Canadians, another writer used American values as a reference point for defining Canadian values:

> To refer to my own experience, there are certain Canadian values and cultural beliefs that I prefer to the American ones: a distaste for violence and grandiose aggressiveness, a stronger sense of the importance of the community in relation to the individual. (Regan 1995)

A journalist for the *Vancouver Sun* also defined Canadian values in terms of their opposition to American values: "We are not Americans. Not as violent, not as rude, not as vulnerable to the vagaries of life behind our security blanket of cradle to grave social programs" (Sheppard 1995). Thus, the writers implied that the American society is characterized by devotion to individualistic, warlike (or violent), uncaring, and sometimes immoral behaviors. They also suggested that Americans are too active (or aggressive).

Brian Jewitt argued that Quebec must separate to save itself from this "violence, lack of morality, and high youth suicide rates," byproducts of Canada's position as a "sovereign colony of the U.S." (Cited in Shahin 1995). Other writers spoke of Americans' "preoccupation with violence" (Chessman 1995) and said that they are "killing themselves off" (Morton 1994). In talking about Canada's gun control laws, one Canadian commented on the need to enact sensible gun laws and to avoid the "'Americanization' of our streets" ("Gun Owners," 1994). Thus, these journalists suggested, either explicitly or implicitly, that Americans are anti-social, warlike, immoral, and uncaring.

Some Canadians also saw American politics as immoral (Blizzard 1994); others associated the Americanization of Canada with conservative political values (Gessell 1994; "CUPE Alarmed," 1994). Other writers, however, decried the Canadian media's negative commentaries on American society. For example, one writer observed sarcastically:

I behold the media as they fulminate with dire warnings of our impending Americanization. As one who has spent the last four-plus years on the fringes of the workforce, I am not exactly quaking in fear of the terrible spectre of full employment and lower taxation. (Jackson 1995)

This article implied activity and competence in the American approach to dealing with workplace-related issues.

Some also described Americans as manifesting values such as imagination, individualism, independence, competitiveness, and achievement-orientation: "The American spirit of entrepreneurship is not bad. Americans take big strides. They have curiosity, creativity and enterprise" (Jaremko 1994). The value of efficiency was at the heart of a statement by Jane Fulton, Deputy Minister of Health in Alberta, who said that the Americanization of Canada's health system could result in greater efficiency in delivering health care services (Arnold 1995).

Another writer suggested that Americans have been progressive in their approach to women's issues: "American culture has given us the progress of feminism" (Ruttan 1994).

It is interesting to note that almost all positive comments originated in Alberta, a province that identifies closely with the United States. Many Americans visit, reside in, and do business with Albertans. The American consulate in Calgary claims to serve the "world's largest concentration of U.S. expatriates" (Ward 1994). In fact, the American community in and around Calgary refer to themselves as "Amergarians." The Prairies and the Western provinces are also known historically to have strong psychic ties with their neighbors to the south. Many believe that they have more in common with the Western United States than with Eastern Canada. As one writer noted, there is a "generally positive feeling toward Americans in Calgary" (Ward 1994).

Conclusion

It is interesting because researchers such as Hofstede (1980) have concluded that Canadians are close to Americans in their value sets. Yet Canadians would agree more with Lipset (1990), who sees Americans as holding a set of societal values that are quite distinct from Canadians. Canadians often define themselves as the antithesis of American culture. They also believe that they understand and know more about Americans than Americans know about Canada—an opinion that may be based in reality since Canadians make twice as many visits to the U.S. each year as Americans make to Canada.

In fact, this study does demonstrate that Canadians were able to identify many of the values that Americans claim to hold. Both survey and content analysis results showed that Canadians rated Americans high on the positive end of the materialistic, achievement-oriented, competitive, and dominant scales—both in the survey and newspaper coverage. Survey respondents also saw Americans as highly patriotic; however, Canadian newspapers did not discuss this topic. These five values show up repeatedly when Americans define their own values. Despite the fact that Canadians recognized the existence of these values in American society, they did not often see the values as ones that they would want to emulate. On the contrary, they see the values as extremely threatening in sovereignty terms. This perception surfaced repeatedly in newspaper articles that described the reactions of Canadian business (e.g., to the entry of Wal-Mart into Canada), sports (e.g., the takeover and changing of the Canadian Football League), telecommunications and culture (e.g., "Death Star" satellite broadcasting), and health care models (privatization of health care).

Significant differences surfaced in Canadian and American responses to the instrumental values of peaceful, caring, moral, responsible, egalitarian, and cultured. Canadians tended to see Americans as displaying the opposite characteristics: warlike or violent, uncaring, immoral, irresponsible, non-egalitarian, and uncultured behaviors—which would suggest that Canadians do not see Americans as manifesting the instrumental values that they claim to hold as standards. Some recent U.S. studies have shown trends in the direction of increasing stress on the values of honesty and integrity; other studies have demonstrated the growing influence of the Christian Right and fundamentalist religions in the U.S. However, survey respondents did not appear to recognize these trends when they rated Americans low on morality, caring, and responsibility.

Especially strong consistency in survey and content analysis results occurred with respect to the terms warlike, uncaring, and non-egalitarian. Uncultured did not appear in the results of the content analysis, and survey respondents showed little agreement on this point. Immoral and irresponsible had a strong showing in the survey results but appeared only occasionally in the content analysis. Individualism, on the other hand, emerged as a strong value in the content analysis but less definitively in the survey.

The tendency of Canadian media to depict Americans in negative terms probably derives, at least in part, from Canadian fears of the "economies of scale" between the two countries. Americans outnumber Canadians by almost 10 to 1. Also history demonstrates that trends that begin in the U.S. often move into Canada within decades. Some current American trends that Canadians would not like to inherit include urban decay, violence, and the erosion of the universal social safety net. Variation in the responses of Albertans can be explained by the large numbers of Americans living in that province and the historical tendency of Albertans to identify more strongly with Western Americans than with Eastern Canadians.

In closing, it is important to note that future studies should seek to identify differences in the perceptions of anglophones and francophones in Canada, in relationship to U.S. image. Many Quebecers spend their retirement years in the southern U.S. Also, French-speaking Canadians are probably less threatened by American television, radio, and other cultural products than are English-speaking Canadians. Therefore, significant differences may exist in how francophones and anglophones perceive Americans.

References

Adler, R.B., and G. Rodman. (1994). *Understanding human communication*, 5th ed.. Fort Worth: Harcourt Brace.

Adorno, T. W., E. Frenkel-Brunswick, D.J. Levinson, and R.N. Sanford. (1950). *The authorian personality*. New York: Harper.

Allport, G.W. (1954). *Personality*. New York: Holt.

Allport, G.W., P.E. Vernon, and G. Lindzey. (1950). *Study of values*. Boston: Houghton Mifflin.

Althen, G. (1988). *American ways: A guide to foreigners*. Yarmouth, Me.: Intercultural Press.

Alwin, D.F., and J.A. Krosnick. (1985, Winter). The measurement of values: A comparison of ratings and rankings. *Public Opinion Quarterly* 49: pp. 535–552.

Arnold, T. (1995, July 19). Klein backs Fulton's health push. *Calgary Herald*, p. A2.

Badaracco, C. (1992). Religious lobbyists in the public square. *Public Relations Quarterly* 37 (1): pp. 30–36.

Baer, D., E. Grabb, and W.A. Johnston. (1990). The values of Canadians and Americans: A critical analysis and reassessment. *Social Forces* 68 (3): pp. 693–713.

Ball-Rokeach, S.J., M. Rokeach, and J.W. Grube. (1984). *The great American values test*. New York: The Free Press.

Bearden, W.O., R.G. Netemeyer, and M.F. Mobley. (1993). *Handbook of marketing scales*. Newbury Park, Cal.: Sage.

Beatty, S.E., P.M. Homer, and L.R. Kahle. (1988). Problems with VALS in international marketing research: An example from an application of the empirical mirror technique. In M.J. Houston (Ed.), *Advances in Consumer Research*, Vol. 15, pp. 375–380). Ann Arbor: Association for Consumer Research.

Beatty, S.E., L.R. Kahle, P. Homer, and S. Misra. (1985, Winter). Alternative measurement approaches to consumer values: The list of values and the Rokeach Value Survey. *Psychology and Marketing* 2: pp. 181–200.

Belk, R.W. (1984). Three scales to measure constructs related to materialism: Reliability, validity, and relationships to measures of happiness. In T. C. Kinnear (Ed.), *Advances in Consumer Reasearch*, Vol. 11, pp. 291–297. Provo, Utah: Association for Consumer Research.

Belk, R.W. (1985, December). Materialism: Trait aspects of living in the material world. *Journal of Consumer Research* 12: pp. 265–279.

Bem, D.J. (1970). *Beliefs, attitudes and human affairs*. Belmont, Cal.: Brooks Cole.

Berman, J.J. (1970). *Cross-cultural perspectives*. Lincoln: University of Nebraska Press.

Blizzard, C. (1994, November 13). High gear: mayoralty race is tight as candidates on last lap. *Toronto Sun*, p. 24.

Cairns, A.C. (1975). Political science in Canada and the Americanization issue. *Canadian Journal of Political Science* 8 (2): pp. 191–225.

Campaign blasts Axworthy reforms: Council vows to upset 'Americanization" of welfare. (1994, October 12). *Gazette*, p. A9.

Cantril, H. (1965). *The pattern of human concerns*. New Brunswick, N.J.: Rutgers University Press.

Carter, R.E. (1956, April). An experiment in value measurement. *American Sociological Review* 21: pp. 156–163.

Chessman, M.E. (1995, April 21). European heritage worth promoting. *Edmonton Journal*, p. A15.

Crissman, P. (1942). Temporal changes and sexual differences in moral judgments. *Journal of Social Psychology* 16: pp. 29–36.

Crosby, L.A., M.J. Bitner, and J.D. Gill. (1990, March). Organizational structure of values. *Journal of Business Research* 20: pp. 123–134.

CUPE alarmed by Tories. (1994, November 9). *Toronto Sun*, p. 39.

Doran, C. F., and J.P. Sewell. (1988, May). *The Annals of the American Academy* 497: pp. 105–119.

Dunn, B. (1995, May 8). U.S. clothing labels are hot; Canadian manufacturers focus on exports as they lose retail battle to giant manufacturers. *Gazette* (Montreal), p. F15.

Easterlin, R.A., and E.M. Crimmins. (1991). Private materialism, personal self-fulfillment, family life, and public interest: The nature, effects, and causes of recent changes in the values of American youth. *Public Opinion Quarterly* 55 (4): pp. 499–533.

Film, TV industry: Foreign allies needed to fight Americanization. (1994, December 17). *Ottawa Citizen*, p. D10.

Ger, G., and R.W. Belk. (1990). Measuring and comparing materialism across countries. In M.E. Goldberg, G. Gorn, and R.W. Pollay (Eds.), *Advances in Consumer Research* 17, pp. 186–192. Provo, Utah: Association for Consumer Research.

Gessell, P. (1994, December 11). Sellout of Canadian film industry rapped. *Calgary Herald*, p. C4.

Gun owners have backs to the wall: The question is: Are they the threat or the threatened? [Editorial]. (1994, September 12). *Vancouver Sun*, p. A11.

Hamilton, G. (1995, March 21). New wrinkles at Scott Paper could spell changes at Hull plant. *Ottawa Citizen*, p. C3.

Hauka, D. Dueling opinions: Impending gun controls get both sides of debate picking favorite targets. (1995, February 19). *The Province* (Vancouver), p. A17.

Hawes, M.K. (1989, January/February). Mulroney and the Americans: A new era? *International Perspectives*, pp. 9–12.

Hofstede, G. (1980). Motivation, leadership, and organization: Do American theories apply abroad? *Organization Dynamics* 9: pp. 42–53.

How not to run a social safety net. [Editorial]. (1994, September 16). *Toronto Star*, p. A20.

Inglehart, R. (1981, December). Post-materialism in an environment of insecurity. *American Political Science Review* 75: pp. 880–900.

Innis, H., (Ed.). (1972). *Issues for the Seventies: Americanization*. Toronto: McGraw-Hill Ryerson Limited.

Jackson, N. (1995, June 19). [Letter to the editor]. *Toronto Sun*, p. 10.

Jaremko, G. (1994, November 20). Our American cousins: 'Amerganians' give thanks for Calgary. *Calgary Herald*, p. A11.

Kahle, L.R. (1983). *Social changes and value change: Adaptation to life in America*. New York: Praeger.

Kahle, L.R. (1986). The nine nations of North America and the value basis of geographic segmentation. *Journal of Marketing* 50: pp. 37–47.

Kahle, L.R., S.E. Beatty, and P. Homer. (1986, December). Alternative measurement approaches to consumer values: The List of Values (LOV) and Values and Life Style (VALS). *Journal of Consumer Research* 13: pp. 405–409.

Kahle, L.R., B. Poulos, and A. Sukhdial. (1988, February/March). Changes in social values in the United States during the past decade. *Journal of Advertising Research* 28: pp. 35–41.

Kainz, A. (1994, November 29). Controversy brewing over make up of panel on direct- to-home broadcasting: Possible selection of Gordon Ritchie raises questions of conflict of interest. *Ottawa Citizen*, p. D4.

Kalish, R.A., and K.W. Collier. (1981). Exploring human values: Psychological and philosophical considerations. Monterey, Cal.: Brooks/Cole.

Kempton, W., J.S. Boster, and J.A. Hartley. (1995). *Environmental values in American culture*. Cambridge: The MIT Press.

Kennedy, M. (1994, October 8). The Americanization of Canada's safety net. *Ottawa Citizen*, p. B1

Kluckhohn, F.R., and F.L. Strodtbeck. (1961). Variations in value orientations. Westport: Greenwood Press.

Lamorie, A. (1976). *How they sold our Canada to the U.S.A.* (2nd ed.). Toronto: NC Press Limited.

Lapierre, L. (1994, November 5). Nash fails to answer CBC riddle. *Financial Post*, p. S6.

Lasswell, H. (1967). *Power and personality*. New York: Viking.

Laxer, J. (1994, October 23). NDP Waffle group's ideas still relevant 25 years later. *Toronto Star*, p. E3.

Leonard-Barton, D. (1981, December). Voluntary simplicity lifestyles and energy conservation. *Journal of Consumer Research* 8: pp. 243–252.

Lichtenstein, D.R., R.G. Netemeyer, and S. Burton. (1990, July). Distinguishing coupon proneness from value consciousness: An acquisition-transaction utility theory perspective. *Journal of Marketing* 54: pp. 54–67.

Lipset, S.M. (1963). The value patterns of democracy: A case study in comparative analysis. *American Sociological Review* 28: pp. 515–531.

Lipset, S.M. (1964). Canada and the United States—A comparative view. *Canadian Review of Sociology and Anthropology* 1: pp. 173–185.

Lipset, S.M. (1967). *The first new nation*. New York: Anchor Books.

Lipset, S.M. (1986). Historical traditions and national characteristics: A comparative analysis of Canada and the United States. *Canadian Journal of Sociology* 11: pp. 113–155.

Lipset, S.M. (1990). The values of Canadians and Americans: A reply. *Social Forces* 69 (1): pp. 267–272.

Litt, P. (1991). The Massey Commission, Americanization, and Canadian cultural nationalism. *Queen's Quarterly* 98 (2): pp. 375–387.

Mardiros, B. (1995, July 11). Fulton protesters were not naive. *Edmonton Journal*, p. A9.

Maslow, A.H. (1954). *Motivation and personality*. New York: Harper.

McLeod, J. (1995, June 15). Canadian business: The American way. *Daily News* (Halifax), p. 22.

McQuarrie, E.F., and D. Langmeyer. (1985, Winter). Using values to measure attitudes toward discontinuous innovations. *Psychology & Marketing* 2: pp. 239–252.

Miller, D.C. (1991). *Handbook of research design and social measurement* (5th ed.). Newbury Park, Cal.: Sage.

Mitchell, A. (1983). *The nine American lifestyles*. New York: Macmillan.

Moffett, S.E. (1972). *The Americanization of Canada*. Toronto: University of Toronto Press.

Morton, B. (1994, November 17). Residents win fight against gun-sale plan. *Vancouver Sun*, p. B5.

Moschis, G.P., and G.A. Churchill, Jr. (1978, November). Consumer socialization: A theoretical and empirical analysis. *Journal of Marketing Research* 15: pp. 599–609.

Munson, J.M., S.H. McIntyre, and E.F. McQuarrie. (1988). Shortening the Rokeach Value Survey for use in consumer behavior. In M.J. Houston (Ed.), *Advances in Consumer Research* 15, pp. 381–386. Provo, Utah: Association for Consumer Research.

Ogmundson, R. (1980). Toward study of the endangered species known as the anglophone Canadian. *Canadian Journal of Sociology* 5 (1): pp. 1–11.

O'Leary, J. (1994, August 7). The secret's out; basketball comes to America's 51st capital. *Toronto Sun*, p. M3.

Orchard, D. (1993). *The fight for Canada: Four centuries of resistance to American expansionism*. Toronto: Stoddart.

Osgood, C.E., G.J. Suci, and P.H. Tannenbaum. (1957). *The measurement of meaning*. Urbana: University of Illinois Press.

Persinos, J.F. (1994, September). Has the Christian Right taken over the Republican party? *Campaign and Elections*, pp. 21–24.

Prakash, V., and J.M. Munson. (1985, Winter). Values, expectations from the marketing systems and product expectations. *Psychology & Marketing* 2: pp. 279–298.

Raths, L.E., M. Harmann, and S.B. Simon. (1966). *Values and teaching*. Columbus: Charles E. Merrill.

Regan, T. (1995, July 3). An immigrant looks home: My hunger for things Canadian tells me why newcomers want to hold on to their cultures. *Daily News* (Halifax), p. 10.

Richins, M.L. (1987). Media, materialism, and human happiness. In M. Wallendorf and P. Anderson (Eds.), *Advances in Consumer Research* 14, pp. 352–356. Provo, Utah: Association for Consumer Research.

Richins, M.L., and S. Dawson. (1990). Measuring material values: A preliminary report on scale development. In M.E. Goldberg, G. Gorn, and R.W. Pollay (Eds.), *Advances in Consumer Research* 17, pp. 169–175. Provo, Utah: Association for Consumer Research.

Roelofs, H.M. (1992). *The poverty of American politics: A theoretical interpretation*. Philadelphia: Temple University Press.

Rokeach, M. (1960). *The open and closed mind*. New York: Basic Books.

Rokeach, M. (1968). *Beliefs, attitudes and values*. San Francisco: Jossey-Bass.

Rokeach, M. (1973). *The nature of human values*. New York: Free Press.

Rokeach, M. (1979). *Understanding human values*. New York: Free Press.

Ruttan, S. (1994, October 24). Immigrant kids, parents often in conflict. *Calgary Herald*, p. B1.

Samovar, L.A., and R.E. Porter. (1995). *Communication between cultures* (2nd ed.). Belmont, Cal.: Wadsworth.

Schreiner, J. (1995, June 20). Americanization pays off for Loewen Group. *Financial Post*, p. 25.

Scott, C., and W.J. Lundstrom. (1990). Dimensions of possession satisfaction: A preliminary analysis. *Journal of Satisfaction, Dissatisfaction and Complaining Behavior* 3: pp. 100–104.

Scott, W.A. (1959, June). Empirical assessment of values and ideologies. *American Sociological Review* 24: pp. 299–310.

Shahin, M. (1995, February 21). Sovereignty hearing: Draft bill not precise enough, commission hears; Outaouais residents want more details to make choice about their future. *Ottawa Citizen*, p. B2.

Sheppard, J. (1995, May 6). Pillars of identity topple as different Canada emerges: Erosion of cultural icons fuels ongoing national debate. *Vancouver Sun*, p. A10.

Simon, S.B., L.W. Howe, and H. Kirschenbaum. (1972). *Values clarification*. New York: Hart.

Smith, J. (1988). Canadian confederation and the influence of American federalism. *Canadian Journal of Political Science* 21 (3): pp. 443–463.

Starkman, R. (1995, April 8). Hockey's future: Big nets and colored pucks? Many worry Canadian game won't survive 'Americanization.' *Toronto Star*, p. A1.

Statistics Canada. (1992). *Canada a portrait* (54th ed.). Ottawa: Supply and Services Canada.

Steele, E.D., and W.C. Redding. (1962). The American value system: Premises for persuasion. *Western Speech* 26: pp. 83–91.

Stewart, E.C., and M.J. Bennett. (1991). *American cultural patterns: A cross-cultural perspective*. Yarmouth, Me.: Intercultural Press.

Tashchian, A., M.E. Slama, and R. Tashchian. (1984). Measuring attitudes toward energy conservation: Cynicism, belief in material growth, and faith in technology. *Journal of Public Policy & Marketing* 3 (2): pp. 134–148.

Thurstone, L.L. (1959). *The measurement of values*. Chicago: University of Chicago Press.

Trenholm, S., and A. Jensen. (1992). *Interpersonal communication* (2nd ed.). Belmont, Cal.: Wadsworth.

Unger, L., and J.B. Kernan. (1983, March). On the meaning of leisure: An investigation of some determinants of the subjective experience. *Journal of Consumer Research* 9: pp. 381–392.

Vinson, D.E., J.M. Munson, and M. Nakanishi. (1977). An investigation of the Rokeach Value Survey for consumer research applications. In W. E. Perreault (Ed.), *Advances in Consumer Research* 4, pp. 247–252. Provo, Utah: Association for Consumer Research.

Wallendorf, M., and E.J. Arnould. (1988). My favorite things: A cross-cultural inquiry into object attachment, possessiveness and social linkage. *Journal of Consumer Research* 14 (4): pp. 531–547.

Ward, S. (1994, November 20). Film-making boom puts U.K. in the picture. *Calgary Herald*, p. D8.

Williams, R.M., Jr. (1970). *American society: A sociological interpretation* (3rd ed). New York: Alfred A. Knopf.

Williams, R.M., Jr. (1979). Change and stability in values and value systems: A sociological perspective. In M. Rokeach (Ed.), *Understanding human values*, pp. 15–46. New York: Free Press.

Yamauchi, K.T., and D.I. Templer. (1982). The development of a money attitude scale. *Journal of Personality Assessment* 46: pp. 522–528.

Yankelovich, D. (1981). *New rules: Searching for self-fulfillment in a world turned upside down*. New York: Random House.

13

The Paradoxical Brazilian Views Concerning American Media Products

ALEX FERNANDO TEIXEIRA PRIMO

Introduction

This chapter will discuss the consumption of American media products in Brazil, highly criticized by Brazilian scholars. Much of the body of knowledge available in Brazil holds that American television programs, movies, music, and other cultural products have an alienating power and constitute a form of imperialism, cultural invasion, and neocolonialism conducted by the United States to maintain its international hegemony and generate high profits. At the same time that scholars publish their critiques, the Brazilian audiences fill movie theaters showing American movies, buy a great many compact discs (CDs) and tapes of American music, and stay tuned to American television programs.

This research intends to report the main critiques of American media found in the body of knowledge available in Brazil through a review of literature. Later, data concerning the percentage of American movies, programs, and music present in Brazilian television and radio stations, and data from a survey conducted to evaluate the public's perception and preferences, are discussed and confronted with the theories analyzed.

The American Cultural Industry

To understand the concept of cultural industry, it is first necessary to understand that it is a phenomenon of industrialization. Coelho (1989) remarks that it emerges through changes in human work, which determine a particular

179

industry (the cultural one) and a type of culture (the mass culture). For this industry to succeed, it is necessary to create a market that can consume the industrial production of "culture." Because these cultural products will reach a huge market, they are produced for the masses, with their characteristics simplified to an extent that they may be understood by the greatest amount of people. This simplification does not demand any effort from the consumer apart from the purchase of the products.

Because of the ephemerality of the industrial culture, it only serves as entertainment, and, thus, as a form of escaping from reality, never as a mean of looking at reality and criticizing it. It serves as a reinforcement to the social norms. It encourages social compliance, instead of social criticism. It sedates the critical mind and forces a conformist behavior, paralyzing social development.

Coelho reminds that every product brings traces of the productive system in which it was generated. Thus, imported American media products bring within them the ideology of the United States. Thus, they have an alienating characteristic as they divulge an alien ideology, which is consumed without discussion. Moreover, as the effects of those products are unidirectional (from the source to the receiver), Coelho states that the result of that process is conformation and alienation; it is formation instead of information.

But why are the cultural industry's messages alienating? According to Coelho, the messages are superficial and mainly use the type of signs called indices in semiotics. There is no time for a logical analysis; the messages are fast, transitory, and ephemeral. There is no revelation, just confirmation. The cultural industry's effects are very broad. It generates a standardization of food, clothes, music, TV programs, business styles, and linguistic conventions.

Soifer (1992), analyzing the impact of television on children, criticizes the great quantity of American movies, series, and cartoons on Brazilian television. According to her, those television products portray alien cultural traces and may harm a child's learning of Portuguese. Those American products are dubbed into Portuguese, but still maintain American idioms and, thus, the American way of representing reality through language. Because the dubbed dialogues still have to follow the gestures of the characters, a difficulty shows up. English has short words and brief sentences, making it different from Portuguese (bigger words and richer sentences). Hence, to dub those products it is necessary to translate the dialogues in an artificial, sharp, and brief way.

> [Brazilian] children get used to a lexicon where monosyllables and interjections prevail. This restricts the possibilities of enlarging their idiomatic knowledge, which added to the fact that, by watching television, they do not read, and as the language constitutes the vehicle

by excellence for the expression of ideas and feelings, the difficulty for family and social communication is incremented by the poverty of the employed language. (36)

Furthermore, Soifer adds that the most popular American movies and series show situations that have almost nothing to do with Brazilian reality. Cowboys, gangsters, the Mafia, and family dismemberment are disconnected from the Brazilian context. "By seeing [Brazilian] children showing interest for those subjects or imitating those situations, it is not possible to regret that they do not know what happens in their own country, its living style and what are and were its problems" (p. 37).

American movies and series shown in Brazilian television are called "canned" programs (*enlatados*), a comparison to canned food: ready for consumption. Vieira (1978) states that the "canned" programs are more profitable (as it is cheaper to import a finished product than to produce a brand new one), but a more harmful option. It harms the technicians and actors, who lose employment in their own country, and also generates cultural alienation and colonization. Brazilian values and themes are forgotten, and Brazilian homes are invaded by programs that show all the violence and problems of the United States. Vieira concludes that there is a colonized psychology in Brazil. That is the belief that anything that comes from abroad is better than the national equivalents.

> As we suffocate the national values and substitute them by the American ones in the American fiction, as it is more present among us, we are blocking the formation of a cultural consciousness, alienating culturally our children, destroying the national soul, and could hardly take the mass media to commit a more serious crime against nationality. We are, with these resources, forming a people without a root in the land, without a connection to its history, without a connection to its future, a people without identity and, hence, without independency, easily maneuvered, capable of being molded as water. (Vieira 1978, 89)

Much of this argumentation is confronted by the remarks of Silva (1985). According to this author, it is not necessary to still insist that the American influence on television is so strong. The programming of the Globo network (the single most powerful and most watched network in Brazil) and of other networks, after 5:00 P.M., during prime time, and often until 11:30 P.M. consists of programs entirely produced in Brazil. Globo has even substituted an American series shown in the afternoon for a national daily series targeted to teen audiences. Thus, according to the statistics showing the average amount of time that Brazilians stay in front of television, and the period of the day that they watch that medium, it is possible to conclude that Brazilians are mainly exposed to Brazilian programs.

Imperialism

The word *imperialism* means the international relationship where a central and powerful country has dominating power over poor and peripheral countries, which are reduced to the condition of its "colonies." The Latin American countries were for a long period of time colonies of Spain and Portugal. A century and a half ago, these countries rid themselves of that colonial condition. However, Beltrán and Cardona (1982) state that during this century Latin American countries have been submitted to the dominant influence of the United States. The resemblance to that colonial condition is such that it can be characterized as a state of "neocolonialism."

According to those authors, American imperialism can be detected in the economy, politics, and culture, economic imperialism being most prominent. The United States maintains an economic relationship with Latin countries that is characterized by inequalities:

> Latin America is forced to sell its raw material at low prices to the United States, at the same time that it has to pay high prices for the importation of American manufactured products. As a consequence, there is a chronically unbalanced market determining an increasing deficit, which affects greatly the plans and actions for development. (Beltrán and Cardona 1982, 27)

According to Hamelink (1993), American economic restrictions have significant impact on nations' domestic politics, which often contribute to the rise of poverty in developing countries. Transnational lobbyists ask for their industries the same incentives and treatment as are given by the governments to national industries. Furthermore, they are pressuring governments for guaranties and permanent settlement to eliminate certain taxes imposed on transnational industries, which, in turn, eliminate the protection for domestic industries. Moreover, during the discussion on intellectual property, the industrialized countries have demanded legislation that favors foreign technology.

> We, Brazilians, Argentineans, Mexicans, relate to the United states as debtors. In this sense, what happens there, affects us. Debtors of a perverse debt, imposed by a system that offered us modernity by the cost of an eternal debt, and that did not deliver the promised merchandise but demands the payment of the installments. (Berger 1993, 45)

Political imperialism contributes to the maintenance of Latin America's economic submission. Traditionally, the United States has positioned itself on the side of conservative governments in Latin America, thereby guaranteeing their dominance. The United States has also opposed social, political, and economic changes in those countries. In the case of actual changes that could harm American interests, the United States has employed economic sanctions, diplomatic pressure, propaganda campaigns, secret operations, and direct military operations.

Finally, cultural imperialism can be characterized as the imposition of the culture of the imperialistic country over the neighboring countries, harming their cultural integrity. To "imperial" countries, cultural domination is vital to the maintenance of hegemony. Beltrán and Cardona list a series of instruments that contribute to American cultural domination: (a) international news agencies, (b) international advertising agencies (as industries become internationalized, their advertising agencies are forced to open branches abroad), (c) international companies of public opinion, market research, and public relations, (d) transnational corporations advertising their products, (e) exporters of material for print and audiovisual programming, (f) exporters of communication equipment and technologies, (g) official propaganda organisms, (h) international telecommunication companies, (i) official organs and security centers.

To understand American cultural imperialistic politics, it is also important to note that it has been part of the American total diplomacy doctrine. Ianni (1976) states that since World War II, the United States has invested material and intellectual resources for the consolidation and extension of its hegemony.

Mattelart (1994) adds that Walt Disney was named the "good will ambassador" during the war to bring the Latin countries closer to the United States. Popular figures of Brazil, Mexico, and the Andes were represented by characters created by the Disney studios who "starred" in movies such as *Los Tres Caballeros* and *Saludos Amigos*. Zé Carioca, the Disney character representing Brazilian men, is still popular today. This comic magazine, which is published only in Brazil, sells 120,000 copies per month (Almanaque Abril 1995). Carmen Miranda, a popular singer in Brazil in the 1940s and 1950s, was taken to Hollywood to star in musicals, singing Brazilian songs. This also helped to align the United States and Brazil. That "diplomatic" doctrine, with clear imperialistic connotations, was intensified and gained new meaning after World War II and during the Cold War.

Marcondes Filho (1986) criticizes the critics of so-called "cultural imperialism." According to him, analysis of the presence of American media products in Brazil follows a predetermined script: it is always the same villain, the cultural imperialism, that chases the heroine of the story, the (virgin) popular culture. In all studies that follow that vein, there is a same preoccupation: "the terror that comes from abroad." The United States was elected the villain, which became a comfortable model. Instead of criticizing the spirit and capitalist practice, the theorists attacked its agents. Marcondes Filho concludes that "the struggle is against those enemies and not against that ideology: turn down the imperialists for us to be the executors of capitalism at home" (19). He remarks that those studies took for granted the ideological and imperialistic power of those media products upon the Latin countries, underestimating the reaction power of the "dominated," transforming the media into a fetish, and fearing the media as such.

Moreover, Marcondes Filho discusses the theories of cultural penetration and the industrialization of cultural goods. He disagrees that the United States is destroying the peripheral cultures. The penetration of American songs, for example, will not provoke the disappearance of Brazilian music. Those songs only constitute fashionable industrialized products that, as fashion, will soon disappear. What really happens is the transformation of culture due to the contact with culture from other origins. Marcondes Filho understands that culture is a continuous process of human activity. Hence, it is natural that it develops as new influences are received.

Mattelart (cited in Caparelli 1989) asks how Brazil can discuss its cultural dependency upon the North when Globo, the biggest Brazilian communication network, exports its television programs to more than a hundred countries around the world. This is really a hard critique for Brazilian theorists to answer. At the same time that the Brazilian scientific community argues against the foreign cultural industry and cultural imperialism, other countries debate the invasion of Brazilian television products.

"God help us, there are too many Brazilian soap operas." This was a complaint from a Portuguese journalist in the newspaper *Correio da Manhã* (cited in Duran 1993). Of eleven soap operas being shown on Portuguese television in 1993, eight were from Brazil. The Portuguese newspaper then blamed Brazil for cultural invasion:

> The Brazilians seem not to forgive the Portuguese for, in 1500, Pedro Álvares Cabral landing with his ships in the Vera Cruz lands. Five centuries later, the colonization happens by reverse, namely through television, this powerful communication medium, and, also, of manipulation. (12)

Neocolonialism

Morin (cited in Melo 1985) was one of the first to recognize the colonialist effects of the cultural industry. According to him, with industrial development, colonialist strategy shifted from territorial domination to a type of "second colonization," which maintains the image of national autonomy but still bestows economical dependency. The cultural industry still observes one of the main colonialist strategies: the imperative to inject the culture and ideology of the colonizer, seeking to transform colonization into a less hated process.

Melo (1985) remarks that after World War II, the Latin American cultures fell under significant influence from the United States. In those countries, the development of the cultural industry was part of a modernizing effort to adapt them to the new international division of labor. This process was accelerated after the Cuban revolution, when the United States recognized that the presence of its media was not just a resource of economic and cultural domination, but also an instrument to discourage possible nationalistic revolutions.

The television industry grew in Brazil significantly in the early 1960s, during the rule of a military regime (a dictatorial regime that would just end in 1982) under the technological and cultural influence of the United States. Melo concludes that this dependency generated a form of neocolonialism in Brazil, as the cultural industry reproduced an alien cultural model.

"As the role of the mass media, within a specific country, is to legitimate the domination of one class over the others, within various countries, it serves to legitimate the imperialism of a country over another" (Guareschi 1981, 21). The mass media works then as an efficient instrument to perpetuate the dependency of the colonized peoples.

Sarti (1979) criticizes the discussion on cultural dependency and cultural colonialism. He states that much of that discussion is simplistic as it does not consider the power of local dominant classes and as it grants all the "malignity" to the "external enemy." The peoples in "dominated" countries are normally considered to be mere passive receivers of the ideological process, without having the possibility of reacting. Whenever those studies identify local elite and external agents, the United States is always presented as the agent that produces and spreads the capitalistic ideology that is to be adopted by the local elite, who have the job to transmit it to the people. Sarti states that those studies forget that the dominant classes are not monolithic blocs that have the power to control the people at the level of conscience. Sarti also remarks that the popular classes are not as passive as they are portrayed. History indicates that the oppressed classes have always had the potential for organization and resistance, even in the most oppressive regimes. Thus, those dependency studies just repeat the old formula of the passive colonized peoples and do not perceive that ideology is produced locally and responds to dominant local interests. Sarti concludes that while these interests may identify themselves with other capitalistic centers, they do not need "foreign lessons" to exercise their domination.

News Agencies

Brazilian media are greatly dependent on foreign news agencies. These agencies have a natural tendency to disseminate the political and social views of the countries where they originate. This produces some distortions. There is a great space for foreign news in Brazilian newscasts, papers, and magazines. Furthermore, newspapers do not just grant space for American news, but also present a substantial number of editorials on the same subjects. According to Coelho (1989), one of the effects of that is that Brazilians are compelled to worry about realities that are not theirs and that will have no effect on them.

The massive discussion about the O.J. Simpson case is a good example. Before the case, Simpson was just a comedy actor in the Brazilian perception (Brazilians did not know he was a famous football player, as the sport is not played in Brazil). But because of the massive coverage by American agencies and CNN of the case, it gained a great space in Brazilian media and provoked Brazilian curiosity.

Moreover, Beltrán and Cardona (1982) conclude that besides feeding the Latin media with news distorted by American ideology, the American news agencies ignore the facts in Latin America, except when the facts fit the traditional news model: anything that is uncommon, such as "man bites dog." According to those authors, the American news agencies select information about Latin America based on the structure of dominance. Also, the news agencies inform Latin Americans about a Latin America that is not the one that they live in, compelling them to believe in the image portrayed because of the power of such agencies.

> Therefore, the central point of the problem is not the few facts that are informed, but also what is not informed, who informs and how. And research demonstrates that, intentionally or accidentally, the news coverage on Latin America done by the United States is systematically superficial and constantly distorted. (51)

New Technologies

Mass media technology has been positioned as a revolution to mask its imperialistic anti-revolutionary function. According to Guareschi (1981), this fact resembles the *green revolution*, where the dissemination of technologies of new fertilizers and new machinery was done on a universal basis, which later guaranteed the dependency of the underdeveloped countries upon that industry. Accordingly, the communication revolution and the announcement of the information age forecasts a similar relationship, as it hides the identity of its origins and the true function of the messages that are spread heralding the new system advertised, i.e., that in order to enter the information age it is necessary that the underdeveloped countries purchase hardware and software from developed countries.

That technology was developed in accordance with the culture where it was produced. Thus, as it carries cultural characteristics within its products, the countries that buy those products also buy a new social establishment. Furthermore, as it is expensive to develop technology adapted to each singular culture in the world, it is more profitable to force the adaptation of other countries to the culture where the technology is produced.

Brazil's dependency on American technology was created with the development of mass media in the country. In the period of 1964–1984, ninety-four television stations were planted in Brazil. According to Caparelli (1989), 77 percent of the equipment needed was imported from the United States. During the 1960s, the Globo network guaranteed its development in Brazil with an illegal association with the Time-Life group. Because of a constitutional restriction on foreign investments in telecommunications, Globo and Time-Life Inc. signed a contract of technical assistance. Globo then sold the building where it was located to Time-Life Inc. and signed a rent contract under which Globo would pay 45 percent of its liquid profit.

Machado (1990) sees some dangers in such technological concentration. The excessive centralization can easily be converted into a mechanism of control over and selection within the communication flux. According to him, the "international" satellite consortiums have a major part of their stocks in the hands of the countries that control the technology. It is important to remember that there is limited orbit space for satellites, but the industrialized countries (such as the United States) defend the idea of "open sky," that is, whoever arrives first, stays.

> Obviously, this race is undertaken with unfavorable condition for the poor countries, or with sacrifice to its prioritary goals, but, as the development model is given by the industrialized nations, to stay out of this race means deepening the delay and becoming available to the international waves invasion. (33)

Methodology

After discussing scholars' criticisms regarding the presence of American media products in Brazil, this research intends to test their assertions with numbers about the Brazilian audience and its consumption of American media products. The numbers to be discussed were collected in various forms, showing different aspects of that consumption.

First, the presence of American media products in the daily programming of TV Globo will be analyzed. The data comes from the institute Ibope (the Brazilian institute of public opinion and research on media audiences). The numbers were collected in April 1995, and show the month's average percentage of television sets turned on to each American program (Correa 1995). The table will also demonstrate the share of each program compared to the other programs being shown at the same time on the other networks.

Second, the programming of the FM radio station *Atlântida* will be analyzed. The intent here is to quantify the percentages of songs in English, Portuguese, and Spanish. This quantification was done based on the daily playlists used by all the disk jockeys of that radio network in the state of Rio Grande do Sul. The playlists for seven consecutive days in the period 12/28/95–01/04/96 (the playlist of Sunday, 12/31/95, was not quantified because the station does not distribute playlists on Sundays), from 7:00–12:00 A.M. and 2:00–11:00 P.M., were quantified. This radio station, *Atlântida* FM, was selected because it was elected in two consecutive years (1994–1995) the most popular radio station in the state of Rio Grande do Sul, according to a research conducted statewide by the business magazine, *Amanhã*.

Third, all the movies played on the Net (the biggest cable company operating in Pelotas) cable channels in the months of November and December 1995 were quantified and separated by their origins. For this analysis, all the movies listed in the magazine furnished by Net were quantified. The percentage of American movies transmitted was then calculated; the percentage of movies from other countries was also calculated. It is important to note that the movies analyzed here were just the ones shown on cable channels. The movies transmitted by broadcast networks were not included in this analysis.

Fourth, a survey was conducted in the city of Pelotas—a city of 291,100 inhabitants (1991), located in the south of the state of Rio Grande do Sul (the most southern state in Brazil). This survey intended to quantify the public's preference among movies, songs, and television programs according to the origins of those products. The survey also intended to investigate the public's perception of the great presence of American media products in Brazil, and the validity of the images about the American way of life portrayed in American media products. This was an intentional stratified survey applied to 400 people, between the ages of fifteen and sixty-four, during the period of 12/12–16/1995. The questionnaires were administered in an area of the city of Pelotas called *calçadão* ("big sidewalk"). This is a downtown street, with the length of four blocks, closed to vehicles, where stores targeted to all social classes are located. The greatest part of the shopping done in the city of Pelotas is done in this area, as Pelotas does not have shopping malls. The *calçadão* was particularly busy in that period because of Christmas shopping, a fact that favored this research because representatives of all social classes, ages, and of both genders were present at the same location.

The sample was stratified by gender and age, representing the percentages in which they are found overall in the city of Pelotas. According to Richardson (1989), this intentional stratified survey has a validity of 95 percent (two sigmas), and an error margin of 5 percent.

Results and Discussion

Table 13.1 shows the programs produced in the United States and transmitted by the Globo network nationwide. Some of the programs are shown in the table with the names they have in Brazil. It was taken for granted in this research that the movies shown were from the United States, a trend that is rarely changed by the exhibition of movies from other countries (something that happens rarely).

The analysis of the Ibope table shows that the American television programs transmitted by the Globo network have a massive audience and a high share in the specific time period. This means that the Brazilian public nationwide demonstrates a favorable opinion of and response to American programs.The analysis of the songs played during the day on the FM radio station *Atlântida* provided the following results. During the time period, *Atlântida* played 1,098 songs, of which 566 (51.55 percent) were sung in English, 381 (34.70 percent) were in Portuguese, and 151 (13.75 percent) were in Spanish. All the songs in Portuguese were produced in Brazil and sung by Brazilian singers and groups—Brazilian radio does not play songs from Portugal or other Portuguese-speaking countries. However, it was not possible to determine with certainty the origins of the songs sung in English and Spanish. There is no danger of overgeneralization in stating that just a minority of the songs in English come from countries other than the United States. Concerning the songs in Spanish, it is important to state that until one year ago Brazilian radio stations did not play songs in that language. However, because of the integration of the markets in the south of South America (Mercosul), the radio stations in the state of Rio Grande do Sul began playing songs in Spanish. These songs have had favorable acceptance by the audience. However, the radio stations' preference for American songs is a paradox, as the majority of Brazilians cannot understand English. Spanish is so similar to Portuguese that a Brazilian can understand a great part of a song's lyrics even without having studied the language.

The third phase of this research quantified the number of movies from the United States and other countries shown during the months of November and December 1995 on the cable channels transmitted by the Net cable company. A total of 1,184 films were analyzed; however, it was not possible to determine

Table 13.1. U.S. Programs on Globo Network in Brazil

Program	Time	Week	Audience Percent	Total Viewers	Share
Sessão da Tarde (movie)	15:35	Mon-Fri	20	10,443,913	59
Tela Quente (movie)	21:30	Mon	36	23,165,273	69
American series	21:30	Wed	33	21,346,011	56
Mini-series	22:30	Tue-Fri	21	12,168,843	52
movie	00:00	Mon-Thu	6	3,133,174	48
Nova Iorque contra o crime (NYPD Blue)	00:00	Fri	8	3,961,949	48
Corujão I (movie)	00:30	Fri	8	4,123,661	54
Corujão II (movie)	2:30	Fri	3	1,536,266	58
The Simpsons	12:00	Sat	14	7,405,071	49
Sessão de Sábado (movie)	16:00	Sat	17	9,220,964	50
Supercine (movie)	21:30	Sat	27	15,645,656	57
Sessão de Gala (movie)	23:30	Sat	12	6,387,632	50
Corujão I (movie)	1:30	Sat	5	2,577,288	62
Corujão II (movie)	3:30	Sat	5	2,560,443	53
Cobra	9:30	Sun	11	6,188,861	55
Cartoon festival	10:00	Sun	9	4,639,119	47
Vida de Cachorro (cartoon)	10:25	Sun	10	5,221,957	48
Thunder in Paradise	10:20	Sun	13	7,314,108	53
The Simpsons	10:50	Sun	10	5,289,337	47
Beverly Hills 90210	11:10	Sun	14	7,782,400	47
Dinosaurs	11:15	Sun	10	5,289,337	46
Laurel and Hardy	11:40	Sun	12	6,387,632	49
Weird Science	12:15	Sun	18	10,127,227	49
Temperatura Máxima (movie)	14:40	Sun	21	12,593,338	50
E.R.	22:00	Sun	17	10,366,426	36
Casa do Terror (terror episodes)	22:00	Sun	22	11,933,013	41
Domingo Maior (movie)	23:20	Sun	5	2,577,288	28

the origin of one movie transmitted in December. The analysis of this data provides a relevant result. The great majority of movies transmitted by the Net cable channels were produced in the United States: 88.11 percent in November (532 films), and 89.1 percent in December (523 films). The percentage of 1.2 percent (November), and 0.7 percent (December) of the movies shown in both months were co-productions of the United States with other countries.

The numbers demonstrate that today the distribution of American media products in Brazil is still very high. The majority of songs played on Brazilian FM stations are American. The movies shown on Brazilian television are almost all American, with few exceptions. American television series also occupy an important space in daily programming. It can then be concluded that the Brazilian audience is exposed daily to a great quantity of information imported from the United States.

The following are the quantitative results from the public opinion survey applied to a sample of 400 people in Pelotas, RS. It is important to remark that the amount of non-answered questions and invalid answers to each question will not be reported.

Asked about their movie preferences, 58.75 percent preferred American movies, 25 percent Brazilian, 4.25 percent French, and 11.25 percent answered that they preferred movies from other countries. Concerning the consumption of music, the great majority (71.50 percent) answered that they would rather listen to a Brazilian song, 13.50 percent preferred American music, 6.50 percent music in Spanish, and 7.50 percent from other countries not listed in the survey.

The survey also aimed to find out the sample's reaction to songs in English. Asked if they were frustrated to listen to an American song without understanding the lyrics, 51 percent declared that they did not mind if they didn't get the message of the song, 28.25 percent said they were frustrated in those situations, and 20.50 percent were frustrated just a bit. However, if there was a choice of choosing between a song in English and a song in Spanish, 39.25 percent said that they would prefer a song in Spanish, 21 percent would prefer to listen to a song in English, and 39.50 percent would listen to any song; the language would not interfere in their decision.

The great number of songs from the United States on FM stations does not mean that the public prefer the songs produced in that country. Actually, 71.50 percent prefer Brazilian songs, and just 21 percent of the sample interviewed answered that they would prefer to listen to a song in English instead of a song in Spanish. This can probably be explained by the high percentage of people (48.75 percent) that are somehow frustrated by not understanding the lyrics of songs in English. The percentage of 51 percent that answered that they do not mind not understanding the lyrics proves that the audience values the rhythm of American songs and not their contents. Thus, it is difficult to state that American songs play an alienating role. It is also simplistic to say that this presence of American songs on Brazilian radio stations threatens to destroy the national culture. In Brazil, American music movements have inspired ways of dressing and dancing, but the behavioral and philosophical ideas reflected in many of them have no impact in the country because of the difficulty that Brazilians have in understanding the lyrics. For instance, the grunge movement, represented mainly by Seattle rock groups, was an ephemeral fashion in Brazil. The songs and the way of dressing were momentarily fashionable, but were soon replaced by other fashions

Concerning the transmission of American television programs on Brazilian television channels, 40 percent said that they liked them more or less, 23.75 percent answered that they liked American TV programs, and 33.75 percent did not like them. The sample was asked to indicate which country produced the best television programs in six different categories. The great majority showed (see Table 13.2) their preference for the programs produced in Brazil.

The results show that the interview sample showed their preference for national products. The Brazilian mini-series of 5–20 episodes normally depict important books from Brazilian literature or current problems and situations in Brazilian life. Thus, it can be concluded that the audience prefers to watch programs that show their own context and deal with national themes. This result goes against the theoretical assertions that the public does not have a critical mind and that the Brazilian audience is a passive and colonized mass. The results show, however, that American series and video clips are preferred, most probably because of their expensive production and the action that they present.

A similar type of question aimed to find out the sample's preference about the origin of soap operas (the preferred television program in Brazil occupying prime time in Brazilian television). The results demonstrated the high quality of Brazilian soap operas: Eighty-two percent preferred Brazilian soap operas, 0.50 percent American soap operas, 0.25 percent Mexican, and 17 percent answered that they did not watch that type of program.

This research also sought to investigate whether the sample knew about the American way of life and how they knew about it. In this question, the sample could provide more than one answer. The results showed that 56.25 percent received their information about the American lifestyle from the media, 29.25 percent answered that they got information about it from interpersonal contacts, 9 percent had already gone to the United States, 0.25 percent had information from other sources, and 27.50 percent said that they did not know anything about the American way of life. A majority (41 percent) stated that the American way of life was better than the Brazilian, 19 percent think the Brazilian way of life was better, and 10.50 percent answered that both lifestyles were equal. The sample was also asked if the American television programs showed American society as it really is. The answers were divided: 35 percent said the American programs did not show society as it really is in the United States, 13.25 percent said those programs portrayed a faithful image of the American society, and 22.75 percent said that they did not know about it. These two last questions were not asked to the individuals who answered that they did not have any information about the American way of life.

Finally, the last question of the questionnaire asked if the American television programs were alienating: 35.25 percent said they were, 29 percent did

Table 13.2. Preferences of TV Program in Brazil

Type of TV program	Brazil	U.S.	Other countries
Comedy	77.75%	11.25%	0.75%
Children's	66%	10.50%	0.75%
Series of 1 episode per week	35%	36.50%	1.25%
Mini-series of 5–20 daily episodes	58%	18.25%	1.25%
Video-clip	22.75%	51.50%	1.50%
Documentary	60.25%	18.25%	5.50%

not believe they were alienating, and 33.25 percent said that they did not know if they were or not.

These results demonstrate that the public has a critical capability of confronting the information from other media with the messages received from television programs. The public seems to be aware that television programs deal with fiction and entertainment and that their information is not necessarily a faithful picture of the American reality. This, added to the amount of people (35.35 percent) who answered that American programs are alienating, shows that the Brazilian audience is not as passive and uncritical as the scholars may think. However, a better discussion on this subject would require long-term qualitative in-depth research.

Conclusions

Brazilian scholars blame American media products for contributing to alienation, damaging the local culture, and serving as an imperialistic instrument to maintain the United States' hegemony. The literature in Brazil states that the massive consumption of those products has an explosive colonizing impact over the vulnerable audience.

At the same time, though, that the scholars say that the American media products are not beneficial for the Brazilian public, audiences for American films and television programs, and the consumption of American music are very substantial. This research defends, however, the idea that the Brazilian audiences are not as passive and vulnerable as the majority of Brazilian literature defines them. Even though the consumption of imported media products is high, the public still prefers and values the national television programs and music that reflect their own culture. Brazilian movies are not in the public's preference because of a long-term crisis in the national film industry.

Criticism of foreign products is a natural nationalistic behavior that exists in many (if not all) countries—it is a self-protective behavior. But often these xenophobic attitudes are paired with expansionist markets. Brazil criticizes the entrance of great quantities of American movies, programs, and songs, while the country exports its own soap operas, series, and songs to more than a hundred countries. The same happens in the United States: the American public criticizes the entrance of many Japanese products at the same time that the U.S. controls an international market of American products.

References

A tela se enche a sombra da Embra [The screen is filled by Embra's shadow]. (1995, December 27). *Zero Hora*, p. 6 (Segundo Caderno).

Adorno, T.W. (1978). Indústria cultural [Cultural industry]. In G. Cohn (Ed.), *Comunicação e indústria cultural* [Communication and cultural industry] (4th ed.), pp.287–295. São Paulo: Companhia Editora Nacional.

Almanaque Abril. (1995). São Paulo: Abril.

Barbero, J.M. (1986). Identidade tecnológica e alteridade cultural [Technological identity and cultural differences]. In A. Fadul (Ed.), *Novas tecnologias de comunicação: impactos políticos, culturais e sócio-econômicos* [New communication technologies: political, cultural and social-economic impacts], pp. 121–132. São Paulo: Summus.

Beltrán, L.R., and E.F. Cardona. (1982). *Comunicação dominada: os Estados Unidos e os meios de comunicação da América Latina* [The United States and the communication media in Latin America]. Rio de Janeiro: Paz e Terra.

Beltrão, L., and N.O. Quirino. (1986). *Subsídios para uma teoria da comunicação de massa* [Subsidies for a mass communication theory]. São Paulo: Summus.

Berger, C. (1993). De quando as incertezas nos espreitam por todos os lados [When the uncertainties glance at us from all sides]. In D.F. Haussen (Ed.), *Sistemas de comunicação e identidades na América Latina* [Communication systems and identities in Latin America], pp 41–48. Porto Alegre, RS, Brazil: Edipucrs.

Caparelli, S. (1989). *Ditaduras e indústrias culturais no Brasil, na Argentina, no Chile e no Uruguai* [Dictatorships and cultural industries in Brazil, Argentina, Chile and Uruguay]. Porto Alegre, RS, Brazil: Editora da Universidade.

Coelho, T. (1989). *O que é indústria cultural* [What is cultural industry] (12th ed.). São Paulo: Brasiliense.

Correa, E. (Especial, 1995). *Ibope prepara o índice nacional de audiência*. Mercado Global , pp. 65–73.

Duran, C. (1993, July 31). *Portugal enfrenta invasão via TV* [Portugal faces invasion via television]. Caderno 2. *O Estado de São Paulo*, p. 12.

Guareschi, P. (1987). *Comunicação e poder: a presença e o papel dos meios de comunicação de massa estrangeiros na América Latina* [Communication and power: The presence and the paper of the foreign mass communication media in Latin America] (7th ed.). Petrópolis, RJ, Brazil: Vozes.

Hamelink, C.J. (1993). Globalização e cultura do silêncio [Globalization and the silence culture]. In D.F. Haussen (Ed.), *Sistemas de comunicação e identidades na América Latina* [Communication systems and identities in Latin America], pp 15–28. Porto Alegre, RS, Brazil: Edipucrs.

Ianni, O. (1979). *Imperialismo e cultura* [Imperialism and culture]. Petrópolis, RJ, Brazil: Vozes.

Machado, A. (1990). *A arte do vídeo* [Video Art] (2nd ed.). São Paulo: Braziliense.

Marcondes Filho, C. (1986). *Quem manipula quem: Poder e massas na indústria da cultura e da comunicação no Brasil* [Who manipulates who: Power and masses of the cultural industry and of communication in Brazil] (4th ed.). Petrópolis, RJ, Brazil: Vozes.

Martelart, A. (1994). *Comunicação-mundo: História das idéias e das estratégias* [Communication-world: History of the ideas and of the strategies]. Petrópolis, RJ, Brasil: Vozes.

Melo, J. M. (1985). *Para um leitura crítica da comunicação* [For a critical reading of communication]. São Paulo: Paulinas.

Sarti, I.A. (1979). Comunicação e dependência cultural: Um equívoco [Communication and cultural dependency: a mistake]. In J. Werthein (Ed.), *Meios de comunicação: Realidade e mito* [Communication media: Reality and myth], pp. 231–251. São Paulo: Nacional.

Schiller, H.L. (1993). As corporações multinacionais de mídia e a transição democrática na América Latina [The media multinational corporations and the democratic transition in Latin America]. In D.F. Haussen (Ed.), *Sistemas de comunicação e identidades na América Latina* [Communication systems and identities in Latin America], pp 15–28. Porto Alegre, RS, Brazil: Edipucrs.

Silva, C.E.L. da (1985). *Muito além do Jardim Botânico* [Beyond the Botanical Garden] (2nd ed.). São Paulo: Summus.

Soifer, R. (1992). *A criança e a TV: Uma visão psicanalítica* [The child and TV: A psychoanalytic vision]. Porto Alege, RS, Brasil: Artes Médicas.

Vieira, R.A.A. (1978). Alienação na comunicação (o caso Brasileiro) [Alienation in communication (the Brazilian case)]. In R.A.A. Vieira (Ed.), *Comunicação de massa: o impasse Brasileiro* [Mass communication: the Brazilian impasse], pp. 49–126. Rio de Janeiro: Forense Universitária.

14

From an Island Nation

Maltese Perception of the U.S.

PEGGY BIEBER-ROBERTS AND PAULINE ABELA

Introduction

The formation of audiences' world view in developing nations is an important and enduring topic in international communication research. For the purposes of policy making and the reader's personal enlightenment, this type of research describes and explains the opinions of people about whom we hear little. For our study, we focused on one of these nations, Malta, which has attracted little attention regarding public opinion and mass media research.

A densely populated, tiny island located in the center of the Mediterranean almost halfway between Sicily and Libya, Malta considers itself part of the Western hemisphere and has good bilateral relations with the U.S. Malta's politically neutral position, however, is a rarity in the Euro-Asian, Near East, and North African regions—parts of the world experiencing dramatic conflicts and changes.

With international currents of thought passing through the island, the Maltese people offer an interesting facet of world opinion about the U.S. The central premise of this study is that Maltese perceptions are comprised of both sociocultural and mass media outlooks. To identify these perceptions, we gathered together six Maltese citizens for a discussion in Fall 1995.

Malta

Consisting of three islands—Malta itself, the smaller Gozo, and Comino— this nation was part of an important trade route in the ancient Mediterranean and host to several civilizations that flourished in the region (Frendo 1993, 169–173). Once the seat of the famous knights of St. John (1530–1798), Malta in 1989 celebrated its twenty-fifth anniversary of independence from Britain and is now a republic in the British Commonwealth. With a population of about 360,000 and an area of 316 square kilometers, the island maintains a thriving trade and tourism economy (Lockhart and Ashton 1991, 22–32). Tourist arrivals in 1995 totaled 901,679. Decreasing arrivals from the U.K. and Germany were partially offset by gains recorded in other continental European markets (Malta's Economic Indicators, July-September 1995).

Maltese and English are the nation's official languages, but Italian is also widely spoken. As an educational requirement, the Arabic language was recently discontinued. Arab influences in Malta are primarily cultural, whereas Italian and British influences are largely economic.

The nation's two major opposing political parties, the Nationalist Party and the Malta Labour Party, dominate Maltese politics. The center-left Malta Labour Party, in control during the 1970s and 1980s, sought alliances with Libya and the former Soviet Union mainly to obtain stronger financial commitments from traditional European patron-states. During this time, Malta obtained aid from Italy, Libya, the former Soviet Union, (Regional Report Europe, October 1989, 54) as well as China and North Korea. The center-right Nationalist Party won elections in 1987 and shifted swiftly toward a more liberal brand of capitalism, building stronger ties with Western Europe (Jones, November 1989, 262–266). Malta applied for membership in the European Union in July 1990 and is currently working to increase its business connections with the U.S.

Given the island's small physical size and strategic location, its population looks outward, acutely conscious of the diversity and conflicts in the surrounding area. Many Maltese people have travelled abroad, but most have not visited the U.S. On occasion, the Maltese people have encountered Americans in Malta and in other nations.

Mass media

Domestic and international mass media are important in informing the Maltese people about events beyond their borders. Because most Maltese have few actual experiences with the U.S., the mass media are expected to produce a number of important shared views. The agenda-setting function of the media is responsible for this, with the mass media telling audiences what public events are important as well as what attitudes to assume toward those events (McCombs and Shaw, Spring 1995, 62). Media imperialism (Reeves 1993, 53–60), the one-way flow of programming and accompanying values from developed to developing nations, is also responsible for creating shared world views.

However, the Maltese people, like audiences in other parts of the world, are not merely passive "readers" of the media texts. They interpret media imagery and messages from their own cultural perspectives, converting them according to preconceived notions of the world. In addition, the Maltese people discuss what they see and read with each other, obtaining personal collective outlooks that may or may not be compatible with mass mediated messages and imagery. Thus, audiences' views are socially constructed and dependent upon the knowledge, approval, prejudices, and resistance that audiences themselves bring to the media text.

Print media

Maltese print and broadcast media contain particular characteristics that are embedded in the nation's political and economic structures. Print media revenues are derived from advertising and power interests. Originating as the partisan press, the print media constitute a wealth of daily and weekly newspapers on the island, published in both English and Maltese (Vassallo 1978, 31). Henry Frendo pointed out the unique partisan origins of the print media:

> Maltese journalism . . . was more seriously conditioned by colonialism than is generally understood . . . the national daily press began in the 1880s as a direct effect of pro-British and anti-British currents. From the very start . . . we had journalism whose main aim was propagandistic and partisan. We have never grown out of this. (1978, 23)

Peter Serracino Inglott claimed that "the current media are always and inevitably associated with some kind of officialdom, whether State, or Church, Britain or Italy, party or Union; and hence that they do not peer behind closed doors" (1978, 38). Along the same line of thought, Saviour Chircop compared Maltese media to "ideological billboards" and the major newspapers in Malta to political "notice boards" (1994, 364–365).

The leading newspapers in Malta are English-language ones, and Frendo contended that "many advertisers will scorn a 'Maltese' newspaper because they are prone to see in it a second-class scandal sheet, a cheap sensational instrument" (1978, 26).

Broadcast media

Radio and television were not immune from political pressure. The two major political parties have traditionally clashed over broadcast policies. One policy, adhered to by the Malta Labour Party, contended that Malta could not afford multiple broadcasting channels (Chircop 1994, 362). A second policy, maintained by the Nationalist Party, argued that the media were to serve as a forum on national issues (Chircop 1994, 362) and as a powerful vehicle for pluralism.

When the Nationalist Party came into power in 1987, the change resulted in new broadcasting legislation. The legislation was implemented in 1992 as a reaction to several decades of public service monopoly in the broadcast industry. Provisions in the Broadcasting Act favored pluralism and choice, and restricted monopolistic practices. The principal aims were to "create a lightly regulated privately run commercial sector and to redimension and develop a public sector out of the former quasi-state run Xandir Malta" (Malta Broadcasting Authority 1993, 10). The gradual development of the media in Malta reached a peak in 1994 when twelve radio stations and three television stations, one of which is available only on cable, were in operation.

An audience survey (Applied Economics Consulting Ltd. 1995) carried out in 1995 concluded that a high percentage (seventy-eight percent) of the population listens to radio programs. Female listeners exceed by far male ones. Audiences prefer music, local and foreign news, and phone-in discussions.

Television audiences are evenly divided between men and women with ninety-two percent of the population tuning in. In programming taste, foreign news takes precedence over local news. Feature films on television were as popular as music on radio.

The most widely watched television stations are Italian, and they belong to the Berlusconi group. These were followed by TVM (Television Malta), which is publicly owned by the Public Broadcasting Services; another Italian group RAI; the extraterrestrial stations; and Super 1 which is privately owned by the Malta Labour Party. Viewership is marginal for the remaining Italian channels and Malta's privately owned cable television channel Smash.

Lifestyle

Maltese people embrace a collectivist society. For example, generally American parents expect their children to "go out on their own" at the age of eighteen, but Maltese parents provide overprotective child rearing, so much so that some parents are concerned with their offspring even after their children are married. Thus, in Malta, the extended family is a common occurrence, but there are exceptions to the rule because sociologically speaking Malta is in transition (Tabone 1995).

Adherence to family and the compactness of the island contribute to a strong personal communication network. Local news spreads by word of mouth faster than through the media. According to Serracino Inglott (1978):

> [Maltese people] talk to each other a lot; they talk in the shops, on buses, in the streets; some even telephone their friends immediately

if they have seen or heard something unusual happening . . . thus word of mouth circulates fast and intensely . . . with the adjunction of embellishment, distortion and speculation. (37)

It leads one to conclude that investigative journalism is a risky business in an island where everyone knows everyone else.

Methodology

In November 1995, six Maltese citizens were brought together in a focus group to talk about their impressions and opinions about the U.S. and the American people. While focus groups are not designed to be representative of a population's views, they offer a flavor of reaction that is normally missing in quantitative research.

Three males and three females comprised the group. Their ages varied from twenty-three to fifty-two. Representing the professional class, four participants worked as a teacher, student, archeologist, and anthropologist. Two participants were lecturers at the University of Malta. Four of the participants had studied abroad in England and Italy.

We solicited participants' opinions on a range of topics. Their responses comprised two hours in time, spoken mainly in the Maltese language. The tape recordings were translated into English. Topics included:

1. The imagery that comes to mind when they hear the word America.
2. America's strong points.
3. America's weak points.
4. American family life.
5. American education.
6. Crime in America.
7. Health care in America.
8. Environment in America.
9. Values in America.

Results

The six participants displayed few significant differences in views about the U.S. As a result, this paper does not attempt to examine individual differences in this focus group, but presents the interpretations of participants as representative of the group.

Participants' thoughts show two distinct patterns relating to the U.S.—a mixed positive/negative perception of individual character in contrast to a primarily negative perception of national character. Positive perceptions of individual Americans included their innovation, curiosity, spontaneity, optimism, and efficiency. Personal liberty was also cited. On the negative side, participants thought that Americans were arrogant and domineering, and that people had to fend for themselves.

Concerning negative views of the United States' national character, participants cited injustices toward certain racial and ethnic groups, deficiency in education, failure of U.S. families, and a self-serving foreign policy. The few positive attributes included U.S. support for freedom. This was important and considerable, according to the participants. The U.S. was also perceived as being inventive and charismatic.

Table 14.1 presents participants' opinions about the U.S. Sources of their views, when specified during the conversation, were marked in parentheses as being derived either from mass media (mm) or personal communication (p).

Discussion

The creation of public opinion is a complex process, consisting of the views of numerous elite and mass groups. Our elite group of participants is one element of the larger public, and like any other group, it expresses multifaceted opinions.

For this paper, we extracted the multifaceted views and examined five major themes. We will address the nature of Maltese perceptions of the U.S. and the contributions by mass media and personal communication in shaping them.

Theme #1: Freedom

Freedom was the core idea behind much of the discussion in this focus group. Asserting that freedom in the U.S. is a uniquely American phenomenon, participants meant that U.S. governmental support for freedom is directly related to personal freedoms, which gives rise to innovative and successful individuals. They also claimed that vast expanses in the U.S. lead to mobility and separation from others, which allow the individual to be free to explore and invent; and these conditions have produced a highly advanced technological society.

Freedom in the U.S. was not a concordant idea, though. Participants asserted that while freedom provided opportunities for innovation, it destroyed families and isolated individuals, leaving them to fend for themselves. The loss of freedom, according to the group, coincided with social injustices, racial troubles, and other problems. (This led the group to a lengthy discussion revealing the powers of the mass media in stereotyping ethnic and racial groups.)

Table 14.1. Maltese Opinions about the United States

Individual Character		
Positive	*Neutral*	*Negative*
For freedom/liberty (mm)	Litigious (mm)	Arrogant
Efficient	Consensus-building (mm)	Liking violence (mm)
Optimistic	Conflict-solving (mm)	Not sophisticated
Childlike/disarming		Loud (p)
Confident		Egoistic
Bravado (p)		Domineering
Curious		Have to fend for selves
Spontaneous (p)		

National Character		
Positive	*Neutral*	*Negative*
Charismatic	Spacious (mm)	Superficial (p)
Inventive	New nation	No longer promised land
Supports freedom	Consumer society	Fragmented families
	Nation of immigrants/diverse	Educational deficiency
	Lacking in history	Liberty doesn't exist in reality (p)
		Lacking social justice (p)
		Excess focus on technology
		Ignorant
		Used to offer something new
		Self-serving foreign policy

Turning her attention to Malta, one female participant pointed to the Maltese extended family as the responsible party for depriving individuals of liberty, saying "willing or not, years go by and you realize that in fact you have been deprived from a lot of things." Another female participant joined in with "and as women, we feel it more." Thus, the participants came to the conclusion that in the U.S., freedom results in isolated individuals; whereas in Malta, the cohesive family results in diminished freedoms. The tradeoffs are innovation versus personal security.

Theme #2: Spacious country

Seen from this tiny nation, participants commented about the large distances between places in the U.S. Participants believed that vast expanses in the U.S. lead to Americans' disinterest in other regions of the world. Yet positive aspects of spaciousness included population mobility which allowed for personal liberty. Participants asserted that this type of individualism is missing in Malta because of its tiny land mass and close-knit personal relationships.

Theme #3: Community

Lack of communal activity in U.S. cities was another point of interest. According to the participants, European cities allow for intimacy whereas U.S. cities produce isolated individuals. One participant expanded on this criticism:

> In Europe I felt that there was a sense of community in spite of the fact that it was a big city. After work people go out and meet in a common place. From films I imagine that America is a place where everyone fends for his or her own self, a place where you go to work, return home. . . . I think life is more isolated. (Personal interview 1996)

Theme #4: American diversity

The topic of diversity came up periodically throughout the two-hour discussion. Participants see the U.S. as a nation of immigrants—not necessarily troublesome groups as U.S. mass media often suggest, but people who have made significant contributions in building the nation. According to one participant, the U.S. was the beneficiary of highly educated World War II immigrants of German and Jewish ancestry: "The best of the country left for America." The contributions of these immigrants were perceived as projecting the U.S. into a dominant technological position in the world.

The discussion on diversity was also framed in the context of Maltese homogeneity. The group discussed "strange and foreign feelings" in Malta—that is, if you're different from others. One participant asserted that, while the U.S. strives for individualism, the Maltese people strive to adapt to the same behavior.

Theme #5: The Persian Gulf War

Acknowledging Cable News Network's role in presenting the Gulf War to world audiences, participants proceeded to interpret U.S. involvement in a critical manner. Thus, while the mass media did set the agenda in telling Maltese audiences what to think about, they did not necessarily tell audiences what to think.

One participant severely criticized the U.S. for its motives in the Gulf War, asserting, "All they (the U.S.) wanted to do was drop the bombs on innocent people." As a U.S. friend, the Maltese description of U.S. motives was unexpected and in obvious conflict with the imagery and messages emanating from CNN reports. CNN had concentrated its coverage on the U.S. avoiding harm to the Iraqi people by destroying non-human targets.

Resistance to media messages was obvious in the personal context, too. One Maltese participant pointed to a conversation with an American consultant in Malta who said, "it wasn't in our brief to take [Saddam Hussein] out." An argument ensued therewith, and this participant came to the conclusion that it was convenient to the U.S. to not remove Saddam Hussein from power during the Persian Gulf War.

It should be pointed out that this statement could also represent many U.S. viewers. The two short excerpts, however, illustrate the power of mass media to put the Gulf War on the world agenda and the power of audiences to resist the dominant pro-war imagery presented by CNN.

Mass media effects

Film was cited frequently as influencing participants' views of the U.S., especially involving social topics, such as family and individual behavioral characteristics. One participant summarized the power of film to shape audiences' views this way: "America is a place . . . where reality merges into celluloid and again most of what I know about America comes again from films and most films I know come from America, so for me it's hard to separate the two" (Personal interviews 1995).

Major news events, on the other hand, are received primarily via television. Participants pointed to television's capacity to create spectacles and performances like the Gulf War—that "you see it on CNN . . . it's a point of view perhaps more than a value but it's a way of commoditizing the world."

Other media served as sources of information as well. These were academic books, popular novels, nonfiction books, and poetry.

The idea of media imperialism was raised when a participant asserted that the Maltese people know a lot about the U.S., but they know little of other nations. The participant asked whether the group felt compelled to look at the world through American eyes. Acquisition of perceptions from an American point of view through U.S. media was an obvious concern of the group.

Personal communication effects

In the international context, the Maltese communication process begins with a flow of mass media messages and imagery, primarily from film and television, to the individual. From there, information is discussed within the group context or with another individual. The resulting outlooks are comprised of a complex of mass and personal opinions. The diffusion of local information in

Malta, in contrast, involves an even stronger personal component, where information about Malta is often acquired first from personal conversations and later from the mass media.

For this group, shared views were acquired often in conversation with neighbors, friends, and relatives, resulting in a strong personal interpretive community. In addition, interaction with American friends and observation of American behavior were two important communication mechanisms, particularly in acquiring information about U.S. education and the personality traits of Americans.

Conclusion

This focus group study offers a picture of the U.S. containing the reflections of six Maltese citizens. Rather than acquiring their world views solely from the mass media, participants tapped several mediated sources, the most important being film, television, academic literature, and personal conversations.

Particularly notable is the focus on an important U.S. characteristic that Americans take for granted—freedom. According to the participants, freedom goes hand in hand with innovation and technological progress. But it also produces a population of fractured families and isolated people—much different, participants believe, from the Maltese altruistic society, which champions personal cohesiveness and security. However, the strong Maltese togetherness happens often at the expense of personal liberty and individualism. Repeated references to individual freedoms in the U.S. may also be a subtle response to the pro-socialist Malta Labor Party's autocratic rule during the preceding two decades and the new political freedoms evolving in the current period.

Mass media were clearly important in shaping participants' views of the U.S. Film was cited frequently as a source of ideas about individual behavior, and participants pointed to television as the source of information about major news events. However, personal communication also played an important role. In this focus group, evidence of audience resistance to mass media messages was present in their reported conversations with others. It leads us to tentatively conclude that social circumstances coupled with exposure to media culture are important influences on Maltese participants' views about the U.S.

Finally, the participants were obviously aware of media imperialism; that is, how the importation of U.S. information and entertainment television programs and film influences their views of the world. It is a considerable influence, they conclude, and participants wonder if they do have an independent view about important events and other nations.

It is clear in this study that a combination of mass media, academic literature, and personal communication served as arbiters of reality in the formation of Maltese perceptions about the U.S. The discussion contained accurate views of the U.S. and some misperceptions, a topic that is beyond the scope of this paper. Additional research is required to more thoroughly examine how perceptions are formed; how media imagery and personal communication are related during the formation of perceptions; how misperceptions emerge; and how audiences develop resistance to dominant mass media imagery.

References

Applied Economics Consulting Ltd. (1995). *Broadcasting survey 1995*. Malta.

Chircop, S. (1994). As we sit together, should we use the phone?: A research agenda for the study of media in Malta. In R.G. Sultana and G. Baldacchino (Eds.), *Maltese society: A sociological inquiry*, pp. 356–368. Malta, Blata 1-Bajda, Malta: Broadcasting Authority.

Frendo, A.J. (1993). Some observations on the investigation of the Phoenicians/Canaanites in the ancient Mediterranean world. *Journal of Mediterranean Studies* 3(2): pp. 169–174.

Frendo, H. (1978). Milestones in the development of mass communications in Malta. In G. von Lojewski (Ed.), *Manipulation of the mass media*, pp. 19–30. Sliema, Malta: San Gwakkin Press.

Jones, C.B. (1989, November). Malta after 25 years of independence. *Contemporary Review* 255: pp. 262–266.

Lockhart, D.G., and S.E. Ashton. (1991). Tourism in Malta. *Scottish Geographical Magazine* 107(1): pp. 22–32.

Malta Broadcasting Authority. (1993). *Annual report 1992, broadcasting authority*. Malta, Blata 1-Bajda, Malta: Broadcasting Authority.

Malta's economic indicator. (1995, July-September). Malta.

McCombs, M.E., and D.L. Shaw. (1993, Spring). The evolution of agenda-setting research: Twenty-five years in the marketplace of ideas. *Journal of Communication* 43(2): pp. 58–67.

Regional Report Europe. (1989, October). A house divided. *World Press Review* 36(10): p. 54.

Reeves, G. (1993). *Communications and the Third World*. New York: Routledge.

Serracino Inglott, P. (1978). The diffusion of information in Malta. In G. von Lojewski (Ed.), *Manipulation of the mass media*, pp. 37–44. Sliema, Malta: San Gwakkin Press.

Tabone, C. (1995). Maltese families in transition—A sociological investigation. *Casa Leone*. Sta. Venera, Malta: Ministry for Social Development.

Vassallo, J.G. (1978). The readership and the audience in Malta. In G. von Lojewski (Ed.), *Manipulation of the mass media*, pp. 31–35. Sliema, Malta: San Gwakkin Press.

15

What Does America Symbolize to the Urban, Educated Youth in India?

UDITA DAS

Introduction

All societies make sense of the world, and the meaning they make of it is always culture specific. Culture denotes a historically transmitted pattern of meanings embodied in symbols, a system of inherited conceptions expressed in symbolic forms by means of which people communicate, perpetuate, and develop their knowledge about their attitudes toward life. Culture is the collective property of a body of people. It transcends the individual, though it must be articulated through her. Culture consists of people's beliefs, their ideas, their values, their very conception of reality itself. It is found in religion, law, arts, sciences, cinema, advertising, food habits, fashions; the list is endless. Cultural things are indeed all-pervasive.

In this age of multimedia, the advancement in technological innovation and invention is quite apparent. Also significant is the growing media culture strengthening the established consumer society. The modern means of communication has a specific role to play in the sociocultural changes taking place in the world today. In this century, the continuous experimentation in the fields of science and technology has added a new dimension to the flow of culture and communications. Slowly but steadily mass media has come to occupy a personality of its own, and the audio-visual media have started affecting society in a very visible manner.

A media culture has emerged today, in which images, sounds, and spectacles help produce the fabric of everyday life, dominating leisure time, shaping political views and social behavior, and providing the materials out of which people forge their very identity. Radio, television, films, and other products of the culture industries provide the models of what it means to be male or female, a success or failure, powerful or powerless. Douglas Kellner rightly indicates the connection between media, culture, and social and political identity. Media culture not only shapes the prevalent view of the world in any given culture, but it also defines what is considered good or bad, positive or negative, moral or evil. Media stories and images provide the symbols, myths, and resources that help constitute a common culture for the majority of individuals in many parts of the world today.

In the new global order where the boundaries between nations are getting blurred by the growing market for satellite television, the emergence and universalization of popular Western (read American) cultural symbols is quite significant. This has to be seen within the context of the sociopolitical developments taking place in the world today with the individual being subjected continuously to an unprecedented flow of signs. Economic liberalization, relaxing controls, allowing foreign equity increase, all these factors have combined to make India a land of possibilities, especially for foreign investors. While economic liberalization has its definite advantages, without concomitant social progress, political awareness, and cultural tolerance, it is just not feasible. Forced liberalization is bound to have unintended consequences.

There is undoubtedly a steady decline in the demand for American hardware ranging from computers, automobiles, home appliances to steel. However, American software, movies, music, TV programming, and home video account for a sizable proportion of its annual trade surplus. America's top sellers in the world at large and India in particular range from fast food, jeans, carbonated drinks, toys, comics, soap operas, films, pulp fiction, rock music, shoes, sun glasses, cosmetics to chewing gums.

Purpose

This study is primarily interested in understanding the implications of such seemingly alien values for the urban, educated youth in India. It is an accepted fact that most major markets are growing younger and more affluent each year. Coupled with this is the interesting phenomenon of the emergence of a single, somewhat homogenous global youth culture becoming more apparent all the time. Needless to say, this global consumer culture is strongly influenced by Western (read American) popular culture. According to advertisers, the reason why there is a conscious segmentation of the consumer market on the basis of age include the following:

1. there is a legitimate market of considerable size represented by the youth (18–30 years), the increase in aging population notwithstanding;

2. it is believed that the purchasing patterns formed at this age will extend into their lifetime; and finally
3. it is generally understood that youth influence the purchasing behavior of younger and older people.

However, the critics claim that the advertisers' preoccupation with the youth stems from the fact that visually it makes a more attractive copy, and culturally, and to some extent biologically too, youth is believed to be the most active and physically stimulating period of one's life.

Ever since the launch of a policy of radical liberalization introduced in June 1991, the Indian economy has undergone tremendous changes. To foreign investors, India has come to represent untapped market potential. This new way of life has led to increased production, leading to a much wider choice in the consumer market. India is in a state of economic unrest, and with liberalization it stands the risk of being shaken to its very sociocultural roots. About three-quarters of the Indian population is rural. Even though the budget claims to provide for the rural poor, it is an accepted norm that the fruits of liberalization will be used up by the minority of the urban elite. The significant yet marginalized group of the urban slum dwellers also have no share in the liberalization pie. Blind faith in the power of the market is bound to give rise to a distorted notion of reality itself.

Influence of Advertisements

We now look at a small sample of advertisements from the print media in India. All advertising is a message and, like all messages, involves a source of utterance, a point of reception, and a channel of transmission. Advertisements in the print media are a combination of a linguistic message (text) and an iconic message (image/design). The common theme running through the advertisements of this sample is the repeated use of certain socially accepted symbols of America. Much of everyday life is obviously permeated by popular culture, if not subsumed under it. Phenomena such as fads, fashions, commonly used expressions, dominant tastes, gastronomic fantasies, as well as the routine viewing of television, listening to the radio, reading magazines and the newspaper, and watching movies—all of these everyday phenomena are undoubtedly influenced by the dominant culture. The following analysis reiterates the emergence of a global order.

I use the semiological analysis as a technique for interpreting advertisements. We take the Saussaurian position; according to this, semiology essentially studies what signs are and how they function by focusing on the internal mechanisms through which meaning is generated in texts. Semiology cuts across the apparent naturalness of objects or actions to show that their meaning is founded on shared assumptions and conventions. Roland Barthes claimed that any advertising message contains two messages. The first is constituted by the text/image taken in its literalness, setting aside its advertising intention. It is a perfectly constituted message, including a level of expression and a level of content. This is called the message of denotation. The second has nothing of the analytical character of the first, it is a total message, and it derives its totality from the singular character of its signified, which is unique and always the same in all advertising messages and which is the excellence of the product announced. The signifier of the second message is in fact formed by the first message in its entirety. Therefore, one might say that the second message connotes the first. However, it need not be assumed that the second message of connotations is hidden behind the first, of denotation; on the contrary, what we immediately perceive is the advertising character of the message, its second signified, the excellence of the product.

In advertising, what needs to be explained is the role of the message of denotation. It is this double message that helps to persuade by developing a certain argument. The first message serves to naturalize more subtly the second; it takes away its interested finality. For the trivial invitation "buy" it substitutes the spectacle of a world where it is "natural" to buy a certain product. On the other hand, it may be seen that advertisements generally work on the fact of the appropriation of signifiers, resulting in the capture of the signified. Therefore, buying the right product is the only way to be a part of a certain class, status, and lifestyle.

Analysis of a Sample of Indian Advertisements

CLUB SHOES™ (SOURCE: CINE BLITZ, *April 1994*)

This advertisement for Club Shoes™ makes interesting reading primarily because of the linguistic message that comes with it. Visually, it is a happy, bright, and very sporty picture of eight individuals against a red backdrop. There are three children (all boys) and two women along with three men, all in smart, white sports shoes. One happy boy in the foreground is in red boxing gloves. In an age where *WWF* has acquired such popularity, boxing too is seen as a happy sport devoid of sweat, pain, and brute physicality. Another striking feature is the absence of young girls, who one assumes would be busy playing with Barbie™ dolls. Women are not considered to be athletically inclined; therefore, we have 25 percent representation of 50 percent of the population. The two who manage to find a place here are shown as wearing their shoes without socks, as if they are being worn only for the picture and will be taken off soon after. It may also be noted that the young lady at the extreme left corner is holding a baseball bat (which, incidentally, looks like the object *club*), which denotes a very popular American sport, and not a hockey stick or a cricket bat, as one might presume.

The two structural relationships, paradigmatic, that of choice, and syntagmatic, that of combination, are well illustrated by the linguistic message. It is possible to divide it into two paradigms, one in bold letters and the other in italics in the ad.

BOLD	*ITALICS*
1. Colors of the world	2. Means to an end
3. People and places	4. Friends and foes
5. Survival	6. Harmony
7. And success	8. The chosen one

The word *club* is repeated four times in varying print sizes. *Club* shoes signify *Class* for people all over the world is the dominant message of this ad. The eight individuals present in this ad are joined together as members of an association or *club* by virtue of their sporting the same shoes, and this in turn gives them the status and prestige which they are quite obviously very happy about. The source of the high status of these shoes in turn comes from the claim "India's Highest Exporter."

The *colors of the world* are represented by four racial types: two blacks, three browns, one yellow, and two whites. Lest we get carried away by the seemingly egalitarian character of this advertisement, we are immediately told, *means to an end*. Followed by a statement of fact, *people and places;* that is, different types of people are found in different kinds of places. We are then warned *friends and foes*. Among this eight seemingly jolly set of people, there are some who are friends, and there are others who are not, implying that there is more to these different people, not a simple division but an immutable stratification. One look below the surface brings us face to face with the not so happy reality of racial discrimination, aggression, bitterness, and alienation. But life goes on, and through it all *survival* is the most basic Darwinian necessity, which eventually leads to *harmony*. Here once again, the emphasis is not on the harmonious coexistence of people but that which comes with the *success* of the *chosen one*, the fittest. Success is the value par excellence, and the **means** to attain it do not matter . . . only the end does.

In the end, **CLUB SHOES**™ bring *world technology to your feet*. In an era, where it is firmly believed that technology holds the key to every problem, what could be a taller claim?!

WRANGLER™: AMERICA'S #1 JEANSSOURCE
(SOCIETY ANNUAL 1994)

The most significant aspect of this advertisement is the nature of the binary opposites used in this one frame, visual as well as linguistic. It establishes the barren landscape of the American Wild West, complete with galloping stallion and a lone cowboy, in a setting that brings to mind many successful Hollywood westerns.

Appearance is used to send messages about personality, social status, and, particularly, conformity (or the lack of it). The man on the horseback here is dressed in the conventional cowboy fashion and therefore makes for easy decoding. Each type of clothing constitutes a paradigm, and together they combine to form a syntagm, the important aspect being the rules by which the individual units are combined. The typical cowboy hat, the scarf tied around the neck, unbuttoned shirt, a casually worn denim jacket, the rough and tough jeans, no-nonsense boots, and a lasso in the right hand complete the picture. To this extent, it may be noted, the meaning of the jeans in question is determined largely by the relationship they share with the other elements in the syntagm.

The dominant message of this ad may be seen as part of the binary opposites. Binary opposition is a system of two related categories that in its purest form comprise the universe. This process, according to Levi-Strauss, is the fundamental, universal sense-making process.

BINARY OPPOSITES

Hang out	Meet purposefully
Outdoors	Indoors
Informal	Formal
West	East
Wild	Developed
Masculine	Feminine
Individual	Society
Nature	Culture

These binary opposites make interesting reading because they conform to the dominant myth of the cowboy, which was made immensely popular by Hollywood Westerns and gave the initial impetus to the present status of jeans as a symbol of America, all over the world. There are many American brands of jeans to be found in the markets of the world, but this is *#1* by virtue of being the *Western Original*. The wild American West is best understood when contrasted with the developed American East, which is far too formal and structured and therefore not in congruence with the values that make up the *cowboy cult*. At one level, the opposition is between the outdoors and the indoors, but it is also about the opposition between nature and culture where the typical cowboy hero, almost always, rides away as a free loner back into nature, as the final titles roll.

In this particular advertisement, the main copy reads *hanging out with the boys*. This has to be seen along with other print advertisement campaigns of the same brand, *working out at the gym* (with the cowboy chopping wood), *a quick bite at the canteen* (with the cowboy fixing a meal at a makeshift fire of what looks like a can of baked beans in a frying pan). One may then conclude that for the loner here, the only interesting company is that of his horses. Therefore, this advertisement for *Wrangler*^{TM} *Jeans* is once again working on the minds of the readers through the myth of the cowboys. Using these very obvious symbols, the image of America is reinforced as being the *#1*, not simply the original, first *(World)* but also the best.

PAPER ROSE CARDS^{TM} *(SOURCE: FEMINA, 23 December 1994)*

The iconic message of this advertisement comprises of three pictures in a row of a sweet little boy of about 5–6 years of age with an endearing smile. He is sitting on his haunches, dressed casually, and sporting a cap two sizes too big for him, worn sideways, with an inverted cricket bat in his hands. He looks straight into the camera with big eyes full of mischief. The advertisement wants us to believe that he is thinking (and not saying) what is signified by three progressively decreasing circles connecting the kid's head and the written words above each of the three pictures. Conventionally, the iconic representation of thinking persons almost always has them looking away from the camera or the spectator. Since here the child is supposed to be thinking from his heart, or so the copy tells us, the kid's ability to be all there and look one straight in the eye, and yet be thinking can be explained.

He is thinking about the kindness of an older person of the female species who could be a mother (most likely), sister, or an aunt. *She did get me my GI Joe . . . , And that deadly WWF poster. . . Maybe I should say I am sorry. If it's in your heart, it's in a Paper Rose Card.* In this day and age when nobody really has the time to sit, think, and write down thoughts for people, the market for ready-made cards is expanding rapidly. There are cards not just for birthdays and anniversaries, but also thank you cards, sorry cards, change of address cards, birth of a baby cards, get well soon cards, good luck cards, welcome home cards, bon voyage cards, write soon cards, missing you cards, let's be friends cards, missed your birthday cards, I love you cards, I hate you cards, you are invited cards, do get lost cards, just to say hi cards, and just like that cards . . . the list seems endless.

There is a card for every mood or emotion that one would like to express, and the credit for it goes to America where there are special days, not just Christmas or Easter, but Mother's day, Father's day, Sister's day, Brother's day, Uncle's day, Aunt's day, Valentine's day, Cousin's day, Secretary's day, Boss' day, Fool's day: There are cards to go with each of these. In a society based on mass production, the individuality of a message that has not been reproduced earlier has little value. No wonder then, in the artificial world that we live in, that which is in your heart may, most likely, be found in Paper Rose Cards™ and not in the fragrance of fresh roses.

The child in the advertisement values the symbols of America and seems very pleased with the perennial fighting soldier doll, G. I. Joe™, in a culture that glorifies militarism. It is a gift *she* got for him. He appears to be happy about the *deadly WWF poster* too, which about five years back, in India, would have conjured up images of the elusive snow leopard in stark, white mountainous terrain or the supremely elegant cheetah gliding through a thick forest, brought out by the *World Wildlife Fund*. But today *WWF* has a different meaning, and the images invoked are of Randy Savage, Hulk Hogan, and the likes of the *World Wrestling Federation* fame. *WWF* is an immensely popular show on the Star TV Network, in which long-haired, scantily clad hulks pretend to wrestle with each other and indulge in a lot of gimmickry in previously set-up matches. The prize money for both the contenders is the same, which explains the violently boisterous and obviously ridiculous humor that characterizes the show.

Even though the kid is very young, he is shown to be quite worldly wise, and why not, he will one day be the man of the house. The reason why we feel this advertisement is working on stereotypes is that at a very young age the notion of gender identity is introduced to us through various means, and the toys we are given to play with is one of them. Boys play with guns and soldiers and girls with dolls and stuffed toys. Girls are emotional and cry easily, and they also can feel sorry instantly, but boys do not cry, and even at a very young age they consider logically whether or not to feel sorry. Therefore, in our opinion, it is not the social consequences of innate sex differences that must be questioned, but the way in which these differences are put forward as a warrant of our social arrangement.

Needless to say, while the most important message of all these advertisements is the excellence of the product announced, the other message, which is far more striking, is that the popular symbols of the American culture wield a lot of power over Indian youth. The forces of culture presently in India are such that the majority of the urban Indian population prefers a lifestyle that exalts the American way of life.

Method

This study consists of a survey conducted in the three metropolitan cities of India, Delhi, Bombay, and Bangalore. Primary research was conducted among the youth in these three cities through a detailed questionnaire comprised of a number of open-ended questions. An equal number of female and male respondents were interviewed in these cities. The sample size was as follows:

Bombay	150
Bangalore	150
Delhi	150
Total	450

Results

The survey indicates that the first two Americans who come to mind among Indian youth are Bill Clinton and George Bush. Apart from holding (or having held) a very prominent political position in the world, both are white and male. The third position is shared by Michael Jackson, John F. Kennedy, Andre Agassi, and Abraham Lincoln. Hillary Clinton, the First Lady, also white, is the ninth person on the list. Madonna follows her in the twelfth position. Seventy-eight percent of the respondents recall white males, while fourteen percent recall white females. Six percent think of black males, while only two percent think of black women when asked to name any two Americans. Eighty percent of these very respondents have indicated that their perception of the U.S. is influenced primarily by television, while eight percent seem to be influenced by newspaper and other print media. One can see a connection between the type of media imagery and the resultant perception. It is an accepted fact that the media in general, and the electronic media in particular, work toward maintaining the social order in any society because it is largely governed by the market forces existing at a given time. Consequently, the images also do not deviate from the accepted stereotypes. It is not natural for people to think of America as predominantly white, but it is a cultural fact, governed by economic, social, and racial constraints. Similarly, the fact that one tends to think of men and not women can be seen as an extension of the stereotypical representation of men in socially powerful positions and women in supporting roles in the dominant media.

The three most striking features of America are listed as:

- Affluence and a High Standard of Living
- Powerful Media
- Advance Technology

The most positive contribution of America to the world is perceived to be scientific progress, while the most negative contribution is nuclear weapons; ironically, the negative contribution could not have been possible without the positive. Interestingly, when asked to react to four statements that were meant to provoke, certain negative aspects of the U.S. were highlighted. The statements were:

- "America is a racist country."
- "America symbolizes equality of opportunity."

- "America is a male-dominated society."
- "American involvement in international politics is justified."

While seventy-two percent of the respondents strongly agree that America is racist, only twenty percent think it is male dominated. Fifty-three percent of the respondents are of the opinion that America stands for equality of opportunity. Class, race, gender, or country of origin is largely inconsequential, for America is perceived to be a "performance and result oriented" society. While for forty-one percent, America's involvement in international politics is justified because it is an accepted "super power," and it is seen as contributing to "peaceful efforts," fifty-eight percent of the respondents are of the opinion that its interference in the affairs of other nations is unjustified and that it behaves like the "super cop." It is therefore quite apparent that, unless provoked, the tendency is to ignore the uncomfortable realities of the U.S.

The most popular American brands are Levi's™ jeans and Coke™ (and Pepsi™). Jeans are the universally held symbol of America, and the results of this study also reiterate the fact. With the opening of the skies, the Star TV Network has become immensely popular. Seventy-eight percent of the respondents watch Star TV, and Star Plus is the favorite channel. The following soap operas top the list:

Santa Barbara
The Bold and the Beautiful
Bay Watch
Beverly Hills 90210
Wonder Years

The renewed interest in animated films is very clear. The following Walt Disney Productions are the current favorites:

The Lion King
Aladdin
Tom and Jerry

The following are perceived as the best of American products:

Food: Cheeseburger
          Pizza
Drink: Coke™
          Pepsi™
Film: *Disclosure*
          Basic Instinct
Actress: Demi Moore
          Julia Roberts

Actor: Sylvester Stallone
        Clint Eastwood
Rock Star: Michael Jackson
            Madonna

While ninety percent of the respondents never use slang in formal writing, seventy-seven percent do not use it in formal speech. Fifty-three percent may use it in informal writing, and fifty-six percent may use it in informal speech.

To pursue further studies, America (40 percent) was the first choice, followed by India (34 percent), England (15 percent), and Australia (11 percent). The reasons for choosing America range from a better education system and reputable universities to superior research facilities. The best-taught subjects in the U.S. according to the respondents are computers, followed by science.

Conclusion

The study reiterates the significance of change in the form of the dominance of the American way of life. It reemphasizes the emergence of a technology-intensive society based on scientific progress. Change is and has been a feature of all societies at any given point in time. It can be more rapid in some and less so in others. India, at present, seems to be undergoing a fast-paced change, and this is most apparent among the youth. The shift in tastes, with fast/junk food being the most preferred taste, the dress code, way of life, the dominant media influence, all symbolize the shift in the cultural capital of the world.

For the urban educated youth in India, America symbolizes the land of opportunities and high standard of living. The media imagery reinforces this myth. Myth universalizes the world as self-evident and without contradictions; the dominant order is presented as the natural order. While on the one hand America stands for freedom, liberty, progress, modernity, a promise of wealth, power, and social status, one cannot ignore the fact this very land of opportunities is also the land of AIDS, racism, sexual violence, and child abuse. Does technological advancement and an upwardly mobile, rapidly changing society come as a package deal along with psychopaths and alienated individuals? Does not the emerging media culture appear to include only the lowbrow elements from the dominant, universal mass culture, be it Western, American, or Indian? It similarly rejects elements from Western high culture and underplays the classical elements of Indian culture as well. The perception of the youth all over the world is strongly influenced by the media which highlights those issues that work toward the maintenance of the social order rather than changing it. A new paradigm of sociocultural development which will be progressive, sensitive, and culturally sustainable is imperative today.

References

Barthes, R. (1967). *Elements of semiology*. London: Jonathan Cape.

Barthes, R. (1972). *Mythologies*. London: Jonathan Cape.

Crane, D. (1992). *The production of culture: Media and the urban arts*. London: Sage.

Featherstone, M. (1991). *Consumer culture and post-modernism*. London: Sage.

Fiske, J. (1989). *Understanding popular culture*. Boston: Unwin Hyman.

Kellner, D. (1995). *Media culture: Cultural studies, identity and politics between modern and post-modern*. London: Routledge.

Lull, J. (1995). *Media, communication, culture: A global approach*. Cambridge: Polity Press.

Olsen, B. (1990). Roland Barthes: From sign to text. In C. Tilley (Ed.), *Reading material culture: Structuralism, hermeneutics and post-structuralism*. Oxford: Basil Blackwell.

16

Imperfect Paradise

The Image of the U.S. on Chinese TV

ERSU DING

Introduction

For the last decade or so, one of the hot academic topics in the West has been so-called Orientalism. Put most briefly, this intellectual movement initiated by Edward Said is a self-critique on the part of some Western intellectuals of the institutionalized style of dealing with, "restructuring and having authority over the Orient." Given the fact that the world history of the past four hundred years is basically a story of Western military conquest and trade expansion, Orientalism certainly provides an important perspective in cross-cultural studies in the sense that it forces us to reexamine the Western episteme toward the East by laying bare the power relationship that has always existed between the dominating and the dominated.

It should also be pointed out, however, that while emphasizing the effect of superior Western economic and military power in the study of the East-West relationship, Orientalism tends to view the "distortion" of other cultures as a one-way cultural activity. Said (1979) himself has this to say in his influential book *Orientalism*:

> [I]deas, cultures, and histories cannot seriously be understood without their force, or more precisely their configurations of power, also being studied. To believe that the Orient was created—or, as I call it, "orientalized"—and to believe that such things happen simply as a necessity of the imagination, is to be disingenuous. The relationship between Occident and Orient is a relationship of power, of domination, of varying degrees of a complex hegemony, and is quite accurately indicated in

the title of K.M. Panikkar's classic *Asia and Western Dominance*. The Orient was orientalized not only because it was discovered to be "Oriental" in all those ways considered commonplace by an average nineteenth-century European, but also because it *could be*—that is, submitted to being—*made* Oriental. (5–6)

The short passage quoted above contains two implicit dimensions of cause-effect relationship. One of them is that, because Western nations want to acquire and then maintain control over Eastern nations, they therefore reconstruct the latter's cultures in accordance with their imperialistic aim. The connection here is not too difficult to see and is now widely accepted as valid. It is not the case, however, with the second cause-effect relationship: in the interactions or exchanges of various sorts between the West and the East, the former is stronger than the latter, and it therefore orientalizes its opponent. The proposition appears valid, but only on the surface level, for once we transform the sentence into its antithesis (if the West were not the stronger of the two, it would not have orientalized the Orient), the logical necessity of the effect following the cause no longer stands. As a matter of fact, when we dig into the historical records of any nation regarding other cultures, we often find that they do not correspond to "realities" either, the descriptions of dominant cultures made by dominated people being no exception. This means that reconstructing, filtering, and even "distorting" other people's world in the interest of one's own is not the monopoly of the strong; on the contrary, it is a much more universal meaning-producing mechanism, which is described by many semioticians as myth-making.

The question to ask then is how and why a particular people construct another culture the way they do, and in our case, how do contemporary Chinese mythologize the U.S. and why? The answer to this, of course, varies with each individual, depending on his or her unique social and intellectual background. Nevertheless, as far as knowledge about the outside world is concerned, the Chinese people can still be regarded as a fairly homogeneous collective. It is true that China now has more diplomats, journalists, business people, and students than ever who have travelled to America, and these people certainly formulate their own ideas of that country, but compared to the population of China as a whole, their number is so small that their marginal opinions are almost negligible. For the rest of the Chinese population who are not allowed to travel abroad freely or cannot afford to do so for economic reasons, the main source of information about the U.S. still comes from official media such as newspapers, books, and television programs.

Media Products

It is interesting to note here that, in the last few years, there have appeared on the Chinese book market a noticeable number of best-sellers that specifically tell stories to the audience at home about life in other countries: *A Chinese Woman in Manhattan, Shanghai Natives in Tokyo, My Fortune Is in Australia*, etc. The one that concerns us is *A Chinese Woman in Manhattan*, which happens to be the most successful of them all and has been turned into a TV series of ten episodes shown on the Chinese Central TV Station in prime time right after the evening news program, watched by millions of households all at the same time. The television production, renamed *A Beijing Native in New York*, was an instant hit and even months after it was first shown, people were still talking about the sensational series that contains so many direct and vivid images of the U.S. The program was afterwards rebroadcast on various local stations, and the copyright was sold to several Chinese communities across Asia. There are many explanations for the success of *A Beijing Native in New York*, but none of them, as the following analysis will show, is as convincing as that it has plucked a string in the Chinese "mythic unconscious."

The plot of the story is fairly simple: a Beijing artist by the name of Wang Qiming goes to New York, the symbol of America, in search of wealth. In order to survive in a totally different culture, he has to give up his music career and works first in a Chinese restaurant, then in a clothing factory. After a few twists and turns, he is finally able to beat his American counterparts and become a very successful businessman. The story itself is by no means extraordinary, for there are a lot of overseas Chinese who have done much better in terms of social success, and some even became Nobel prize winners in science, but the way in which it is presented is worthy of semiotic studies. Roland Barthes puts it very well in his *Mythologies*: "[P]sycho-analysis, structuralism, eidetic psychology, some new types of literary criticism of which Bachelard has given the first examples, are no longer concerned with facts except inasmuch as they are endowed with significance. Now to postulate a signification is to have recourse to semiology. I do not mean that semiology could account for all these aspects of research equally well: they have different contents. But they have a common status: they are all sciences dealing with values. They are not content with meeting facts: they define and explore them as tokens for something else" (Bathes 1972). It is this "something else" that the present paper tries to explore behind the story of *A Beijing Native in New York*.

Media Portrayals

As has been pointed out by many semiotics scholars, myth usually works "in dichotomic fashion." The diagnosis certainly fits the underlying structure of *A Beijing Native in New York*. Throughout the series, New York is portrayed as a paradise full of wonders as opposed to the non-paradise of Beijing. This mythic signified is established by the director's emphasis on only certain aspects of New York life. Here we should not overlook one otherwise insignificant detail in the making of the program; that is, the work is one of very few Chinese TV series or movies that are shot exclusively outside China. As can be expected, the cinematic crew are said to have been so "shocked" by what they saw in the biggest city of the world that "they were working under its influence virtually the whole time" (*Zhongshan Bimonthly*, 1st issue of 1994, 128). The producers' infatuation with New York inevitably shows itself in the series. The most noticeable is the protracted lingering of the camera over the impressive evening skylines, the Brooklyn Bridge, and the boulevards of New York City, plus the awe-inspiring American anthem as its background music at the beginning of each episode. It is exactly these grandiose American sceneries that also appeal to the Chinese audience, most who have never seen human wonders of this kind at home. In consistence with this, the director did not waste too many shots in the entire series on the true life of Wang Qiming who washes dishes twelve hours a day in a Chinese restaurant and shares one tiny dingy room with several other compatriots, which is usually what happens when one comes to America as an overseas student; instead, what the audience sees in closeup after closeup are the beautiful components of a breakfast shared by Wang and his wife when she comes to join him from China, or the expensive gifts that his daughter receives at her birthday party, or the luxurious style of the honeymoon of an American and Wang's ex-wife. Also relevant to the image of the West as paradise is Wang's ownership of a factory, his Cadillac™, and his house in Long Island. None of these can be accomplished in China, where money is short and technology backward.

One thing that is not lacking or outdated, however, is the supposed Oriental moral strength that has been maintained by Chinese emigrants to the U.S. and proven to be very powerful and superior to the American capitalist spirit. This constitutes another mytheme in *A Beijing Native in New York*. In the series, Wang is depicted as hardworking, able to endure all kinds of adversities, and smart, which finally leads him to his financial success. When he first arrives in New York, he can barely speak English, nor does he have enough money to go to school, let alone start a business, and he also faces racial discrimination because of the yellow color of his skin, but he manages to overcome all these difficulties with his hard work in a Chinese restaurant and his unwavering perseverance in a clothing factory. On the contrary, the American males in the series are generally depicted as self-centered and immature. For example, David, Wang's American competitor in business as well as in love life, is portrayed as a boss who easily loses his temper at his employees and is therefore capable of destroying his career in a matter of seconds, which is what actually happens in the story.

When it comes to the portrayal of women characters, the contrast between the Chinese and the Americans is even sharper. The former are always depicted as loving, sensitive, understanding, hardworking, attractive, and morally decent; while the latter are usually portrayed to be selfish, insensitive, and morally loose. There are two major female Chinese characters in the series, and both of them are presented as martyrs ever ready to sacrifice for the moral principles they uphold and for the people they love. The central figure, of course, is Guo Yan, who epitomizes the Chinese sense of female decency. When her husband is struggling for his survival in a new country, she is with him all along. Besides being a help and comfort at home, she works very hard in a clothing factory run by David for which she wins the admiration of her boss. Only when Wang later stoops to the American logic of running a business, that is, seeking profit at the cost of human warmth and moral values, does she leave him for David, albeit not without a lot of sincere effort on the part of David. Wang and David become business competitors, and the former faces bankruptcy because of the latter. Out of compassion and not intending to hurt David, Guo leaks some business information to her ex-husband. When David finds out about this, the couple quarrel and part company. Guo does not go back to Wang, who is now successful, but works instead as a janitor in a university hospital while receiving her graduate education. After that, she returns to China, where she eternally belongs. The same can be said about the other female character, Chun, who is second generation Chinese American. She speaks perfect English and knows very well the American way of doing things, but she maintains many Oriental values that she inherits from her ancestors. She is a good friend of Wang and is willing even to sell her own business to help Wang to get back on his feet. She is also a very unselfish lover after Wang's divorce, and the relationship proves to be more understanding and less motivated than anything that could ever exist between two human beings. As it happens, there is no major American female character in *A Beijing Native in New York*, and the absence can be accounted for by the fact that it is a story about some Chinese living in America. However, the series does contain a short scene in which Wang is intimately involved with an American woman. Even this brief appearance is made into one of prostitution where the American is willing to do anything for money: She is paid to say, "I love you," many times. Also worth mentioning is the characterization of Linlin, Wang's daughter, who comes to New York at a very early age and is soon Americanized. Like her American school peers, Linlin is portrayed as sexually promiscuous, first losing her virginity to a schoolmate and then purely for economic reasons becoming a partner of that boy's father.

West-East Confrontation

The story as a whole is much more complicated than the simple contrast of characters presented above, but the audience is never left in doubt as to which side gets the better hand in the West-East confrontation. There is a time when Wang becomes avaricious, and his business practice is hardly separable from that of his American counterparts. In that sense, he succumbs to the capitalist logic that businesses should be run with one's mind, not one's heart, yet it is exactly this corruption in character that also brings about his downfall. If not for his ex-wife, who out of compassion gives him some important information, and later his girlfriend, who out of devotion sells her own business and lends him a big sum of money, Wang would never be able to stand up again. Apart from the two shining female characters who symbolize Chinese moral strength, the whole series seems to impart a pervasive sense of emptiness, just like in the casino where Wang later becomes a frequent visitor and where there is a lot of money going around but few decent human beings. Against the background of magnificent highrises, buzzing highways, and well-lit store windows of New York City, one sees the ruthless schemes of business people, the endless fights in almost every family which eventually lead to divorce, and above all, the almost unbearable high pressure that the capitalist system exerts on every individual who lives in it. As the script writer puts it in the guiding caption at the beginning of each episode, "If you love him, send him to New York, for it's Paradise; If you hate him, send him to New York, for it's Hell." Paradise here certainly refers to the material aspect of the U.S., and Hell refers to its undesirable moral condition.

Discussion

Needless to say, *A Beijing Native in New York* has not presented to its Chinese audience at home the "reality" of life in New York. First, not all buildings in the city are as impressive as those repeatedly shown on the TV screen. If one goes to the Bronx or Queens, the dilapidated buildings there will certainly give a very different impression. Second, it is extremely difficult, if not impossible, for a new immigrant who has little knowledge of the language and culture and zero capital to start a business and become financially very successful within his lifetime. There are many first-generation immigrants who have never purchased a new car in their entire lives, let alone a Cadillac™ or a Mercedes™. This makes unconvincing Wang's ability to purchase a house in Long Island in a matter of a few years. Third, there are good people and bad people everywhere in the world, be they Chinese or American, businessmen or peasants, men or women. As a matter of fact, prostitution, which to the Chinese is the symptom of Western moral corruption, constitutes less a social problem in the U.S. than in China and most other Asian countries. All these make *A Beijing Native in New York* a "distortion" of the reality of American life.

The next question is why the U.S. is presented the way it is. The answer lies in the particular social and psychological functions of mythology. Etymologically speaking, the word "myth" means a story about gods that gradually takes its shape from ancient religious rituals, and many subsequent theories were built upon that premise of early human ignorance and superstition. But in recent years, scholars have expanded the definition to include stories that concern the more practical side of human life. Joseph Campbell (1970), for example, suggests the following four as the functions of what he calls "mythologies":

- Reconciliation of consciousness with the preconditions of its own existence;
  Formulating and rendering an image of the universe, a cosmological image in keeping with the science of the time and of such kind that, within its range, all things should be recognized as parts of a single great holy picture;
- Validating and maintaining some specific social order, authorizing its moral code as a construct beyond criticism or human emendation; and
- Shaping individuals to the aims and ideals of their various social groups, bearing them on from birth to death through the course of a human life. (138–141).

These four mythic functions were taken over for analytic purposes by Halbrook and Hirschman in their book *Semiotics of Consumption* and also given their categorical names as "metaphysical, cosmological, sociological and psychological" (Holbrook and Hirschman 1993, 147). The motivations behind *A Beijing Native in New York* certainly belong to the latter two categories, and it is the task of semiotic workers to trace the link between the myth in question and its ideological background. As Algirdas Greimas (1987) once put it:

The interpretation of myths brings into being a new "ideological" language, because this is indeed what happens: An analysis of signification must necessarily lead to a new "terminology," a new metalanguage. In other words, mythologists translate mythological language into "ideological" language. (3–4)

Conclusion

From the textual analysis presented above, a dominant theme seems to emerge from the series: America is a paradise full of material riches, but the place is inhabited by less perfect people, less perfect in the sense that their life is characterized by excessive sensuality and lack of human warmth which eventually will lead Americans to their downfalls. Given the current political and economic position that China takes in relation to the West in general and the

U.S. in particular, it is not hard to see what ideological purposes *A Beijing Native in New York* is meant to serve. On the one hand, the economic and technological backwardness of China has to be emphasized if the government wants to instill into the minds of its people the necessity of opening up to the outside world. Less than twenty years ago, China was still totally isolated from the international communities, the official ideology of the country at that time was that the Chinese were the luckiest of all peoples, and "two-thirds of the world population lived in misery." Inheriting a country on the verge of collapse and facing massive discontent from its citizens, the new leaders decided to adopt an open-door policy to court Western money as well as technology as an effort to revive its own economy, hence the much repeated mytheme of the U.S. and other Western countries as paradise. On the other hand, the national pride of the Chinese as the greatest of all peoples on earth has to be maintained, hence the mythic stereotype of Westerners as intellectually immature and emotionally insensitive.

References

Barthes, R. (1972). *Mythologies*. New York: Hill and Wang.

Campbell, J., (Ed.). (1970). *Myth, dreams, and religion*. New York: E.P. Dutton & Co.

Greimas, A.J. (1987). *On meaning: Selected writings in semiotic theory*. Minneapolis: University of Minnesota Press.

Holbrook, M.B., and E.C. Hirschman. (1993). *The semiotics of consumption*. Berlin: Mouton de Gruyter.

Said, E. (1979). *Orientalism*. New York: Vintage Books.

Part IV

U.S. Image and the Entertainment Factor

Today, more than ever before, the mass communication media contribute to the formation of opinions and perceptions of "others" throughout the world. In this section, the authors focus on the influence of media contents on the ways in which various cultures perceive the U.S. and its people. Shinichi Saito explores the relationship between television viewing and perceptions of America in Japan. He also examines whether positive or negative images of American society are cultivated by television. Hennie J. Groenewald, Annelie M.E. Naude, and Lynnette M. Serfontein assess perceptions of the U.S. and its people as portrayed in magazines, television, and films in South Africa. Daradirek "Gee" Ekachai, Mary Hinchcliff-Pelias, and Rosechongporn Komolsevin present results of a survey relative to the Thais' perception and characterization of the U.S. based on their exposure to the U.S.-produced media contents. Thimios Zaharopoulos examines the relationship between young people's television viewing behavior in Greece and their perception of the U.S. Dafna Lemish writes about "Americanization" of Israeli society, the influence of World Wrestling Federation (WWF) television programs on Israeli youngsters, and their impressions of the U.S. Rania M. Hegazi and Beverly Jensen explore the genesis of the American image in Arabic literature dating back to the 1600s. Hussein Amin examines the impact of American television programs, direct satellite broadcasts, and Hollywood movies on the Egyptian perception of the U.S. Finally, Joanne M. Lisosky explores reactions from around the world to U.S. images presented in a popular American children's television program, *Mighty Morphin Power Rangers*^{TM} (MMPR), broadcast in more than thirty countries.

17

Television and Perceptions of U.S. Society in Japan

SHINICHI SAITO

Introduction

The mass media both in the U.S. and in Japan often report a growing dislike or distaste toward America in Japan, and say that a new form of anti-Americanism is especially strong among the young generation (e.g., Honma and Eto 1991; Rapoport 1991; Weisman 1991). The perception of America in Japan has varied over the years, but it is said that we now face the deepest division between the two countries since World War II.

K. Suzuki (1992), however, calls this situation "a pseudo-crisis," which is created and amplified by the mass media. Although some tensions and conflicts in fact exist between Japan and the U.S. regarding trade imbalance and the U.S-Japan security treaty, some prominent journalists claim that the mass media place too much emphasis on the negative aspects of U.S.-Japan relations, thereby contributing to the creation of negative images of American people and society among the Japanese (e.g., Ando 1991; K. Suzuki 1992).

Because many Japanese have limited direct contact with America and Americans, most commonly held Japanese beliefs and conceptions about America can be considered the results of exposure to portrayals in newspapers and magazines and, above all, on television. Do the Japanese media, particularly television, really contribute to the formation and maintenance of negative or unfavorable images of America? I address this issue here by exploring the relationship between exposure to television and perceptions of U.S. society in Japan from the perspective of cultivation theory.

Cultivation theory

While there are several different approaches to the influence of the mass media on the social construction of reality (see Adoni and Mane 1984), research concerning the contribution of television to our perceptions of social reality has often been guided by cultivation theory (Gerbner and Gross 1976; Gerbner, Gross, Morgan, and Signorielli 1980, 1986). Cultivation theory postulates that the more time people spend watching television, the more likely it is that their conceptions of social reality will reflect what they see on the screen. Furthermore, the theory contends that heavy consumption of television contributes to a homogenized view of the real world.

A number of researchers have questioned or challenged Gerbner et al.'s assumptions, methodologies, and findings; an extensive review of such criticisms is beyond the scope of this article. (For a more extensive review of this research tradition, see Hawkins and Pingree 1982; Morgan and Signorielli 1990; Potter 1993.) Here, I examine message uniformity, one of the central issues in cultivation theory.

Gerbner and his associates insist that the message elements that lead to cultivation are those which cut across most programs and genres, and that audiences watch television in a relatively nonselective fashion. It follows that the amount of television viewed is far more important than what is viewed. Many researchers, however, disagree with this assumption. They have observed that measures of exposure to specific genres are associated more strongly with cultivation effects than is the total amount of viewing (e.g., Hawkins and Pingree 1981; Potter and Chang 1990). They argue that the overall amount of viewing is not the most relevant factor in explaining cultivation effects because cultivation relationships may be "content-specific." Hawkins and Pingree (1981) conclude that discarding the assumption of message uniformity and using a measure of exposure to specific genres strengthens cultivation theory rather than weakening it.

Cultivation Studies Focusing on Images of the United States

Although many studies on cultivation theory focus on TV violence, the theory also has been applied to a wide variety of topics, including images of America and Americans (Tamborini and Choi 1990; Tan, Li, and Simpson 1986; Tan and Suarchavarat 1988; Weimann 1984).

Weimann (1984) reported that heavy television viewers in Israel demonstrated a strong and consistent tendency to paint a rosy picture of life in the U.S. Other researchers have found that negative images of the U.S. were cultivated by American-made programs. Tan et al. (1986), for example, asserted that some American programs in Taiwan and Mexico create unfavorable images of Americans. In their opinion, the influence of American television programs "can either be positive or negative, depending on which programs are watched, and the symbols present in these programs" (810), because different and conflicting images of Americans are presented in different programs. Tan and Suarchavarat (1988) produced similar findings in their sample of Thai students. They stated that American television was a major source of social stereotypes about Americans, and that their subjects' images were mixed and included both positive and negative traits.

Tamborini and Choi (1990) reported complex results. They studied the effects of the American Forces Korean Network (AFKN) on Korean college students in regard to various perceptions of crime, drug abuse, sexual permissiveness, and affluence in the U.S. They stated that "while AFKN-TV crime/adventure show viewing was a relatively good predictor for 'mean world' perceptions of U.S. society, several other AFKN-TV viewing measures (i.e., total viewing, information program viewing, entertainment program viewing) showed no association with perceptions of crime in the United States" (167).

The existing cultivation studies that focus on images of America and Americans deal with the impact of U.S. programs on non-American audiences, because such programs are readily available in the investigated countries. Weimann (1984), for example, reported that in Israel more than sixty-five percent of broadcasting time was allocated to imported (mostly American) programs.

In Japan, on the other hand, only a few American-produced programs have been shown in recent years (Kawatake 1988, 1994). As I will discuss later, programs produced in Japan often depict America and Americans; therefore not only programs produced in the U.S. but other types of programs as well may influence perceptions of the U.S.

Depictions of America on Japanese Television

The mass media in Japan often report on foreign countries in great detail. The coverage of foreign countries, however, is slanted disproportionately toward the United States. In a content analysis of TV programs about foreign countries and people, for example, Hagiwara, Midooka and Nakamura (1987) indicated that Japanese TV portrays the United States much more frequently than other countries.

Programs Produced in the United States

It is argued that American-produced programs may not contribute much to the formation of images of America (e.g., Kawatake 1988). Dramas and movies imported from the U.S. were popular in the 1960s in Japan. The popularity of American programs declined during the 1970s, however. In recent years, Japanese TV has relied very little on imported programs. Imported (mainly American) programs have constituted only five percent of total broadcasting time since the 1970s.

Although their broadcasting time is not substantial, certain types of U.S.-produced programs may have a strong impact on Japanese perceptions of U.S. society because messages from such programs could be more salient than those from domestically produced programs. (According to Kawatake and Hara (1994), about sixty percent of the American dramas and movies shown on Japanese TV are action/adventure stories or thrillers.)

News

Kawatake's (1988) study revealed that nearly half of all TV news in Japan included some reference to foreign countries, and forty-five percent of all foreign news was related to the U.S. In a more recent study conducted by the NHK Broadcasting Culture Research Institute and the Mansfield Center for Pacific Affairs, about thirty-three percent of all international news in Japan dealt with the U.S. or U.S.-Japan relations (Kohno, Hara, and Saito 1994). Thus one can argue that TV news is a very important element in forming images of America among Japanese viewers.

The study by NHK and the Mansfield Center showed that TV news in Japan covered many aspects of the U.S. such as societal issues and events (e.g., violence and crime), cultural subjects (e.g., education), economics, and business. The study also revealed that much of the TV news conveyed neither positive nor negative images, but that about thirteen percent of the news stories analyzed in their study showed some negative pictures of the U.S., and only 4.3 percent conveyed positive pictures (Kohno et al. 1994).

Programs Produced in Japan

Among all programs (excluding news and commercials) broadcast from November 7 to November 13, 1993, those that contained some kind of foreign image accounted for 21.2 percent of total broadcasting time (15.8 percent Japanese-produced and 5.4 percent imported) (Kawatake 1994). Among the 217 Japanese-produced programs containing foreign images, 90 concerned cooking, shopping, and travelling, 52 were documentaries, 22 were music programs, 21 were educational or cultural, and 16 were about sports. Kawatake (1988) stated that many of the documentaries dealing with the U.S. depict negative aspects such as high school education in crisis or children of divorced families. He also commented that negative portrayals of the U.S. might create biased images of U.S. society in the Japanese audience.

Commercials

Commercials also convey images of America. According to M. Suzuki (1992), approximately thirty percent of all commercials aired between 7 and 9 P.M. show aspects of foreign countries, and thirty-five percent of these contain portrayals of the U.S. In general, commercials on Japanese television depict positive images of America, emphasizing concepts such as openness, brightness, or grandness. Most American characters are portrayed as cheerful, progressive, or civilized.

In sum, depictions of America on Japanese TV include both positive and negative images. In general, however, Japanese TV is more likely to depict negative than positive aspects.

Research Questions

This study is guided by the following research questions:

1. Does television in Japan have negative effects on perceptions of America? This is the fundamental question in the present study. As mentioned earlier, some social critics argue that the mass media in Japan may a have negative influence on the Japanese audience's perceptions of the U.S. because the media emphasize unfavorable aspects of U.S.-Japan relations or U.S. society. A limited number of content-analytic studies suggest that although TV portrayals of the U.S. are not totally negative, they tend to depict more negative than positive images. Does TV in Japan cultivate negative perceptions of the U.S.? In this study I attempt to shed some light on this question.

2. What elements of television have the most measurable impact on perceptions of America? This subquestion of the first question asks whether total television viewing time or the viewing of specific genres (e.g., news and U.S.-produced programs) has a greater power to predict perceptions of U.S. society.

Method

The sample for this study was drawn from Sendai, the largest city in the northeastern region of Japan. Five hundred people twenty years old or over who lived in Sendai City were selected on a stratified probability sampling method. Questionnaires were administered in person by trained interviewers from April 17 to April 30, 1993. The final sample comprised 403 completed interviews; the response rate was 80.6 percent.

The sample included 48.1 percent males and 51.9 percent females. Respondents ranged in age from 20 to 82 ($M = 48.0$, $SD = 16.8$): 36.5 percent were 20–39 years old, 31.75 percent were 40–59, 31.75 percent were 60 or over. As to the level of formal education, 11.0 percent were junior high school graduates, 45.1 percent were senior high school graduates, 25.4 percent had graduated from junior college (or the equivalent), 17.5 percent were college students or graduates, and 1.0 percent had attended graduate school.

Experience in Visiting the United States

Respondents were asked whether they had visited the United States, and if so, how long they had stayed. Only 13.4 percent of the sample had visited the United States (other than Hawaii). 44.4 percent of this group had stayed less than one week. Only six respondents had stayed more than three months. Most of the sample thus does not have substantial direct experience with the U.S. Therefore such experience would not be expected to play a substantial role in forming their images of U.S. society. (Despite this lack of experience, 88.1 percent of the respondents regard the U.S. as the country most important to Japan.)

Measures of TV Exposure

The total amount of television viewing was measured with two questions asking respondents to indicate how many hours of television they usually watched (a) on weekdays and (b) on the weekend. An index of viewing level (total TV viewing) was constructed by averaging the weekday and weekend viewing hours ($M = 3.2$, $SD = 1.6$ per day). The amount of TV news viewing was measured by asking how much time they usually spent watching TV news ($M = 1.2$, $SD = 0.8$ per day). Respondents also were asked to indicate how often they watched U.S. programs, on a six-point scale ranging from "almost never" to "more than four times a week." Thirty-five percent said they did not watch U.S. programs, 32 percent did so once a month, 12 percent two to three times a month, 13 percent once a week, and only 8 percent more than two or three times a week.

Measures of Perceptions of the United States

The questionnaire was long and contained items assessing a variety of images and beliefs about America. Because of space limitations, I report the results of only selected items.

Crime-related perceptions of U.S. society. Two items measured to what extent, on a four-point scale, respondents considered the U.S. to be dangerous: (a) "Which of the following most closely reflects your opinion about the frequency of violent crime in the United States?" (1 = almost never; 2 = seldom; 3 = somewhat frequent; 4 = very frequent); and (b) "Suppose you are staying in a big city in the U.S. How would you feel about walking alone on the street during daytime?" (1 = not afraid at all; 2 = not very afraid; 3 = somewhat afraid; 4 = very afraid). The former dealt with perceptions on the societal level; the latter, with perceptions on the personal level.

Beliefs about gender and racial equality in U.S. society. I used forced-choice questions to assess respondents' images of gender and racial equality in U.S. society. Respondents were asked to choose the response from each pair which they considered to be closer to reality. The gender equality item read "Though many women are becoming more active as members of society, the United States is still a male-dominant society" (coded 0); " In the United States, men and women have completely equal opportunity in all aspects" (coded 1). The racial equality item read "Many people in the United States believe that regardless of his/her race every human being is equal" (coded 1); "Many people in the United States have racial prejudice" (coded 0).

Statistical Analyses

First, I conducted cross-tabular analysis. This method is quite simple, but is an important feature of Gerbner et al.'s cultivation analysis. Contingency tables compare responses of light, medium, and heavy viewers in various control conditions.

Although cross-tabular analysis provides baseline information, it does not guard fully against spuriousness. Therefore, in the second analysis, I computed partial correlations between the TV exposure measures and the items regarding perceptions of the U.S.

Results

Perceptions Related to Crime

Tables 17.1 and 17.2 summarize the results of the items on crime-related perceptions of the U.S. Table 17.1 shows the percentages of respondents who think that violent crimes happen "very frequently" in the U.S.; Table 17.2 presents the percentages of respondents who said they would feel "very afraid" of walking alone during daytime in a big American city.

Table 17.1 shows that both total TV viewing and viewing of U.S. programs were associated with the image of the U.S. as crime ridden. The results of cross-tabular analysis indicate that heavy viewers (either in total TV viewing or in U.S. program viewing) were more likely to perceive the U.S. as crime ridden. For example, forty-eight percent of the heavy total TV viewers said that violent crimes occur "very frequently" in the U.S., but only

Table 17.1. Percentages of Respondents Who Think Violent Crimes Occur "Very Frequently" in the United States, by Total TV Viewing, TV News Viewing, and U.S. Program Viewing

	Total % (N)	Total TV				TV News				U.S. Programs			
		Light %	Heavy %	CD[a]	Partial r	Light %	Heavy %	CD	Partial r	Non %	Frequent %	CD	Partial r
Overall	38 (403)	34	48	+14***	.14***	37	38	+1	-.04	34	49	+15*	.16**
Sex													
Female	39 (209)	42	43	+1	.06	40	35	-5	-.10*	35	48	+13	.11*
Male	37 (194)	27	60	+33***	.28****	33	43	+10	.03	33	50	+17*	.21**
Age													
20–39	42 (147)	39	57	+18	.09	40	45	+5	-.05	35	52	+17	.19*
40–59	36 (128)	27	46	+19**	.17**	27	33	+6	-.08	30	50	+20*	.12*
60 or over	36 (128)	33	44	+11	.15*	42	37	-5	-.09	36	42	+6	.15*
Education													
Low	36 (225)	27	47	+20****	.22****	33	36	+3	-.02	30	49	+19	.17**
High	40 (176)	41	53	+12	.06	43	41	-2	-.07	42	50	+8	.11*
Newspaper													
Light	39 (159)	38	50	+12	.14**	35	52	+17*	.05	36	48	+12	.19**
Heavy	37 (240)	30	48	+18**	.13**	39	35	-4	-.10*	31	50	+19*	.13*

Note: Total television viewing, TV news viewing, and U.S. program viewing are divided into light, medium, and heavy viewing based on an approximate three-way split. For purposes of space, medium viewers are omitted from this table.

[a]CD = cultivation differential: percentage of heavy viewers (or frequent viewers) giving response minus percentage of light (or non-) viewers giving response (significance for c^2 test). Correlations are fifth-order (sixth-order for overall) partials controlling for sex, age, education, amount of newspaper reading, information from others, and direct U.S. experience.

* $p < .10$; ** $p < .05$; *** $p < .01$; **** $p < .001$

Table 17.2. Percentages of Respondents Who Say They Would Feel "Very Afraid" of Walking Alone During the Day in a Big City in the United States, by Total TV Viewing, TV News Viewing, and U.S. Program Viewing

	Total % (N)	Total TV				TV News				U.S. Programs			
		Light %	Heavy %	CD[a]	Partial r	Light %	Heavy %	CD	Partial r	Non %	Frequent %	CD	Partial r
Overall	32 (403)	25	48	+23****	.14***	28	37	+9	.00	44	23	–21***	–.06
Sex													
Female	39 (209)	38	48	+10**	.07	34	40	+6	.00	53	25	–28**	–.13**
Male	24 (194)	14	48	+34****	.25****	20	32	+12	.02	33	21	–12	.02
Age													
20–39	22 (147)	24	38	+14**	.12*	21	28	+7	–.04	28	21	–7	–.09
40–59	30 (128)	19	39	+20	.15**	23	33	+10	.00	40	25	–15	.00
60 or over	45 (128)	33	59	+26*	.12*	46	48	+2	–.03	58	26	–32*	–.15**
Education													
Low	36 (225)	18	53	+35****	.20***	26	42	+16	.07	44	28	–16	–.08
High	27 (176)	30	33	+3	.09	31	28	–3	–.09	44	19	–25***	–.05
Newspaper													
Light	33 (159)	21	62	+41****	.25***	27	63	+36*	.16**	41	29	–12	–.08
Heavy	30 (240)	27	40	+13*	.06	28	30	+2	–.10*	45	20	–25***	–.04

Note: Total television viewing, TV news viewing, and U.S. program viewing are divided into light, medium, and heavy viewing based on an approximate three-way split. For purposes of space, medium viewers are omitted from this table.

[a]CD = cultivation differential: percentage of heavy viewers (or frequent viewers) giving response minus percentage of light (or non-) viewers giving response (significance for c^2 test). Correlations are fifth-order (sixth-order for overall) partials controlling for sex, age, education, amount of newspaper reading, information from others, and direct U.S. experience.

* $p < .10$; ** $p < .05$; *** $p < .01$; **** $p < .001$

thirty-four percent of the light total TV viewers chose this answer (CD = +14, $p < .01$). The relationship remained even after controlling simultaneously for several third variables (sixth-order partial $r = .14$, $p < .001$). The magnitude of associations varied depending on the subgroups: Male respondents, the less educated, and light newspaper readers showed stronger correlations. In this item, total TV viewing and U.S. program viewing had almost equal predictive power.

As displayed in Table 17.2, the cross-tabular analysis showed that heavy total TV viewers were more likely to say they would feel "very afraid" to walk alone on the street during daytime in a big city in the U.S. That is, heavy total TV viewers had a more fearful image. Frequent viewing of U.S. programs, however, was associated with a less fearful image.

The relationship observed in the cross-tabular analysis between total TV viewing and this personal-level perception remained when third variables were controlled simultaneously (for example, sixth-order partial $r = .14$, $p < .01$). The results also reveal some specifying variables: significant associations were found only among male respondents, the less educated, and light newspaper readers. The association between U.S. program viewing and this item, however, declined significantly after implementation of simultaneous controls of third variables: Significant correlations with U.S. program viewing were found only in female respondents and the elderly. In other subgroups, correlations were reduced to nonsignificant levels.

As mentioned previously, the items on crime-related U.S. images deal with both personal- and societal-level perceptions. Some researchers have pointed out that the television message could affect beliefs on the societal level, but not on the personal level. Doob and MacDonald (1979) remarked, "Television may well act as a source of information with regard to questions of fact, whereas it does not change people's view of how afraid they should be" (179). Tyler and Cook (1984) provided further evidence supporting this *impersonal impact hypothesis*. The results in the present study, however, do not support this hypothesis. Our data demonstrate that both personal- and societal-level perceptions were correlated significantly with the amount of total television viewing.

Image of Gender Equality

Table 17.3 summarizes the results of cross-tabular analysis and partial correlation analysis for the gender equality item. The table shows the percentages of respondents who chose the answer "In the United States, men and women have completely equal opportunity in all aspects."

Table 17.3 demonstrates that the amount of TV news viewing was a reliable indicator for the gender equality item. Both cultivation differentials

Table 17.3. Percentages of Respondents Who Say "In the United States, men and women have completely equal opportunity in all aspects," by Total TV Viewing, TV News Viewing, and U.S. Program Viewing

	Total % (N)	Total TV				TV News				U.S. Programs			
		Light %	Heavy %	CD[a]	Partial r	Light %	Heavy %	CD	Partial r	Non %	Frequent %	CD	Partial r
Overall	61 (403)	58	61	+3	.03	50	72	+22***	.17****	55	61	+6	.07
Sex													
Female	66 (209)	67	66	−1	.02	54	78	+24***	.20***	61	68	+7	.03
Male	55 (194)	52	50	−2	.08	45	62	+17	.12*	48	55	+7	.10
Age													
20–39	59 (147)	59	46	−13	−.04	53	65	+12	.18**	45	62	+17	−.07
40–59	60 (128)	60	61	+1	.01	47	71	+24	.14	70	54	−16	−.04
60 or over	63 (128)	55	70	+15	.13	49	78	+29**	.21***	53	71	+18	.23***
Education													
Low	64 (225)	62	67	+5	.10	45	78	+33****	.28****	58	65	+7	.07
High	57 (176)	56	47	−9	−.02	59	61	+2	.04	50	59	+9	.07
Newspaper													
Light	60 (159)	59	60	+1	.04	51	78	+27**	.25****	53	69	+16	.17**
Heavy	62 (240)	59	63	+4	.04	53	70	+17	.13**	59	57	−3	.00

Note: Total television viewing, TV news viewing, and U.S. program viewing are divided into light, medium, and heavy viewing based on an approximate three-way split. For purposes of space, medium viewers are omitted from this table.

[a]CD = cultivation differential: percentage of heavy viewers (or frequent viewers) giving response minus percentage of light (or non-) viewers giving response (significance for c^2 test). Correlations are fifth-order (sixth-order for overall) partials controlling for sex, age, education, amount of newspaper reading, information from others, and direct U.S. experience.

* $p < .10$; ** $p < .05$; *** $p < .01$; ****$p < .001$

(CDs) and partial correlations indicate that heavy TV news viewers were more likely than light TV news viewers to regard the United States as a nonmale-dominant society. Overall, seventy-two percent of heavy TV news viewers said "Men and women have completely equal opportunity" in the U.S., but the corresponding figure among light TV news viewers was fifty percent (CD = +22, $p < .01$). The pattern observed by crosstabular analysis remained after the third variables were controlled simultaneously (partial $r = .18$, $p < .001$). The results also reveal stronger associations among females, the elderly, the less educated, and light newspaper readers, who depend most strongly on TV. In some subgroups, the level of U.S. program viewing was also correlated with the gender equality item (partial $r = .23$, $p < .01$ for persons age 60 or older; partial $r = .17$, $p < .05$ for light newspaper readers). This item, however, was not correlated with the amount of total television viewing.

Image of Racial Equality

Table 17.4 summarizes the results of cross-tabular analysis and within-group partial correlation analysis for the racial equality item. This table shows the percentages of respondents who chose the answer "Many people in the United States believe that every human being is equal regardless of his/her race" and partial correlations.

The results of cross-tabular analysis indicated that heavy total viewers of television and of TV news were more likely to think that people in the U.S. are self-identified nonracists. The associations were stronger for females, the less educated, and light newspaper readers. Partial correlations remained significant, however, only for females (partial $r = .18$, $p < .01$ with total TV viewing). Some of the partial correlations also were marginally significant ($p < .10$), but most were not significant.

Discussion

In regard to perceptions of crime, the results indicate that the amount of total television viewing (and, for the societal-level perceptions, the level of U.S. program viewing as well) were associated with more strongly negative images of U.S. society. It is reasonable for many Japanese to think of the U.S. as unsafe because violent crimes are much more frequent in the U.S. than in Japan, as shown clearly by crime statistics. Yet, the crime-ridden image of U.S. society among the Japanese seems somewhat exaggerated. For example, approximately half of the heavy total television viewers believe that violent crimes occur "very frequently" in the U.S., and they would feel "very afraid" to walk alone during the day in a large American city. (In addition, most of the respondents greatly overestimated the number of people involved in violent

Table 17.4. Percentages of Respondents Who Say "Many people in the United States believe that every human being is equal regardless of his/her race," by Total TV Viewing, TV News Viewing, and U.S. Program Viewing

| | Total | Total TV | | | | TV News | | | | U.S. Programs | | | |
	% (N)	Light %	Heavy %	CD[a]	Partial r	Light %	Heavy %	CD	Partial r	Non %	Frequent %	CD	Partial r
Overall	35 (403)	29	37	+8	.07*	30	41	+11	.06	31	36	+5	00
Sex													
Female	37 (209)	24	44	+20**	.18***	34	49	+16***	.10*	33	39	+6	-.01
Male	33 (194)	33	24	-9	-.07	23	28	+5*	-.02	28	32	+4	-.01
Age													
20–39	39 (147)	32	49	+17	.07	33	53	+20	.09	35	38	+3	-.06
40–59	31 (128)	33	36	+5	.06	27	31	+8	.02	33	27	-6	-.04
60 or over	34 (128)	18	30	+12***	.08	27	41	+14	.05	27	45	+18	.11
Education													
Low	32 (225)	27	38	+11	.10	22	37	+16*	.07	28	34	+6	.04
High	38 (176)	32	36	+4	.04	41	47	+6	.04	38	38	0	-.05
Newspaper													
Light	28 (159)	24	33	+9	.10	25	33	+8	.13*	27	23	-4	-.04
Heavy	40 (240)	34	40	+6	.07	42	43	+1	.04	35	44	+9	.04

Note: Total television viewing, TV news viewing, and U.S. program viewing are divided into light, medium, and heavy viewing based on an approximate three-way split. For purposes of space, medium viewers are omitted from this table.

[a]CD = cultivation differential: percentage of heavy viewers (or frequent viewers) giving response minus percentage of light (or non-) viewers giving response (significance for c^2 test). Correlations are fifth-order (sixth-order for overall) partials controlling for sex, age, education, amount of newspaper reading, information from others, and direct U.S. experience.

* $p < .10$; ** $p < .05$; *** $p < .01$; **** $p < .001$

crime in New York and the number of people who carry a gun for personal safety.) Thus, television in Japan may cultivate an extreme view of America as a crime-ridden society.

The results show that the image of gender equality was associated with the amount of TV news viewing (and of U.S. program viewing in some subgroups): Heavy viewers had a rosier image of U.S. society, contrary to the prediction that television in Japan cultivates negative perceptions of the U.S. Although the available content analysis data provide few clues indicating why heavy TV news viewers had more positive gender equality perceptions of the U.S., the following reasoning might explain this finding. TV news often reports on American women such as female executives or politicians working actively in U.S. society, but seldom refers to the existing gender inequality in the U.S., presumably because such a report is not so newsworthy in Japan. It seems reasonable to assume that, when answering the survey question on the gender equality image, heavy TV news viewers retrieved from memory some instances of American female professionals more quickly and easily than light TV news viewers (See Shrum 1995 for a related argument). If so, heavier TV news viewing may result in a more gender-equal image of the U.S.

In the overall results, the perception of racial equality in the U.S. was not associated with TV viewing. Among female respondents, however, total viewing showed a positive association with this item, indicating that heavy viewers were more likely than others to believe that the U.S. was a nonracist country.

Further analysis for this item revealed that the racial equality image was associated more strongly with newspaper reading (overall sixth-order partial $r = .18$, $p < .001$) than with any of the three TV exposure measures. The investigation of the newspapers' independent influence on perceptions of the U.S. is beyond the scope of this article, but certainly the image of America reported in major Japanese newspapers, as on television, has a major impact on Japanese perceptions of U.S. society. Further study is needed to address this issue.

In sum, the findings of this study show that television in Japan may cultivate not only negative images of the U.S. but also some positive images. However, we found evidence showing that television viewing was negatively associated with some aspects of the images of America. The results also indicate that measures of exposure to specific genres (e.g., news or American programs) may be more reliable indicators for specific images.

While many of the current tensions or conflicts between Japan and the United States tend to be considered in the political or economic domains, we should not overlook the underlying "cultural friction" behind these problems. Distorted and often negative images and perceptions can be thought of as one of the main sources of the cultural friction. Paying attention to negative effects of television, we need to examine more fully the relationship between exposure to television and the perceptions of the U.S. in Japan.

References

Adoni, H., and S. Mane. (1984). Media and social construction of reality. *Communication Research* 11: pp. 323–340.

Ando, H. (1991). *Nichibei Joho Masatsu* [The Japan-U.S. information conflict]. Tokyo: Iwanami.

Doob, A.W., and G.E. MacDonald. (1979). Television viewing and fear of victimization: Is the relationship causal? *Journal of Personality and Social Psychology* 37(2): pp. 170–179.

Gerbner, G., and L. Gross. (1976). Living with television: The violence profile. *Journal of Communication* 26: pp. 172–199.

Gerbner, G., L. Gross, M. Morgan, and N. Signorielli. (1980). The mainstreaming of America: Violence profile no. 11. *Journal of Communication* 30(3): pp. 10–29.

Gerbner, G., L. Gross, M. Morgan, and N. Signorielli. (1986). Living with television: The dynamics of the cultivation process. In J. Bryant and D. Zillmann (Eds.), *Perspectives on media effects*, pp. 17–48. Hillsdale, N.J.: Lawrence Erlbaum.

Hagiwara, S., K. Midooka, and M. Nakamura. (1987). Terebi no naka no gaikoku gaikokujin [Foreign countries and people in the world of television]. *Shimbungaku Hyoron* 36: pp. 57–72.

Hawkins, R.P., and S. Pingree. (1981). Uniform content and habitual viewing: Unnecessary assumptions in social reality effects. *Human Communication Research* 7: pp. 291–301.

Hawkins, R.P., and S. Pingree. (1982). Television's influence on social reality. In D. Pearl, L. Bouthilet, and J. Lazar (Eds.), *Television and behavior: Ten years of scientific progress and implications for the eighties*, Vol. 2, pp. 224–247. Washington, D.C.: U.S. Government Printing Office.

Honma, N., and J. Eto. (1991, June). Nihonjin wa naze amerika ga kiraika [Why do Japanese dislike America?]. *Bungei Shunju*, pp. 94–109.

Kohno, K., Y. Hara, and K. Saito. (1994). Terebi wa aite-koku wo dou tsutaete iruka (2) [American and Japanese television news coverage of the other (2)]. *Hoso Kenkyu to Chosa* 44(7): pp. 2–25.

Kawatake, K. (1988). *Nippon no Imeiji* [Image of Japan]. Tokyo: Nippon Hoso Shuppan Kyokai.

Kawatake, K. (1994). Nihon wo chushin to suru terebi joho furo no genjo to mondai-ten [Television flow to and from Japan: Present situation and problems]. *Johotsushin-Gakkaishi* 43: pp. 54–63.

Kawatake, K., and Y. Hara, Y. (1994). Hihon wo chushin to suru terebi bangumi no ryutsu jokyo [The distribution of TV programs centering on Japan]. *Hoso Kenkyu to Chosa* 44(11): pp. 2–17.

Morgan, M., and N. Signorielli. (1990). Cultivation analysis: Conceptualization and methodology. In N. Signorielli and M. Morgan (Eds.), *Cultivation analysis: New directions in media effects research*, pp. 13–34. Newbury Park, Cal.: Sage.

Potter, W.J. (1993). Cultivation theory and research: A conceptual critique. *Human Communication Research* 19(4): pp. 564–601.

Potter, W.J., and I.C. Chang. (1990). Television exposure measures and the cultivation hypothesis. *Journal of Broadcasting & Electronic Media* 34: pp. 313–333.

Rapoport, C. (1991, May 6). The big split. *Fortune*, pp. 38–48.

Shrum, L.J. (1995). Assessing the social influence of television: A social cognition perspective on cultivation effects. *Communication Research* 22(4): pp. 402–429.

Suzuki, K. (1992). *Nichibei "kiki" to hodo* [Japan-U.S. crisis and media coverage]. Tokyo: Iwanami.

Suzuki, M. (1992). *Terebi: Dare no tame no media ka* [Television: Whose medium is it?]. Tokyo: Gakugei Shorin.

Tamborini, R., and J. Choi. (1990). The role of cultural diversity in cultivation research. In N. Signorielli and M. Morgan (Eds.), *Cultivation analysis: New directions in media effects research*, pp. 157–180. Newbury Park, Cal.: Sage.

Tan, A.S., S. Li, and C. Simpson. (1986). American TV and social stereotypes of Americans in Taiwan and Mexico. *Journalism Quarterly* 63(4): pp. 809–814.

Tan, A.S., and K. Suarchavarat. (1988). American TV and social stereotypes of Americans in Thailand. *Journalism Quarterly* 65(4): pp. 648–654.

Tyler, T.R., and F.L. Cook. (1984). The mass media and judgments of risk: Distinguishing impact on personal and societal level judgments. *Journal of Personality and Social Psychology* 47(4): pp. 693–708.

Weimann, G. (1984). Images of life in America: The impact of U.S. T.V. in Israel. *International Journal of Intercultural Relations* 8: pp. 185–197.

Weisman, S.R. (1991, October 16). Japanese coin word for their unease about U.S. *The New York Times*, p. A14.

18

Is the American Way
Really the Right Way?

A South African Perspective

HENNIE J. GROENEWALD, ANNELIE M.E. NAUDE,
AND LYNNETTE M. SERFONTEIN

Introduction

The South African media scene is dominated by American films (about 90 percent of films are American productions) and television programs. The South African Broadcasting Corporation has three television channels and viewers from at least eleven different cultures. Its daily broadcasts consist of between 50 percent to 65 percent American-oriented programs. M Net (Multi-choice Network), a subscription service owned by the major newspaper groups in the country, obtains more than 80 percent of its program material from America. This channel provides viewers with at least three to four films every day.

Although radio, newspapers, books, and magazines report important events and disseminate a lot of information, films and television programs open a window for South Africans on America. Today, *Dances with Wolves* and *Jurassic Park* are well known in many South African homes, together with television programs such as *Melrose Place*, *Murder She Wrote*, *Santa Barbara*, and *The Cosby Show*.

Against this background, an investigation of a sample of South Africans' perceptions of and attitudes to the U.S. and its people as portrayed in films, television, and magazines are reported in this chapter.

Theoretical background

People's perceptions of and attitudes about the global village are largely formed by their exposure to mass media. The effect of mass media and especially of television on what people believe the social world is like has been investigated in various communication studies (Shrum and O'Guinn 1993, 463–467). Social scientists such as Schutz, Berger, Luckmann, and Gergen developed the theory of the social construction of reality while Gerbner, Gross, Morgan, and Signorelli, among others, put forward the cultivation theory (Littlejohn 1992, 190–198, 358–360; Potter 1993; Shrum and O'Guinn 1993). Although these two theories are independent, it is clear that the concept of a mass mediated construction of social reality cuts through both of them (Peck 1989; McLeod et al. 1991). It is important to note that both these theories were used only as broad theoretical frameworks in this study, and it was not the intention to conduct a standard cultivation analysis.

The theory of social construction of reality is concerned with the processes by which individuals account for the world and their experience (Gergen 1985). The mass media, according to Lipmann and Park, create pictures in the heads of people, and these pictures do not necessarily relate to reality. Most people today experience the outside world through their exposure to mass media, and in particular audio-visual media such as television and film. (De Fleur and Ball Rokeach 1989; O'Neill 1991; Black 1982; Naude et al. 1994).

Cultivation theory, which was developed by George Gerbner and his colleagues, deals with the sociocultural outcomes of mass communication (Littlejohn 1992). The concept of cultivation refers to the long-term formation of perceptions of and beliefs about the world as a result of exposure to the mass media. Gerbner stressed the need to look beyond examining the short-term effects of the media and to investigate how the media have subtle but cumulative effects over a long period of time. He claimed that "changes in the mass production and rapid distribution of messages across previous barriers of time, space, and social groupings bring about systematic variations in public message content whose full significance rests in the cultivation of collective consciousness about elements of existence" (Potter 1993, 564).

Gerbner (1991) focused the theory of cultivation mainly on the effect of television on people. According to him, television is a homogenizing agent in culture. Television is the means to a common experience for almost everyone and has the effect of providing a shared way of viewing the world. It is important to realize that cultivation analysis is concerned with the totality of the pattern communicated cumulatively by television over a long period of exposure rather than with any particular content or specific effect. Instead of referring to specific effects, it makes a statement about the culture of the viewers as a whole (Littlejohn 1992). Television exposure is usually conceptualized in terms of time. "It does not matter what a person watches, only how much he or she watches" (Potter 1993, 570). Media users in this study were classified in terms of light, medium, and heavy usage of different mass media.

The assumption of uniform messages states that television is a world consistently presenting viewers with a set of monolithic messages. According to Gerbner and his colleagues, the world portrayed on television is uniform across programs and time. Some types of presentations are repeated so often that viewers come to believe that the real world also operates the same way the television world does. Supporters of cultivation theory claimed that programs such as crime or police stories cannot and need not relate to specific elements of those or other shows. These programs should be seen as generalized responses to the central dynamics of the world of television drama (Potter 1993).

Cultivation theory predicts a difference in the social reality of heavy television viewers in contrast to light viewers. Heavy viewers will believe in a reality that is consistent with the television world although this may differ from the real world (Littlejohn 1992).

Based on the abovementioned assumptions, this study was conducted to determine if there were any correlations between light, medium and heavy users and their perceptions of the American reality as portrayed by the media in South Africa.

Empirical investigation

In order to investigate the perceptions and attitudes of South Africans of America and its people, an empirical investigation was launched during the latter half of 1995. This study focused on television, film, and magazines because these media contained the highest American content.

Aims of the Study

The following aims were set:

- To determine the media usage patterns of respondents with regard to television, magazines, and film;
- To determine South Africans' perceptions of and attitudes toward the U.S. as a country and the American people;
- To determine the respondents' preferences for American content in television programs, magazines, and film;
- To determine if different media usage patterns correlate with perceptions and attitudes toward American people and the U.S.

Method

A nonprobability sample which relied on available subjects (Babbie 1992) was used to obtain responses nationwide. Six hundred questionnaires were distributed and collected by senior students in their home towns or cities. A response rate of 97.0 percent was obtained. A structured questionnaire with questions on media usage patterns, media content preferences, as well as perceptions of and attitudes toward American people and the U.S. as a country was used. Perceptions and attitudes were mostly measured with the use of 7-point semantic differential scale and 5-point Lickert-type scale.

The data obtained were processed by the use of the Statistica computer program. Several re-codings were done in the process, especially with regard to media users as light, medium, and heavy users. One-way frequency tables, Pearson's correlation coefficients, cross-tabulations and chi-squares were calculated. Owing to the relatively large sample size, the statistical significance of most of the correlation coefficients was high, while the r-values did not indicate any significant correlations.

These results were interpreted by means of the Effect size test (Steyn and Engelbrecht 1990), which indicates the practical significance of a correlation. According to the Effect size test an r-value of up to 0.3 indicates a low effect, an r-value between 0.3 and 0.5 indicates a medium effect and an r-value higher than 0.5 indicates a high effect. All results were rounded off to the first decimal.

Results

Demographic profile

Table 18.1 represents the demographic profile of the respondents. The majority of the respondents were Afrikaans speaking and under the age of thirty years.

The Television Audience

A distinction was made between weekday and weekend television viewers. In the case of weekday viewers, a light viewer was seen as a person watching less than an hour of television every weekday. A medium viewer was defined as a person who watched between one and three hours of television every weekday, while a heavy viewer was defined as a person watching more than three hours of television per day.

Most of the respondents (62.1 percent) seem to fall in the category of medium television viewers on weekdays, while 28.8 percent were light viewers

Table 18.1. Demographic Profile of Respondents in South Africa

	Percentage	*Number*
Gender		
Male	50.2	290
Female	49.8	292
Age		
18–30	59.5	347
31–45	20.8	121
46+	19.7	114
Geographical distribution		
Urban	57.0	332
Rural	37.6	219
Unknown	5.4	32
Language		
Afrikaans	66.6	388
English	7.4	43
Afrikaans & English	9.1	53
Southern Sotho	3.3	19
Tswana	8.9	52
Xhosa	1.2	7
Zulu	0.5	3
Other	3.1	18

and only 9.1 percent ($N = 583$) were identified as heavy television viewers on weekdays. Figure 18.1 represents the viewing patterns of the light, medium, and heavy weekday viewer.

A light weekend television viewer was defined as a person who watched less than an hour of television on a weekend. A medium viewer was seen as a person watching between one and three hours of television during a weekend and a heavy viewer as a person watching more than three hours.

Once again, most respondents (61.6 percent) were identified as medium television viewers, but on a weekend there were more heavy viewers (24.4 percent) than on weekdays and 14.1 percent ($N = 583$) were light viewers. The viewing patterns of weekend viewers are graphically displayed in Figure 18.2.

In order to determine the relationship between light, medium, and heavy viewers regarding exposure to American content, a further analysis of the content of the programs watched was made. It seems as though light viewers don't watch television programs with a South African background. On a 5-point scale with 5 indicating very often, most of the respondents (28.0 percent) chose

Figure 18.1. Viewing Patterns of Weekday Viewers in South Africa

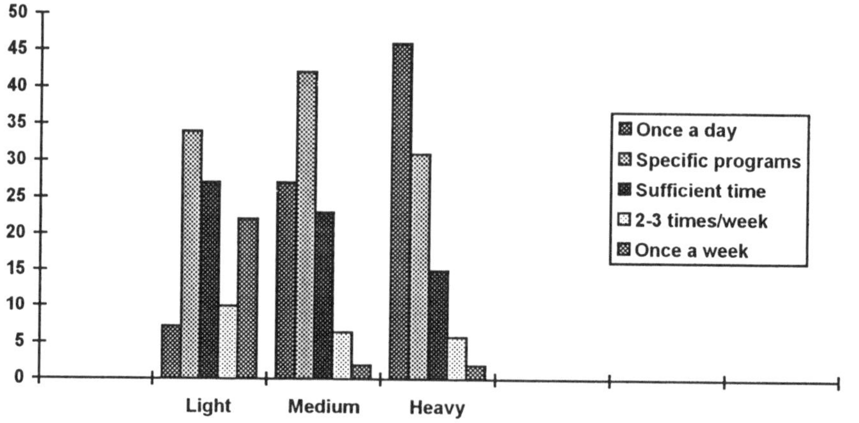

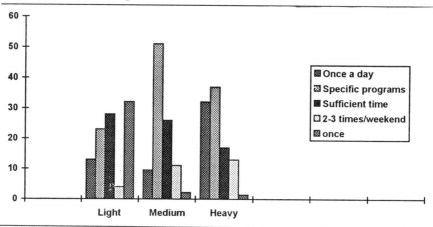

Figure 18.2. Viewing Patterns of Weekend Viewers in South Africa

1. 20 percent chose 2 and 26.0 percent chose 3. Only 14.0 percent and 12.0 percent (*N*=162), respectively, chose options 4 and 5. Basically, the same trend was noted regarding the heavy viewer. Options 1, 2, and 3 were chosen by respectively 25.0 percent, 25.0 percent, and 26.0 percent of the respondents. Only 9.4 percent and 15.0 percent chose options 4 and 5. Regarding the medium viewer no clear trend could be identified. Respondents varied between

Figure 18.3. Viewing Patterns of the Film Audience in South Africa

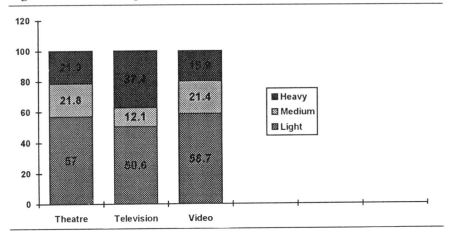

19.0 percent and 21.0 percent for each option. Contrary to what was expected, the heavy viewer didn't seem to get more exposure to American content.

The film audience

In order to describe the film audience, a distinction was made between persons going to a theatre to watch a film, watching a film on television, and renting a video to watch a film. In all instances, a light viewer was defined as a person who only watched a film if it was a special film, a medium viewer as a person who watched one or two films a months, and a heavy viewer as a person watching more than three films a month. Figure 18.3 indicates the viewing patterns of the film audience.

A further analysis was made to determine a distinction in preference toward American films by light, medium, and heavy viewers. In all three instances (film, television, and video), light, medium, and heavy viewers indicated that they preferred American films. Therefore, it can be concluded that the film audience was exposed to a large number of American films, but it must also be kept in mind that the light viewer was the dominant category.

Magazine readers

In defining magazine readers, once again a distinction was made between light, medium, and heavy readers. A light reader was seen as a person who read a magazine only when he had time, while a medium reader was defined as a person reading one or two magazines a week, and a heavy reader was seen as reading three or more.

Most of the respondents (48.3 percent) were light readers, i.e., reading a magazine only when they had sufficient time. There were 27.8 percent medium readers and 23.9 percent (N = 553) heavy readers.

A further analysis of the content regarding the U.S. and its people revealed that the majority of the light readers (37.0 percent) indicated on a 5-point scale that they never read articles on the U.S. and its people, and only 4.5 percent (N = 266) indicated that they often read articles on the U.S. and its people. Much the same trend was noted regarding medium readers: 29.0 percent chose option 1 indicating that they never read articles with American content, and this was supported by 27.0 percent (N = 154) of the respondents choosing option 2. Only 5.2 percent (N = 154) indicated that they often read articles on Americans.

Regarding the heavy reader, an interesting trend emerged. While only 16.0 percent of the respondents chose option 1, indicating that they never read articles on the U.S. and its people, 24.0 percent of the respondents chose option 2—still indicating that they rarely read articles on Americans. Most of the respondents (32.0 percent) were undecided and chose option 3, while 16.2 percent and 12.0 percent (N = 132) respectively chose options 4 and 5, indicating that they often read articles on Americans.

Most respondents indicated that they didn't read the magazines listed in the questionnaire. This can be ascribed to the fact that almost half the respondents were light readers of magazines.

Perceptions of American people

The results of most of the twenty-one semantic differential scales clustered around the middle of the scale. There were, however, a few exceptions:

- Uneducated(1)/Educated(7):   Mean = 5.1 (N = 543)
- Not creative(1)/Creative(7):   Mean = 5.3 (N = 543)
- Ambitious(7)/Not ambitious(1):   Mean = 5.4 (N = 543)
- Unsociable(1)/Sociable(7):   Mean = 5.5 (N = 543)
- Non-materialistic(7)/Materialistic(1): Mean = 2.1 (N = 543)

Although the mean of the Aggressive(1)/Non-aggressive scale was close to the middle value (3.6), 46.6 percent of the respondents (N = 268) chose the first three values (that is, the more negative side) of the scale.

It seems that respondents' perceptions of the acceptability of American people were somewhat influenced by how much they wanted to live in America. A practically significant correlation (medium effect according to the Effect size test) was found between these two variables ($r = 0.3543$; $N = 542$; $p < 0.000$). This means that the respondents who reacted positively toward living in America also experienced Americans as more acceptable than respondents who did not want to live in America.

Respondents' attitudes toward the statement, "The American way is the right way," seemed to influence their perceptions of American people, although the Effect size test indicated only medium effects in this regard. The conclusion can be made that the respondents who agreed with the statement tended to evaluate Americans more positively, as can be seen in Table 18.2.

Media usage and perceptions of American people

Contrary to what was expected, no high correlations between media usage and perceptions of Americans were obtained for television viewers, film viewers, or magazine readers. In every instance the value of r was less than 0.20, which indicated only a slight correlation and an almost negligible relationship (or small effect) (Williams 1986). The highest correlations obtained for each medium will be mentioned briefly. The following statistically significant correlations were obtained for frequency of television watching during the week:

Attractive/Unattractive	($r = 0.1691$; $p < 0.000$; $N = 543$);
Uneducated/Educated	($r = 0.1059$; $p < 0.01$; $N = 543$);
Untrustworthy/Trustworthy	($r = 0.1017$; $p < 0.02$; $N = 543$);

It can be deduced that the frequency of television watching has only a small effect (according to the Effect size test mentioned earlier) on the perceptions of the respondents. Thus, high television viewers tended to evaluate Americans more positively than light or medium television viewers.

No statistically or practically significant correlations were obtained for television viewers over weekends, or for films watched in film theatres, films watched on television, or magazine readers. It seems as if respondents' different media usage patterns with regard to the media mentioned do not show any relation to their different perceptions of American people.

With regard to films on video the following significant correlations were obtained (note that the Effect size test indicates that these correlations represent only a minimal effect, due to the low value of r):

Unsympathetic/Sympathetic	($r = 0.1152$; $p < 0.008$; $N = 534$);
Attractive/Unattractive	($r = 0.1002$; $p < 0.02$; $N = 534$);
Immoral/Moral	($r = 0.1041$; $p < 0.02$; $N = 534$);

Table 18.2. Pearson R-Correlations between the Acceptance of the Statement "The American Way is the Right Way" and Perceptions of Americans

Perceptions	r	p <	Effect
Friendly/Unfriendly	0.325	0.000	medium
Trustworthy/Untrustworthy	0.302	0.000	medium
Acceptable/Not	0.326	0.000	medium
Wise/Unwise	0.351	0.000	medium
Hardworking/Lazy	0.346	0.000	medium
Honest/Dishonest	0.311	0.000	medium
Moral/Immoral	0.338	0.000	medium

It can be deduced that respondents who watched films on video frequently were more inclined to evaluate Americans positively than the medium or lighter viewers in this regard.

Preferences for media content and perceptions of American people

Further analysis of the data was done to determine relations between media preferences and perceptions of Americans. Respondents were asked how much they preferred to read magazine articles on American people or watch television programs/film with an American content.

Television. The correlations found between preferences for American content on television and perceptions of American people were lower than 0.3 in all instances but one. According to the Effect size test, this comprises a minimal effect and is thus of a low practical significance. The exception was the semantic differential scale Attractive/Unattractive ($r = 0.3040$; $N = 538$; $p < 0.000$). An r-value of between 0.3 and 0.5 represents a medium effect. This means that the preference for American content on television had a medium effect (positive correlation) on viewers' perception of the attractiveness of Americans.

A minimal effect worth mentioning was found in two other instances as well: Acceptable/Not acceptable ($r = 0.2292$; $N = 538$; $p < 0.000$) and Unsociable/Sociable ($r = 0.2649$; $N = 538$; $p < 0.000$). Thus, preferences for American content had a minimal effect on viewers' perceptions of the sociability and acceptability of American people.

An interesting negative relationship was found between the opinion of the respondents regarding the number of American programs on South African television and their perception of the attractiveness ($r = -0.2194$; $N =$

541; $p < 0.000$) and acceptability ($r = -0.2015$; $N = 541$; $p < 0.000$) of American people. Although the Effect size test indicated that this was only a minimal effect, it means that the more attractive/acceptable Americans were experienced to be, the more the respondents felt that there were not enough American programs on South African television.

Film. With regard to preferences for American film the Effect size test indicated the same correlations as were the case with television programs discussed above. A medium effect (r between 0.3 and 0.5) was found between Attractive/Unattractive ($r = 0.3405$; $N = 536$; $p < 0.000$) and Acceptable/Not acceptable ($r = 0.3163$; $N = 536$; $p < 0.000$) on the one hand, and respondents' preferences for American films. A minimal effect was also found between these preferences and the sociability ascribed to Americans ($r = 0.2736$; $N = 536$; $p < 0.000$).

Magazines. No practically significant correlations were found. The highest correlation was found between preferences for American content in magazines and the attractiveness ($r = 0.2298$; $N = 541$; $p < 0.000$) ascribed to American people. Thus, the preferences for American content had a minimal effect on the perceptions of the attractiveness of Americans.

Perceptions of the U.S. as a country

The means of these thirteen scales clustered mostly around the middle of each scale. There were, however, a few exceptions:

> Undeveloped(1)/Modern(7):   Mean = 6.3 ($N = 554$)
> (In this case, 48.6 percent [$N = 281$] chose value 7 [most positive side] of the scale.)
> Capitalistic(7)/Socialistic(1):   Mean = 5.4 ($N = 554$)
> Progressive(7)/Backward(1):   Mean = 5.6 ($N = 554$)
> Undemocratic(1)/Democratic(7):   Mean = 5.3 ($N = 554$)

Although the mean of the Criminal(1)/Criminal-free(7) scale was close to the middle value (3.2), 59.2 percent of the respondents ($N = 342$) chose the first three values (that is, the more negative side) of the scale. The same tendency was found for the Polluted(1)/Unpolluted(7) scale (Mean = 3.4): 51.5 percent ($N = 296$) chose options 1, 2, 3, that is, the more negative ones.

The responses to three other scales were more positive than negative—although the mean of each was 4.8, which is close to the midpoint of 4. For each of these scales, 59.6 percent ($N = 343$) chose options 5, 6, or 7: A healthy economy/An unhealthy economy; Closed/Open; A strong government/A weak government.

It seemed as though respondents' perceptions of the acceptability of the U.S. as a country were influenced by how much they wanted to live in America ($r = 0.3965$; $N = 556$; $p < 0.000$) as well as their opinion on the statement, "The American way is the right way" ($r = 0.3286$; $N = 557$; $p < 0.000$). Practically significant correlations (although a medium effect according to the Effect size test in both instances) were found between these variables. Accordingly, it can be deduced that respondents who wanted to live in America and agreed with the above-mentioned statement, also viewed the U.S. as an acceptable country.

No practically significant correlations were found between the respondents' perceptions of the U.S. as a country and their attitudes toward the number of American programs on South African television or their views on the extent to which South Africans follow the American way of thinking. Likewise, the respondents' opinion of the extent to which South Africans strive to be like Americans also did not seem to influence their perceptions of the U.S. as a country.

Media usage and perceptions of the U.S.

Contrary to what was expected, no high correlations between media usage and perceptions of the U.S. were obtained for television viewers, film viewers, or magazine readers. In every instance the value of r was less than 0.20, which indicated only a slight correlation and an almost negligible relationship (or small effect) (Williams 1986). The highest correlations obtained for each medium will be mentioned briefly.

The following correlations were calculated between frequency of television viewing (weekdays) and perceptions of the U.S.:

Poor judicial system/ An excellent judicial system	($r = 0.1343$ $p < 0.002$; $N = 554$);
Polluted/Unpolluted	($r = 0,1103$; $p < 0.009$; $N = 554$);
Acceptable/Unacceptable	($r = 0.1168$; $p < 0.006$; $N = 554$);
Strong government/ Weak government	($r = 0.1084$; $p < 0.01$; $N = 554$).

According to these correlations, the frequency of television watching on weekdays had a slight positive effect on the perceptions of the respondents on the U.S. with regard to the abovementioned scales. The same could apply to frequency of television watching during weekends, which slightly influenced the acceptability of the U.S. ($r = 0.1264$; $p < 0.003$; $N = 557$).

With regard to films watched on television, the highest correlation was calculated for Healthy economy/Unhealthy economy ($r = 0.1196$; $p < 0.005$; $N = 555$). This means that the respondents who watched more films on television were slightly more inclined to evaluate the American economy positively than respondents who watched films on television less frequently.

The following two scales produced statistically significant correlations when correlated with frequency of films watched on video:

Strong government/	($r = 0.1150$; $p < 0.007$; $N = 545$);
Weak government	
Acceptable/Unacceptable	($r = 0.1189$; $p < 0.005$; $N = 545$).

According to the Effect size test these correlations indicate only a slight effect, thus respondents who watch films on video more frequently were slightly more inclined to evaluate the acceptability of the U.S. and the strength of their government more positively.

No statistically or practically significant correlations could be found between frequency of films watched in theatres and frequency of magazine reading.

Preferences for media content and perceptions of the U.S.

No practically significant correlations were found between the respondents' preferences for American television programs on South African television and their perceptions of the U.S. as a country. However, a minimal effect was found between the acceptability of the U.S. and preferences for American content on television ($r = 0.2071$; $N = 551$; $p < 0.000$). This means that the respondents' preferences for American content on South African television had only a minimal effect on their perceptions of the acceptability of the U.S.

With regard to preferences for American film, practically significant correlations were also not found, with the exception of a minimal effect on perceptions of the healthy/unhealthy American economy ($r = 0.2279$; $N = 550$; $p < 0.000$).

The same trend appeared with regard to preferences for American content in magazines. Only a minimal effect could be found on the perceptions of the U.S. as backward/progressive ($r = 0.1957$; $N = 551$; $p < 0.000$).

Attitudes toward Americans and the U.S.

Most respondents indicated that they strongly disagreed with the statement that "The American way is the right way"; on a 5-point scale 39.0 percent ($N = 582$) of the respondents chose option 1.

In replying to the question whether South Africans strove to be like Americans, 13.9 percent chose option 1, indicating that South Africans never strove to be like Americans, while most of the respondents chose option 2, still indicating that they didn't think South Africans wanted to be like Americans. Much the same trend emerged on the question whether South Africans followed the American way of thinking; most respondents (38.5 percent, $N = 582$) chose option 2, indicating that they didn't think the American way was the right way.

Most respondents (44.0 percent, $N = 578$) were indecisive on the question whether there were too many American programs on South African television and chose option 3.

To summarize, it seems as if South Africans, contrary to popular belief, don't idealize Americans. This was substantiated by the data showing that on a 5-point scale the most respondents (31.3 percent) indicated that they never wanted to live in America, while only 13.3 percent ($N = 581$) wanted to live there. Most of the respondents (73.8 percent, $N = 583$) didn't have any American friends, while 64.7 percent ($N = 583$) of the respondents had met Americans.

In contrast to the abovementioned, it seems as if Americans are seen as world leaders on certain aspects. The exception was the case of Americans being world leaders regarding personal freedom. On a 1-point scale most respondents (34.4 percent) chose option 2, followed by 26.9 percent ($N = 581$) of the respondents choosing option 2. Thus, more than half of the respondents indicated that they didn't think Americans were leaders regarding personal freedom.

Most respondents (30.3 percent) were indecisive on the question of whether Americans were leaders regarding a healthy family life and chose option 3, but this was closely followed by 28.6 percent ($N = 577$) of the respondents choosing option 2 and therefore indicating that they thought Americans were leaders regarding family life.

In the case of pop music (47.0 percent, $N = 577$) and junk food (64.2 percent, $N = 578$), America was clearly identified as a world leader.

It seems that South Africans see Americans as achievers. On a 5-point scale most respondents (45.6 percent) chose option 5, indicating that they thought that achievement was important to Americans, while 36.6 percent ($N = 577$) of the respondents chose option 4.

Media usage and attitudes

The highest correlations obtained for each medium will be mentioned briefly.

Television (weekdays). Statistically significant correlations were found in two instances. However, according to the Effect size test these correlations indicate only a small effect ($r < 0.3$). It seems as if frequency of television watching had a slight effect on viewers' evaluation of the statement: "The American way is the right way" ($r = 0.1240$; $N = 536$; $p < 0.004$). Heavy television viewers were thus more inclined to agree with the statement. Accordingly, a small effect was detected between frequency of television watching and the degree to which the respondents believed that South Africans strove to be like Americans ($r = 0.980$; $N = 536$; $p < 0.023$). No practically significant correlations were found between attitudes and frequency of television watching during weekends.

Film theatres. The only correlations worth mentioning were those between the film audience and their willingness or desire to live in America. Statistically significant correlations were found for films watched in theatres and on television, as well as films watched on video. However, these correlations showed only a small effect, according to the Effect size test ($r < 0.3$). Therefore, it can be deduced that frequency of films watched in theatres ($r = 0.1349$; $N = 536$; $p < 0.002$), films watched on television ($r = 0.1362$; $N = 536$; $p < 0.002$), and films watched on video ($r = 0.1425$; $N = 536$; $p < 0.001$) had only a slight effect on respondents' desire to live in America. However, the respondents that were in the heavy film viewer category tended to have a greater desire to live in America than the medium or lighter film viewers. As mentioned before, the respondents who wanted to live in America only comprised 13.3 percent.

No statistically or practically significant correlations were found between *frequency of magazine* reading and attitudes toward Americans and the U.S. It seems, therefore, that the number of magazines read by the respondents had no effect on their attitudes in this regard.

Preferences for media content and attitudes of the U.S.

A statistically significant correlation (practical significance = medium effect) was found between respondents' preference for American content on television and their attitudes toward the number of American programs on South African television ($r = -3083$; $N = 536$; $p < 0.000$). This means that the more respondents preferred American content on television, the more they felt that there were too few American programs on South African television.

With regard to the extent to which South Africans strove to be like Americans, a small relationship (slight effect according to the Effect size test) was found with preferences for American content on South African television ($r = 0.2448$; $N = 536$; $p < 0.000$). It can thus be deduced that respondents who preferred American content on television were somewhat more inclined to think that South Africans strove to be like Americans than those who did not prefer American content on television. It also seemed as if the respondents who preferred American content on television felt more positive about living in America than respondents with different program preferences ($r = 0.2431$; $N = 536$; $p < 0.000$). Note however, that according to the Effect size test, this relationship was also very small ($r < 0.3$).

Respondents who preferred American content in magazines also indicated that they were more positively inclined toward living in America than the rest of the respondents ($r = 0.2379$; $N = 536$; $p < 0.000$). However, the effect of their preferences for a certain type of magazine content on their desire to live in America was very small according to the Effect size test.

As was the case with the other media, preferences for film with an American background showed a slight relationship (small effect) with the extent to which respondents wanted to live in America ($r = 0.2847$; $N = 536$; $p < 0.000$) as well as the extent to which they believed that South Africans strove to be like Americans ($r = 0.2822$; $N = 536$; $p < 0.000$).

Discussion

The main finding of the study was that, contrary to popular belief, there wasn't a clear correlation between media usage and attitudes and perceptions toward America and its people. It is important to note that it would be impossible to deduce a direct relationship between media usage and media preferences on the one hand, and perceptions and attitudes on the other. Perceptions and attitudes are also influenced by several other factors. All the results and interpretations in this study must be seen against the background of the following characteristics of the sample

- Most respondents in this study were not heavy users of the mass media. With regard to television, the majority were medium viewers, during both weekdays and weekends. Most magazine readers and film viewers were also light users of these media. This could be the reason why most of the practically significant correlations were found between television viewing and perceptions and attitudes. Only in the case of films did the respondents indicate that they preferred American content. The implication of this is that the respondents weren't necessarily exposed to a large amount of media content referring to America and its people.
- Most of the respondents indicated that they didn't want to live in America and that they didn't think South Africans strove to be like Americans. They also strongly disagreed with the statement, "The American way is the right way," and didn't follow the American way of thinking. In this regard, it was found that respondents who did not want to live in America perceived Americans as less acceptable than respondents who wanted to live in America.

- In most instances the respondents had moderate views on America and American people. Some of the exceptions on the negative side were their views regarding Americans as being materialistic and fairly aggressive. The U.S. as a country was seen as fairly polluted and with a high crime rate. In general, respondents who agreed with the statement, "The American way is the right way," had more positive perceptions of Americans than the respondents who disagreed with the statement. Some of the positive exceptions included respondents who regarded Americans as sociable and ambitious and their country as progressive.
- It seemed as if respondents who preferred American content on films and television viewed Americans and their country as more attractive and acceptable than the other respondents. Accordingly, respondents who viewed Americans as unattractive and unacceptable also preferred less American content. Respondents who preferred American films had a more positive view of the American economy.

According to the cultivation theory, it was expected that the media usage patterns and the perceptions and attitudes of the respondents would correlate. However, this was not found in this study. This may be due to the characteristics of the respondents, as mentioned above, especially because of the lack of high media users in the sample.

Conclusion

Although the sample in this study is not representative of the population, it seems that South Africans are not heavily influenced by the U.S. and its people. One reason may be the heightened awareness since the mid-eighties among the eleven major population groups in the country of the importance of their different languages and cultural heritage (Prinsloo and Malan 1987). Since the dramatic political changes in 1990, different cultural groups have been very sensitive to any attempt to decrease television programs in their own language and view these attempts as a undermining of their culture. In the light of this, the importance of American media content might have declined. It seems as if South Africans still prefer American films.

References

Babbie, E. (1992). *The practice of social research*. Belmont: Wadsworth.

Black, E.R. (1982). *Politics and the news*. Toronto: Butterworth.

DeFleur, M.L., and S.J. Ball-Rokeach. (1989). *Theories of mass communication*. London: Longman.

Gerbner, G. (1991). Symbolic functions of violence and terror. In Y. Alexander and R.G. Picard (Eds.) *The camera's eye: news coverage of terrorist events*, pp. 3–10. Washington: Brassey's.

Gergen, K.J. (1985). The social constructionist movement in modern psychology. *American Psychologist* 40: pp. 266–275.

Littlejohn, S.W. (1992). *Theories of human communication*. 4th edition. Belmont: Wadsworth.

McLeod, M., G.M. Kosicki, and Z. Pan. (1991). On understanding and misunderstanding media effects. In J. Curren and M. Gurevitch (Eds.), *Mass media and society*. London: Edward Arnold.

Naude, A.M.E., L. Serfontein, P.J. Schutte, D. Van der Waldt, and H.J. Groenewald. (1994). Students of the PU for CHE's sources of political information and expectations of the New South Africa. *Communicare* 13: pp. 67–85.

O'Neill, J. (1991). *Plato's cave: desire, power and the specular functions of the mass media*. Norwood, N.J.: Ablex.

Peck, J. (1989). The power of media and the creation of meaning: A survey of approaches to media analysis. In B. Dervin, M.J. Voigt (Eds.), *Progress in Communication Sciences. Volume 9*. Norwood: Ablex.

Potter, W.J. (1993). Cultivation theory and research. A Conceptual critique. *Human Communication Research* 19: pp. 564–601.

Prinsloo, K.P., and C. Malan. (1987). Cultures in contact: Language and the arts in South Africa. In C.H. Marais (Ed.), *South Africa: Perspectives on the future*. Pinetown: Owen Burgess.

Shrum, L.J., and T.C. O'Guinn. (1993). Processes and effects in the construction of social reality. Construct accessibility as an explanatory variable. *Communication Research* 20: pp. 436–471.

Steyn, H.S., and J.P. Engelbrecht. (1990). *Praktiese statistiek vir die geesteswetenskappe*. Potchefstroom: Potchefstroomse Universiteit vir Christelike Hoër Onderwys.

Williams, F. (1986). *Reasoning with statistics: How to read quantitative research*. New York: Holt, Rinehart & Winston.

19

Where Are Those Tall Buildings

The Impact of U.S. Media on
Thais' Perceptions of Americans

DARADIREK EKACHAI, MARY HINCHCLIFF-PELIAS,
AND ROSECHONGPORN KOMOLSEVIN

Introduction

Prateep* left her native Bangkok and its nearly six million residents to live in midwestern America. She did this in order to begin graduate studies in communications at a U.S. university. As had happened with numerous international students before her, the midwestern American university environment and its attendant culture came as quite a shock to her.

One might ask, why is this the case? Obviously, an individual as intelligent as Prateep, who graduated from a prestigious Bangkok university and who was accepted into a competitive graduate program in the U.S., should have expected cultural differences between her native Thailand and the U.S. Certainly, language was not the problem, for her facility with English was quite good. What, then, was it that contributed to her confusion and discomfort upon arriving in the U.S? One possible explanation is that her expectations of America and Americans were not met. Indeed, she might have asked herself upon arriving in the U.S.: where are all the glamorous people?, or, where are all the swimming pools?, or, as the title of this chapter suggests, where are all the tall buildings?

---

*This is a fictitious name. The account is a composite of remarks made by individuals known by the authors.

Prateep, like many of her generation and similar social and economic circumstances in urban Bangkok and throughout Thailand, grew up on a steady diet of U.S. media exports, especially entertainment products, most specifically movies and television. Thus, popular television shows such as *Dallas, Falcon Crest, Hart to Hart, Magnum P.I.*, and *LA Law*, and theatrical releases including such movies as *Jaws, Raiders of the Lost Ark, The Breakfast Club, The Towering Inferno, Fatal Attraction*, and the numerous *Rocky, Rambo*, and *Die Hard* movies, likely engendered in Prateep and her fellow Thai citizens certain images of the U.S. and its inhabitants. Additionally, televised sporting events exported from the U.S. such as boxing, American football, and NBA basketball added to the Thais' image formation regarding Americans. This latter medium in particular (i.e., television) probably contributed most significantly to these images. Tan, Li, and Simpson (1986) tell us that American television is for many foreign viewers either the primary or only main source for information about American people and their culture.

These media images are, to some degree, as varied as American life. However, they most often seem to resonate as icons of opulence, power, fortune, indulgence, passion, violence, and excess. Perhaps these expected characteristics, based on her formed perceptions of Americans, did not match the reality Prateep encountered when she arrived at her U.S. university. Or perhaps the found reality actually exceeded her expectations. Whatever the case, it was clear that she had arrived in the U.S. with preconceived notions about Americans. Those notions, accurate or erroneous, consistent or incompatible, formed the basis of her expectations for future communication interactions with Americans. Therefore, it is both an interest and concern for the importance and potential repercussions of this impression formation that the reported study was undertaken. We believe that a fuller understanding of the relationship between Thais' U.S. media consumption and their perceptions of Americans should help us form a more complete picture of this complex relationship and direct us to continued research focused on the relationships between the people of these two nations.

Study Focus

In this chapter we examine the relationship between Thai citizens' exposure to U.S. media and the perceptions they hold of Americans. Specifically, this chapter reports the results of a study exploring how Thais perceive and characterize Americans based on their consumption of U.S. media products such as movies and television programs.

The U.S. exports more media products to more places globally than any other country (Varis 1984). Although not necessarily a staple of every individual Thai's life, it is likely that U.S. media products do constitute some significant portion of many Thais' media consumption. Television programming, the most widely received media product from the U.S., is primarily entertainment, although some educational programs are exported (Tan et al. 1986). The study reported in this chapter did not limit the questions related to media exposure to entertainment television viewing. However, entertainment television and movies are the two genres that represent the overwhelming majority of the reported U.S. media consumed by the Thai study respondents. Thus, they are assumed to be the primary sources upon which the Thai respondents based their reported perceptions of Americans.

Theoretical Base for the Study

Research focused on the media's (especially television's) influence on social learning is informed by cultivation theory (Gerbner, Gross, Morgan, and Signorielli 1986, 1994). Cultivation theory suggests that media exposure shapes and sustains one's perceptions. More specifically, it suggests that it is through an individual's exposure to television and other media that one learns about one's culture and one's society (Gerbner et al. 1986, 1994). Cultivation theory postulates that the more a person is exposed to a construction of reality (e.g., a television program's portrayal of a particular racial or ethnic group), the more that construction of social reality is believed. As the name implies, cultivation theory suggests that through repeated exposure, the media may indeed "cultivate" sets of beliefs and/or ideals in its consumers.

Cultivation analysis research does have its critics, particularly concerning methodological issues related to measurement (Potter 1994). However, the basic theoretical assumptions informing such analysis (i.e., those of cultivation theory) have guided numerous studies, spanning more than two decades. Gerbner and his associates affirm that cultivation analysis is particularly well suited to multinational and cross-cultural comparative study (Gerbner et al. 1994).

Research focused on the American image abroad has received some attention in recent years. Weimann (1984) found that Israeli high school and college students who were heavy consumers of U.S. media had an "idealized" or "rosy" image of life in the U.S. Tan, Li, and Simpson (1986) found mixed perceptions engendered by media exposure in their study of social stereotypes of Americans held by television viewers in Taiwan and Mexico. They concluded these results could be accounted for by the different programs viewed (e.g., *Dallas* vs. *Three's Company*) and the conflicting images presented therein. Tan and Suarchavarat (1988) report similar findings in their study of Thai students. They state that "the picture projected by American television is mixed and includes both positive and negative traits" (652). However, they do conclude that U.S. television is "a major source of social stereotypes held by Thai students" (654).

Pingree and Hawkins's (1981) examination of Australian students' consumption of U.S. media found another cultivation effect. They discovered that the students' exposure to U.S. television (particularly crime and adventure programs) was related to their perceptions of Australian "Violence in Society" and "Mean World" indices (Gerbner et al. 1994), but these perceptions did not hold for the U.S. The results of a study examining media exposure among Koreans indicate that heavier exposure to U.S. television correlated with greater hostility towards the U.S. among male students (Kang and Morgan 1988). All of these reported studies lend strong support for the theory of cultivated image formation based upon exposure to U.S. media for foreign consumers. The study reported in the next sections of this chapter aims to build upon and extend this knowledge base.

The Study

Research Questions

This study investigates the Thais' media exposure, particularly to U.S. media, and its apparent impact on the Thais' perception of Americans. The research questions guiding the study are: (1) What images or characteristics do the Thais associate with Americans?, (2) Do the Thais think that the portrayals of Americans in the U.S.-produced TV programs are accurate?, (3) Are levels of media exposure related to the Thais' perception of Americans' image and their perceived accuracy of Americans' depictions on T.V.? and (4) Does the media exposure predict the Thais' overall image of Americans, their perception of the accuracy of Americans on television, and the individual images of Americans, held by the Thais?

Method

Between September and November 1995, the self-administered questionnaires were distributed to Thai undergraduate students at three universities in Bangkok, of which two are public (Chulalongkorn University and Thammasat University) and one private (Bangkok University). A total of 582 questionnaires were completed, 265 from Bangkok University, 174 from Thammasat, and 143 from Chulalongkorn University. The instrument measuring the variables in the next passage was translated into Thai by the first and third authors, for whom Thai is their native language. The questionnaire was pre-tested with a group of students at Bangkok University. Minor changes of wording were made after the pretest.

Americans' Image

To measure images of Americans, we used the measure of social stereotypes adapted from Karlins, Coffman, and Walters (1969) by Tan (1982) and later used in Tan et al. (1986) and Tan and Suarchavarat (1988). The respondents were asked to rate thirty-six adjectives on a five-point scale according to whether they agreed that Americans have those characteristics. They were also asked whether the overall image of Americans they received from the U.S. media was positive or negative, and whether they thought the depictions of Americans on U.S. television programs were accurate.

Media Exposure

Media exposure was operationalized by asking the respondents three questions: how often they watch U.S. movies (both at movie theaters and on television), how many U.S. movies they see a week, and how many hours of television they watch a day. Each media exposure variable was categorized into three levels: low, medium, and high.

For the frequency of U.S. movie viewing, the respondents who seldom or never saw U.S. movies were infrequent viewers. Those who occasionally watched U.S. movies were medium viewers, and those who watched them frequently were frequent viewers. Similarly, the categories of the amount of U.S. movies seen per week are light viewers (one movie or none), medium viewers (two to three movies), and heavy viewers (four movies and more). The categories of the amount of daily television viewing are light TV watchers (three hours or less), medium TV watchers (four to five hours), and heavy TV watchers (six hours or more).

Other Measures

We also examined other variables that might have had an influence on the respondents' image of Americans. They are: how often they had contact with Americans, whether they had been to the United States, and whether they wanted to visit the United States.

Results

Of 582 respondents from the three universities, 159 were male, 423 were female, and 60 percent of them were juniors and seniors. Their average age was 20.8 years old. Most of them (97.6 percent) had a television set at home; but only one-third (32.7 percent) had access to cable channels at home. They watched television 4.7 hours a day. A large proportion of the Thai students

(61 percent) frequently watched U.S. movies, with an average of 2.5 movies per week.

Similar to Tan and Suarchavarat's study in 1988, the Thai respondents had limited contact with Americans. Sixty-three percent of the sample had infrequent or no contact with Americans. The majority of the respondents (85 percent) had never been to the United States, 62 percent expressed that they would like to visit the country.

To answer the first research question, Table 19.1 lists the characteristics of Americans perceived by the Thais. They are, in order of frequency ratings, individualistic, pleasure loving, scientifically minded, athletic, sensual, musical, impulsive, passionate, practical, efficient, and persistent. The traits that the respondents did not agree characterized Americans were naive, loyal to family, and traditional.

The overall impression of Americans held by the majority of the respondents was neutral (68 percent), while 21 percent had a positive image, and 11 percent had a negative image.

For the second research question, the respondents were asked how accurately they thought the U.S.-produced movies or TV programs portrayed Americans. The majority of the respondents (52 percent) did not feel one way or the other, while 40 percent said the portrayals were somewhat correct or correct.

The respondents reported that they were exposed to U.S. media products via, in order of frequency, movie theaters, Channel 7, Channel 3, videotapes, *Thai Rath* (newspaper), Channel 5, Channel 9, and radio. They identified that the U.S. movies they saw at movie theaters as the most influential factors in shaping their images of Americans. Other media channels were videotapes, Channel 7, cable TV (IBC), Channel 3, AM-FM radio stations, and Channel 9*. The press didn't seem to influence the Thais' views toward Americans (See Table 19.2).

Crosstabular Analyses

To answer the third research question, cross-tabular analyses were conducted to compare responses of light (or infrequent), medium, and heavy (or frequent) viewers regarding their overall perception of Americans' image and

---

*Thai public television stations are controlled by the government and operated by different groups under the auspices of the National Broadcasting Services of Thailand. Royal Thai Army operates Channel 5, and the Mass Communication Organization of Thailand operates Channel 9. Two private groups operate channels 3 and 7 under license from the government. Channel 11, an educational station, is operated by the government-owned Television of Thailand.

Table 19.1. Characteristics Attributed to Americans, Ranked by Means

Characteristics	Mean*
Individualistic	4.72
Pleasure loving	4.50
Scientifically minded	4.43
Passionate	4.39
Impulsive	4.38
Athletic	4.35
Musical	4.32
Persistent	4.26
Practical	4.26
Efficient	4.25
Sensual	4.20
Intelligent	4.17
Industrious	4.12
Ambitious	4.09
Artistic	3.95
Stubborn	3.95
Ostentatious	3.90
Straightforward	3.86
Mercenary	3.86
Aggressive	3.73
Honest	3.72
Materialistic	3.62
Sensitive	3.60
Rude	3.55
Conceited	3.54
Arrogant	3.47
Cruel	3.36
Sincere	3.31
Kind	3.31
Neat	3.14
Courteous	3.01
Quiet	2.64
Lazy	2.62
Loyal to Family	2.50
Naive	2.43
Traditional	2.42

*Mean is computed on a five-point scale where 1 = strongly disagree, 2 = disagree, 3 = neutral/no opinion, 4 = agree, 5 = strongly agree.

Table 19.2. Frequency of Media Attributed as Source of Influence of Image of Americans

Media Source	Mean*
Theaters	4.24
Videotapes	3.86
Channel 7	3.40
IBC (Cable Channel)	3.35
Channel 3	3.32
Radio	3.16
Channel 5	3.14
Channel 9	3.06
Bangkok Post	2.90
Thai Rath	2.94
The Nation	2.89
Daily News	2.56
Matichon	2.42
Kaosod	2.30
Channel 11	2.26

*Mean is computed on a six-point scale where 0 = don't know, 1 = least, 2 = little, 3 = moderate, 4 = much, 5 = very much

their perception of the accuracy of American portrayals in U.S. movies and TV programs.

Table 19.3 shows that only the frequency of U.S. movie watching had a significant association with the Thais' overall image of Americans. Frequent American movie viewers (24 percent) were more likely to hold positive image of Americans than were medium viewers (16 percent) and infrequent viewers (18 percent) ($p < .01$).

However, all media exposure variables (frequency of watching U.S. movies, number of U.S. movies seen per week, and number of hours of daily TV viewing) showed significant associations with the respondents' perception of the accuracy of American depictions in the media. Specifically, among the frequent viewers of U.S. movies, 47 percent were more likely to believe that portrayals of Americans in the movies or on television were accurate than were the medium viewers (32 percent) and infrequent viewers (24 percent) ($p < .0001$). Also, of the heavy viewers (those who saw four or more American movies a week), 56 percent tended to think that those depictions were correct, compared with 43 percent of medium viewers and 33 percent of light viewers ($p < .01$).

Furthermore, the number of hours spent watching television had an impact on the Thai respondents' perception of Americans. Among the heavy TV watchers (watching television six or more hours a day), more than half (53 percent) believed that Americans were portrayed accurately in the media, while

Table 19.3. Percent of Respondents Who Say the Image of Americans is Positive and Depictions of Americans in Media are Accurate

	IMOV %	MMOV1 %	FMOV %	LMOV %	MMOV2 %	HMOV %	LTV %	MTV %	HTV %
Positive image	18	16	24*	24	23	15	24	19	21
Accurate depictions	24	32	47**	33	43	56*	33	37	53*

*p < .01
**p < .0001
IMOV = Infrequent movie viewers
MMOV1 = Medium movie viewers
FMOV = Frequent movie viewers
LMOV = Light movie viewers (one or none/week)
MMOV2 = Medium movie viewers (2 to 3 movies/week)
HMOV = Heavy movie viewers (4 or more movies/week)
LTV = Light TV viewers (3 hours or less/day)
MTV = Medium TV viewers (4 to 5 hours/day)
HTV = Heavy TV viewers (6 hours or more/day)

only one-third of the medium and light watchers (37 percent and 33 percent respectively) thought so (p < .01).

In addition, the Thai students' wish to visit the United States and their frequency of contact with Americans were significantly associated with whether they thought Americans were correctly characterized in the U.S. media products. Forty-eight percent of those who would like to visit the United States (compared with 20 percent of those who don't care), and 54 percent of respondents who talked with Americans on a regular basis (compared to 38 percent of those who had limited contact) believed the media depictions of Americans were right (p < .0001 and .05 respectively). Moreover, one-fourth of the people with higher level of direct contact with Americans held a positive image of Americans, compared with 17 percent of those with limited or no contact.

Regressional Analysis

We used stepwise regression analysis to examine the last research question. The dependent variables put in the equation were the Thais' overall image of Americans, their perception of the U.S. media characterizations of Americans, and all thirty-six individual traits. The predictors were all three variables measuring the Thais' media exposure, frequency of contact with Americans, previous visit to the United States, and the desire to visit the country.

While the overall American image was best predicted by the frequency of U.S. movies viewing (beta = .12, p < .05), both the frequency and the number of American movies seen per week predicted whether the Thais perceived the

Table 19.4. Overall Image and Characterization of Americans and Predictors

Traits	Frequency of Seeing U.S. movies	No. of U.S. movies seen per week	No. of hours watching TV per week	Frequent contact with Americans	Want to visit U.S.	Have been to U.S.
Overall Image	.1166*			.1077*		
Accurate Image	.1436**	.1840***		-.1247**	.2711***	
Aggressive		.1091*			.1097**	.1266*
Arrogant	-.1329*	.1415**	.1302*	.1457***		.1146*
Artistic			.1132*			
Athletic						
Conceited				.1455**	.1225*	
Courteous					.1281*	
Cruel		.1311*	.1400**	-.1135*	.1672**	
Honest		-.1419**		.1099*		
Individualistic					.1933***	.1128*
Industrious		.1460**	.1596**			.1204*
Intelligent		-.1343*	.1693**			
Lazy						
Materialistic			.1526**			-.1761***
Mercenary				-.1093*	.1700**	
Musical		.1183*				
Neat	-.1165*	.2687***				
Naïve	-.1299*	.2813***			.1000*	

Table 19.4. (continued)

Traits	Frequency of Seeing U.S. movies	No. of U.S. movies seen per week	No. of hours watching TV per week	Frequent contact with Americans	Want to visit U.S.	Have been to U.S.
Passionate		.1382**				
Persistent		.1851***				
Pleasure Loving		.1327*			.1189*	
Practical			.1226*			
Quiet		.1575**				.1095*
Rude		.1401**	.1275*			.1127*
Sensitive		.1265*	.1097*	.1885***		
Sensual		.1071*				
Sincere				.1523**		
Straightforward	.1226*			.1041*		
Stubborn		-.1478**	.1134*			

Notes: Cell entries are beta weights of significant predictors from stepwise regression.
*p < .05, **p < .01, *** p < .001)

depictions of Americans in the media as accurate (beta = .14, $p < .05$, and beta = .22, $p <.001$, respectively).

All three media exposure variables were found to significantly predict twenty-one of thirty-six traits of the Thais' characterization of Americans. As Table 19.4 shows, the number of movies watched per week was the most frequent significant predictor of social stereotypes of Americans: seventeen of thirty-six traits. The number of U.S. movies watched was a positive predictor that the Thai students would see Americans as aggressive, arrogant, cruel, industrious, intelligent, musical, neat, naive, passionate, persistent, pleasure loving, quiet, rude, sensitive, and stubborn. It was, however, a negative predictor of the characterizations of Americans as honest and sensual.

The number of hours of daily TV viewing positively predicted characterizations of Americans as arrogant, artistic, cruel, materialistic, practical, rude, sensitive, and stubborn. Interestingly, frequent exposure to American-produced movies or programs had an opposite influence on the Thais' perceptions of Americans. In other words, the more often the Thais watched American movies, the less they perceived Americans as arrogant, intelligent, neat, and naive.

Other independent variables in the regression equation were also found to be significant predictors, particularly the frequency of contact (or talk) with Americans, the respondents' desire to visit the United States, and previous travel to the country.

Frequent interpersonal exposure to Americans predicted the Thais' positive image of Americans, and their disbelief that the American portrayals in the movies were correct. Moreover, frequent contact with Americans contributed to mostly positive characterizations of Americans. The Thai respondents who regularly talked with Americans perceived them as arrogant, honest, sensitive, sincere, and straightforward, but not as conceited, cruel, and mercenary.

The Thais' aspiration to visit the United States also significantly predicted their accuracy perception of the media characterizations of Americans, and their rating of Americans as aggressive, athletic, conceited, courteous, individualistic, mercenary, and pleasure loving.

The respondents' direct experience of travel to the United States also influenced their perceptions of Americans. Those who had been to the United States perceived Americans as aggressive, arrogant, individualistic, industrious, and scientifically minded. They didn't see Americans as lazy.

Conclusion and Discussion

This study set out to examine the relationship between Thais' exposure to U.S. media and the perceptions they have formed of Americans based upon the exposure. From the analysis, it is clear that U.S. media exposure had an impact on the shaping of Americans' image among our Thai sample.

Consistent with previous series of research conducted by Tan and his colleagues, our study provides evidence that U.S. media products, in the form of films and TV programs, are an influential source of image formation of Americans among the Thai sample.

Although the majority of Thai respondents in this study held a neutral image of Americans, frequent viewers of American movies were more likely to harbor a positive attitude toward Americans. They also tended to believe that the Americans' characterizations in the movies were true.

The exposure to U.S. media was related to twenty-one characteristics, both positive and negative, attributed to Americans by the Thai respondents. Other factors affecting the formation of social stereotypes of Americans were their aspiration to visit the United States, frequent interpersonal communication with Americans, and previous travel to the country. The latter two contributed to mostly positive attributes of Americans.

Given that most of the findings of this study were consistent with previous investigations, we found that the social stereotypes instrument, conceived by Karlins et al. in 1969, is still viable and useful for future international cultivation research. However, one must caution that not all thirty-six traits could be translated with complete connotations in other languages. This was also the case in this study.

In conclusion, we undertook this study to extend the understanding of the complex relationship between media cultivation and its effects on social reality among the Thais. Our study provides evidence that frequent exposure to U.S. media products as well as hours of TV viewing are related to Thais' perception of Americans.

Future research should address more directly the issue of the interpersonal dimension and direct experience, which appeared to have a positive influence on the image formation in this study.

References

Gerbner, G., L. Gross, M. Morgan, and N. Signorielli. (1986). Living with television: The dynamics of the cultivation process. In J. Bryant and D. Zillmann (Eds.), *Perspectives on media effects*, pp. 17–48. Hillsdale, N.J.: Lawrence Erlbaum Associates.

Gerbner, G., L. Gross, M. Morgan, and N. Signorielli. (1994). Growing up with television: The cultivation perspective. In J. Bryant and D. Zillmann (Eds.), *Media effects: Advances in theory and research*, pp. 17–41. Hillsdale, N.J.: Lawrence Erlbaum Associates.

Kang, J., and M. Morgan. (1988). Culture clash: U.S. television programs in Korea. *Journalism Quarterly* 65: pp. 431–438.

Karlins, M., T. Coffman, and G. Walters. (1969). On the fading of social stereotypes. *Journal of Personality and Social Psychology* 13: pp. 1–16.

Potter, W. (1994). Cultivation theory and research: A methodological critique. *Journalism Monographs* 147: pp. 1–34.

Tan, A. (1982). Television use and social stereotypes. *Journalism Quarterly* 59: pp. 119–122.

Tan, A., S. Li, and C. Simpso. (1986). American TV and social stereotypes of Americans in Taiwan and Mexico. *Journalism Quarterly* 63: pp. 810–814.

Tan, A., and K. Suarchavarat. (1988). American TV and social stereotypes of Americans in Thailand. *Journalism Quarterly* 65: pp. 648–654.

Varis, T. (1984). The international flow of television programs. *Journal of Communication* 34: pp. 143–152.

Weimann, G. (1984). Images of life in America: The impact of American TV in Israel. *International Journal of Intercultural Relations* 8: pp. 185–197.

20

Television Viewing and the Perception of the United States by Greek Teenagers

THIMIOS ZAHAROPOULOS

Introduction

The United States is the largest exporter of television programming in the world. This single fact has been examined in communication research through various scholarly approaches, including media/cultural imperialism, cultivation hypothesis, social construction of reality, and in terms of the political economy of the international television market.

The purpose of this study is to look at U.S. television abroad, specifically in Greece, in terms of its role in helping to construct an image of the country and the people of the United States in the minds of Greek teenagers. The approaches used here are social construction of reality and cultivation. As Pingree and Hawkins (1981) asserted, imported TV programs may have a stronger impact on the attitudes of foreign viewers about what the United States is like, given that most viewers overseas have no direct experience of the United States; thus, television becomes a significant source of knowledge for them. Similarly, Adoni and Mane (1984) state that television's influence will be greater when direct experience is limited.

The cultivation hypothesis suggests that television "is a medium of the socialization of most people into standardized roles and behaviors. Its function is, in a word, acculturation" (Gerbner and Gross 1976, 175). Thus, as the social learning theory also suggests, we learn from television, and viewers without direct experience with what is to be learned may be the most influenced by television.

279

Greek television has historically included a good deal of U.S. television programming since its inception in the late 1960s. Up until the late 1980s, when there were only two Greek television channels, both public, they averaged between thirty-eight and forty-eight percent in imported programming, the majority of which came from the United States (Zaharopoulos 1990). In 1984, programs from the United States accounted for around eighteen percent of all programming on the two Greek channels, most of which was in the form of movies, series/serials, and children's programs (Zaharopoulos 1985, 185). Since 1989, the introduction of private television in Greece has revolutionized the market. Initially, imports from the United States were the main source of programming for the new private stations, sometimes making up more than fifty percent of their total programming (Zaharopoulos and Paraschos 1993). Slowly, however, the major Greek stations increased their local production, and the share of U.S. and other foreign programming per major station decreased. Nevertheless, when all stations are taken into account—more than 200, instead of just six major ones—more hours of U.S. television programming are flowing into Greece now than ever before.

At the same time, Greece has had a very important relationship with the United States in two other respects: First, there has been extensive Greek emigration to the United States, starting primarily in the 1920s; and second, Greece has been a traditional ally of the United States, as well as its political and economic client, since the Truman Doctrine in 1947. As such, Greek perceptions of United States could conceivably be influenced by three major factors: Greeks in the United States; the close political/economic relationship between the two nations; and the great amount of U.S. cultural products, particularly television programs, that can be found in Greece.

Review of Related Literature

The cultivation hypothesis states that the more television people watch, the more likely they are to hold a view of reality that is close to television's depiction of reality. This is the main theme of the work of George Gerbner and his colleagues (Gerbner and Gross 1976; Gerbner et al. 1977). Their work starts with the cultural indicators project, which first looks at the content of television programming, particularly in terms of violence, and then relates it to the views of heavy versus light viewers of television about violence in society (Gerbner et al. 1978). This process examines whether heavy viewing of television content cultivates a television-inspired view of the world. And in most studies of televised violence, it does.

Nevertheless, cultivation, according to Morgan (1990), is highly culture specific. "The symbolic environment of any culture reveals social and institutional dynamics, and because it expresses social patterns it also cultivates them" (226). When this approach is used to study U.S. television overseas, cultivation predictions cannot be as certain (see Wober 1986). For example, in an Australian study of more than 1,000 students, Pingree and Hawkins (1981) unexpectedly found that watching violent U.S. television programs was more related to conceptions of reality in Australia than about the reality of violence in the United States (103). On the other hand, a study in Israel (Weimann 1984) found that high school and college students who were heavy viewers of U.S. television had more of an idealized image of life in the United States (involving wealth) than light viewers of same programs.

In a study of how Lebanese college students perceive American social reality, El-Koussa and Elasmar (1995) found evidence that American television programs do have an impact on certain elements of that reality. While heavy viewers gave a higher estimation of certain (not all) elements of social reality in contrast to light viewers, interpersonal factors also played an important role in shaping that reality.

Studying the relationship between television viewing and the perception of affluence in the United States, Fox and Philliber (1978) found that although perceptions of affluence are indeed positively related to the amount of television viewing, this relationship does not hold up in all cases. For example, when variables such as education, income, and occupational prestige are taken into account, the relationship gets very weak, or disappears. At the same time, controlling for age, gender, and race does not affect the positive relationship.

Tan, Li, and Simpson (1986) used social learning theory to examine the relationship between viewing U.S. television and social stereotypes held of Americans by residents of Taiwan and Mexico. They found that watching certain U.S. programs tended to relate to holding certain stereotypes of Americans. Most of those cultural stereotypes were negative. Similarly, Tan and Suarchavarat (1988) in a perception study in Thailand found that total viewing of U.S. television programs was the most frequent predictor of social stereotypes of Americans held by Thai students, while income was also an important predictor. In addition, the authors report that there is evidence that "frequent viewing of American television programs is related to the self-reported probability that the respondent would visit the United States" (654).

The two studies above looked at specific television programs, not simply total hours of viewing, thus responding to a criticism of cultivation hypothesis, that it traditionally does not look at specific television content, but only total television viewing. Another important issue in this type of research is how realistic the viewers perceive television programming to be (Potter 1986). Again, one would expect that foreign viewers of U.S. programs would differ from American viewers on this matter. Elliott and Slater (1980), in a study in the United States for example, found that frequent viewers of certain programs tend to see them as more realistic, and that those with direct positive experience (in this case with the police) perceived the programs as less realistic. Generally, however, Gerbner et al. (1979) believe that "heavy television viewers perceive social reality differently from light TV viewers even when other factors are held constant" (193), and this social reality is influenced by the amount of television viewing (Gerbner et al. 1980). In the 1980 study, they found that among young people, heavy TV viewers tended to perceive older people in more unfavorable and negative terms.

The research questions of this study are generally two: How do Greek teenagers perceive the United States in terms of the character of Americans, the comparative crime rates of Greece and the United States, U.S. lifestyle, and U.S. affluence? And second, how do those perceptions relate to the TV viewing habits of Greek teenagers? More specifically, what variables, socioeconomic and otherwise, account for differences in the perception of the United States in terms of the aforementioned constructs?

Method

Two Greek senior high schools, or *lycea*, were chosen for this research, one in a middle-class section of Athens, and another in a more rural area, in the town of Amalias, which has a population of about 17,000, in southwestern Greece. These schools were chosen because they represent the urban/rural dichotomy of Greece, because they represent the Greek middle class—without extreme socioeconomic characteristics—and because access to these schools was much easier, in terms of cooperating teachers and principals.

A survey questionnaire was designed first in English, using questions similar to ones used in similar studies around the world. It included Lickert-type questions, as well as some open-ended ones. This questionnaire was initially translated by the author and later polished and proofread by professional proofreaders in Greece. Following approval of the proposed research by the Greek Ministry of Education and its Pedagogical Institute, which examined the questionnaire, the instrument was administered at the two schools during the month of March 1995. One teacher at each school was trained to talk to other teachers and train them so they could administer it in their classes during the same day.

This study examines the relationship between the dependent variables listed above, and such independent variables as perceived realism of television programming, amount and type of TV programs viewed, the participants' English language skills, political identification, travel experiences, contact with people in the United States, and various other demographic characteristics.

Results

Of the 508 usable surveys, 255 came from Amalias, and 253 from Athens. Males make up 40.9 percent of the sample (208), and females make up 58.5 percent (297), while three did not respond to this question. The Greek senior high school is made up of three grades, and students were equally divided between the three: 170 from the tenth, 168 from the eleventh, and 170 from the twelfth grade. The students' ages ranged from fifteen to nineteen years old. Amazingly, 48.7 percent of the respondents reported having friends or relatives in the United States, although only 31 percent actually correspond with those friends or relatives.

Television Viewing

The students, on average, watch three hours of television each day, including weekends, although they watch more on weekends than on weekdays. A Pearson correlation reveals that those watching more television tend to watch U.S. programming more often during an average month (r [$N = 476$] = .25; p = .000).

In terms of viewing U.S. television programming, of the 403 students answering the open-ended question, "from which nation other than Greece do your favorite television programs come?," 323 or 63.6 percent named the United States. Regarding how often they watch U.S. programs, 18.5 percent of the respondents reported watching U.S. television programs on a daily basis, 45.4 percent on a weekly basis, 18.1 percent on a monthly basis, and 18.1 percent reported that they rarely or never watch U.S. shows. Overall, the respondents reported an average of a little over three hours a week watching U.S. programs. Those who watch at least some U.S. programs report that they spend an average 37.5 percent of their total viewing time watching U.S. television programs.

Generally, males watch more television overall than females (199 minutes per day vs. 176 minutes for females) (F [1, 484] = 6.11; p < .014). However, females seem to watch more hours of U.S. programming, although this relationship is not significant. A significant difference does exist between males and females in the portion of their total TV viewing time devoted to Greek programs. Males spend 60 percent of their TV time watching Greek shows, while females spend 53.7 percent of their time doing the same (F [1, 434] = 8; p < .005). As expected, males and females also differ in terms of which U.S. programs they watch. More males watch such programs as NBA basketball, *Married with Children*, and crime/adventure programs, while more females watch such shows as, *Beverley Hills 90210*, *Dr. Quinn: Medicine Woman*, *Melrose Place*, *Full House*, *Moonlighting*, and soap operas such as *The Bold and the Beautiful*, *The Young and the Restless*, *Loving*, and *Santa Barbara*.

When asked to evaluate U.S. television programs on a five-point scale, the research participants were not particularly kind to U.S. programs, even though they watch a lot of U.S. television: 40 percent said the shows were generally exciting—24 percent boring; 19 percent said the shows were generally instructive—60 percent wasteful; 28.2 percent said they were fast—25 percent slow; 28.3 percent said they were good—25.8 percent bad; 59 percent said the shows were violent—23 percent non-violent; 60.1 percent said the shows were luxurious—20.1 percent poor; and 16.6 percent said the shows were ethical—56.6 percent unethical. A great majority of the respondents (69 percent) believe U.S. shows have much sexual content. Furthermore, 55.5 percent said they love or like U.S. music videos, while 15 percent said they do not like, or actually hate such videos.

Generally, the students were divided as to whether U.S. programs accurately portray real life in the United States—38 percent felt they generally do, 32.6 percent had no opinion or did not know, and 29.4 percent said U.S. programs do not generally portray real life in the United States accurately.

U.S. Character

A plurality of Greek students surveyed (46 percent) disagree with the statement, "Americans are generally happy." Similarly, 37 percent disagree that "Americans are generally friendly," although the majority, around 45 percent had no opinion on either of the above statements. Similarly, around 40 percent of the sample disagree with the statement, "Americans generally can be trusted" (56 percent no opinion). And 30.8 percent disagree with the statement, "Americans are generally polite" (48.8 percent no opinion). Within this rather negative perception of the character of Americans, women tend to hold a less negative view than men ($F [1, 492] = 26$; $p = .0000$), (Males mean = 3.5, Females = 3.2).

In a factor analysis, the four statements above were found to be highly loaded, with an eigenvalue of 3.72, and were grouped into a hypothetical variable of U.S. character (see table 20.1).

A Pearson product-moment correlation shows a significant positive relationship exists between a positive perception of U.S. character and how often students watch U.S. television in Greece ($r [N = 486] = .19$; $p < .0001$). Furthermore, having friends or relatives in the United States is not related to how one perceives U.S. character. A stepwise regression analysis with U.S. character as a dependent variable indicates that a number of variables account for 100 percent of the variance in this variable. The strongest predictor is the perceived degree of realism of U.S. shows (beta = .768; $p < .0002$). The more re-

Table 20.1. Greek Teenagers' Characterization of Americans

	Factor Loading Table		
	Factor 1	Factor 2	Factor 3
Americans are generally happy	.56		
Americans are generally friendly	.76		
Americans are generally trustworthy	.77		
Americans are generally polite	.76		
Percent of U.S. families who			
can afford a trip to Europe each year		.78	
own a luxury car		.83	
own at least a $100,000 dwelling.		.81	
have an income of at least $36,000 per year		.74	
An average citizen has a greater chance of being			
murdered in the U.S. than Greece			.75
The crime rate in the United States is higher than that of Greece			.75

alistic the shows seem to respondents, the more positive a perception of U.S. character they have (r [$N = 478$] $= .20; p < .0001$).

Another strong predictor is the reason viewers watch (beta $= .319; p < .0003$). Those who watch because they like the particular show have a more positive perception of U.S. character (F [2, 454] $= 3.24; p < .039$). Also, the type of U.S. shows students watch is a strong predictor (beta $= -.008; p < .008$), and according to a Chi-square test, those who watch soap operas and *Melrose Place* are more likely to have a positive perception (X^2 [169, $N = 349$] $= 212; p < .012$). Other weaker predictors include: the students' family income (beta $= .39; p < .0003$); the likelihood of watching music videos on their VCR (beta $= -.209; p < .0002$); the likelihood of renting video tapes (beta $= .094; p < .0004$); nations to which they have travelled (beta $= -.099; p < .0004$); newspapers that their parents read (beta $= -.039; p < .0008$); and their city of residence (beta $= .017; p < .004$).

In addition, there is a significant correlation between a more positive view of U.S. character and reading newspapers more often (r [$N = 484$] $= -.09; p < .033$); having fewer friends (r [$N = 492$] $= .089; p < .05$); watching fewer movies on television (r [$N = 402$] $= -.89; p < .05$); and liking U.S. television programs (r [$N = 413$] $= .16; p < .001$). Finally, those who view the United States as more affluent tend to perceive the U.S. character more positively (r [$N = 402$] $= 11; p < .019$), as do those who see Greece as being more violently dangerous than others (F [2, 480] $= 7.14, p < .0009$).

American Affluence

Questions regarding the perception of the affluence of the United States and Greece involved asking the participants open-ended questions for which they had to give percentages of American and Greek families (as in Fox and Philliber 1978 and Weimann 1984) who do the following: Take a yearly trip to Europe—on the average, they said 51 percent of Americans and 27 percent of the Greeks could; own a luxury car—on the average they said 54 percent and 30 percent, respectively; own a $100,000 home—48.8 percent of Americans and 24 percent of the Greeks do; have an income of at least $36,000 per year—48 percent and 22 percent, respectively. These four items were found to be highly loaded in a factor analysis (eigenvalue = 4.1, see Table 20.1) and were combined into the variable American Affluence. A similar hypothetical variable was constructed about Greek Affluence (eigenvalue = 1.6). Statistical information available about the above topics indicates that the students over-estimated U.S. wealth in terms of taking a yearly trip to Europe and owner-ship of a luxury automobile, but were right on the mark in their estimates of U.S. family income and the value of their homes.

A stepwise regression analysis pointed to five variables, which account for 99 percent of the variance in this variable. They are: perception of the quality of U.S. shows (Good/Bad on a five-point scale) (beta = .50; $p < .0000$); income (beta = $-.558$; $p < .0000$); frequency of reading a newspaper (beta = .451; $p < .0001$); frequency of watching movies on television (beta = .182; $p < .0023$); and frequency of listening to radio (beta = .46; $p < .0056$).

Furthermore, it was found that those devoting a larger percentage of their TV time to viewing U.S. shows are more likely to perceive Americans as more affluent ($r [N = 357] = .12$; $p < .018$). Also, there is a strong correlation between perceiving Greeks as more affluent and perceiving Americans as more affluent ($r [N = 403] = .21$; $p < .0001$). Males and females also seem to differ in their perception of American affluence, as females perceive Americans as more affluent ($F [1, 404] = 4.39$; $p < .04$). Similarly, those in the twelfth grade seem to perceive Americans as significantly less affluent than those in the other two grades ($F [2, 404] = 6.3$; $p < .002$).

U.S. Lifestyle

Students were asked to respond to a number of statements about how they perceive life in the United States. They were evenly divided in responding to the statement, "Americans seem to have a boring life" (32.5 percent strongly agreed or agreed, 34.5 percent had no opinion, and 33 percent disagreed or strongly disagreed; mean = 2.97). However, 55.5 percent agreed that "Americans seem to have a comfortable life" (mean = 2.6).

A stepwise multiple regression analysis shows that eight variables account for 100 percent of the variance in the degree of perception of life in the United States as boring. Those more likely to perceive life in the United States as boring are those who feel safest in a Greek city at night (beta = –.60; $p < .0004$) (F [2, 484] = 4.3; $p < .14$); those who dislike U.S. music videos (beta = –.40; $p < .0005$) (r [$N = 485$] = –.11; $p < .001$); those who spend a greater portion of their TV viewing time watching Greek shows (beta = –.14; $p < .001$) (r [$N = 434$] = –.12; $p = .012$); and those whose mother's political affiliation is more to the left (beta = –.0798; $p < .0024$) (r [$N = 393$] = .11; $p < .026$). Other predictor variables include corresponding with people in the United States (beta = –.2988; $p < .0005$); perceived pace of U.S. programs (beta = .24; $p < .0005$); source nation of imported TV shows (beta = .03; $p < .0032$); and average daily TV viewing (beta = .0119; $p < .03$).

Similarly, a number of variables account for all the variance (adj. R^2 = 1.0) in the degree of perception of life in the United States as comfortable. Those more likely to perceive life in the United States as comfortable are those who feel U.S. television shows are good (beta = –.651; $p < .0001$) (r [$N = 415$] = .10; $p < .037$) and those who perceive U.S. shows as less violent (beta = .311; $p < .0001$) (r [$N = 420$] = –.12; $p < .008$). Other predictor variables include perceived realism of Greek TV shows (beta = .3836; $p < .0001$); perceived Greek affluence (beta = –.4775; $p < .0001$); degree of perception of U.S. shows as luxurious (beta = –.20; $p < .0002$); reason for watching television (beta = –.25; $p < .0004$); frequency of watching adventure programs (beta = .062; $p < .0004$); using the VCR to record a program that was on while in school (beta = .015; $p < .0026$); and people with whom they watch television (beta = .001; $p < .012$). Finally, those who have a more positive image of Greek culture are less likely to perceive that Americans have a comfortable life (r [$N = 497$] = –.17; $p < .000$).

Generally, Greek teenagers in the study did not agree that their U.S. peers had less personal freedom than they (mean = 3.5). In fact, more than 57 percent tended to either disagree or strongly disagree, as opposed to 18.9 percent who strongly agreed or disagreed with that statement.

A stepwise multiple regression analysis reveals a number of variables that account for 99 percent of the variance in this variable. The strongest predictor is how students feel about ownership of foreign, expensive goods as adding to one's prestige. Those who are more likely to agree with the statement that U.S. teenagers have less personal freedom than Greek teens, are those who tend to feel that ownership of foreign, expensive items add to one's prestige (beta = –1.22; $p < .0000$) (r [$N = 491$] = .10; $p < .025$). Other predictor variables include the frequency of watching movies on television (beta = .70; $p < .0000$); the perception of safety at night in a Greek city (beta = –.40; $p < .0000$); the likelihood of renting videos (beta = .388; $p < .0001$); the frequency of watching TV game shows (beta = .185; $p < .0058$); and corresponding with someone (friend/relative) in the United States (beta = .0678; $p < .0232$). Another important aspect of this variable is that males, rather than females, are significantly more likely to agree with the statement that young people in the United States have less personal freedom than young people in Greece (F (1, 198) =11.46; $p < .0008$).

Comparable Crime Rates

Two questions were used to gauge the students' perception of crime in the United States as opposed to crime in Greece. More than 81 percent of them said the chances of being murdered in the United States are higher than in Greece. Similarly, 88 percent correctly stated that the crime rate in the United States is higher than Greece's crime rate.

The two questions were found to be highly loaded in a factor analysis, with an eigenvalue of 1.5 (see Table 20.1), and were combined into a hypothetical variable of comparable crime rate. The following nine variables were found to account for 100 percent of the variance in this variable: The perceived degree of violent content of U.S. programs (beta = $-.6928$; $p < .0000$), as those perceiving U.S. shows as being more violent are more likely to strongly agree that the crime rate in the United States is much higher than that of Greece (r [$N = 420$] = .15; $p < .001$); amount of radio listening (beta = $-.022$; $p < .0002$), as those who listen to radio less are more likely to strongly agree that the crime rate in the United States is much higher than that of Greece (r [$N = 496$] = .09; $p < .042$); the perception of the degree of ethical content in U.S. programs (beta = .088; $p < .0001$), as those who perceive the content to be more unethical are more likely to agree that the crime rate in the United States is much higher than that of Greece (r [$N = 415$] = $-.096$; $p < .05$); and the perception of the degree of the luxurious nature of U.S. programs (beta = .0011; $p < .0072$), as those who perceive the programs as less luxurious are also more likely to agree that the crime rate in the United States is much higher than that of Greece. Other significant predictors of this variable include: perceived realism of U.S. television programs (beta = .52; $p < .0000$); the perception of ownership of foreign items as affecting the degree of one's prestige (beta = $-.964$; $p < .0000$); the number of hours spent in out-of-school tutoring (beta = .25; $p < .0000$); the number of video tapes rented each week (beta = .10; $p < .0001$); and father's education (beta = .011; $p < .0006$).

Three other variables were found to be significantly related to the perception of comparative crime rate: City of residence, as Athenians are more likely to perceive the United States as much more crime ridden (than Greece) than residents of Amalias (F [1, 498] = 6.55; $p < .02$); gender, as males are more likely to perceive the United States as much more crime ridden than females

$(F[1, 495] = 9.49; p < .003)$; and school class, as those in tenth grade are more likely to perceive the United States as much more crime ridden (than Greece) than those in twelfth grade $(F[2, 497] = 4.4; p < .02)$.

However, more than 56 percent of the respondents did not believe that their chances of being involved in a car accident were higher in the United States than in Greece, which is also statistically correct. The variance in this variable was 100 percent accounted for by nine variables. The most significant predictors are, amount of TV news and information viewing (beta = −1.06; $p < .0002$), as the more one watched, the more likely the respondent was to disagree that the accident rate was higher in the United States $(r [N = 494] = −.08; p <.05)$; the amount of series/serials on television one watches (beta = −.3758; $p < .0002$), as the more they watched the more likely they were to disagree $(r [N = 495] = −.18; p < .0000)$; and how often one reads a newspaper (beta = .0298; $p = .0028$), as the more one reads the more likely s/he is to disagree $(r [N = 488] = .012; p < .012)$. Other significant predictors of the variable of comparative accident rate were the perception of the pace of U.S. shows (beta = .458; $p < .0002$); the perception of the quality of U.S. shows (beta = −.2375; $p < .0003$); the amount of viewing of TV magazine shows (beta = .476; $p < .0004$); the amount of time one spends reading non-school books (beta = .0298; $p < .0028$), and with whom the respondents watch television (beta = .0042; $p < .0236$). Finally, another significant relationship was found between this variable and the specific U.S. television programs someone watches $(X^2 [52, N = 350] = 136; p < .002)$. Those more likely to agree that the U.S. automobile accident rate is higher than that of Greece are more likely to watch *Full House* and NBA basketball, whereas, those on the opposite side of this issue are more likely to watch *Melrose Place, Moonlighting, Beverly Hills 90210, Married with Children*, MTV, movies, and soap operas. However, this seems to be related more to gender than specific U.S. programs.

Conclusions

The purpose of this study was to examine the relationship between television viewing and Greek teenagers' perception of the United States. The students' perception of the United States is gauged through the following dependent variables: Their perception of U.S. character, comparative crime rates, U.S. lifestyle, and U.S. affluence.

Greek high school students questioned in the study seem to have an image of the United States that in some respects is accurate, but in evaluating that image the students are either neutral or negative. For example, Greek teenagers perceive Americans to have a rather comfortable life, but are split evenly as to whether they lead a boring life. At the same time, they do not see Americans as happy, friendly, trustworthy, or polite. However, they see their peers in the United States as having at least equal, if not more, personal freedom than they have.

The study's participants see the United States as rather affluent, and although they overestimate an average family's ability to take a yearly trip to Europe, or their ability to own a luxury car, they do accurately estimate the median income of a U.S. family, as well as the value of their homes. Similarly, they accurately perceive that the crime rate in the United States is higher than that of Greece, and that the automobile accident rate is higher in Greece than in the United States.

The results of this study generally indicate that U.S. television programs do play a role in the way Greek teenagers perceive the United States. At the same time, however, other factors play a role as well, and maybe even a larger one.

Generally, Greek high school students watch almost as much television as students in the United States, but Greek males watch more television than females. The more television they watch, the more likely they are to watch more U.S. programs. Obviously this age group does not represent Greeks in general. For example, of more than 100 different Greek and foreign shows the students stated they make an effort to watch, by far the most popular is *Beverly Hills 90210*.

The findings indicate that the more U.S. television these students watch, the more favorable perception of the character of Americans they have, and those devoting a greater portion of their TV time watching U.S. shows are more likely to perceive the United States as more affluent. And although this is not, strictly speaking, a cultivation study, because programs were not content analyzed, generally the U.S. programs they watch do portray life in the United States as, if not affluent, at least very comfortable—as do shows such as *Beverly Hills 90210*, *Full House*, and various soap operas. At the same time, the students are evenly divided as to whether U.S. television programs accurately portray life in the United States. However, those who see them as realistic have a more positive perception of U.S. character.

The students' perception of U.S. programs was also found to relate to how they perceive Americans and the United States. Generally, their views of U.S. programs lean toward the negative. Those who like U.S. shows have a more positive image of U.S. character and believe Americans have a more comfortable life, and those who perceive a more affluent U.S. lifestyle have a more positive image of U.S. character. Similarly, those who believe U.S. shows are less violent tend to think that Americans have a comfortable life, and that the United States does not have the relatively high crime rate that others believe it has in comparison to Greece. On the other hand, those who believe U.S. shows have more violent and more unethical content, perceive a much greater crime rate in the United States.

Furthermore, the specific U.S. television programs students watch do seem to have at least a limited role in their perception of the United States. For example, watching certain shows like soap operas is related to a more positive perception of U.S. character, and is related to how they see the comparable auto accident rates between the two nations.

However, gender is also a variable that plays a role in the Greek students' perception of the United States, and this seems to interact with their television viewing behavior. For example, males watch more Greek programs than females, and watch different U.S. shows than females. But females have a less negative image of U.S. character, perceive the United States as being more affluent than males, perceive it as relatively less violent in comparison to Greece than males, and believe that their peers in the United States have more personal freedom, than is perceived by males.

Other demographic variables that seem to play a role in some areas include the students' city of residence and school class. For example, Athenian teenagers, more than teenagers from a more rural environment, and students in earlier grades, tend to believe that the United States has a much higher crime rate in comparison to Greece. Students in earlier school grades also believe the United States to be more affluent.

Income also seems to play a role in the teenagers' perception of the United States. Those with higher incomes tend to believe that the United States is more affluent, and those who view Greece as more affluent tend to think of the United States as more affluent as well. However, two other variables expected to have a role in many of these relationships did not appear to have much of a role at all: The number of years a student has been studying English, and whether students have friends or relatives in the United States.

In many of the relationships discussed above, there seems to be one variable that plays a key role—a variable that was not quite foreseen: degree of Greek ethnocentrism. This seems to be represented most in people who feel safest in Greece, watch more Greek shows, and who have a high positive perception of Greek values and culture. They tend to perceive the United States as less affluent, more crime ridden, and see Americans as having a less comfortable lifestyle, a more boring life, and see American teenagers as having relatively less personal freedom than they do. These teenagers, more than others, also dislike U.S. television shows, including music videos. Some of these teenagers are also characterized by their mother's leftist political leanings.

Another media consuming behavior that seems to play a limited role in the perception of the United States is the frequency of reading Greek newspapers. For example, those who read more often have a more positive image of U.S. character, and definitely see Greece as more accident ridden than the United States—as do those who watch more news and information programming on Greek television.

Total amount of television viewing (as the cultivation hypothesis indicates) does not seem to have a role in how Greek teenagers perceive Americans and the United States. However, frequency of viewing U.S. programs, viewing certain U.S. programs, and their evaluation of these programs, all play a role in their overall perception of the United States. Other variables that play a role include gender, income, perceived realism of U.S. shows, newspaper reading, school class, political affiliation of the mother, and correspondence with people in the United States.

References

Adoni, H., and S. Mane. (1984). Media and the social construction of reality: Toward an integration of theory and research. *Communication Research* 11: pp. 323–340.

El-Koussa, H.H., and M. Elasmar. (1995). *The influence of imported U.S. TV programs on the perceptions of U.S. social reality among students in Lebanon.* Paper presented at the Broadcast Education Association convention, Las Vegas.

Elliott, W.R., and D. Slater. (1980). Exposure, experience and perceived television reality for adolescents. *Journalism Quarterly* 57 (3): pp. 409–414, 431.

Fox, W.S., and W.W. Philliber. (1978). Television viewing and the perception of affluence. *The Sociological Quarterly* 19 (1): pp. 103–112.

Gerbner, G., and L. Gross. (1976). Living with television: The violence profile. *Journal of Communication* 26 (2): pp. 173–199.

Gerbner, G., L. Gross, M.F. Eleey, M. Jackson-Beeck, S. Jeffries-Fox, and N. Signorielli. (1977). TV violence profile No. 8: The highlights. *Journal of Communication* 27 (2): pp. 171–180.

Gerbner, G., L. Gross, M. Jackson-Beeck, S. Jeffries-Fox, and N. Signorielli. (1978). Cultural indicators: Violence profile No. 9. *Journal of Communication* 28 (3): pp. 176–207.

Gerbner, G., L. Gross, N. Signorielli, M. Morgan, and M. Jackson-Beeck. (1979). The demonstration of power: Violence profile No. 10. *Journal of Communication* 29 (3): pp. 177–196.

Gerbner, G., L. Gross, N. Signorielli, and M. Morgan. (1980). Aging with television: images on television drama and conceptions of social reality. *Journal of Communication* 30 (1): pp. 37–47.

Morgan, M. (1990). International cultivation analysis. In N. Signorielli and M. Morgan (Eds.), *Cultivation analysis: New directions in media effects research*, pp. 225–247. Newbury Park: Sage.

Pingree, S., and R. Hawkins. (1981, Winter). U.S. programs on Australian television: The cultivation effect. *Journal of Communication* 31 (1): pp. 97–105.

Potter, W.J. (1986, Spring). Perceived reality and the cultivation hypothesis. *Journal of Broadcasting and Electronic Media* 30 (2): pp. 159–174.

Tan, A.S., S. Li, and C. Simpson. (1986). American television and social stereotypes of Americans in Taiwan and Mexico. *Journalism Quarterly* 63 (4): pp. 809–814.

Tan, A.S., and K. Suarchavarat. (1988). American TV and social stereotypes of Americans in Thailand. *Journalism Quarterly* 65 (3): pp. 648–654.

Weimann, G. (1984). Images of life in America: The impact of American television in Israel. *International Journal of Intercultural Relations* 8: pp. 185–197.

Wober, J.M. (1978, Fall). Televised violence and paranoid perception: The view from Great Britain. *Public Opinion Quarterly* 42 (3): pp. 315–321.

Zaharopoulos, T. (1985). Foreign mass communication in Greece: Its impact on Greek culture and influence on Greek society (Doctoral dissertation, Southern Illinois University at Carbondale). *Dissertation Abstracts International* 47: p. 03-A.

Zaharopoulos, T. (1990, March). *The dimensions of Greek television.* Paper presented at the Broadcast Education Association convention, Las Vegas.

Zaharopoulos, T., and M. Paraschos. (1993). *Mass media in Greece: Power, politics, and privatization.* Westport: Praeger.

21

"America, The Beautiful"

Israeli Children's Perception of the U.S. through a Wrestling Television Series

DAFNA LEMISH

Introduction

In the winter of 1994, the media informed the Israeli public of a phenomenon that was of great concern to staff members of many elementary schools: violent behavior by children, which was associated with a wrestling television series called the *World Wrestling Federation* (WWF). Public and political concern presented us with an unusual opportunity to reconsider the relationships between television violence and violent behavior under well-defined, focused conditions. As a result, a multistage study was initiated by the Israeli Council of Cable Broadcasts to examine several facets of the phenomenon: the uses and gratifications associated with viewing WWF; the visible effects viewing had on children's behavior; and the coping strategies adopted by the educational system in Israel to confront the phenomenon. (For summary of primary findings see Lemish, forthcoming; Lemish 1996a; Lemish 1996b).

In addition, an unanticipated theme has emerged in the interpretation of the data: Children's perceptions of the United States and its culture. The study reported below is the result of an attempt to document and analyze this aspect of the larger project.

WWF: A Wrestling Television Series

The World Wrestling Federation's (WWF) programs present coverage of wrestling matches performed in a wrestling arena in front of live audiences.

WWF—the largest and most popular wrestling federation in the United States—functions under the guise of sport and has become not only a booming entertainment industry, but a unique cultural phenomenon (Maguire and Wozniak 1987, 264).

This form of wrestling is distinctly different from other televised sporting events: there are no clear rules or agreed-upon code of behavior; almost every form of violent act is allowed and possible until the most brutal defeat of the enemy. According to Fiske (1987), the WWF programs are a form of sport-parody. The rules of the game are there to be broken; the referee exists so he can be ignored.

While in other forms of sport, opponents start as equals and have an equal chance at winning the competition, the differences between WWF opponents are emphasized from the start: "good guys" and "bad guys" are identifiable to viewers through their names, costumes and appearance, the gadgets they use, their reactions to the audience, their body language and facial expressions, and the like. The "good guys" are often handsome caucasians promoted in Euro-American culture as images of the good and powerful. On the other hand, the "bad guys" are often dark skinned, physically grotesque, ridiculously dressed, and non-Euro-American in appearance. They purposely break the rules, ignore the referee, cheat on their own partners, and evoke feelings of meanness in an excited audience.

Each opponent acts on two complementary levels—as an athlete and as an actor. Their professional training teaches them not only to master technical skills, but theatrical ones as well, as part of the development of their symbolic identity (Rosenberg and Turowetz 1975). Hence, WWF is not only a physical confrontation, it is a clashing of symbolic cultural and institutional identities (Henricks 1974).

As suggested by Fiske (1987), the active audience is part of the show's excitement—yelling, waving, offering advice and help, jumping up and down.

These elements of wrestling as theater, rather than as a sporting event, are emphasized in the semiotic analysis of wrestling (Barthes 1972; Webley 1986). Here, the audience is seen to have no interest in the sporting nature of the match. Further, in the semiotic view, the audience is seen to completely submit itself to the actual experience of the event, detached from motives or consequences. What is important is not what viewers think, but what they see: extreme expressions of emotions and desires. Above all, the "struggle" represents the quest for justice, the mythological victory of "good" over "evil." It therefore allows justice to ultimately make itself understood (Barthes 1972).

WWF in Israel

WWF was broadcast in Israel on the Second Channel as well as on the cable Sport Channels during different days and hours of the week. Rating data available suggested limited viewership among elementary school children—an average of two to three percent. Yet strong public concern developed in the winter of 1994. The Chair of the Knesset's (Parliament) Education Committee made a direct request to policy makers in the television industry to stop broadcasting the series or at least to broadcast the program in the late night hours. The Second Channel stopped broadcasting the program after one season, for various reasons. However, the cable Channels continue to broadcast several times a week.

Overall, the prominence of WWF as a social phenomenon declined after one season of broadcasting. Several complementary explanations for this decline are possible: The discontinuation of broadcasting by the Second Channel; the loss of the novelty effect; the preventive measures taken by the schools; first- and second-hand experiences of injuries; growing realization that the program is a staged drama rather than a sporting event.

Children and Cultivation of World View

The literature on child development and television suggests that the medium may play the role of an alternative school for children, teaching an unplanned curriculum and serving as an important socializing agent (see for example Liebert and Sprafkin 1988; Palmer and Dorr 1980).

More specifically, the cultivation hypothesis, offered originally by Gerbner and colleagues (Gerbner et al. 1980, 1994), was suggested as an explanatory hypothesis accounting for the possible role television might be playing in the shaping of children's world view. Violence and racial and gender portrayals are three of the issues explored in relation to children's world view, arguing that heavy exposure to television is related to more stereotypical perceptions of the social world (Berry and Asamen 1993; Van Evra 1990).

According to cognitive developmental psychology, children's cognitive skills develop on the average until the age of twelve. As a result, they perceive and interpret television programs differently than adults (Bryant and Anderson 1983; Palmer and Dorr 1980). While children, like older viewers, are active negotiators of meaning, they bring with them to the particular viewing experience an accumulating world view, affected by many socializing agents (Hodge and Tripp 1986). Previous experiences with media products, either directly or through adults' mediation, may serve as contributing factors to this world view, framing further selective exposure to television as reinforcers rather than as providers of oppositional meanings. Researchers are particularly in agreement that in contrast to adults, children's limited real-life experiences and alternative sources of information in a given area make them more vulnerable to television's portrayals (Comstock 1991; Van Evra 1990).

Very little is known specifically about television's contribution to children's knowledge and perceptions of other societies. Cross-cultural cultivation studies have been done mostly with college students. In Israel, for example,

Weimann (1984) found that high school and college students' heavy television viewing was related to an idealized image of the standard of living in the United States. Recently, several studies that explored children's emotional reactions to television's coverage of the Gulf war (in Greenberg and Gantz 1993) have touched incidentally on its role in disseminating knowledge about world politics. Parents' mediating role in reducing or escalating anxiety related to television's coverage of the war is of particular interest in an attempt to understand the dynamics of the socialization processes.

The current study attempts to highlight television's potential in regards to cultivating children's perceptions of other cultures. As became apparent through children's talk, the WWF series may provide an interesting case study.

Method

The study developed through three phases—school survey, in-depth interviews, and school visits. An analysis based on 285 questionnaires filled out by school principals provided initial mapping of the phenomenon. This was followed by seventy-five in-depth phone interviews with school principals (Lemish 1996).

The third phase of the research, on which this study is based, consisted of case studies of nine elementary schools. Schools were selected according to four main variables—socioeconomic status of the school's population, urban versus rural, religious versus non-religious school, and availability versus non-availability of cable television in the school's residential area. In addition, an effort was made to include schools from different geographical areas. The main constraints affecting the choice of the schools included the willingness of the principals to cooperate and attaining permission from the regional authorities in the Ministry of Education. It should be emphasized that while the schools chosen do not constitute a random representation of Israeli elementary schools, the nine schools do offer a representative sample of common profiles of Israeli society and provide a very wide cross-section of elementary school children. Included were religious and secular schools; a wide range of populations—from children just under the poverty line up to higher class; schools from the northern border through the heavily populated center part of the country and the isolated southern Israeli desert; schools from older and newer urban areas as well as from rural kibbutz and agricultural settlements.

Each school was visited for a full school day by the researcher and an assistant. A three-page questionnaire was administered to one class at each grade level from third to sixth grade. The questionnaire included open-ended and closed questions. The questions asked for information about television viewing behaviors (program preferences, programs viewed the day before); habits of viewing WWF; the students' description of the nature of the program; likes and dislikes in relation to the program; frequency and forms of playing WWF games; frequency and forms of others observed playing WWF games; perceptions of the cultural origin of the program. Finally, children were asked to name peers who they felt were frequently involved in violent behavior.

Overall, 901 filled questionnaires were collected, coded, and statistically analyzed. Of the questionnaires, 46 percent (413) were completed by girls.

In addition, all the children in these classes were invited to participate in a personal interview with the researcher in a private room for the purpose of discussing the issues in the questionnaire. These interviews were conducted with individuals, pairs, and occasionally groups of three students, according to the children's choice. Interviews were an average of ten minutes in length and were recorded. The main purpose of the interviews was to listen to the children discuss their own concerns, in their own language, and with examples they chose to bring. A second area of interest was to enable the interviewees to react to, explore, and challenge notions suggested by the adults.

There was a very high interest among the children in participating in the interviews for various reasons, not all of which directly related to the issue at hand (such as an opportunity to miss a lesson, curiosity, a false assumption that the interviewer was a television personality, and the like). Many children used the opportunity to share their feelings and ideas about the role television has in their lives and to express wishes and desires. Others unloaded their social distress in relation to violence in their school and expressed a hope that the researcher would change the situation.

Overall, 254 interviews were conducted and recorded. Forty-four percent of the interviews (114) were with girls. The content analysis was completed through qualitative techniques.

Findings: Children's Perception of the U.S.

Viewing Frequency

Analysis of children's questionnaires suggested that viewing frequency of WWF was significant: 92 percent of all children during both the current year and the previous year admitted to having watched the program or at least to being familiar with its nature. Less than a quarter claimed they did not watch, but were familiar with the program. In contrast, 40 percent of the children in the current year and more than 50 percent in the previous year watched it every week or occasionally.

Popularity of the program was significantly higher among boys, urban children, lower socioeconomic status children, and among children rated as violent by their peers. No age-related differences were recorded (for more details see Lemish 1996).

Identifying WWF as an American Program

More than 80 percent of the answers to an open-ended question in the 901 questionnaires identified the origin of the WWF series in the United States. This general agreement was reconfirmed in the personal interviews. However, conversations with the children suggested that for many of them there was a confusion between the United States and other English-speaking countries—mainly England—and with other famous locations in the world. For example, one sixth grade girl explained that: "The program is from the United States, because that's where all the states are—that is many countries—such as New York, Disneyland, Paris, France. Most of the audience comes from there . . . you can tell that they are yelling the names in English." A fifth grade boy suggested: " England is a very developed country where they make all kinds of programs. They've got there Hollywood, EuroDisney, and all kind of places where they make movies. . . . United States is bigger, but England is inside the United States."

The children's answers were varied when asked for reasons for identifying the series as American. One explanation was that English is the language spoken in the program, and audience members shout "USA!" and frequently mention names of places, such as Chicago, New Jersey, Florida, and the like.

A second type of response suggested that "they looked American." Prompting questions revealed that "looked American" meant white and mostly blonde. A prototype perpetuating this image was the most admired character "Lex Luger"—an "all-American" masculine blonde caucasian, who dresses in short red, blue, and white pants and wraps himself in the American flag. Opponents who were clearly non-caucasians were identified as foreigners who came from other countries, a group that included Asian, African-American, and Native American wrestlers. America, according to many of the children, is an all white-country.

A related third type of argument strengthening children's perception that WWF is an American production was the use of auxiliary gadgets, such as flags, bandannas, decorations. These were clearly interpreted by the children as "American."

Finally, several children recalled reading in TV magazines or other sources of information that WWF was an American organization.

Describing WWF as an American Cultural Product

Children who identified WWF as being an American series were asked to respond to a series of open-ended questions in the personal interviews that enabled them to explain why they thought WWF was produced and popular in the United States. Many elaborate explanations were provided by the interviewees, which suggest insights into their mythical view of this culture. The following were among the most common themes they mentioned:

United States is "The" United States—the richest, the biggest, the most developed country known to mankind. Examples of this "awe" and admiration for the U.S.:

A fifth grade boy explained: "Many stars come from there. America is "The"—it's the most developed . . . it is very big and all the big things are in Hollywood." Similarly, a sixth grade boy suggested: " Because it is the country were everything develops from, it is the most developed country in the world, the biggest continent and it develops lots of things." A fourth grade girl said: " Because the United States is always like that, it seems to me that it is such a country that has everything. Hollywood and all." And a sixth grade boy explained: "Because they are much better then Israel in industry . . . a more developed country, more people, kind of professors. It's a kind of a different country . . . they do everything big—not a small amusement park, but Disneyland."

Having "more people" was repeated by many children. A third grade girl explained: "In America there are lots of people and fifty-two States, and probably they have quite a lot of people in the audience to admire things like this." And another third grade girl described the specific situation in sporting events: " In sports matches there are always Americans, and they are the most. And most of the people come especially to America because everybody is familiar with it."

A related theme to "development" and "bigness" was money. A third grade boy said: "They've got winners, and they also have more money than in this country, and they are the richest in the world." A third grade boy incorporated "imported" terms to express this power, but at the same time to suggest a shred of criticism: "Because the United States got lots of Rating. They were looking for ratings that will make children enthusiastic and attract the money from the parents."

The United States, it seemed from children's talk, is clearly the leading country of the world. It was described with a great deal of enthusiasm, admiration, and self-confidence.

United States is the strongest yet most violent and dangerous country.
While the first theme was presented mostly in positive terms, this one was

clearly framed negatively. The sweeping statements on the violent nature of American society were striking because of their extremism.

A fourth grade boy explained: "That's where they have the most out of control people. They have more crimes, more chances for disturbed people. They have more people and also more criminals." A fifth grade girl said: "When you walk in the streets in the United States you don't know what will happen, anyone can attack you." And her female classmate argued: "they are probably the stupidest. People that don't understand themselves. Write down—hell, because I hate it." A third grade girl explained: "There are many movies about the United States with hitting. In America everyone is strong . . . I can tell by the way they hit each other. The name of America is strong." And a fourth grade boy got a bit carried away as he enthusiastically related: "Because they fight freely there, they are free and have lots of disorder. They think it is fun. They don't think very well. They don't have brains. They hit each other freely . . . all the children there go crazy."

Such prejudiced opinions were expressed by many children. A fifth grade girl was trying to provide a logical explanation for this violence: "Most of the fashions start in the United States, in New York. Because this is a State where the citizens encourage more of this kind of things. There are nations that are kind of more intelligent. But there [New York] it is wilder, because that's where all the fashions start, and the citizens encourage it, and it attracts all of the citizens . . . people in that region are more attracted by violence than by peacefulness." Similarly, a sixth grade boy argued: "Because the Americans are more out of control, in my opinion. They are the only ones that will make a show like this. You can tell also by what you see in the movies. You don't have Israeli movies where a guy just takes everybody's heads off and such. In the United States they've got lots of movies like that, because that's the kind of head they have—more disturbed." And a fifth grade boy explained: "There are all kinds of systems to different countries. . . . In America the system is cutting off heads. You can tell from the movies that you see, for example, Van Damme."

Americans, therefore, are perceived as violent, out of control people, who have adopted norms of behavior unaccepted elsewhere. Various movies and other television programs were quoted as sources of information and as "proof" for the truthfulness of these arguments. This perception, however, was treated with mixed feelings by the children. Gender differences were particularly prominent: While girls were more critical of violence in general and in WWF in particular, many of the boys related to the unusual levels of violence associated with the United States with a great deal of curiosity and enthusiasm, a mixture of contempt and awe. (For further discussion of gender differences see Lemish 1996).

United States is the most creative country, where the "American Dream" is alive and well. A fifth grade boy explained: "America is the most developed country of all other countries, in Israel I don't think anyone will invent something like that. It can't take place in Egypt for example, because they don't have such developed cultures."

A fifth grade boy with business aspirations provided his version of market research: "America is the country where a new thing enters. . . . Let's say I wake up in the morning with a new product or a new television program and I have the power to make it, it will catch on very quickly if I have commercials." Another fifth grade boy said: "You have to start in the right place. If you want to be a cheese chef—go to Holland. You go to the country of the source . . . to check the content of the thing and to penetrate in a different place it won't work." And his friend continued the sentence: "And America is the place for movies and programs." Relating to a news item about an American pilot who was rescued in former Yugoslavia, a third grade girl concluded: "They also invent all the solutions to the problems."

Inventing new things was a dominant theme in discussing different types of sports, as a third grade boy explained: "In Israel they hardly have an interest in that athletics (WWF), because they have there things, sports, that we don't do here, sports that develop such as long jump, diving, Judo . . . because here it is a real small country and it takes time to develop a new sport, and there [U.S.], they invent, like the skateboard, they have a tournament, and in Israel we don't, jumping up in the air on a board."

The United States, according to these children, is the best place for new ideas and new inventions—it is innovative and creative and gives a sense of dynamics and constant progress.

United States has the best infrastructure for WWF. Many children argued that WWF was developed in the United States since that country has the biggest wrestling halls, most elaborate arenas, largest studios, best players, and the like. Such examples were the following quotes. A third grade girl: "Here in Israel there is no place for it. No arena and nothing. No studio. There they have all the American viewers who come to watch." And a third grade boy: "In Israel there isn't such a big hall that so many people can come in. America is much bigger."

The United States, then, developed WWF as a result of practical reasons—it has the appropriate facilities to accommodate both the fights and the large audiences interested in them.

Framing WWF as "Their" Cultural Phenomenon Rather than "Ours"

Discussion of the American nature of WWF was often contrasted or balanced against the children's own culture—Israel. Israel, in comparison to the United States, was perceived as not being as rich, big, developed, creative, etc.

In addition, children brought up several enlightening ethical explanations for the improbability of a program such as WWF developing in their homeland. Such, for example, was the explanation provided by a fifth grade boy: "This [WWF] is kind of boasting, and here we have religious people. . . . I don't think they will agree." A third grade boy explained as well: "In Israel we don't do things like this . . . because afterwards everyone . . . will not like it. Israelis don't do things like this. The Prime Minister did not agree to it." Bringing into the conversation authoritative figures to strengthen the argument was repeated many times. A fourth grade girl, for example, said: "In Israel it is un-educational, we study Bible, and we are not related to such things. Take for example in (name of her town), XX (name of the Mayor) will not want such a thing here. No one will allow it here. "And her female classmate added: "Because here no one will agree, the Prime Minister and the President will not agree to things like this that only bring violence to the world and to our country and it is not good."

Many children incorporated themes related to the Israeli-Arab conflict and to stereotypical perceptions of the Arab as The Enemy in their perceptions of the program as violent and inappropriate for their country. A third grade boy, for example, said: "In Israel there aren't such violent people that do such things except for the Arabs." A sixth grade girl, however, suggested that the program could not have been produced in Israel because Israel "is on the verge of peace treaties and it will do everything for peace and it doesn't want wars." She continued to talk at length about peace agreements, evacuation of the Occupied Territories, and the perception that a violent program such as WWF would not fit in the process of peace. A third grade boy gave this line of argumentation another twist: "We already have enough fighting between Arabs and Israelis, so we don't need WWF. In the United States they need it, because they don't have enough."

Incorporating WWF in Other Sources of Information about the U.S.

As was quoted earlier, children often supported their claims in relation to WWF with other sources of information. Many used other cultural products as proof for their arguments and as an answer to the question: "How do you know?" A third grade girl explained: "There are many movies about America of fighting. Everyone there is strong." And another third grade girl specified: "America, they are strong. I see in programs. Especially in action movies." A fifth grade boy related: "like many American movies that I like that have pistols and guns and fighting." Names such as Sylvester Stallone ("who is a boxing champion and he has already killed several people and won them in matches"—third grade boy); Arnold Schwarzenegger, Jean-Claude Van

Damme, Chuck Norris, and the like were cited often as familiar examples demonstrating violence in American culture.

While such confusion between the symbolic reality portrayed in television programs and movies and the reality of life in the United States was very typical in the interviews, several children made references as well to the world of news and current events. For example, a sixth grade boy argued: "There is more violence in America than in Israel or other countries. You can see it on television in the news and everywhere."

A supporting source of information was second-hand personal experience, such as "my mother told me," "I have a cousin who visited there," and the like. What was striking about these examples was that they were not used to balance or contradict media experiences, but on the contrary, were incorporated in them. Such, for example, was the description given by a fifth grade boy: "because in America there are many children in gangs, they have pocketknives, pistols, guns—maybe you haven't heard—they catch a child in this gang, and they kill him, and they don't leave him alive. That's why children go to gangs, children are afraid to walk there. That's why I don't go to America. I am very scared for my cousin who lives in America. He walks several steps—and each time he sees a gang—he takes his pocketknife out." Similarly, a fourth grade boy shared: "My mother was there. All the children there go crazy. She had a television set in the hotel, and she saw that children are involved in extreme violence just for fun." And a sixth grade boy: "All the people there are fighting in the streets. How do I know? I hear people talking about it, rumors. I have an uncle in America."

Second-hand experiences with life in the United States seem to be a weaker form of persuasion in comparison to the accumulated perception created by media messages. Rather than moderate the belief in the extremely violent nature of the entire American culture, they are incorporated in the existing belief system as additional supporters. This mutual reinforcement between everyday experience and television was named, by Gerbner et al., "resonance" which amplifies the cultivation effect.

Conclusion

Clearly, WWF was identified as representing a foreign ideology and culture, different from the children's own. This culture is characterized by an extreme form of "more-ness": "More" in the positive sense—richer, bigger, more developed, more creative, more varied. But also "more" as fear and as criticism—more violent, wilder, more dangerous. For many of the children, it was clear that the program conveyed values foreign to their culture and unacceptable to authority figures, such as the Mayor, the Prime Minister, or the President.

These readings of WWF possibly suggest partial resistance to the notion of "Americanization" of Israeli culture: Children enjoy the programs, but they categorize them as "foreign."

On the other hand, results from the larger project, of which this is a part, suggest that despite this critical perspective, many Israeli children are eager to adopt wrestling styles observed on television (Lemish 1996a). In this sense, television may be playing an active role in the cultural reproduction of violent norms of behavior. This may be particularly encouraged in a society torn over security issues, such as Israel, where use of force under certain circumstances is appreciated and glorified.

One interpretation of these findings is that WWF did not create these images, but was incorporated in an existing world view based at least in a significant part—if not mostly—on previous encounters with popular media that present the United States as a violent and rich society in a homogenized stereotypical way, over and over again. In that exciting all-powerful and violent culture called America, WWF was perceived as a natural phenomenon that fits well with existing cultural stereotypes, which at the same time provides further "proof" for its realness. This circular logic seems to support and continue to perpetuate a mythical belief system in the "Mean World" notion of the cultivation effect, with the "world" being reduced to the United States. Even personal experiences are selectively filtered to fit in this social picture (probably not only by the children but also by the adults relating them as well). Furthermore, television may be contributing to the "no change" effect, in resisting possible oppositional readings of the nature of American society, even those based on limited personal or second-hand experiences. In this sense, the question of causality—which came first, television cultivation effect or perceptions of American society?—becomes irrelevant, since children are raised from birth in a symbolic environment which already includes television.

The uniqueness of children's cognitive processes, their lack of personal experience with American society, and their underdeveloped critical media skills make them particularly vulnerable. Once again, so it seems, the media can be most influential where there is the least amount of knowledge and critical skills. This claim in particular is one of the major arguments used for introducing media literacy curricula into the Israeli school system (Lemish and Lemish, forthcoming).

In summary then, popular television programs such as WWF may be significant contributors to the internalization of a misguided mental map of the United States which reinforces emerging beliefs and expectations. Since such programs pertain to a realm of experiences otherwise not available to young viewers, their influence may prove to be lasting by presenting selectively limited mental frames for future reference.

References

Barthes, R. (1972). The world of wrestling. *Mythologies.* New York: Hill and Wang.

Berry, G.L., and J.K. Asamen. (1993). *Children and television: Images in a changing sociocultural world.* Newbury Park, Cal.: Sage.

Bryant, J., and D.R. Anderson. (Eds.). (1983). *Children's understanding of television: Research on attention and comprehension.* New York: Academic Press.

Byrson, L. (1987). Sport and the maintenance of masculine hegemony. *Women's Studies International Forum* 10: pp. 349–360.

Comstock, G. (1991). *Television and the American child.* New York: Academic Press.

Fiske, J. (1987). *Television culture.* London: Methuen.

Gerbner, G., L. Gross, M. Morgan, and N. Signorielli. (1980). The mainstreaming of America: Violence profile no. 11. *Journal of Communication* 30(3): pp. 10–29.

Gerbner, G., L. Gross, M. Morgan, and N. Signorielli. (1994). Growing up with television: The cultivation perspective. In J. Bryant and D. Zillman (Eds.), *Media effects: Advances in theory and research.* Hillsdale, N.J.: Lawrence Erlbaum.

Henricks, T. (1974). Professional wrestling as moral order. *Sociological Inquiry* 44(3): pp. 177–188.

Lemish, D. (forthcoming). Television wrestling in the lives of Israeli children: Uses, perceptions, and behavioral effects. In B. Bachmair and G. Kress (Eds.), *Hell-staged wrestling: Meaning and reception analysis of controversial genres.* München: Kopad [in German].

Lemish, D. (1996a). Israeli schools as wrestling arenas: Reconsidering the violent effects of television. Paper presented at the International Communication Association annual meeting in Chicago, 1996.

Lemish, D. (1996b). Girls can be wrestlers too: Gender differences in the consumption of a wrestling television series. Paper presented at the International Communication Association annual meeting in Chicago, 1996.

Lemish, D., and P. Lemish. (forthcoming). A much debated consensus: Media literacy in Israel. In R. Kubey and B. Ruben (Eds.), *Literacy in the information age.* New York: Transaction Press.

Liebert, R.M., and J. Sprafkin. (1988). *The early window.* New York: Pergamon Press.

Maguire, B., and J.F. Wozniak. (1987). Racial and ethnic stereotypes in professional wrestling. *The Social Science Journal* 24(3): pp. 261–273.

Palmer, E.L., and A. Dorr. (Eds.). (1980*). Children and the faces of television: Teaching, violence, selling.* New York: Academic Press.

Rosenberg, M.M., and A. Turowetz. (1975). The wrestler and the physician: Identity workup and organizational arrangements. In D.W. Ball and J.W. Loy (Eds.), *Sport and social order: Contributions to the sociology of sport.* Reading, Mass.: Addison-Wesley Publishing Company.

Van Evra, J. (1990). *Television and child development.* Hillsdale, N.J.: Lawrence Erlbaum Associates.

Webley, I.A. (1986). Professional wrestling: The world of Roland Barthes revisited. *Semiotica* 58(1/2): pp. 59–81.

Weimann, G. (1984). Images of life in America: The impact of American television in Israel. *International Journal of Intercultural Relations* 8(2): 185–197.

22

The Genesis of the American Image in Arabic Literature (1600s–1800s)

RANIA M. HEGAZI AND BEVERLY JENSEN

Introduction

The contemporary American image in the Arab world was formed through two main channels: travel literature on America and later, the mass media. This chapter is on the American image in Arabic literature, which preceded the emergence of its press image. That former image is of particular relevance not only because of its age, but also due to the kind of literature through which it was formed. The American image in Arabic literature between the 1600s and 1800s was based on the travel notes of Arabs who travelled to America as well as the translated literature of European travellers. In fact, the contacts with Europe and with European sources were major contributors to that image during that early period (Lewis 1982).

Speculations about the presence of a world behind the "Sea of Darkness" date back to al-Idrisi (1100–1160), the Arab geographer who wrote about eight Arab adventurers who sailed from Lisbon in the twelfth century toward the west, in search of what was behind the Sea of Darkness. This manuscript was discovered later among Christopher Columbus's belongings, whom Arab sailors and a translator accompanied on the *Santa Maria* when he crossed the Atlantic in 1492 (Mehdi 1978).

Despite these manuscripts, there is no evidence in the available Arabic literature on what the New World was like before the 1670s, when the Chaldean priest Ilyas al-Musili described his trip to South America between 1675 and 1683. The manuscript of his trip documents the earliest known voyage by an Arab to America. It was discovered in a Syrian Catholic monastery's library in 1905 by Father Antun Rabat. Rabat edited and published the manuscript in the same year in *al-Masriq* (vol. 18 through 23, 1905) under the title "The Trip of the First Eastern Traveler to America." One year later, he published it again as a book, published by the Catholic Press of Beirut. Bernard Lewis (1982) argues that al-Musili was "almost certainly the first Middle Easterner to visit and describe the New World, where he traveled extensively in Peru, Panama and Mexico" (Lewis 1982). Al-Musili's travels in America lasted eight years. He first had decided to visit Jerusalem and some European states, but while he was in Spain, he met the queen, who wanted him to go to the West Indies, i.e., America. Al-Musili stated that such a request was hard on him, but he asked "God's support and obeyed." In 1675, he was aboard a ship heading to America from Cadiz in Spain. He landed approximately forty-five days later in South America, where he visited several places, and eventually reached the present-day Los Angeles as his northernmost point, according to his description.

Al-Musili explained the hardship involved with travelling to America. Not only did the king personally have to authorize anyone's travelling, but the trip itself was also hard. He described how a man died because of the anxiety, and the mixed feelings of stress and sadness among the people aboard his ship. Al-Musili, despite mentioning those feelings, didn't provide a clear picture of the people aboard his ship, nor their purpose in travelling to America. But because he mentioned that the Spanish ships travelled to collect taxes from the colonies, it is clear that among those people were state agents who travelled on duty.

There is consistency in the way al-Musili described the places he visited in his notes. He always started by describing the distance from his last stop, the kind of rule in the village or city, whether under the Spanish or any other authority. Then he would mention the race of the inhabitants, their religion, the ruler's name, the geography of the place, and the people's way of subsistence—agriculture, gold or silver mining, etc. Al-Musili also was careful to describe the church and the buildings in detail if there were any. That was the pattern he always followed in his visits to different locations in America.

Al-Musili's description was limited to a number of themes, which formulated the picture of America he presented in his account. The first involved slavery, beginning when the ship he was aboard passed an English ship carrying slaves from Brazil. It involved the variety of Europeans in America too, as he mentioned English and French ships, indicating the presence of Europeans other than the Spanish in South America. In addition, al-Musili mentioned the presence of pirates, which added to the danger associated with the trip to America. For him, America was a rather violent and dangerous place. He recommended against going there, "lest you get lost and die" in these lands. Most of the stories and events al-Musili recalled, whether they had happened to others in the past or to him personally, concerned pirates, thieves, clashes between the rulers and priests, murder, and the relationship with the American Indians.

America was not only a violent and dangerous place in al-Musili's account, but also full of natural wonders, differences in climate, and with many varied animals and plants. Most importantly, it was also rich in gold and silver, as it had "mountains" of these precious metals. Gold and silver mining was described in extensive detail. Al-Musili was astonished by the sea at La Calera port, which was full of pearls, although they were not harvested. He asked some pilots to gather shellfish for him to eat, and as he opened one oyster he found a big pearl in it. When he asked why the Spanish weren't gathering those pearls, the captain of the ship told him it was due to fear of the Indians.

The geography was also an element to which al-Musili paid particular attention. The variations in the climate was one part, and he mentioned that it rained at times when it didn't in the East. Furthermore, al-Musili experienced earthquakes and described their locations as unstable land. In addition to geography, nature was described in terms of its wildlife and plants. As to the wildlife, he described types of alligators he had never known before and "big birds which could imitate human sounds"—parrots—of which he brought two back with him. He also wrote about different kinds of deer.

Plants were one distinct element in al-Musili's account of American nature. He described the shapes of wild flowers and trees as well as different agricultural crops. Cultivation was the basic means of subsistence. He vividly described the cacao plant, and the steps in gathering and producing the chocolate from it. Cultivation of sugar cane was recorded, and he described the processing of sugar from the cane in detail, too. In his accounts of the cultivations and their related activities, al-Musili noted that all the peasants were "black slaves," which means Indians, as he would always describe them as black, while the Spanish were the operating directors.

The relationship between the Spanish rulers and the American Indians was never judged in explicit terms; although in a number of instances, al-Musili's description implied his opinion. In different contexts and stories, the lower status of the majority of Indians is prevalent, with the exception of one wealthy Indian mentioned in the notes. There was also continuous hostility in interactions between the Spanish and Indians.

Indians were mostly slaves, working in the fields, mining, and working in the Spanish houses. Al-Musili described them as "wicked" a number of times. Even in cases when Indians seemed loyal, such as when an Indian servant saved al-Musili from being killed by another Indian, the former turned against al-Musili later and tried to kill him. Generally, the portrayal of Indians is negative, entailing distrust, disobedience, and violence.

The tone of distrust in al-Musili's description of the Indians continues even with those who are not slaves, but rich people. In the only story where a rich Indian was mentioned, the man had become rich because he had known a place from which he secretly extracted silver. He had not declared his wealth because he had seen Indians before him tortured to death by the Spanish because of their wealth. In a comment on that man's story, al-Musili made his only implicit statement on Spanish injustice in treatment of the Indians, saying that he did not doubt the man's story.

Al-Musili had given religious justification for such treatment in other instances. As a prelude to a description of a battle between the Indians and the Spanish, al-Musili reported that the Indians were "infidels" who worshipped a mountain in front of them called the Red Mountain. When the Indians were attacked, defeated, and captured, they were driven to Cusco (Cuzco, the ancient Inca capital). Its ruler asked the Bishop to "teach them the principles of Jesus and divide them around the country." Al-Musili, in describing this incident, claimed religion as an acceptable justification for attacking and dispersing the Indians, and the whole action as desirable.

Violence and confrontation, although predominantly between the Spanish and Indians, were also elements in depicting the relationships among the Spanish themselves. Al-Musili recalled clashes among the Spanish rulers, and between rulers and priests, which would extend sometimes to the murder or exile of priests.

The Language

Although it was written in Arabic, al-Musili's language was quite poor and his writing full of spelling mistakes, according to Rabat's introduction to the book (*al-Masriq*, 1905, 821). This might be due to the fact that al-Musili's mother language may have been Syrian and not Arabic. Rabat edited the manuscript in *al-Masriq*, not only linguistically, but also by adding more information regarding the names of places and their locations. Even though Rabat's additions were included in the main text of the manuscript published in *al-Masriq*, it documents the earliest Arabic names of locations used for America. As for continental names, America was given the Arabic translation of "India of the West," or West Indies. Later in the manuscript, al-Musili called it "India." Names of cities were either translations or transcriptions of Spanish names. Among many names in the manuscript, he transcribed Caracas, Lima, Mejico or Mexico, and translated Ste. Helena and La Pueblo de Los Angelos (Los Angeles)—the City of Angels—into Arabic.

The relevance of al-Musili's account lies in its age and the detailed image it portrays of America in the earliest available Arabic encounter. Al-Musili's encounter was composed of a number of elements. Violence, hardship in relation to nature and survival, wealth, the turbulent relationship between the Indians and the whites (Spanish, Portuguese, or English), and religion persist as the major components of the picture he drew of America.

In addition to al-Musili's manuscript, another one is available from the late seventeenth century. It is a manuscript of a book called *Al-Fawa'id al-Saniyya min Khawas al-Asgar al-Tibbiyya* (The Characteristics of Materia Medica), written by Monaggem Basi (n.d.-1703), the fortune teller of the Ottoman Sultan Murad IV. The book describes the medical benefits of newly discovered American plants. Basi wrote the book in Turkish and later translated it into Arabic. The Arabic manuscript is available in Bankipore, India (Brockelmann 1937).

Although the book is of secondary importance to the American image in the Arabic literature prior to the eighteenth century, as Basi had not been to America, it reflects a particular element of that image which persisted during that time: America as a land of different flora. In al-Musili's account, which emphasized in detail unusual flowers, trees, and cultivation, this aspect of the American image was established. It persisted as one of the basic elements of the American picture in Arabic literature until the mid-nineteenth century.

The Nineteenth Century

Although al-Musili's manuscript is the oldest, it was not the first known published picture of America presented to the Arabic reader. Al-Musili's manuscript was first made available in 1905, more than seventy years after the publication of two books by Rifa'a al-Tahtawi (1801–1872), the Egyptian educational pioneer and thinker, in 1833 and 1834. Al-Tahtawi's books are then the earliest known presentation of the New World to the Arab reader.

Two of Al-Tahtawi's books included descriptions of America: *Qala'id al-Mafakhir fi gharib 'Awa'id al-'Awa'il wal Awakhir* (Delineations of the Manners and Customs of Various Nations) by Georg Bernhard Depping, which al-Tahtawi translated in its French version and added to (printed in 1833), and *Takhlis al-Ibriz fi Talkhis Bariz* (The Golden Essence of the Parisian Trip), al-Tahtawi's notes on his sojourn in Paris (first published in 1834). In *Takhlis al-Ibriz*, nature persisted as an element in the image as al-Tahtawi described in astonishment how different kinds of palm trees were imported from America and successfully cultivated in France (al-Tahtawi 1834). *Qala'id al-Mafakhir*, on the other hand, had more elements comprising the image it portrays of America. It is an ethnographic description of the different costumes of peoples of the world. The first part of the book, which al-Tahtawi wrote, is an index of names of the different tribes, countries, and geographical places later described in the book. Each entry explains pronunciation and the geographical location of the tribe or country. In some cases, it also includes more description on the race of the people, their culture, religion, and governance. In this index, America is described as part of the "Europe" entry, yet there are separate entries for Mexico, Brazil, Chile, Colombia, Amazon, and Eskimos, as well.

Al-Tahtawi was the first to introduce the image of the United States in Arabic literature. He coined the first Arabic name of the United States, Etazoni or Etazonia, which is a transformed transcription of the French *Etats-Unis*, and gave it a separate entry in his index. The image al-Tahtawi projected of the United States was the first introduction of an urban American society and state. In his description, he noted the different political entities and divisions of the United States and the other states in South and North America. His writings clearly depict a political system, types of government rule, and state borders (al-Tahtawi 1833).

In depicting the United States, two main aspects composed al-Tahtawi's picture. He indicated the political independence of the United States from England. He talked about the arrival of English groups in North America who were under the English rule, then fought for their "freedom and independence (al-Tahtawi 1833, 14). He also drew a connection between the United States religious environment and its being "amongst the greatest civilized countries where worship according to different religions in not prohibited" (14). Thus, al-Tahtawi, too, chose the element of religion among the characteristics to depict of the New World, yet his choice was in terms of setting forth an example of tolerance, diversity and civilization.

The Language

Al-Tahtawi's encounters are the first in Arabic literature to make a clear distinction between North and South America. Furthermore, the United States along with the different regions and states in Central and South America were also referred to as distinct political entities from each other. In his writing, al-Tahtawi always specified which area he was referring to, except when he meant both continents with no separation, then he would use the term "America" or "lands of America." He'd also call it "the New World," "West Indies," and sometimes "Land of Wonders."

Like al-Musili, al-Tahtawi either translated or transcribed names of locations. Whenever there was an Arabic parallel meaning, the Arabic term was used. Otherwise, transcribing the names was the other alternative. The transcription was based either on the English or French names. According to al-Tahtawi, North America was composed of Russian America (Alaska), Agroland (Greenland), lands of New England, lands of Etazonia, lands of Mexico, and lands of Guatemala. Its main cities were Mexico, New York,

Philadelphia, and Washington, which were all transcribed in their Arabic names. In reference to South America, he would either call it South America or Spanish America both in Arabic translations.

Eleven years after the publication of his two books, al-Tahtawi supervised the translation of a travel book on America entitled *Kitab Siyahat Amriqa* (The Book of America's Travel) in 1845. This book was originally written in French by Father Henry Mercham. Its Arabic translation was done by Saᶜd Naᶜam of Madrasat al-Alsun (the School of Languages) in Cairo. The original date of the French publication is not indicated in the Arabic version nor in the later compilation of al-Alsun's translations (al-Sayyal). However, it is most likely that the book was published in the first half of the nineteenth century, since al-Tahtawi, the headmaster of al-Alsun, aimed to translate current French knowledge into Arabic.

Kitab Siyahat Amriqa is important for a number of reasons. First, it represents the later creations of the early American image in Arabic literature and the last prior to American-Arab contact on more direct levels through missionary and diplomatic activities. Second, the book introduced the first Arabic translation of "United States," an initiation to its current Arabic name, in substitution for Etazonia coined earlier by al-Tahtawi. Mercham's account is detailed in reviewing the history of the English and French colonies in North America and the formation of the United States.

The book is distinguished for its comprehensive description of both North and South America, as Henry Mercham traveled throughout the two continents. In his account, a portrayal of the American Indians of both Americas is dominant. Again, their religion is negatively presented as "barbarian," similar to al-Musili's view. Later in his book, Mercham praised the missionaries for "accomplishing the achievement of guiding the Eskimos to the right God . . . which made their morals more civilized and saved their children" (NaCam 1845, 102).

Despite the similarity between al-Musili and Mercham in their approaches toward the American Indian religions, a very strong difference shows in the depth each perceived of violence practiced against them by the Spanish. Mercham, while damning the Indians for sacrificing their children and for infidelity, strongly and directly stated how they were victims of the Spanish: "The Incas king Atahuallpa . . . who suffered harm and distress from his enemies . . . who was attacked and unjustly killed . . . and whose followers also suffered . . . makes anyone frightened of what Pizarro the Spanish had done . . . God curses him" (118). On the other hand, al-Musili had only lightly mentioned the poor conditions of the American Indians. Mercham closed his book leaving the reader with a lasting impression of a rich land whose people were tortured and massacred.

In addition to its portrayal of American Indians, *Kitab Siyahat Amriqa* perpetuated the image of America as a land of different plants. Plants were described, such as potatoes. Wildlife was also a prevalent element and animals different from those described by al-Musili and al-Tahtawi were reported. Penguins and llamas were introduced.

The wealth of the American natural resources was also a component in Mercham's picture. Compared to the emphasis on the prosperity of resources depicted in the earlier images, the portrayal was of diminished wealth due to the Spanish exploitation.

Conclusion

In sum, there is a continuity of elements in the picture of America in the Arabic literature from the 1600s to the 1800s. This picture, mainly of South America, was dominated by the American Indians, with particular emphasis on their religious practices and their conflict with the Spanish. In the earlier account by al-Musili (1668), the American Indians were portrayed as inferior and disloyal to the Spanish, with minor reference to them as victims of the Spanish. Yet, in the later image by Mercham (1845), despite being presented in terms of their violence and infidelity, they were clearly portrayed as victims of the Spanish. Thus, the image of the American Indians changed through the years. But while relations between peoples were dynamic, reports on the flora and fauna of the Americas remained constant in the literature between the 1600s and the 1800s.

In general, the American Indians, the injustice of their treatment, the violence of the Spanish, the spread of Christianity, and the natural resources of wealth, plants, and wildlife continued to be the main elements of the first American images in the Arab world from the 1600s through the mid-nineteenth century.

Along with the continuity of these elements, the United States emerged as a new component of the continental American image through al-Tahtawi's writings. His writings were the first to depict an American state with a well-defined political system and an urban society. Al-Tahtawi's encounter with the United States was created solely through his French experience; America for him was an extension of his encounter with European civilization. Like his picture of modern France, his picture of the United States was the first in the Arabic literature. It was in al-Tahtawi's writings that the United States was not only introduced to the Arab reader, but also given its first Arabic name.

References

Brockelmann, C. (1937). *Geschichte der Arabischen litteratur* [History of the Arabic Literature]. Leiden: Brill.

Hanafi, H. (1991). *Muqadimma fi ʿIlm al-Ilstighrab* [Introduction to Occidentalism]. Cairo: al-Dar al-Faniyya.

Lewis, B. (1982). *The Muslim discovery of Europe*. London: Orion Books.

Mehdi, B.T. (1978). *The Arabs in America 1492–1977: A Chronology and Fact Book*. New York: Oceana Publications.

Al-Musili, I. (1905). Rihlat Awwal Sa'ih Sarqi Ila Amriqa [Trip of the First Eastern Traveler to America]. *al-Masriq* 8: pp. 821–824, 875–886, 931–942, 974–987, 1022–1033, 1080–1088, 1118–1139.

Naᶜam, S. (1845). *Kitab Siyahat Amriqa* [Book of America's Travel]. H. Mercham, Trans. Cairo: Bulaq Printshop.

The New Encyclopædia Britannica. (1995). Vol. 3, p. 817, and vol. 9, pp. 489–490. Chicago: Encyclopædia Britannica, Inc.

Al-Sayyal, G. (1951). *Tarikh al-Targama wal-Haraka al-Thaqafiyya fi Misr* [History of Translation and Intellectual Movement in Egypt]. Cairo: Dar al-Fikr al-ᶜArabi.

Al-Tahtawi, R. (1833). *Qala'id al-Mafakhir fi Gharib 'Awa'id al-Awa'il wal Awakhir* [Delineations of the Manners and Customs of Various Nations]. G.B. Depping, Trans. Moeurs et Usage des Nations. Cairo: Bulaq.Printshop. (Original work in French, 1812).

Al-Tahtawi, R. (1834). *Takhlis al-Ibriz fi Talkhis Bariz* [The Golden Essence of the Parisian Trip]. M.F. Hegazi, (Ed.). (1975). Cairo: General Egyptian Book Organization.

The Times Atlas of the World. (1992). 9th Edition. London: Random House.

23

American Programs on Egyptian Television

Prospects and Concerns

HUSSEIN Y. AMIN

Introduction

Arab countries import a large number of American programs. Almost one-third of the imported programs in Arab countries are American (Varis 1993). This is borne out in Egypt, where more than twenty percent of Egyptian television programming is American in origin (Varis 1984).

American programs on Egyptian television are quite popular and attract a great number of viewers. In general, these programs portray Americans and America in a variety of ways—from an egalitarian, classless society where hard work is rewarded with success to a vile, corrupt, crime-ridden society where violence predominates and permeates everything. Although this wide range of messages provides conflicting information about America and American society, it may also constitute the basis for Egyptian's perceptions of the country and its culture. This chapter examines the factors that affect the access and availability of American films and television programs on Egyptian television, describes the history and current status of American programming in Egypt, and then discusses the impact of these programs on the perception of Egyptian audiences about Americans and America.

Access and Availability of American Programming in Egypt

The Context

The Arab Republic of Egypt is located in the northeast corner of Africa facing the Mediterranean Sea on the north, bounded on the south by Sudan, on the west by Libya and on the east by the Red Sea, Israel, and Palestine. Cairo is the capital city and also the largest city in the country. There are numerous smaller cities and villages scattered along both sides of the Nile River and in the Nile Delta, with the population mostly engaged in agriculture. Per capita income in Egypt is U.S.$620 annually (World Bank Annual Report 1995).

Egypt has a fast-growing population of sixty million. The official language is Arabic. Islam is the religion of the state, with a large religious minority of almost eleven million Coptic Christians. King Farouk was the last of the kings to rule Egypt. He was appointed by the British and was King of Egypt until the 1952 revolution. The revolution ended British rule over Egypt and was headed by General Mohamed Naguib, who remained in power for almost two years, until Gamal Abdel Nasser seized control of the country in 1954. Nasser remained in power until his natural death in 1971. Nasser's successor, Anwar Sadat, was assassinated in 1981 and was followed by Egypt's current president, Hosni Mubarak (Amin 1986). The current political system of the state is a presidential republic.

The Culture

Islamic society in general and Egyptian society in particular tend to be culturally defensive. The Egyptian individual identifies himself/herself first with the family and second with the religious community. Egyptian people share some social values that are derived from religious traditions, such as kindness, charity, virtue, and hospitality.

Television is the ideal medium for a culture that is very family-oriented and tends to look for its entertainment within the home. Although Cairo and Alexandria are culturally rich, cosmopolitan cities with live music, theaters, cinemas, and sporting activities, the majority of Egyptians cannot take advantage of these activities. Hence, they must stay close to home either because they are not in the proper economic or social position or because they live outside of these large urban areas. Most urban Egyptians live at a subsistence level and cannot afford the cost of entrance tickets, child care, and transportation to these activities. Furthermore, Cairo's overpopulation and tremendous overcrowding increase the difficulty of seeking entertainment outside the home. With the continued development of the country's electric power infrastructure, villages are becoming increasingly television oriented. Often several families share a television set and view the television as not only a status symbol, but also as a way of educating children and family members, if only by giving them a view of the world outside the village (Boyd 1993).

The importance of television and its role as a focal point for the Egyptian family is borne out by the results of a field study conducted in Egypt in 1989. Two researchers, Salem and El Kordy, found that the percentage of children who watch television regularly ranges from 87.2 percent to 95.54 percent. During holidays, the percentage of children watching television daily increases to 97.18 percent–98.10 percent. The researchers found no significant differences among children based on gender or age. Most of the children who watch television watch it all day long, often while doing other activities, such as homework or reading. The programs preferred by the children include children's cinema programs, cartoons, and puppet shows, the majority of which are imported from the U.S. (Salem and El Kordy 1989).

Some of the main concerns regarding foreign programs on Egyptian television are broadly cultural, specifically religious, and inescapably political. These concerns have existed for quite a long time, but the sudden visual impact of popular Western culture, courtesy of television, coupled with radical changes in Western mores as projected in much television programming over the past three decades, intensified these defenses (Schleifer 1995).

The Status of Television Broadcasting in Egypt

Egyptian television opened its first broadcast in the late 1950s with verses from the Holy Koran followed by a speech from Nasser (Napoli *et al.* 1995), and it was obvious from that time that the medium was going to be used as a propaganda tool for the government.

The most important sources of programming for Egyptian television were films, including romance, slapstick comedy, and political films. News was broadcast initially only in Arabic, but later English and French news programs were added. Foreign programs, including British and American programs, were also telecast by Egyptian television until the 1967 war.

After Egypt's defeat in the 1967 war, the number of foreign programs, particularly American programs, broadcast over Egyptian Television decreased substantially. That was due mainly to the breakdown of diplomatic relations between Egypt and the United States and Egypt and Great Britain. The third television channel was closed after the 1967 war, and the British and American programs were deemed unacceptable.

American programming in Egypt was replaced by television programs from the Soviet Union. This situation lasted until the 1973 war. During President Sadat's rule, Egyptian television reoriented itself toward the West, specifically the United States, and became a direct reflection of the Egyptian government's political shift in international relations. Consequently, the number of British and American programs broadcast on the networks increased substantially. This trend has continued throughout Mubarak's regime, and foreign programs continue to appear on the Egyptian television schedule.

In comparison to the two previous Egyptian regimes, and in fact to most regimes throughout the Arab World, Mubarak's regime, undoubtedly allows a great degree of freedom to the media in general (Amin and Napoli 1995). For instance, within the last decade, Egyptian television has begun implementing a plan to decentralize the system by introducing local television channels. Channel 4 was introduced in October 1988 to cover Ismailia, Suez, and Port Said; the first official broadcast was at the end of May 1989 (Goweili 1993). Channel 5, covering Alexandria and surrounding areas, was introduced in December 1990. Channel 6, covering the Delta and the surrounding territories, began broadcasting in May 1994. Channel 7, covering Minia and some parts of southern Egypt, was introduced in October 1994 (Amin 1995). Most of the local television channels are carrying American programs on their broadcast schedule.

Furthermore, within the last six years, the Egyptian government has moved into satellite broadcasting services. Egypt also has a domestic/international mainly English language television service (Nile TV), using a UHF channel. Its service is limited to the city of Cairo and now to southern Sinai with broadcasts in English and French only.

History and Status of American Programming in Egypt

Motion Pictures

From 1965 to 1969, the Egyptian cinema market imported 89.7 percent of all films shown in movie theaters. The United States was the main source of films projected in Egypt during this specific period of time, representing 64.5 percent of all foreign films imported. During the period from 1969 to 1975, Egypt imported 1,074 films. The United States held first position with 336 films, followed by Italy with 125 films, Britain with 110, the Soviet Union with 58, France with 49, and India with 40. Some experts stated that this increase in importation of films from the U.S. was because of the strong relationship between Egypt and the U.S. at that time (Rachty and Sabat 1979).

In 1980, Egypt imported 150 foreign movies, 94 of which were American. In 1981, Egypt imported 113 foreign films, 75 of which were American. In 1985, Egypt imported 116 films including 55 American movies. In 1987, Egypt imported 126 foreign movies including 38 American movies. In 1990, Egypt imported 166 foreign films, 89 of which were American. In 1992, Egypt imported 160 foreign films including 55 American films. In 1993, Egypt imported 81 foreign movies, that included 74 American movies (see Figure 23.1).

Figure 23.1. American Film Imports to Egypt

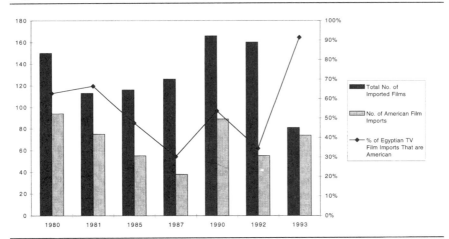

Source: Sayegh 1995.

American movies have constituted a huge portion of the imported films to Egypt throughout history, which is indicative of the fact that there is a large audience for these films (Sayegh 1995).

VCRs

In the Arab World, video cassette recorders (VCRs) are very popular. Their popularity ranges from the rich Gulf states that constitute a virtual videotape world to Egypt and Sudan where videotapes fill a niche left by the state-run television services and where per capita incomes can ill afford the cost of cinema tickets. The penetration of VCRs in pre-invasion Kuwait, Saudi Arabia, Oman, Bahrain, Qatar, and the United Arab Emirate (UAE) is very high, to the point where most homes have a machine. In other Arab countries that have a lower per capita income, such as Egypt and Sudan, penetration is lower than in the Gulf countries. In 1986, it was estimated that 4 percent of Egyptian television homes had a VCR (Boyd and Straubharr 1989). In 1990, the BBC estimated that Egypt had three VCRs for every one hundred people or equivalent to 1,680,000 home video recorders (British Broadcasting Corporation 1990).

The video consumption patterns in the Arab World, particularly in Egypt, should not be examined in a Western context. This is due to the fact that there is a large amount of group VCR viewing by friends and extended family members. Not sharing one's media with others runs against Arab hospitality (Amin and Boyd 1993).

VCRs in Egypt are gaining popularity since it has become economically difficult in recent years for a middle-class family to attend movie theaters. Cinema tickets are expensive and range between U.S.$1.36 to U.S.$2.85 in the larger cities, such as Cairo and Alexandria. A family of four can expect to pay between U.S.$5.60 to U.S.$12 for one cinema outing, in addition to the costs of the trip. It is estimated that one trip can cost the average Egyptian family up to twenty percent of the family's monthly income.

Other reasons that motivate Egyptians to buy a VCR include:

1. Government-Controlled Television News and Entertainment: Entertainment programming is heavily censored to prevent violations of the predominant cultural religious and political norms and values. Many Egyptians were shocked when American prime time soap operas such as *Dallas* and *Dynasty* were banned from Egyptian Television for cultural and moral reasons. Viewers managed to get tapes of these particular programs from video rental stores and watched them in groups.

2. Affluence: Egypt has an affluent upper class that has been able to get television sets and VCRs either in Egypt or from working in the Gulf states.

3. Suppression of Political Activity: When political expression on television is almost forbidden, VCRs become a means for communicating political and religious points of view. Most Egyptians did not witness the assassination of President Sadat on national television, but they have been able to see it on tapes available through video clubs.

Rental costs for a video cassette range from U.S.$0.76 to U.S.$1.14. Official reports listed more than 200 video clubs in the country in 1984, but the number of unregistered video clubs exceeded 500. The number of video clubs in Egypt in 1990 exceeded 2,000 clubs (Amin and Boyd 1993). Overall, the majority of Egyptian people prefer to rent American videos rather than Egyptian. In fact, 65 percent opted for American movies, 20 percent for English movies, 10 percent for Egyptian movies, and 5 percent for Indian movies. American movies that had huge success in the season of 1994–95 were *Lethal Weapon* with Mel Gibson, *Blood Sport* with Jean-Claude Van Damme, *Pretty Woman* with Richard Gere, *Scarface* with Al Pacino, *Bodyguard* with Kevin Costner, and *Forrest Gump* with Tom Hanks (Arab Contractors 1995).

Direct Broadcast Satellite

In October 1990, the Egyptian government approved the establishment of Cable News Egypt (CNE) in a twenty-five-year cooperative arrangement with the U.S. based Cable News Network (CNN). The main purpose of CNE was to retransmit Cable News Network International (CNNI) in Egypt. CNE, a subscription television system, operates over an ultra high frequency channel (UHF) controlled by the Egyptian Radio and Television Union (ERTU), and has a satellite receiving station and transmitter that covers greater Cairo (Foote and Amin 1993).

At the end of 1994, CNE underwent a major change. Cable News Egypt, the name of the original company, was changed to be Cable Network Egypt. The renamed company then made an agreement with a South African-based company (Multichoice Africa) to market CNE in Egypt. Within the framework of this agreement, Multichoice began selling a new decoder and introduced new services such as CNNI, Music Television (MTV), the Kuwaiti space network, Movie Network (Mnet), KidTV, a children's channel carrying mostly American children television programs as well as movies, and Super-Sports, an all-sports channel (Amin and Napoli 1995).

Egypt has been the leader of a new wave of international pan-Arab television transmission for Arab viewers in the region by introducing the Egyptian Space Network followed by Nile TV. Saudi Arabia, realizing the importance of the international television services directed toward the Arabs and Egyptians, launched the Middle East Broadcasting Center (MBC), a London-based news-oriented channel, followed by Arab Radio and Television (ART), television services consisting of four specialized international television networks for children, movies in Arabic and English, sports, and a general network. ART later added a fifth channel in Europe. In 1994, the Saudis launched a new service called Orbit, consisting of thirty-two channels that include the following American networks:

- Orbit-ESPN sports: A package of sporting events and sports programs mainly from the Entertainment Sports Network accompanied by Arabic narration and commentary. This channel covers the major tennis and golf tournaments and gives highlights of American sports, such as the National Basketball Association (NBA) and the National Hockey League (NHL).
- Music Now channel: It provides a variety of songs from around the world and offers regular music shows, such as America's Top Ten and the Album Show. It also covers international and Arabic concerts on the air.
- The Hollywood channel: It telecasts programs related to life in Hollywood and includes show business gossip, game shows, and celebrity interviews.
- The Discovery Channel: It is a retransmission of the American Discovery channel.

- The Fun Channel: It specializes in children's programs, specifically cartoons.
- America Plus: It shows selected American programs, dramas, and TV mini-series.
- All News Channel: It telecasts soft news programs in various fields.
- CNN international: This is a 24-hour news channel.
- C-SPAN: It covers the government of the U.S. in session.

In addition, Orbit is planning to include the Disney Channel on its lineup of American programming ("Orbit on Intelsat 702" 1996).

The Egyptian government has made it clear from the beginning that they are going to adopt an "open window" policy that will allow Egyptians to purchase or rent satellite dishes. A satellite dish allows Egyptians access to services from European countries, including Turkey, and Israel. There are currently about 2.8 million satellite dishes in the Arab World, of which about 800,000 are in Egypt. Different patterns of buying a satellite dish range from full purchase to finance and lease-to-own. Studies have shown that the main motivation behind the purchase of the satellite dishes is to watch Western programs.

American Films and Programs on Egyptian Television

Historically, American programs have represented a substantial percentage of the program material imported by Egyptian television. The presence of American movies on Egyptian television from 1960 to 1968 exceeded all other foreign program materials from all over the world. Of all foreign programs broadcast on Egyptian TV, the United States had a 59.6 percent cut, followed by the former Soviet Union at 16 percent, former Czechoslovakia at 6.2 percent, and the former German Democratic Republic at 4.8 percent. A decline in the percentage of American programs broadcast on Egyptian TV followed the 1967 war with Israel. In 1969 and 1970, Egyptian television did not import any television programs or telefilms from the United States. However, after 1970, American presence began to grow again until it reached a peak in 1978 with 97.3 percent of all foreign films broadcast during that year. After the collapse of the Soviet Union, American programs on Egyptian television maintained a 90 percent and above proportion of all foreign programs broadcast on Egyptian television.

The strong presence of American programs broadcast on Egyptian TV has continued to the present day. The first national network, Channel One, broadcasts a weekly program called the *Cinema Club* during prime time, that presents American movies followed by commentaries on the films by guest experts. Channel One also has a weekly program *Ikhtarna Lak* (We Selected for You) during prime time on Wednesday nights. The program normally shows an American series based on requests from Egyptian audiences. Top American series presented through the program since the seventies include: *Colombo, Hart to Hart, Macmillan and Wife, Mission Impossible, McCloud, Magnum P.I., Knight Rider, Murder She Wrote, The Equalizer, Miami Vice,* and *McGyver* (Author's files).

The second national network, Channel 2, broadcasts a weekly program on Thursday night prime time called *Oscar*, which also shows old as well as relatively new American movies. Channel 2 also broadcasts American movies during non-prime-time hours. This channel also presents American series and soap operas at least once a week. American serials tend to be extremely attractive to the Egyptian audience, especially middle, upper-middle, and upper classes. Some of the most popular U.S. TV serials in the past were *Dallas, Dynasty,* and, more recently, *Falcon Crest, Knots Landing,* and *The Bold and the Beautiful* (Author's files).

Another famous weekly program broadcast on Channel 2 is called *El Alam Yoghani* (The World is Singing), which presents songs by performers from throughout the world, including Madonna, Michael Jackson, Julio Iglesias and Whitney Houston. (Author's files).

American programs are broadcast on all local television channels except Channel 4. A one-month study conducted in 1995 on Egyptian television programming found that during the study period, American programs represented 2.26 percent of all programming on Channel One, 19.84 percent on Channel 2, 7.74 percent on Channel 3, 0 percent on Channel 4, and 2.04 percent on Channel 5. American programs on Channel 2, which has by far the largest amount of foreign programming on Egyptian television, constitute more than 90 percent of the foreign offerings. These figures do not include American cartoons, American video clips, television commercials, visual materials utilized in the opening and closing of programs, and segments of popular American television programs that are frequently broadcast such as *America's Funniest Home Videos, Guinness Book of World Records, America's Bloopers, Bleeps and Blunders,* and *Candid Camera* (Farouk et al. 1995).

The above programming distribution is roughly the same throughout the year except during the month of Ramadan, a period of daily fasting for all Moslems, when television programs are completely different, mostly of religious nature, on all channels (Radio and Television Magazine 1995).

The Impact of American Programs On Egyptian Audiences and Their Effect on the Image of the U.S. in Egypt

At the heart of the debate on the growing internationalization of American media products, mainly films and television series, lies the issue of their impact on viewers around the world. Participants in this debate generally can be grouped into three camps. The first group holds that television's impact is immense and totally pervasive and therefore requires the development of national media policies. The second camp holds that the lack of data makes verification of the degree and nature of television's impact impossible, and therefore an intense research effort is needed to allow policy makers to base decisions on accurate information. The third group maintains that national communication policies restrict the free flow of television programming and that fewer restrictions will right whatever imbalances currently exist (Mowlana 1986). Television does have an impact on its audience. For instance, George Gerbner's often-cited research, conducted in the U.S., documents that heavy viewers of American prime-time programs are increasingly receiving a highly distorted picture of the real world, which they tend to believe more than the actual reality. He also found that there is evidence that television violence induces heavy viewers to perceive their world as a more violent and dangerous place than it truly is. Gerbner found that heavy viewers greatly overestimate the proportion of Americans who are doctors, lawyers, athletes, and entertainers and that there is approximately ten times more crime on television than in real life (Mowlana 1986).

Despite the substantial research done on the impact of media in the U.S., studies relative to the image of the U.S. abroad or the impact of U.S.-produced and exported media products in countries such as Egypt have been generally neglected. In fact, even with the prevalence of American programs on Egyptian television, only a few studies have been conducted to examine the effects of American television programs on Egyptians. One of the reasons is that Arab broadcast organizations do not in general support media research efforts, beyond the counting of transmission hours. In addition, there is a cultural reluctance among the people to answer official questions (Boyd 1993).

Rachty and Sabat (1979), in their study analyzing the activities reflected by American television programs, concluded that chivalry headed the list with 78.33 percent in 120 episodes, followed by cruelty and violence, 65.83 percent, fanaticism 53.33 percent, aggressiveness 47.50 percent, treachery 45 percent, and thievery and kidnapping 38.30 percent. The researchers also noted that the program content reflects a society that holds individualism as a primary value, rests on capitalism, favors fair competition among individuals, is dependent on science as the backbone of any capitalist society, respects science, and strives to safeguard, collectively and individually, public order. In spite of these positive aspects, the researchers concluded that foreign materials broadcast on Egyptian television created a danger for the cultural integrity and mores of Egyptian society and that the negative aspects reflected in the foreign programs do not coincide with Egyptian and Arab values (Rachty and Sabat 1979).

Another researcher, Emad Hassan (1979), analyzed foreign films during a discrete period on Egyptian television and stated that crime and detective films were the most frequently broadcast films during the period of the study. In his research, Hassan used content analysis to determine what character traits were most often ascribed to the main characters in the film. The results of the study show that 79.4 percent of the pivotal characters could be described as "civilized"; "proud" characters 76.5 percent; "disciplined" characters 67.6 percent; "materialistic" 64.7 percent; "liberal" 61.7 percent; "true and keen" 55.9 percent; "good" 52.9 percent; "honest," "attractive," and "meticulous" 47 percent; "compassionate" 41 percent; "tolerant" and "forgivable" 35.3 percent; "joyful" 32.4 percent; "confident" 29.4 percent; "creative" and "generous" 17.6 percent; and "religious" 13.7 percent. An average of 51 percent of the main characters documented in his research demonstrated positive characteristics, as determined by the researcher. Negative characteristics, again defined by the researcher, were "nervous and fanatic" characters 29.4 percent; "severe" 26.2 percent; "depressed" 23.5 percent; "abnormal," "suspicious," "lacking self-confidence," "vicious," and "exaggerating" 17.6 percent; "liar" 14.7 percent; "repulsive" and "unsociable" 8.8 percent; "dull" 5.9 percent; and "uncreative" 2.9 percent. The negative characteristics as a whole totalled 12.2 percent on the average. The research indicated that pivotal characters in foreign films more often reflect positive characteristics than negative ones (Hassan 1979).

As for the objectives the pivotal characters try to reach, it was noted in this study that the objectives of ambition and power came first insofar as they were realized in 14.7 percent of the films. Objectives of honesty, charity, family relations, revenge, nationalism, artistic objectives, and scientific objectives were realized in 8.8 percent, followed by recreation, independence, money and materialistic objectives in 5.9 percent of the films. Love, sex, and legitimacy were each realized in 2.9 percent of the films. Hassan noted that positive objectives were more recurrent and met with a greater percentage of success than harmful objectives. The researcher also documented the methods that the characters used to achieve their objectives. Values documented for reaching these objectives were divided into positive and negative techniques. Topping the positive techniques was persistent work at 32.4 percent followed by struggle and conviction in 29.4 percent of the films. Positive techniques were used on the average of 16.2 percent. Topping the negative techniques was deception at 11.8 percent, followed by violence at 8.8 percent, theft at 5.9 percent, and lies at 2.9 percent (Hassan 1979).

Essam Saleem (1990) analyzed American series on Egyptian television and found that social values derived from the series were endurance, independence, and responsibility, taking the largest percentage at 14.36 percent. Ambition took second place with 14.29 percent. Nobility and goodness came third with 13.71 percent. Faithfulness and gratefulness came fourth with 11.47 percent. Equality came fifth with 6.6 percent. He concluded that American programs are not dangerous to Egyptian society, but rather act as incentive for progress and growth. On the other hand, he indicated that other values had a negative impact on Egyptian society. Malice came first with a percentage of 13.26 percent, weakness of family ties 12.74 percent, violence 9.74 percent, and deception 8.42 percent. He also concluded that extramarital sex and forbidden affairs were depicted in 7.09 percent and considered that a dangerous threat to Egyptian mores, religion, and society (Saleem 1990).

A fourth researcher, Margaret-Anne Epps, conducted a study in 1993 to explore the relationship among Egyptian elite's television viewing, interpersonal contact with Americans, and gender and to assess the impact of cultivation theory, which asserts that the attitudes and beliefs of people toward a given element are cultivated by television (Epps 1993). Epps surveyed students at the American University in Cairo, a private tuition-based university that attracts students from the upper socioeconomic segment of Egyptian society. While the overall conclusion of the study was that attitudes and beliefs about Americans and America are not significantly media-cultivated, it found that television viewership was a statistically significant variable in the case of attitudes and beliefs about American culture. Epps further suggested that a larger sample that is more representative of Egyptian society might lead to different conclusions (Epps 1993).

In an effort to build on Epps's work and to obtain more insight into the effect of American television programs on Egyptian audiences, a group of journalism and mass communication students at the American University in Cairo conducted a similar survey that included subjects outside the university. The survey, carried out under the supervision of the author in July 1995, was designed to examine and explore the impact of American programs, particularly movies, TV serials, and soap operas, on Egyptians' cultural attitudes and beliefs. The data were collected from a convenience sample of 100 respondents, including university students (both private and public), secondary school students, and working elite. The small sample size is due to the legal difficulties and time constraints involved in obtaining permission to conduct a large-scale survey in Egypt.

More than eighty percent of all selected groups who watch television indicated that they watch both Arabic and foreign programs. Twenty percent of students at the American University in Cairo and ten percent of the working elite respondents indicated that they watch foreign programs exclusively. The majority of all groups watch movies and soap operas and have never visited the U.S., although students at the American University in Cairo were more likely to have visited the U.S. than other groups (Farouk et al. 1995).

Figure 23.2. Percentage of Respondents Indicating That American Programs Affect Their Lifestyles

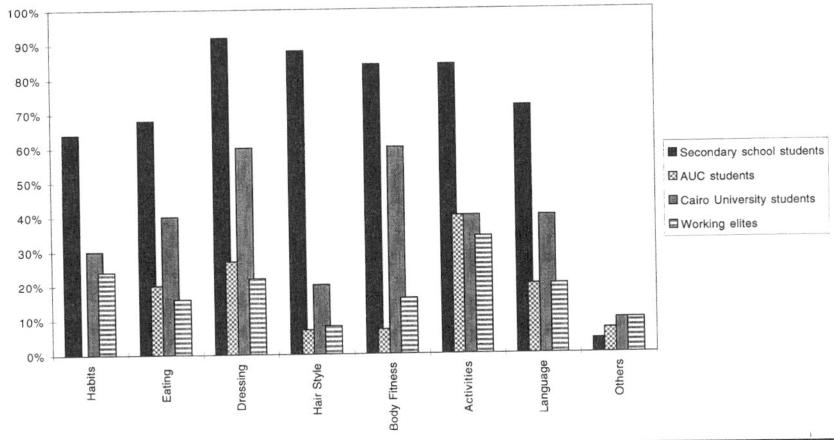

Source: Farouk et al. 1996.

Respondents were then asked how American programs had affected their lifestyles, beliefs, and traditions. Secondary school students were by far the most affected of the four groups in all categories. Respondents' lifestyle attributes that were most affected by the programs include dressing style (fashion), activities, and language (See Figure 23.2).

The highest overall response in terms of how programs affected traditions were in freedom of expression, particularly among secondary school students (See Figure 23.3).

Once again, secondary school students were more affected by the programs in terms of their beliefs than the other groups, particularly in their social beliefs, although all groups responded that the programs had little impact on their religious beliefs (Farouk et al. 1995) (See Figure 23.4).

The majority of respondents indicated that they would like to replace something in their own culture based on their experience of watching American programs. Secondary school students had the highest affirmative response rates to this question, while far fewer working elite agreed with the statement. Responses to a question asking what the respondents would like to change include greater freedom of expression, changing traditions, greater equality for women, more technology, increased optimism, and traffic relief. A large majority of all respondents agreed that American programs represent cultural imperialism, although the term was not defined in the survey instrument (Farouk et al. 1995).

Figure 23.3. Percentage of Respondents Indicating That American Programs Affect Their Traditions

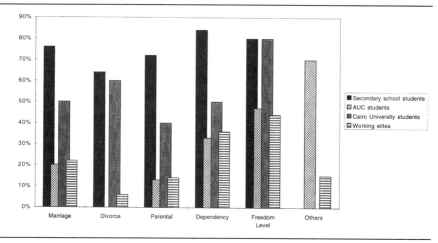

Source: Farouk et al. 1996.

Figure 23.4. Percentage of Respondents Indicating That American Programs Affect Their Beliefs

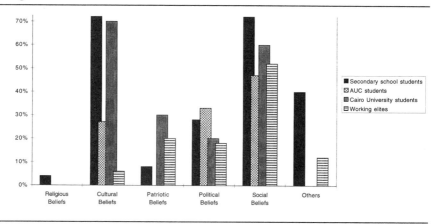

Source: Farouk et al. 1996.

While this study had a number of limitations, it does give an indication that American programs have a substantial impact on the cultural attitudes and beliefs of the Egyptian audience, particularly among impressionable younger viewers.

Conclusion

U.S. television programs and films have been successfully marketed throughout the world, penetrating television broadcast networks in developing as well as developed countries. The debate currently raging in governments around the globe is what effect this influx of American programming has on the host country and on its population.

Research has shown that television programming in Egypt has had an impact on Egyptian viewers as well as on the Egyptian film and television industry. With the increase in the amount of American programming and the introduction and growth of direct broadcast systems in the country, the Egyptian film industry has recorded a sharp decline in the number of films produced each year. Egyptian news broadcasts have altered their format to reflect the production values of American news broadcasts. And audience research has shown that the Egyptian viewers, particularly younger viewers, have felt the impact of American programming in their cultural attitudes, beliefs, and lifestyle.

Television plays an important role in Egypt, where the culture is family-oriented and entertainment centers around the home. Research has shown that Egyptian children are particularly heavy viewers, are often watching American programs that portray distorted images of American life. With the continued growth of direct broadcast systems, both local cable networks and satellite networks, the videocassette industry, the number of cinemas showing American films, and the increase in the amount of American programming on Egyptian television, the potential effects of the programs may also expand.

Further research is needed to study these effects on both Egyptian audiences and the film and television industry, particularly image research, so that decision makers can have adequate data on which to base decisions regarding the need for censorship and controlling or restricting access to programming, as well as deciding what, if any, content such as pornography, general moral values, consumerism, political issues, and so on needs to be controlled. Further studies should also use large heterogeneous samples that cut across socioeconomic boundaries and are more representative of the population. The ultimate effect of foreign programs, particularly American programs, on Egyptian audiences and on the Egyptian media industry will not be known for some time, but, for better or worse, they have already left their mark.

References

Amin, H. Y. (1986). *An Egypt-based model for the use of television in national development*. Unpublished doctoral dissertation, The Ohio State University, Columbus, Ohio.

Amin, H.Y. (1995). Broadcasting in the Arab World and the Middle East. In A. Wells (Ed.), *World Broadcasting*. Oxford: Oxford University Press.

Amin, H.Y., and M. Murrie. (1992). Development and impact of the Egyptian International television network (SpaceNet). *Proceedings of the International Association for Mass Communication Research*, Garuja, Brazil, August 16–21.

Amin, H.Y., and D.A. Boyd. (1993). The impact of home video cassette recorder on Egyptian film and television consumption patterns. *The European Journal of Communication* 18 (1): pp. 77–87.

Amin, H.Y., and J. Napoli. (1995). Clash of communication cultures: CNN in Egypt. *Proceedings of the Twelfth Annual Intercultural/International Communication Conference*, Miami, Florida, Feb. 2–4.

Boyd, D.A. (1993). *Broadcasting in the Arab world: A survey of the electronic media in the Middle East*. Ames, Iowa: Iowa State University Press.

Epps, M.A. (1993). *The effects of American television programs on the Egyptian elite*. Unpublished master's thesis, Department of Journalism and Mass Communication, The American University in Cairo, Cairo, Egypt.

Farouk, D., M. Hagrass, M. Emile, and S. Soliman. (1995). *Impact of American programs in Egyptian TV*. Unpublished paper, Department of Journalism and Mass Communication, The American University in Cairo, Cairo, Egypt.

Foote, J.S., and H.Y. Amin. (1993). Global TV news in developing countries: CNN's expansion to Egypt. Ecquid Novi, *Journal of Journalism in Southern Africa* 14 (2): pp. 153–178.

Goweili, S. (1993). *Agenda setting and local issues on Egyptian regional television broadcasting*. Unpublished master's thesis, The American University in Cairo, Cairo, Egypt.

Hassan, E. (1979). *The influx of foreign films on the Egyptian television*. Unpublished master's thesis, Department of Mass Communication, Cairo University, Cairo, Egypt.

Mowlana, H. (1986). *Global information and world communications: New frontiers in international relations*. New York: Longman.

Napoli, J. (1995). *Assessment of the Egyptian print and electronic media*. Study, The United States Agency for International Development. Cairo, Egypt.

News . . . MTV to launch Middle East package. (1996, January). *Middle East Broadcast & Satellite*, p.20.

Orbit on Intelsat 702. (1996, January). *Middle East Broadcast & Satellite*, p.4.

Rachty, G., and K. Sabat. (1979). *Importation of films for cinema and television in Egypt*. UNESCO Publications.

Saleem, E. (1990). *Arabic and foreign serials in Egyptian television*. Unpublished Ph.D. dissertation, Department of Mass Communication, Cairo University, Cairo, Egypt.

Salem, N., and M. El Kordy. (1989). Field study of the Egyptian child's exposure to mass media. In H. Danner (Ed.), *Mass media and Arab identity: The future and technological challenges*, pp. 142–143. Cairo, Egypt: Dar El Shorouk.

24

Battling Standards Worldwide

Mighty Morphin Power Rangers™ Fight for Their Lives

JOANNE M. LISOSKY

Introduction

The success of the MMPR television program is unprecedented. The Fox network first broadcast *Mighty Morphin Power Rangers* in 1993; immediately it became the number one rated children's television program in the United States—after only five weeks on the air, according to Nielsen ratings. For the week of October 4, 1993, the program boasted a 6.9 rating and 44 share for children two to eleven, a full point-and-a-half better than the next best rated children's program, *Animaniacs* (Schmuckler 1993).

Program Content

Despite the production cost of $350,000 to $400,000 per episode, the production values of the MMPR series are not high quality. In fact, they are reminiscent of Godzilla films of the early 1950s with their formulaic story lines. Ironically, the program itself is a morphin, with much of the action footage lifted from a long-running Japanese television program, *Jyu Rangah*. Curiously, it has been reported that much of the original Japanese violence has been toned down for the American audience (Cody 1994).

The title characters in this live-action program are portrayed as wholesome, California-style teens—four males and two females, including one Asian American and one African American. At the beginning of each program, the off-duty Rangers behave as typical Los Angeles youngsters who complain about homework, shop at the mall, and practice aerobics. But soon these "teenagers with an attitude," as they are referred to in the opening sequence, are clandestinely summoned to save planet Earth. The Rangers then "morph" into brightly-hued Spandex-clad martial artists and kick, karate chop, and punch at various monsters. Their usual victims at this stage, silver-Spandexed, faceless humanoid monsters called "Putties," quickly pop on the screen in great numbers and melt away when pummeled by the Rangers.

Once they defeat the Putties, the battle continues, often with larger, more grotesque monsters. For these battles, the Rangers morph again, this time with "Thunder-zor Power," into individual, robotic, prehistoric creatures that stream across the screen. The Rangers battle briefly at this stage until their opponent *du jour* grows more powerful and overpowers them. They then ready for battle amidst a new setting, often replete with one-dimensional, knee-high skyscrapers. Utilizing stylized action and low-tech special effects, the Rangers morph still again into one large martial arts robot, Megazord, equipped with laser-type weapons and controlled by the Spandex Rangers working in unison in a control booth located somewhere near the center of the oversized robot. Inevitably, Megazord defeats the evil monster and saves the world. Precious little deviation from this plot ever occurs. In multi-part stories, the elements of the plot are simply extended.

Nearly all of this morphing takes place while a catchy theme song plays in the background:

> They've got the power and force you've never seen before. No one will take them down. The power lies on their side. Go, go, Power Rangers. Go, go, Power Rangers. Go, go, Power Rangers, Mighty Morphin Power Rangers. Go, go, Power Rangers. Go, go, Power Rangers®.

The tune is so hypnotizing that it has been reported that even children who have never watched MMPR come home singing the refrain to the theme song (DePaolis 1994).

Additionally, in many countries, a thirty-second "Message from the Power Rangers" follows the credits. Here, the Rangers offer a variety of positive, prosocial messages, and speak directly to the child audience with advice on how not to react with anger, how to share your toys, and essentially how to be good citizens.

The International Battles

The spotlight on the MMPR in recent months, however, has not focused on the positive aspects of the show, but rather, on the reported excessive violence in the program.

Since 1994, a number of countries that had acquired the MMPR from the Los Angeles–based Saban Entertainment, found that the program exemplified behaviors contrary to their cultural norms or broadcast regulations. A review of these objections follows.

England

There was a mild outcry in England in October 1994 when a four-year-old was karate-style kicked by a playmate imitating the MMPR (Orvice 1994). Following the kick, the four-year-old was hospitalized for a bruised kidney. This led the Royal Society for the Prevention of Accidents to issue a warning about the series. Royal Society spokesperson, Cathy Warder said, "It [MMPR] is extremely dangerous. Kids love to copy their heroes and it is time for someone to intervene. Teachers and parents should crack down on copycat play-fighting before there is a real tragedy" (in Orvice 1994, 3).

It was also reported at this time that Britain's Independent Television Commission had received six complaints from parents about the violence in *Power Rangers*. The Commission decided not to act on these complaints because, according to a spokesperson: "We felt the series was cartoon-like in its approach . . . in the line with fantasy programmes" (in Orvice 1994, 3).

Scandinavia

In other parts of Europe, the response to the MMPR resulted in more severe action. In Scandinavia, MMPR aired at 6 P.M. every weekday on a Swedish-owned commercial satellite television station based in London, Scansat TV-3 (Rehlin 1994). According to Torill Mortensen, media scholar and teacher of Mass Communications and Public Information at Volda College in Norway: "TV-3 is not a very important channel in Norway" (personal communication-e-mail, October 28, 1994). Other data show that the satellite penetration in Norway is about thirty-five percent (Ostergard 1992). Despite what appeared to be low viewership for MMPR in Scandinavia, day care centers in Norway reported that the dubbed version of the program was enormously popular among four- and five-year-old children who imitated the Power Rangers using martial arts kicks and blows.

In October 1994, something occurred that caused TV-3 to take drastic action. Following a young girl's brutal killing, debate renewed on the causes of violence in Scandinavian society. This response led Scansat TV-3 to take the MMPR program immediately off the air. Prime Minster Grottarlen Brundtland responded by issuing a public statement saying that Norwegians should think twice before allowing such "free market" violence to be broadcast by commercial networks (in "Rangers Return" 1994). He added that "violence on the screen [could] possibly become violence on the retinas of even small children" (in "Girl's Death" 1994, 12A).

It was reported that the reason for targeting the live-action program was because one of the boys involved in the incident initially told police that teenage boys attacked and killed the girl. Then he chased them away by kicking one of them just like the *Teenage Mutant Ninja Turtles*™ (Zurawik 1994, 10).

This report led TV-3 program director, Ricky Ghal to respond, "As responsible broadcasters, we removed from our schedules all action-oriented children's programming until the exact nature of the incident had been determined. *Power Rangers* was just one of the programs that was temporarily taken off the air" (Hollinger 1994, NEXIS).

And its removal was temporary. Within days of taking MMPR off the air, TV-3 reinstated the children's program. Ghal said that MMPR was returned to TV-3 because "no direct linkage exists between the program and this tragic accident" (in "Rangers Return" 1994, 30).

Germany

In January 1995, *Power Rangers* came under attack from the German Society for the Protection of Children. The Society called for the program to be banned for excessive violence due primarily to complaints by German kindergarten teachers who charged that the program promotes child nightmares (Kindred 1995, found on NEXIS).

Malaysia

Authorities in Malaysia banned the popular children's program in December 1995 in a controversy over its title. Deputy Home Minister Magat Junid Megat Ayob said that the title words "Mighty Morphin" might cause children to associate the characters with the drug morphine, leading them to believe that "the drug could make them strong like the characters in the show" (in "Mighty Morphin" 1995, 2A).

Australia

In August 1994, the Australian Council on Children's Film and Television lodged a complaint with the Australian Broadcasting Authority (ABA), stating that MMPR was too violent for the "G" rating it was given by the network that broadcasts the program. The Council had found that the Office of Film and Literature in Australia had classified MMPR videos as "PG" while the network broadcasts were still given a "G" rating (Personal communication,

Barbara Biggins, Executive Director, Australian Council on Children's Film and Television, March 18, 1995).

In November 1995, after reviewing three episodes of MMPR, the ABA stated that two episodes of the series contained scenes that did not comply with the "G" classification (Lewes 1995). The ABA found that the two episodes breached parts of the "G" violence section of the Commercial Television Industry Code of Practice, where violence could cause distress to children or was out of context. The Authority added that "the depiction of violence may be acceptable or desirable in a situation where one acts in self defense" ("Power Ranger Decision" 1995, 1). The network airing the series in Australia has been allowed to continue to screen the *Power Rangers* in prime children's viewing time, as long as certain scenes are edited out.

New Zealand

To date, the most impregnable regulatory monster the MMPR have battled has been in New Zealand. In August 1994, Television New Zealand "dumped the children's programme, the *Mighty Morphin Power Rangers*, on the advice of the Broadcast Standards Authority" ("TVNZ Dumps" 1994, 1). The series had just finished its initial run, and TVNZ was planning to screen another forty episodes beginning in October (Wakefield 1994).

The press reported that even though TVNZ had edited out some of the violent confrontations with the Putties and the network had added prosocial public service announcements to the end of each program, the Authority claimed that these changes were not enough (Ruth Zanker, New Zealand Broadcasting School, Christchurch Polytechnic, personal communication-e-mail, November 17, 1994). TVNZ spokeswoman, Aline Scanilands said that she believed this was the first time a program had been cancelled in New Zealand by direct result of an Authority decision ("TVNZ Dumps" 1994).

The New Zealand Broadcast Standards Authority (BSA) stated that it had received more adverse comments about MMPR than any other program, since the establishment of the Authority. The Annual General Report of the BSA states

> The Authority received formal and informal complaints about both excessive violence and glamorization of violence in a programme aimed at children. . . . TVNZ's quick and responsible action of cancelling the second series, when advised of the Authority's decision, is a good example of the effectiveness of the standards regime which combines consumer initiated complaints and appeal to an independent body. (Ruth Zanker, personal communication-e-mail, November 15, 1994)

BSA Executive Director, Gail Power, said that the BSA had not banned the program and did not have the legal authority to do so. However, the BSA's written decision stated that the MMPR programs that had aired on TVNZ had breached legally defined standards ("State Television Cans" 1994).

In response to the New Zealand technical knockout of the MMPR, Saban International President Stan Golden said that the company planned steps to appeal the process. He added, "We consider it an unfortunate decision that won't affect the show worldwide" (Wakefield 1994, found on NEXIS).

Canada

Not long after losing the struggle in the New Zealand market, the Rangers were accosted by another regulatory body, the Canadian Broadcast Standards Council (CBSC).

The CBSC is an independent organization whose members include private radio and television stations across Canada. Established by the Canadian Association of Broadcasters (CAB) in 1989, the Council helps Canadians voice their comments and concerns about programming to broadcasters. More than ninety-five percent of CAB member stations are likewise members of CBSC and adhere to the industry codes (Canadian Broadcast Standards Council 1994).

In November 1994, the CBSC ruled that MMPR, estimated to be the most popular children's television show in Canada, was too violent for Canadian television (Lacey 1994). The Ontario Regional Council of the national broadcasters regulatory body unanimously decided that MMPR contravened several articles related to children's programming in the industry's Voluntary Code Regarding Violence in Television Programming. In a news release from the CBSC, the Regional Council agreed that "the program depicted excessive violence and that the scenes of violence were not essential to the plot of the program and the character development" (CBSC 1994).

The Regional Council members added that violence was generally the preferred means of conflict resolution in the program and, in fact, the program offered no alternative to violence in order to resolve conflict. The Regional Council concluded that the program glossed over consequences of violence which in turn invited young viewers to imitate the martial arts techniques depicted in the program (CBSC 1994).

This public statement regarding MMPR was the first decision of the CBSC focusing on the violence code since its inception in January 1994 (Lacey 1994). The code states that "violence on television pertains to all types of programming, from music videos to hockey games. This voluntary code helps broadcasters determine what guidelines to apply to their own communities" (CBSC 1994).

Prior to making this decision, the members of the Regional Council screened ten episodes of MMPR provided by the broadcaster. The Council members found that after removing the opening and closing credits, and the commercials from the calculations of program length, the dramatic action covers approximately seventeen or eighteen minutes of each program. The Council members noted that of that time, fight scenes comprise between 4.5 and 6.5 minutes, or 25 to 35 percent of the dramatic time (Canadian Broadcast Standards Council Ontario Regional Council 1994).

As a result of the CBSC decision, YTV, a youth cable channel, cancelled MMPR, and the Montreal-based French TVA network dropped the series. Global Television, a commercial satellite network and part of CanWest Global, decided to talk to the program's producers, Saban International, to determine if there were ways of altering the program to conform to Canadian criteria (Farnsworth 1994).

In the days following the decision, CanWest Global Systems were inundated with public responses from across Canada, according to Doug Hoover, National Vice-President of Programming at CanWest. Hoover said that his network fielded 100 calls in favor of the MMPR and twenty against the show ("Mighty Morphins Too Violent" 1994). Hoover added:

The vast majority of the responses we have received maintain that watching this program is a personal decision for parents and children to make together and that we should continue to broadcast Power Rangers. A number of parents strongly supported Power Rangers because of its reinforcement of positive social values and role models. (CanWest Global 1994, 1)

Hoover added that his company had reviewed the program and with the consent of the producers had successfully modified the series "to reflect the Canadian environment" (CanWest Global 1994, 1). Hoover said that the portions of the program where the Rangers fight the Putties would be edited to de-emphasize the kicking and hitting in favor of the athletics and action of the conflict. Additionally, each episode will feature a prosocial public service vignette at the end of the program, extolling the virtues of positive behavior (CanWest Global 1994).

Despite these alterations, the volume of complaints to the CBSC office about the excessive violence on the *Power Rangers* has remained about the same (Personal communication, Ron Cohen, CBSC National Chair, March 18, 1995).

When asked about the ramifications of the Canadian decision in the United States, Ronald Cohen noted that the MMPR was not in jeopardy in the United States because no equivalent to the Broadcast Standards Council exists there. He added that the United States is still debating the causal link between television programs and children's behavior. He concluded, "But that part of the debate had already taken place in Canada" (Bash 1994, 3D).

U.S. Response

Cohen is accurate with regard to the debate still waging in the United States over the effect of televisual violence on children. Since the 1950s, research has been piling up in the United States on both sides of this issue. Horst Stipp, Ph.D., Director of Social and Development Research at NBC, said more substantial proof of causal effects of television violence is needed before this content should be regulated. He noted, "Most scientists in the field do not acknowledge that the evidence is so weak" (personal communication, October 25, 1994). Other media critics in the United States suggest that the blame for the proliferation of violent behavior within U.S. society is not solely within the purview of television (Gitlin 1994).

Still others offer conflicting arguments. One research study, conducted in 1994 at California State University-Fullerton, found that watching the *Power Rangers* can be hazardous to a child's health. Students observed that those children exposed to a single episode of the MMPR responded by committing significantly more acts of aggression than children in a control group. In fact, for every aggressive act the researchers observed in the control group children, there were seven aggressive acts committed by the *Power Rangers* viewers. The study also noted that boys committed more aggressive acts than girls after watching the program (Boyatzis, Matillo, and Nesbitt in press).

In 1993, the National Coalition on Television Violence (NCTV) in the United States conducted research that suggested MMPR was twice as violent as any children's television show the organization had monitored in its thirteen-year history. The NCTV screened three programs and observed acts of violence ranging from 257 to 151 per hour. The organization tabulated these aggressive acts on a 1-3-5 point scale that gives one point to a slap, three points to a punch or a kick, and five points for murder or anything deadly (Kiesewetter 1993).

Other U.S. responses included a surprise move by *Parenting* magazine, which named the MMPR one of television's best shows in its December 1994 issue. The *Power Rangers* ranked sixth, between two PBS programs: *The Magic School Bus* (5) and *Reading Rainbow* (7). The magazine described the program as:

> Hall monitors with abs of steel, the five young Rangers fight crime, prejudice, and pollution to make the world safer for nerds like themselves. Don't knock this show just because it has been marketed to death—Rangers is that rare mix of high tech and heart. ("The 10 Best Shows" 1994, 169)

In another surprise move, the entire world watched as the new Speaker of the U.S. House of Representatives, Newt Gingrich, shook hands with the Mighty Morphin Power Rangers who were invited to Washington, D.C., to entertain at the Speaker's opening day celebration. During the festivities, Gingrich remarked that *he* was like the Mighty Morphin Power Rangers. He said, "You ride the waves in America, and if something's hot, it's hot" (*Nightline* 1995).

Months before the world began levelling blows at the MMPR, Margaret Loesch, President of the Fox Children's Network, was asked about the violence in the Power Rangers show and whether she feared children might imitate what they observed. Loesch said, "We're not worried about Power Rangers because frankly we have gotten very little criticism. We've gotten almost no letters of complaints from parents, for example, because it's such a silly show" (in Zurawik, 1D).

Discussion

The sheer volume of international protests to MMPR underscores the extent to which some countries will go to protect their children television viewers. It likewise exposes the lack of content restrictions on children's television in the United States. The Children's Television Act of 1990, the sole regulation of television content in the United States, controls commercial length, but never mention standards regarding violent television content, unlike many other nations. In fact, the added prosocial public service messages that accompany the MMPR would, no doubt, serve to qualify the program for "FCC-Friendly" status under the current interpretations of the Act.

These protests likewise suggest that the United States' laissez-faire attitude toward media content may soon serve to limit distribution of its television programs around the world. This evidence suggests that if the United States wishes to continue to be the primary supplier of children's television, it should consider monitoring its programs more carefully or at least heed the actions of other governments. Increasingly, the international television markets are questioning the value of wholesale mediated U.S. culture. The days of cultural imperialism may be waning.

These initial disputes, focusing on a particular series and the widespread violent content in a program directed exclusively at children, may indicate that the United States is moving further away from other countries in its cultural standards regarding televised violence. In the United States, MMPR supplies role models for children and even appears to be sanctioned by the U.S. Congress. This same program contains levels of violence unacceptable in New Zealand, Canada, and Australia, and perhaps in Great Britain, Scandinavia, and Germany as well.

Regardless of opinions about whether mediated violence develops a causal relationship with violent behavior, unless the United States adheres to global concerns about televisual violence, it may "morph" itself out of the international television market.

References

Bland, K. (1994, October 20). Power Rangers too violent?; Outcry Europe doesn't keep Fox, kids from morphin. *The Phoenix Gazette*, p. A1.

Boyatzis, C.J., G.M. Matillo, and K.M. Nesbitt (in press). Effects of the *Mighty Morphin Power Rangers* on children's aggression with peers. *Child Study Journal*.

Canadian Broadcast Standards Council Ontario Regional Council. (1994, April and May). Decision Concerning *Mighty Morphin Power Rangers* on CIII-TV (Files 9394-270 and 9394-277). Toronto: Author.

Canadian Broadcast Standards Council Pamphlet. (1994). Toronto: Author.

Canadian Broadcast Standards Council. (1994, November 1). *Power Rangers Too Violent, Says Ontario Council*. Toronto: Author News Release.

CanWest Global System. (1994, November 1). *CanWest Global System stations to continue broadcasting "Power Rangers."* Toronto: Author News Release.

Cody, J. (1994, June 10). Power Rangers take on the whole world. *Wall Street Journal*, p. B3(E).

DePaolis, M. (1994, October 21). Sure, you can watch the *Power Rangers*—But your kids shouldn't [SECOND OPINION]. *Star Tribune*, p. 23A.

Farnsworth, C.H. (1994, November 11). Zap! Children's Ninja show ruled alien to Canadian culture. *New York Times News Service*.

Girl's death prompts *Power Rangers* ban. (1994, October 19). *The Atlanta Constitution*. p. 12A.

Gitlin, T. (1994, Winter). Imagebusters: The hollow crusade against TV violence. *The American Prospect* 16: pp. 42–49.

Hollinger, H. (1994, October, 21). Scandi cabler: No link in between Rangers, killing. *The Hollywood Reporter*, p. found on NEXIS.

Kiesewetter, J. (1993, December 17). Top kids show also ranks as most violent. *Cincinnati Enquirer*, n. p.

Kindred, J. (1995, January 28). Critics say a popular children's TV series shows excessive violence. *Deutsche Presse-Agentur*, p. found on NEXIS.

Lacey, L. (1994, November 2). *Power Rangers* suffers body blow to programming. *The Globe and Mail*, p. A15.

Lewes, J.L. (1995, November 13). Australia. *The Hollywood Reporter*, p. found on NEXIS.

Mighty Morphin Power Rangers banned from TV. (1995, December 22). *Seattle Post-Intelligencer*, p. 2A.

Mighty Morphins regarded as "too violent" in Canada. (1994, November 5). *The Straits Times* (Singapore), p. 9.

Nightline (ABC). (1995, January 5). Television program transcripts.

Orvice, V. (1994, October, 19). Copycat dangers of the Power Rangers; Outcry over children's TV heroes after young fan is hurt. *Daily Mail*, p. 3

Power Rangers decision highlights ABA hitches. (1995, November). *Small Screen: News digest of the Australian council for Children's Films and Television* 98: p. 1.

Rangers return to Scandinavia. (1994, October 21). *Daily Variety*, p. 30.

Rehlin, G. (1994, October 19). Rangers pulled from Scandinavia's TV3. *Daily Variety*, p. 10.

Schmuckler, E. (1993, October 18). Fox's *Power Rangers* are new kids smash. *Media Week* 3(42): pp. 1, 8.

State television cans *Power Rangers* after public protests. (1994, August 25). *Agence France Presse*, p. found on NEXIS.

The 10 Best Shows. (1994, November). *Parenting*, p. 169.

TVNZ dumps *The Mighty Morphin Power Rangers*. (1994, August 25). *Dominion*, p. 1.

Wakefield, P. (1994, August 26). Too violent *Rangers* gets yanked in N.Z. *The Hollywood Reporter*, p. found on NEXIS.

Zurawik, D. (1994, October 20). Critics of kid's TV laud Norwegian response to killing of a little girl. *The Baltimore Sun*, p. 1D.

About the Editor and Contributors

YAHYA R. KAMALIPOUR (Ph.D., University of Missouri-Columbia) is professor of mass communications and director of graduate studies at the Department of Communication and Creative Arts, Purdue University Calumet, Hammond, Indiana, U.S.A., where he has taught graduate and undergraduate courses since 1986. He has also taught at universities in Ohio, Illinois, Missouri, Oxford (England), and Tehran, Iran. He is editor of *The U.S. Media and the Middle East: Image and Perception* (1995, 1997), and *Mass Media in the Middle East: A Comprehensive Handbook* (with Hamid Mowlana, 1994). A recipient of several significant awards, including the 1996 Distinguished Scholarship Award from the International and Intercultural Division of the National Communication Association, his articles on media effects, broadcast education, image and perception, and international communication have appeared in professional and mainstream publications in the U.S. and abroad.

PAULINE ABELA is a student in psychology at the University of Malta in Malta. In 1995, she studied at the University of Wyoming through an international exchange program. Her academic interests include international communication and psychology.

PEGGY BIEBER-ROBERTS is assistant professor in the Department of Communication and Mass Media at the University of Wyoming, Laramie, U.S.A. Her research interests include international communication with emphasis in audience studies and mass media in developing countries.

UDITA DAS is doctoral candidate at Jawaharlal Nehru University India, and also a media consultant for the Mudra Centre for Fundamental Communications Research, Ahmadabad, India. Her areas of research interest include mass media and social order, advertising, and gender studies.

ERSU DING is professor in the Institute of Comparative Literature and Culture, Peking University, People's Republic of China. His recent publica-

347

tions include a monograph, *Beyond Ontology: A Study in Marxist Theory of Meaning*, and numerous articles devoted to cultural studies, semiotics and literary theories.

DARADIREK EKACHAI is associate professor of communication in the Department of Speech Communication, Southern Illinois University, Carbondale, U.S.A. Her areas of research include public relations, journalism, and communication studies.

SHERRY DEVEREAUX FERGUSON is associate professor of communication at the University of Ottawa, Canada. She received the 1994 SCA PRIDE Award for her most recent book, *Mastering the Public Opinion Challenge* (1994). In addition to training managers and executives in issue management and strategic planning techniques, she has served as consultant to the Department of Justice, the Privy Council Office, Health Canada, Secretary of State, Communications Canada, the National Research Council, Indian and Northern Affairs, Transport Canada, and other Canadian governmental organizations.

ALEXANDRA FERGUSON is a graduate student in the Mass Communication and Public Relations Program at Boston University, U.S.A. She has worked for the Federal Communication Council of Canada and the Public Relations and Information Services Department at the University of Ottawa, Canada.

HENNIE J. GROENEWALD is director for graduate studies at the Department of Communication, Potchefstroom University for Christian Higher Education, Potechefstroom, South Africa. A former president of the Southern African Communication Association, he has co-authored six books and has published twenty-six articles and fifteen major research reports.

THOMAS HAFEN is a doctoral student in history at the Department of History, University of Chicago, Illinois, U.S.A.

RANIA M. HEGAZI is a graduate student at Stanford University, California, U.S.A. She received a master's degree in mass communication at the American University in Cairo where she was awarded a Graduate Merit Fellow by the School of Business, Economics and Communication in 1994–95. Her research interests include intercultural communication and image studies relative to the Arabic press.

MARY HINCHCLIFF-PELIAS is professor of communication in the Department of Speech Communication, Southern Illinois University, Carbondale, U.S.A. Her areas of research include intercultural communication and communication education.

HILARY HORAN is professor and former director of the Department of Communication at the University of Ottawa, Canada. In addition to serving as a consultant to the Privy Council Office in Canada, he has conducted research in values transmitted by the media and environmental effects in organizational climate.

DINA IORDANOVA is a Rockefeller fellow at the University of Chicago and works on film projects dealing with mass mediation and the Balkan crisis. She has taught East European media and cultural studies at the University of Texas, Austin, U.S.A., and has worked at universities in Bulgaria and Canada. Her areas of research include East European media, cinema, and the Internet.

RICHARD JACKSON HARRIS is professor of psychology at Kansas State University, Manhattan, Kansas, U.S.A. He has published books and research papers on memory for language and discourse, social cognition, bilingualism, deceptive advertising, mass communication, and cultural knowledge. He has also been a Fulbright Professor in Brazil (1982) and Uruguay (1994).

BEVERLY JENSEN teaches marketing communication in the Journalism and Mass Communication Department at the American University in Cairo, Egypt. Her research interests include marketing and public communication processes in the Islamic world.

JOSEPH ANDREW KARAFA is a doctoral candidate in social psychology, Department of Psychology, Kansas State University, Manhattan, Kansas, U.S.A. His research interests include shyness, evaluation anxiety, and cultural estrangement.

ROSECHONGPORN KOMOLSEVIN is assistant professor of communication arts and chair of the doctoral program in Interpersonal Communication at Bangkok University, Thailand. Her teaching and research interests include advertising, organizational communication, and public relations.

JAE-KYOUNG LEE is assistant professor of journalism at Ewha Womans University in Seoul, South Korea. A former TV news reporter for the Munhwa Broadcasting Corporation network in Korea, he teaches news writing and reporting, broadcast news production, and critical communication theory.

DAFNA LEMISH teaches in the Department of Communication at Tel Aviv University, Israel. A recipient of a doctoral degree in communication from the Ohio State University, Columbus, U.S.A., her areas of research interest include media literacy, children and television, and media gender portrayals.

JOANNE M. LISOSKY, a former employee of PBS, teaches communication and broadcasting at Pacific Lutheran University in Tacoma, Washington,

U.S.A. Her research interests include comparative broadcast standards and children's programming.

ROBERT M. MCKENZIE is associate professor of communication in the Department of Speech Communication Studies, East Stroudsburg University, East Stroudsburg, Pennsylvania, U.S.A., where he is also faculty advisor to the campus radio station, WESS-FM. He has published articles on radio news, college radio operation, international newspaper journalism, crisis TV news, and media aurality.

ANNALIE M.E. NAUDE teaches communication studies at the Department of Communication, Potschefstroom University for Christian Higher Education, South Africa. Her research interests include persuasive communication, research methodology, interactive media, and media analysis.

ALLEN W. PALMER is a lecturer in the Department of Communications at Brigham Young University, Provo, Utah, U.S.A. He has also taught at the University of Mauritius and Ricks College in Idaho.

ALEX FERNANDO TEIXEIRA PRIMO is professor of communications at Universidade Federal do Rio Grande do Sul (UFRGS), Brazil. His research interests include mass communication, computer graphics, and media production. He released the first Brazilian 3D book about the Brazilian culture in 1995.

KULDIP R. RAMPAL is professor of mass communication at Central Missouri State University in Warrensburg, U.S.A. As a visiting scholar, he has taught at the Nanyang Technological University, Singapore, and National University of Singapore. He is co-author of *International Afro Media: A Reference Guide* (1996), has written numerous articles on development communication, press regulation, media ethics, and international communication, and is the recipient of several teaching awards, including the 1993 International Communication Award from the government of Republic of China in Taiwan.

SHINICHI SAITO is associate professor, Department of Communication, Tokyo Women's Christian University in Japan. A recipient of a doctoral degree from the Annenberg School of Communication, University of Pennsylvania, U.S.A., his research interests include social and psychological effects of mass communication, international/intercultural communication, and quantitative research methods.

LYNNETTE M. SERFONTEIN teaches mass and political communication in the Department of Communication, Potchefstroom University for Christian Higher Education, Potchefstroom, South Africa. Her research interests include political communication and image studies.

HERBERT I. SCHILLER is professor emeritus, Department of Communication, University of California, San Diego. In addition to teaching and lecturing throughout the world, he has published extensively on culture and communication. His most recent book is *Information Inequality* (1996).

JANE STOKES is lecturer and course director of the Media and Society program at South Bank University, London, England. She has also taught media and communications studies at several institutions in and around London, including London College of Printing and the University of Westminster.

AYSELI USLUATA is associate professor of communication in the Department of Management, Bogazici University, Istanbul, Turkey. The author of two books in Turkish, *Iletism* (1994) and *Proceedings of the Congress Presentations* (1984), she has many papers on image and reality, international communication, and mass communication in Turkey.

MCKENZIE WARK lectures in media studies at Macquarie University in Sydney, Australia, and is the author of *Virtual Geography: Lying With Global Media Events* (1994). A well-known columnist for *The Australian Newspaper*, his articles in cultural and media studies have appeared in many journals in Australia and elsewhere.

LAID ZAGHLAMI, a former journalist for the Algerian Radio and head of research unit on audience measurement and public opinion, is training chief for the Algerian Broadcasting and associate professor of information and communication at University of Algiers. He has taught seminars at universities in England, Australia, and Switzerland. His research areas include media influence, communication technology, international relations, and cultural issues.

THIMIOS ZAHAROPOULOS is chair of Mass Media Department at Washburn University of Topeka, Kansas, U.S.A. The author of *Mass Media in Greece* (1993), he has published numerous articles on U.S. media image of other countries and on Greek radio and television. He teaches in the areas of broadcasting, mass media theory, and international communication.

Index

353